PHILIP'S

STRE...

Powys

ATLAS STRYDOEDD Powys

First published in 2005 by

Philip's, a division of
Octopus Publishing Group Ltd
2-4 Heron Quays, London E14 4JP

First edition 2005
First impression 2005

ISBN-10 0-540-08660-6 (pocket)
ISBN-13 978-0-540-08660-3 (pocket)

© Philip's 2005

Ordnance Survey®

This product includes mapping data licensed from Ordnance Survey® with the permission of the Controller of Her Majesty's Stationery Office.
© Crown copyright 2005. All rights reserved.
Licence number 100011710.

Printed and bound in Italy by Rotolito

Contents

II	**Key to map pages**
IV	**Route planning**
VIII	**Key to map symbols**
X	**Administrative and Postcode boundaries**
1	**Street maps** at 1⅓ inches to 1 mile
134	**Street maps** at 2⅔ inches to 1 mile
154	**Index** of towns and villages
157	**Index** of streets, hospitals, industrial estates, railway stations, schools, shopping centres, universities and places of interest

Digital Data

The exceptionally high-quality mapping found in this atlas is available as digital data in TIFF format, which is easily convertible to other bitmapped (raster) image formats.

The index is also available in digital form as a standard database table. It contains all the details found in the printed index together with the National Grid reference for the map square in which each entry is named.

For further information and to discuss your requirements, please contact Philip's on 020 7644 6932 or james.mann@philips-maps.co.uk

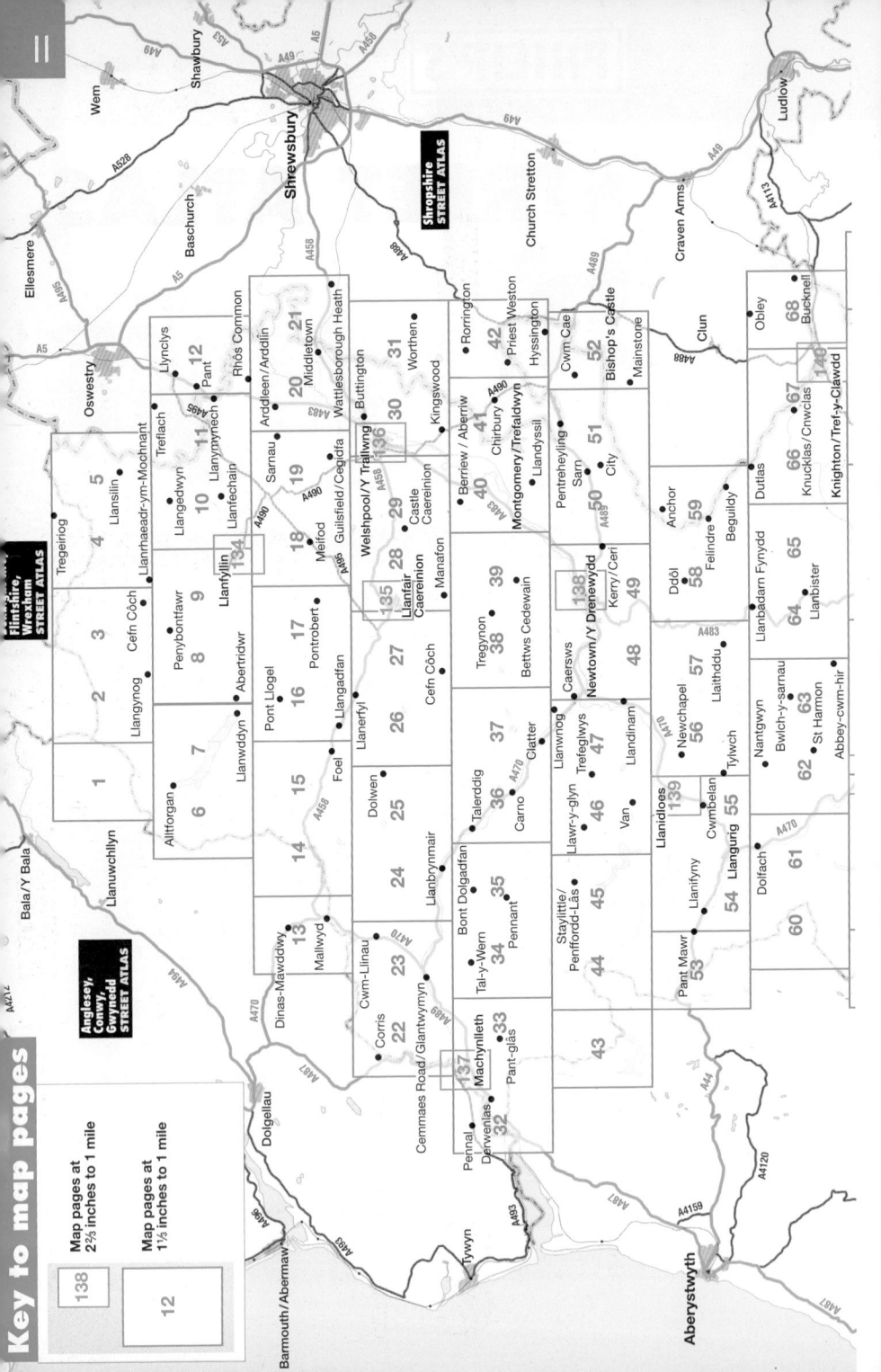

Key to map pages

Shropshire
STREET ATLAS

Flintshire,
Wrexham
STREET ATLAS

Anglesey,
Conwy,
Gwynedd
STREET ATLAS

Map pages at
2¾ inches to 1 mile

Map pages at
1½ inches to 1 mile

138

12

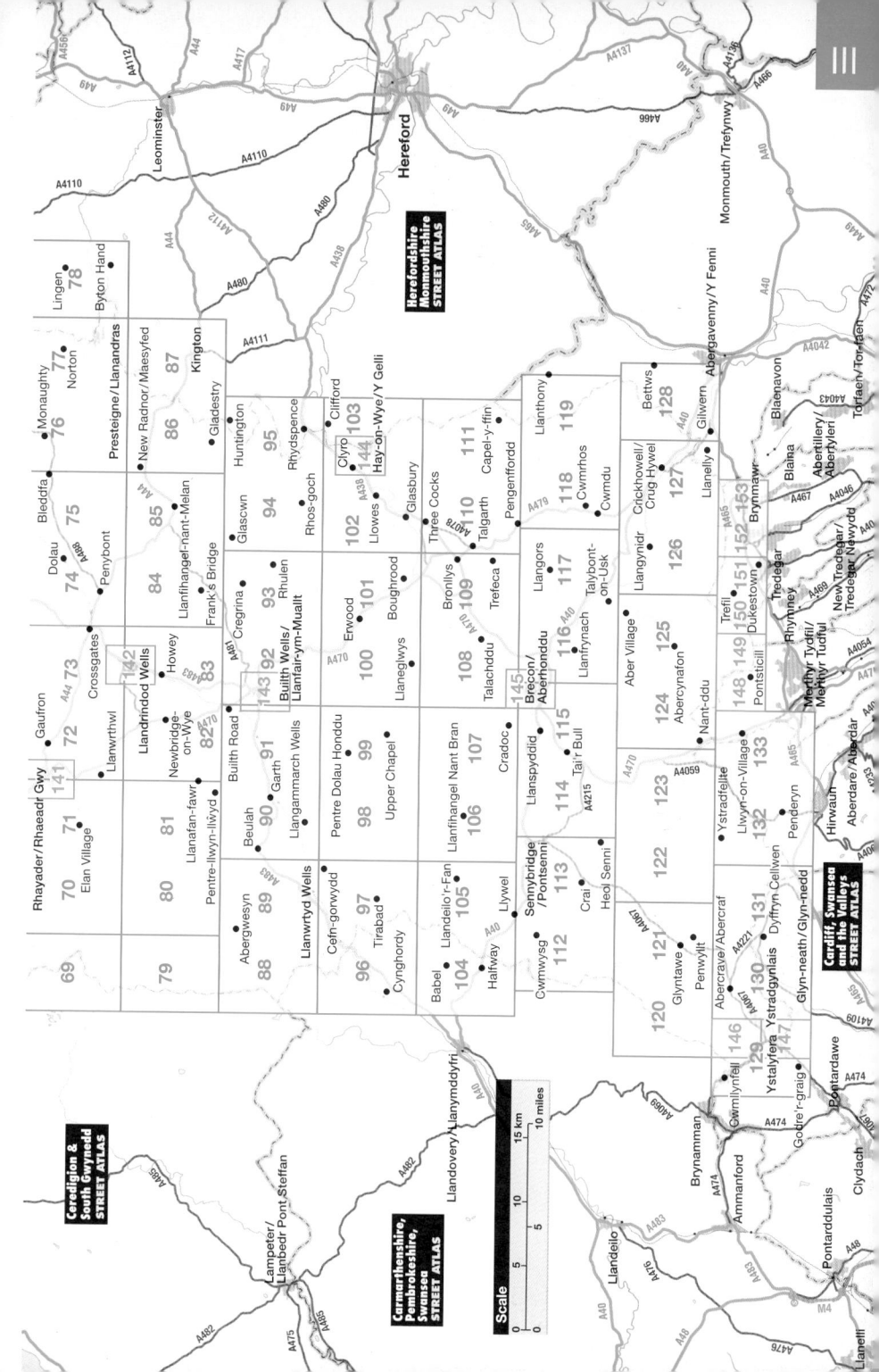

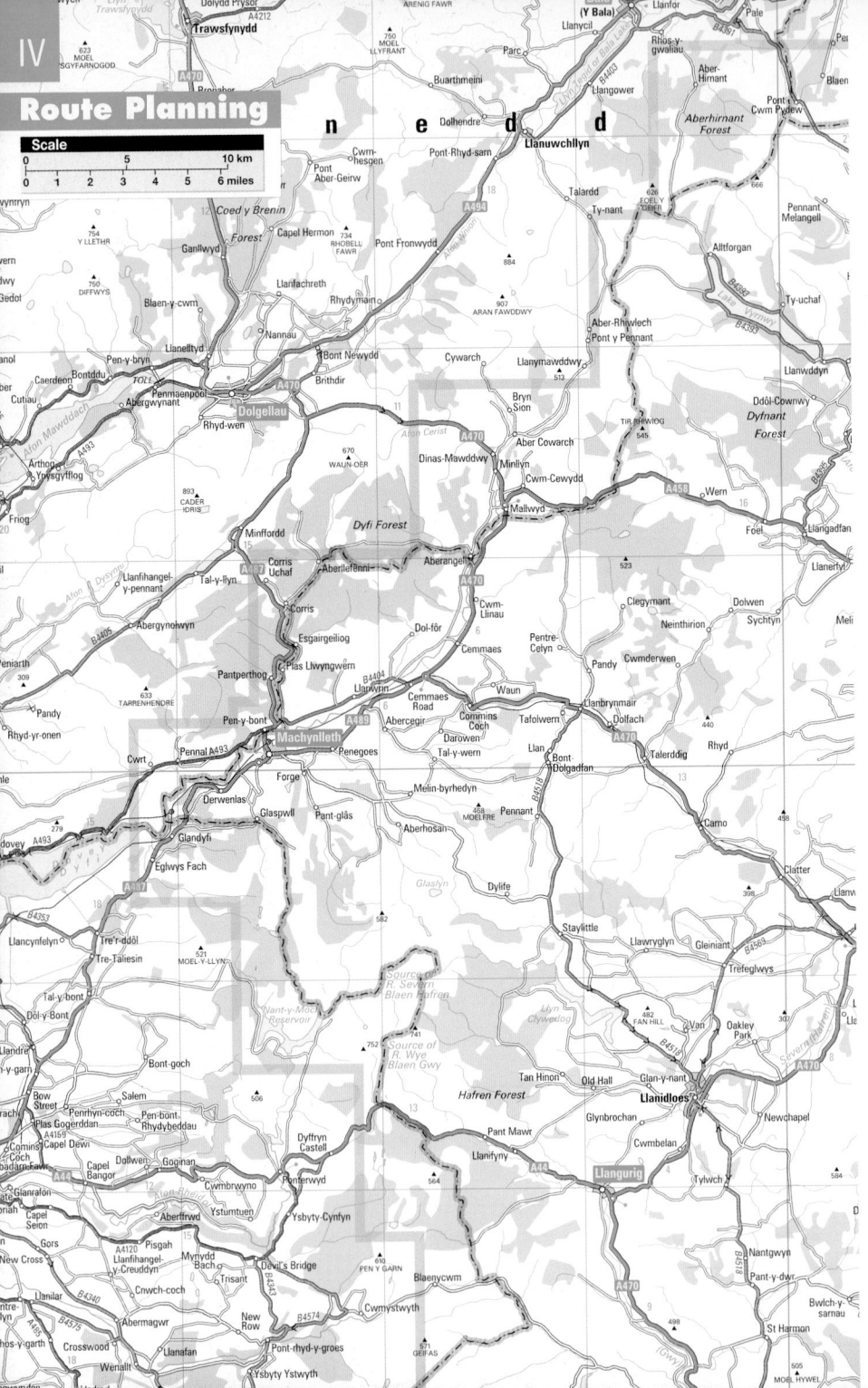

Route Planning

Scale

0 ___ 5 ___ 10 km
0 1 2 3 4 5 6 miles

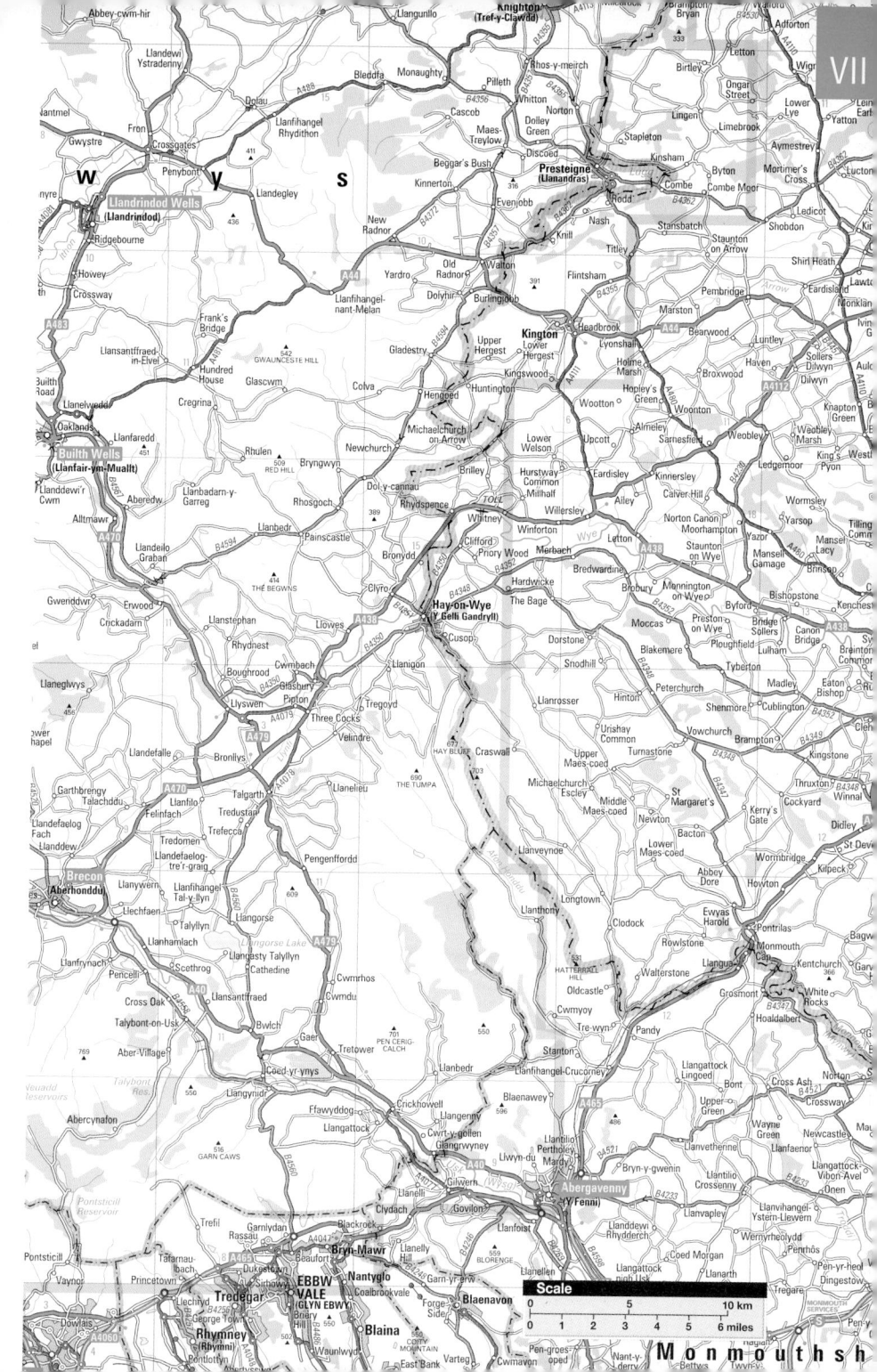

Traffordd gyda rhif y gyffordd (228)	**Gorsaf ambiwlans**
Prif dramwyfeydd – ffordd ddeuol/un lôn	**Gorsaf gwylwyr y glannau**
Ffordd A – ffordd ddeuol/un lôn	**Gorsaf Dân**
Ffordd B – ffordd ddeuol/un lôn	**Swyddfa'r heddlu**
Ffyrdd bychan – ffordd ddeuol/un lôn	**Mynedfa damwain ac argyfwng i'r ysbyty**
Ffyrdd bychan eraill – ffordd ddeuol/un lôn	**Ysbyty**
Ffordd yn cael ei hadeiladu	**Lle o addoliad**
Twnnel, ffordd dan orchudd	**Canolfan gwybodaeth** (a'r agor drwy'r flwyddyn)
Trac gwledig, ffordd breifat, neu ffordd mewn ardal ddinesig	**Canolfan siopa**
Llidiart neu rhwystr i draffig (gall fod cyfyngiadau ddim yn ddilys ar gyfer bob amser neu i bob drafnidiaeth)	**P** **P&R** **Parcio, Parcio a chludo**
Llwybr, llwybr march, cilffordd yn agored i bob trafnidiaeth, ffordd a ddefnyddir yn lwybr cyhoeddus	**PO** **Swyddfa'r post**
	Safle gwersylla
Mân cerddwyr	**Safle carafan**
Ffiniau codau-post DY7	**Cwrs golff**
Ffiniau Sir ac awdurdod unedol	**Safle picnic**
Rheilffordd, twnnel, rheilffordd yn cael ei hadeiladu	**Adeiladau pwysig, ysgolion, colegau, prifysgolion ac ysbytai** Prim Sch
Tramffordd, tramffordd yn cael ei hadeiladu	**Ardal adeiledig**
Rheilffordd ar raddfa fychan	**Coed**
Gorsaf rheilffordd Walsall	River Ouse **Dŵr llanw, Enw dŵr**
Gorsaf rheilffordd breifat	**Dim dŵr llanw** – llyn, afon, camlas neu nant
Gorsaf metro South Shields	**Loc, cored, twnnel**
Atalfa tram, atalfa tram yn cael ei hadeiladu	Church **Hynafiaeth anrhufeinig**
Gorsaf fysiau	ROMAN FORT **Hynafiaeth rhufeinig**

Acad	**Academi**	Inst	**Institiwt**	PH	**Tŷ tafarn**	
Allot Gdns	**Gerddi ar osod**	Ct	**Llys cyfraith**	Recn Gd	**Maes chwaraeon**	
Cemy	**Mynwent**	L Ctr	**Canolfan**	Resr	**Cronfa ddŵr**	
C Ctr	**Canolfan ddinesig**		**hamdden**	Ret Pk	**Parc adwerthu**	
CH	**Tŷ Clwb**	LC	**Croesfan wastad**	Sch	**Ysgol**	
Coll	**Coleg**	Liby	**Llyfrgell**	Sh Ctr	**Canolfan Siopa**	
Crem	**Amlosgfa**	Mkt	**Marchnad**	TH	**Neuadd y dref**	
Ent	**Menter**	Meml	**Coffa**	Trad Est	**Ystad Fasnachol**	
Ex H	**Neuadd Arddangos**	Mon	**Cofgolofn**	Univ	**Prifysgol**	
Ind Est	**Ystad ddiwydiannol**	Mus	**Amgueddfa**	W Twr	**Tŵrdŵr**	
IRB Sta	**Gorsaf bad**	Obsy	**Arsyllfa**	Wks	**Gwaith**	
	achub y glannau	Pal	**Palas brenhinol**	YH	**Hostel ieuenctid**	

Arwyddion dalennau cyfagos a bandiau gorymylon
94
Y mae lliw y saeth â'r band yn dynodi gradd y ddalen gyfagos â'r ddalen gorymyl (gwelwch y graddau islaw)
164

■ Y mae'r rhifau bach o gwmpas ochrau'r mapiau yn dynodi llinelli grid cenedlaethol 1 cilomedr
■ Mae'r ffin llwyd tywyll ar ochr fewn rhai tudalennau yn dynodi nad yw'r mapio yn canlyn ymlaen i'r tudalen gyffiniol

Gradd y mapiau ar y dalennau gyda rhifau glas yw
4.2 cm i 1 km • **2⅔ modfedd i 1 filltir** • **1: 23810**

0 — ¼ — ½ — ¾ — 1 milltir
0 — 250m — 500m — 750m — 1 km

Gradd y mapiau ar y dalennau gyda rhifau gwyrdd yw
is 2.1 i to 1 km • **1⅓ modfedd i 1 filltir** • **1: 47620**

0 — ¼ — ½ — ¾ — 1 milltir
0 — 250m 500m 750m 1 km

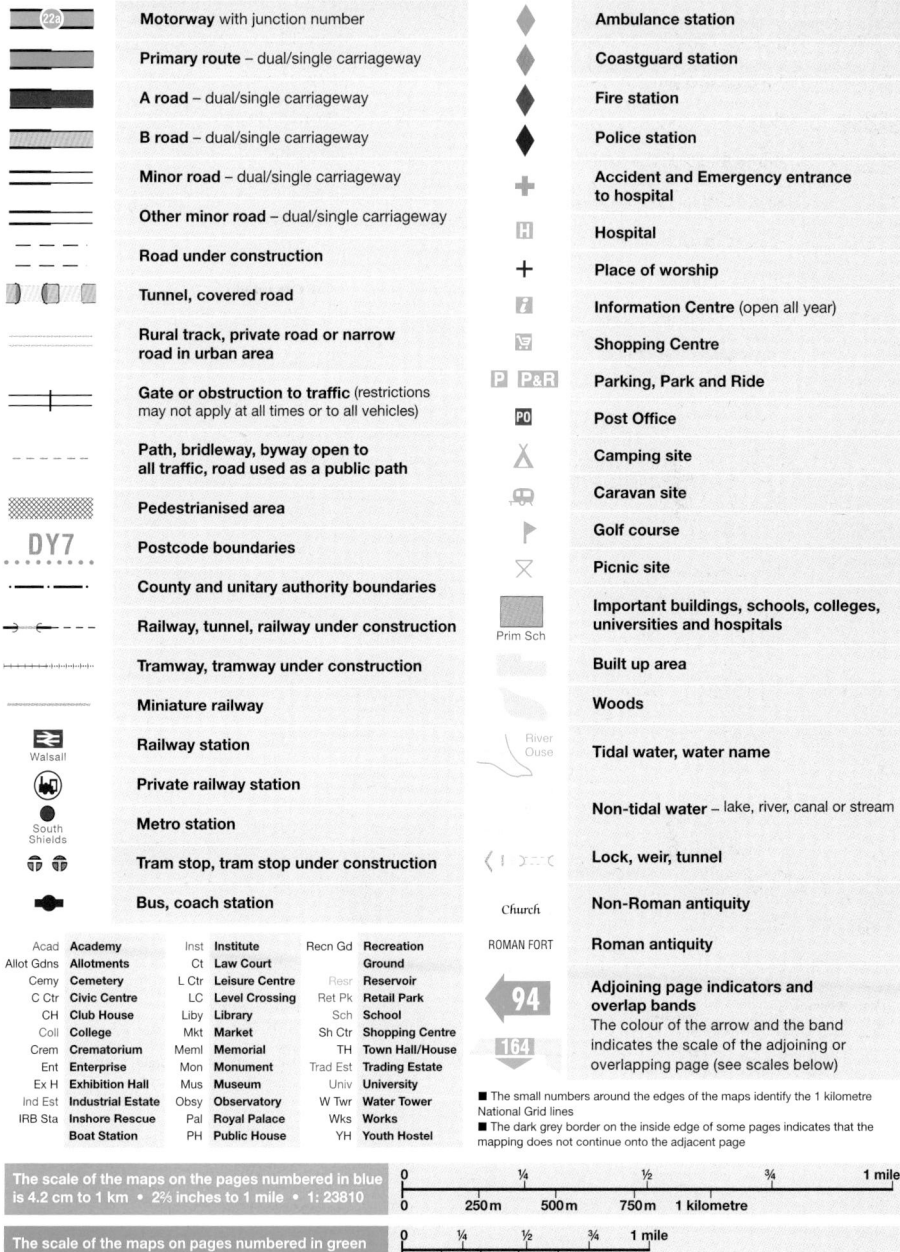

Symbol	Description
	Motorway with junction number
	Primary route – dual/single carriageway
	A road – dual/single carriageway
	B road – dual/single carriageway
	Minor road – dual/single carriageway
	Other minor road – dual/single carriageway
	Road under construction
	Tunnel, covered road
	Rural track, private road or narrow road in urban area
	Gate or obstruction to traffic (restrictions may not apply at all times or to all vehicles)
	Path, bridleway, byway open to all traffic, road used as a public path
	Pedestrianised area
DY7	**Postcode boundaries**
	County and unitary authority boundaries
	Railway, tunnel, railway under construction
	Tramway, tramway under construction
	Miniature railway
Walsall	**Railway station**
	Private railway station
South Shields	**Metro station**
	Tram stop, tram stop under construction
	Bus, coach station

Symbol	Description
	Ambulance station
	Coastguard station
	Fire station
	Police station
	Accident and Emergency entrance to hospital
H	**Hospital**
+	**Place of worship**
i	**Information Centre** (open all year)
	Shopping Centre
P P&R	**Parking, Park and Ride**
PO	**Post Office**
	Camping site
	Caravan site
	Golf course
	Picnic site
Prim Sch	**Important buildings, schools, colleges, universities and hospitals**
	Built up area
	Woods
River Ouse	**Tidal water, water name**
	Non-tidal water – lake, river, canal or stream
	Lock, weir, tunnel
Church	**Non-Roman antiquity**
ROMAN FORT	**Roman antiquity**
94	**Adjoining page indicators and overlap bands** The colour of the arrow and the band indicates the scale of the adjoining or overlapping page (see scales below)
164	

Acad	**Academy**	Inst	**Institute**	Recn Gd **Recreation**
Allot Gdns	**Allotments**	Ct	**Law Court**	**Ground**
Cemy	**Cemetery**	L Ctr	**Leisure Centre**	Resr **Reservoir**
C Ctr	**Civic Centre**	LC	**Level Crossing**	Ret Pk **Retail Park**
CH	**Club House**	Liby	**Library**	Sch **School**
Coll	**College**	Mkt	**Market**	Sh Ctr **Shopping Centre**
Crem	**Crematorium**	Meml	**Memorial**	TH **Town Hall/House**
Ent	**Enterprise**	Mon	**Monument**	Trad Est **Trading Estate**
Ex H	**Exhibition Hall**	Mus	**Museum**	Univ **University**
Ind Est	**Industrial Estate**	Obsy	**Observatory**	W Twr **Water Tower**
IRB Sta	**Inshore Rescue Boat Station**	Pal	**Royal Palace**	Wks **Works**
		PH	**Public House**	YH **Youth Hostel**

■ The small numbers around the edges of the maps identify the 1 kilometre National Grid lines
■ The dark grey border on the inside edge of some pages indicates that the mapping does not continue onto the adjacent page

The scale of the maps on the pages numbered in blue is 4.2 cm to 1 km • 2⅔ inches to 1 mile • 1: 23810

0 ¼ ½ ¾ 1 mile
0 250m 500m 750m 1 kilometre

The scale of the maps on pages numbered in green is 2.1 cm to 1 km • 1⅓ inches to 1 mile • 1: 47620

0 ¼ ½ ¾ 1 mile
0 250m 500m 750m 1kilometre

Administrative and Postcode boundaries

County and unitary authority boundaries
.... Postcode boundaries
Area covered by this atlas

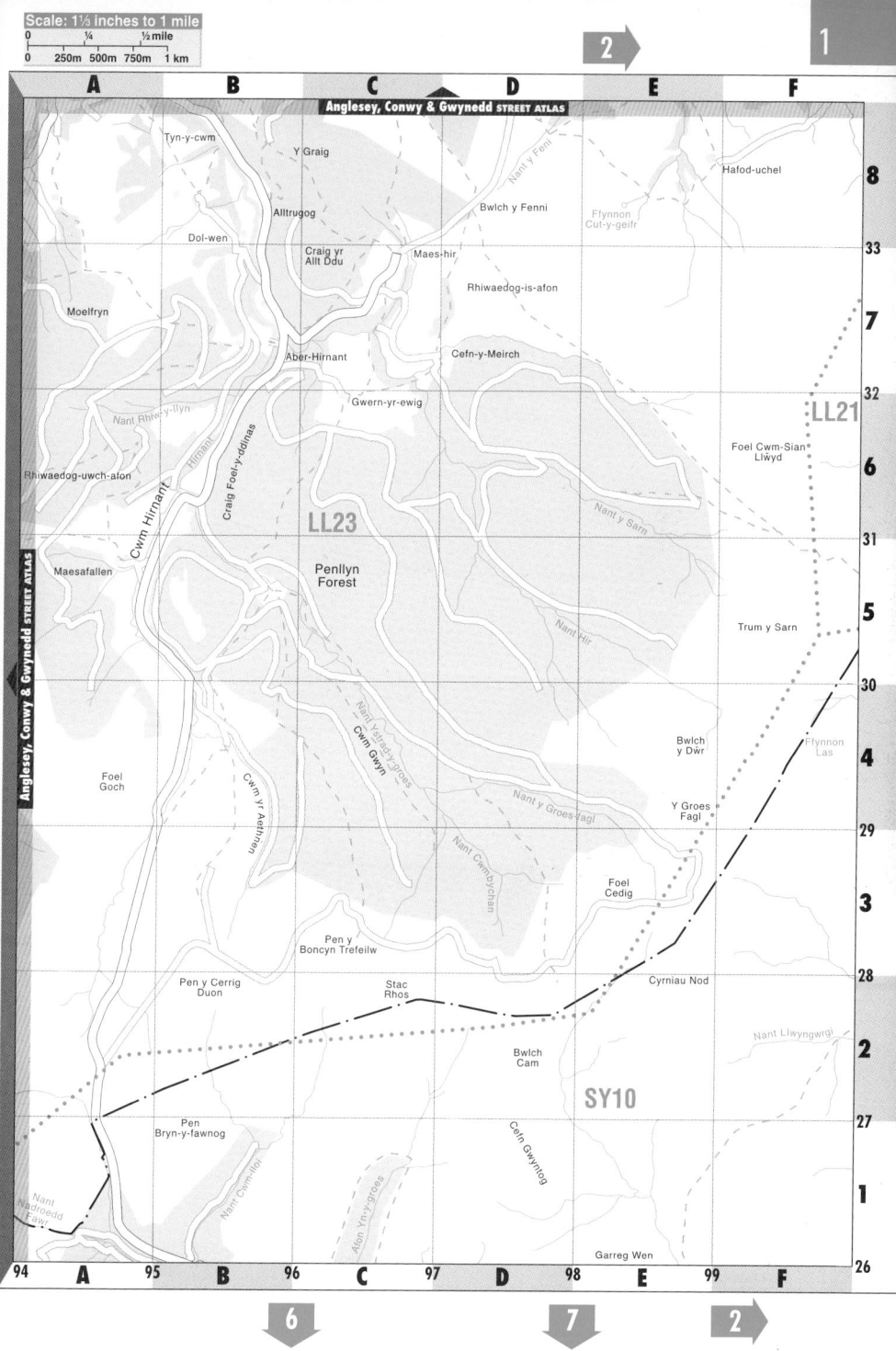

Scale: 1⅓ inches to 1 mile

0   ¼   ½ mile
0   250m 500m 750m 1 km

A   **B**   **C**   **D**   **E**   **F**

Anglesey, Conwy & Gwynedd STREET ATLAS

8

LL23

Rhanneg

B4391

Cwm Sian Llwyd

Dinas

Cefn Llysfyn

Nant Cwm Tywyll

Rhyd-y-Gethin

Pennant

Nant Esgeiriau

33

Bryniau
Gleision

LL21

Nant Cwm Pydew

Blaen-y-cwm

Nant Y Waun

Cwm-pen-llydan

Esgeiriau

7

Nant Crethwy

Yr
Oron

32

6

Pont
Cwm Pydew

Nant Sgrin

Ceunant Coch

31

Cwm y Eithin

Cerrig
Duon

5

Milltir
Gerrig

Blaen Glaswen

Afon Disgynfa

30

Craig Wen

4

Bryn Ysbio

Tre-rhiwarth

Blaen-rhiwarth

Post
Gwyn

29

Hafod
Hir

Craig Blaen-
rhiwarth

Tyn-y-ffynonydd

Cwm Rhiwarth

Bryn
Mawr

3

Nant Llwyngwgil

Craig Boeth

Ty-mawr

Bedd Crynddyn

28

SY10

Craig y
Castell

Llwyn-onn

Tre-y-llan

Afon Ocw

2

Graig
Wen

Blaen y Cwm

Nant Ewyn

Yr
Eithin

Pencraig

Craig Pen-
y-buarth

27

Nant Achlas

Tyn-y-cablyd

Aber
Cysgod

Afon Eirth

Craig
Rhiwarth

1

Nant Tory

**Pennant
+Melangell**

Cwm Pennant

Y Gribin

Llechwedd-
y-garth

Llangynog

B4391

GLENDOWER
CVN PK

PH

26

Trum y Fawnog

CHURCH VIEW 1
CHURCH ST 2

00   **A**   **01**   **B**   **02**   **C**   **03**   **D**   **04**   **E**   **05**   **F**

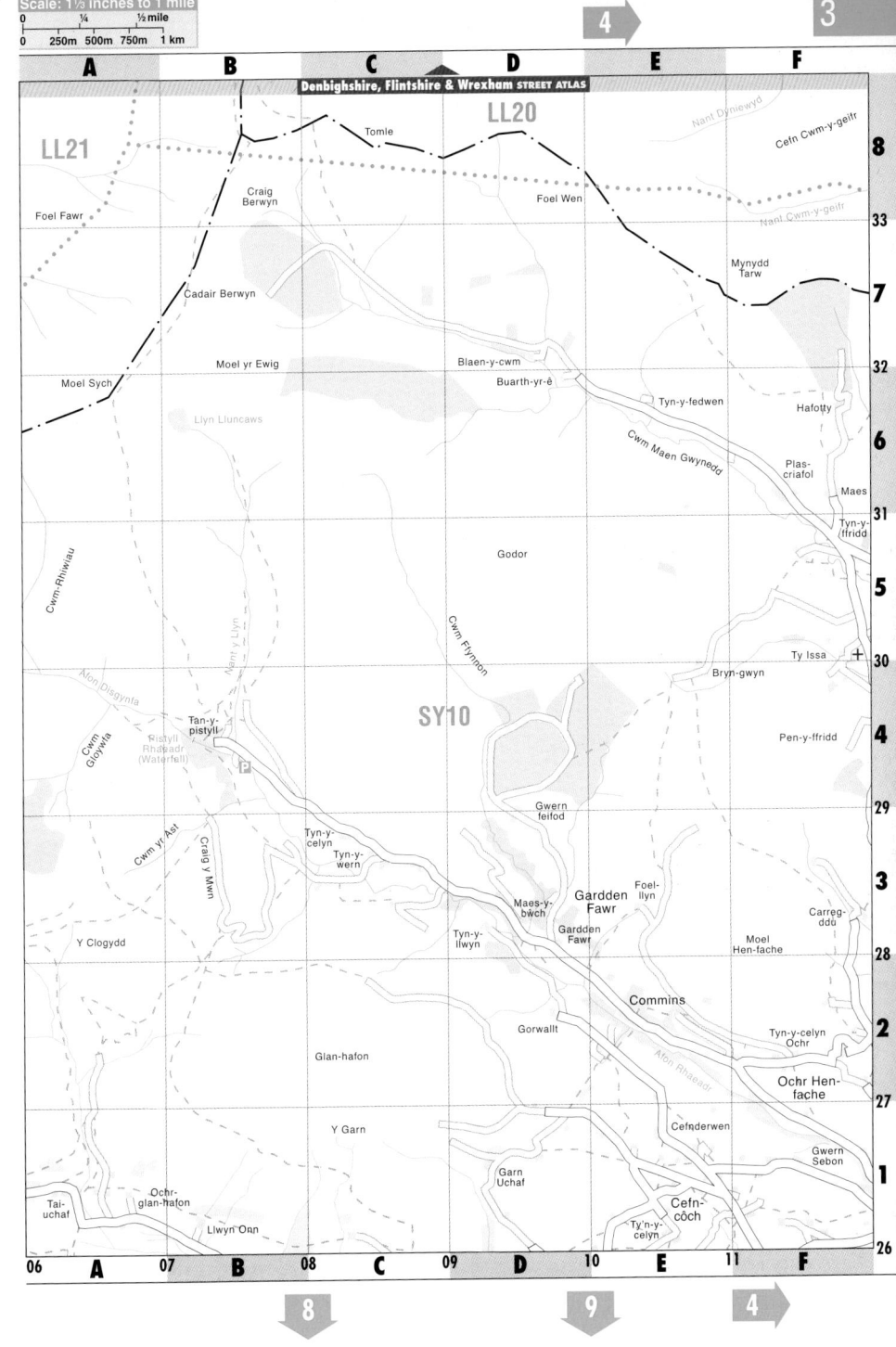

Scale: 1⅓ inches to 1 mile

0   ¼   ½ mile
0   250m 500m 750m 1 km

LL21

LL20

SY10

Foel Fawr

Craig Berwyn

Cadair Berwyn

Moel yr Ewig

Moel Sych

Llyn Lluncaws

Cwm-Rhiwiau

Afon Disgynfa

Cwm Gloywfa

Tan-y-pistyll

Pistyll Rhaeadr (Waterfall)

Cwm yr Ast

Craig y Mwn

Y Clogydd

Tyn-y-celyn

Tyn-y-wern

Maes-y-bwch

Tyn-y-llwyn

Garden Fawr

Gwern feifod

Gardden Fawr

Foel-llyn

Commins

Gorwallt

Glan-hafon

Y Garn

Garn Uchaf

Cefnderwen

Ty'n-y-celyn

Cefn-côch

Tai-uchaf

Ochr-glan-hafon

Llwyn Onn

Tomle

Foel Wen

Blaen-y-cwm

Buarth-yr-ê

Tyn-y-fedwen

Cwm Maen Gwynedd

Godor

Cwm Flynnon

Bryn-gwyn

Ty Issa

Pen-y-ffridd

Moel Hen-fache

Tyn-y-celyn Ochr

Ochr Hen-fache

Gwern Sebon

Cefn Cwm-y-geifr

Nant Dyniewyd

Nant Cwm-y-geifr

Mynydd Tarw

Hafotty

Plas-criafol

Maes

Tyn-y-ffridd

Carreg-ddu

Afon Rhaeadr

Nant y Llyn

3

Scale: 1⅓ inches to 1 mile

0   ¼   ½ mile
0   250m 500m 750m 1 km

Denbighshire, Flintshire & Wrexham STREET ATLAS

8

Glas-aber
Dolwen
Mynydd Bach
Hafod Adams
Ael-y-coryn
MAISEINION
B4500
Tregeiriog

33

River Ceiriog
Afon Ceiriog
Tower
Penybryn
Foel Gôch
Sarffle
Plas Tregeiriog

Nant Cwm-y-geifr
Cae-llwyd
Ty'n-y-fedw
B4500

Nant Sarffle
Ysgol Llanarmon Dyffryn Ceiriog
PORTH-Y-CWM
PH

7

LL20
Llanarmon Dyffryn Ceiriog

Rhos
Maengwyn

32

Cyrchynan-isaf

6

Pen-cae-newydd

Cyrchynan-ucha

Cefn Hir-fyhydd

Hen Graig

31

Garneddwen
LLIDIART-CAE-HIR

5

Cae-hir

Cefn-y-rhodfa
Pant-y-maen
Lawnt

Tyn-y-cae
Cynarfron
Ty-gwyn

30

Tynyfron
Pantglas Ucha

4

Tan-y-ffridd
Cefn Gwyn
Glas-hirfryn
Pantglas Isaf

SY10
Preswylfa
Ty-newydd
Berthlwyd
Nanthirwen

29

Gilfach
Ty-mawr
Bryn-Gwerfil
Tynllyn

Pén-y-graig
Tai-bach
Pen-y-graig
Parc Farm
Llyn Moeltre

3

Bedran
Ceunant-du

28

Llanarmon Mynydd-mawr
Moel Lloran
Oddiar-y-llyn

Sychnant
Plasynglyn
Hafod
Moel y Gwelltyn

2

Penfforddwen
Liety
Tyn-y-ffridd
Tyddyn Maen

Afon Iwrch
Lleiriog
B4580

Bryn Coch
Rhydygaled
Lloran Uchaf

27

Gors-goch
Cefnhirfach
Tynycelyn

Henfache
Cefnhirfawr

1

Llanrhaeadr-ym-Mochnant
1 BACK CHAPEL ST
2 MAES Y DDERWEN
3 CHURCH ST
4 DOL-Y-BONT
Ty-brith
Efail-rhyd
Mynydd-y-briw

WATERFALL ST
Trewern
CROES-STRYT
Parc Uchaf
Ty-draw
Craig Orllwyn

26

Sch
B4580
PARK ST
Pont Tre-wern

MARKET ST
P

5

B4500

LL20

SY10

A B C D E F

Cemy
Cefn-y-braich
Ty-newydd
Foel Wylfa
Pensarn
Blaen Rhiwlas Uchaf
Nant
Rhiwlas
Craig Ysgwennant
Ysgwennant
Llangadwaladr
Gyrn Moelfre
Craig Gamhyll
Pentre
Moelfre
Lloran Isaf
Ty Du
Craig Fawr
Priddbwll
Pentrecwm
Parc Sycharth
Talwrn
Tynewydd
Cefn-y-braich
Glan-yr-Afon
CROES-HIR
BRYN-CELYN
Llansilin
PH
Ysgol Bro Cynllaith
MAES Y LLAN
Penllan
Moeliwrch
Wenffrwd
Bodlith
Hafodty
Bryn-ellyll
Clyrun
Rhydleos
Lledrod
Bwlch
Tyncelyn
Lledrod
Ty-mawr
Felin Newydd
Derwen Deg
Tynygroes
Glanogeu
Hafod
Ty-draw
Tynyfron
Hafodig
Mynydd Lledrod
Tynllwyn
Fron Ucha
Foel Rhiwlas
Craig-yr-hwch
Siambr-gerrig
Pen y Gwely
Ty-uchaf
Bwlchydonge
Cefn Canol
Cefn-y-maes
Cefnbyralit
Gallt-y-wrach
Bank Farm
Bryncoch
Tan-y-graig
Bwlch y rhiw
Cynllaith
Craig-y-rhiw
Rifle Range
DANGER AREA
Coed y-Gaer
Llyn Rhuddwyn
Coed Cochion
Pentregaer
Craig-llwyn
Glascoed
Fron
Mynydd y Bryn
Pentre-cefn
Wern ddu
Pentre
Cefn Coch
Pen-y-gwely Resr
Afon Ogau

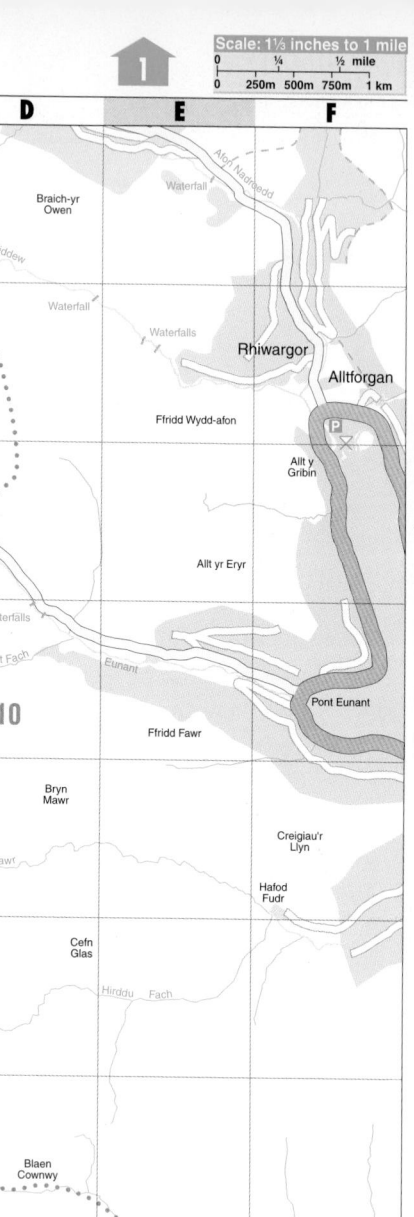

Anglesey, Conwy & Gwynedd STREET ATLAS

Anglesey, Conwy & Gwynedd STREET ATLAS

LL23

LL40

LL23

Braich-yr Owen

Afon Eiddew

Waterfall

Afon Nantnedd

Carreg Clap

Craig yr Ogof

Tan-y-bwlch

Moel y Cerrig Duon

Waun y Gadfa

Viewpoint

Bwlch y Groes

Waun Drawsfan

Craig y Pant

Gallt Ceiniogau

Cwm Cerddin

SY20

Coed Cochion

Cwm Llygoed

Pen-y-gelli

Cwm Pen-y-gelli

Tap Mawr

Carreg y Fran

Carreg y Big

Eunant Fawr

Y Gadfa

Cairn

Earthwork

Waterfalls

Eunant Fach

SY10

Y Berwyn National Nature Reserve

Bryn Mawr

Hirddu Fawr

Cefn Glas

Hirddu Fach

Mynydd Coch

Blaen Cownwy

SY21

Hen Gerrig

Waterfall

Waterfalls

Rhiwargor

Alltforgan

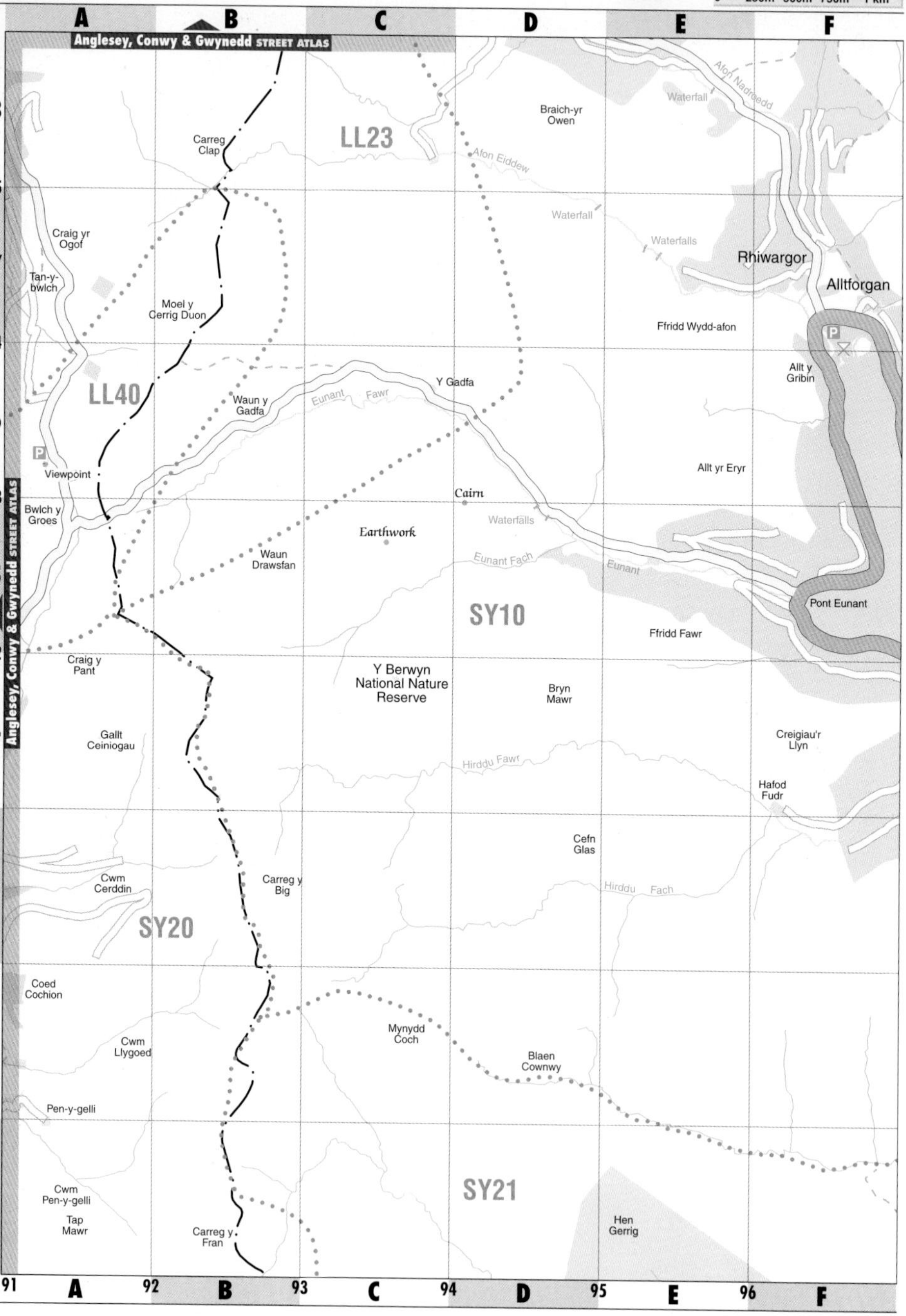

Ffridd Wydd-afon

Allt y Gribin

Allt yr Eryr

Eunant

Pont Eunant

Ffridd Fawr

Creigiau'r Llyn

Hafod Fudr

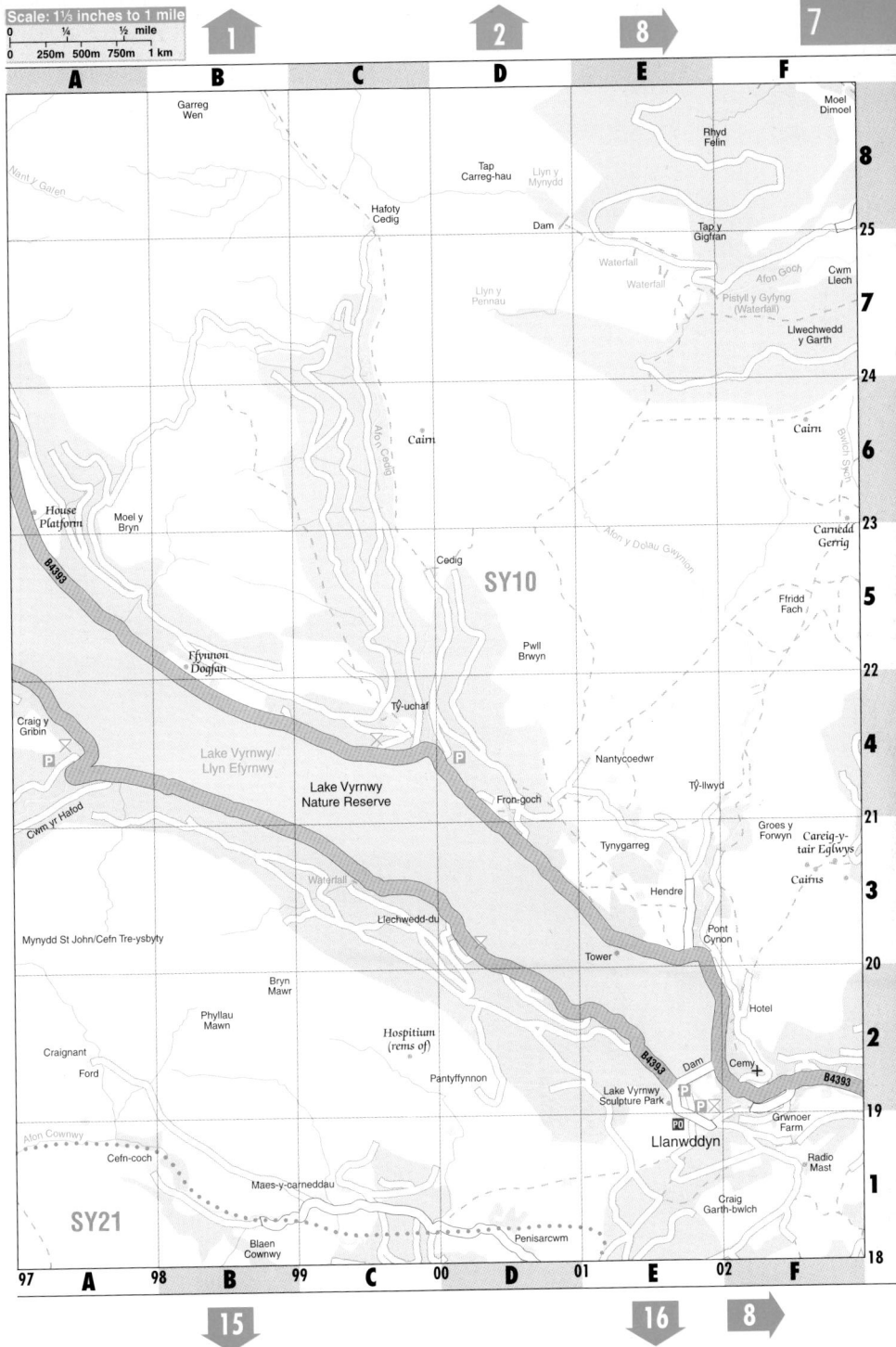

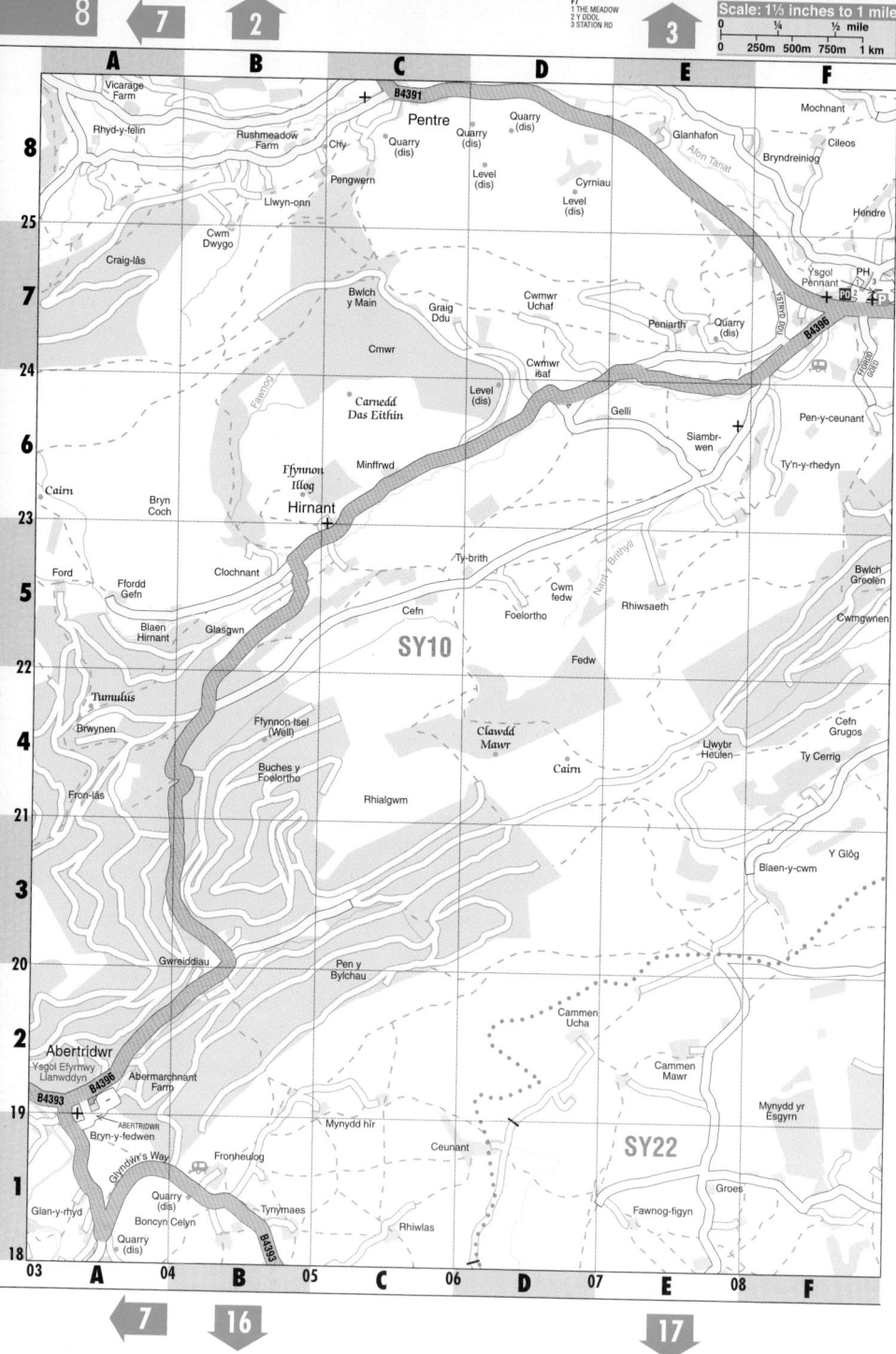

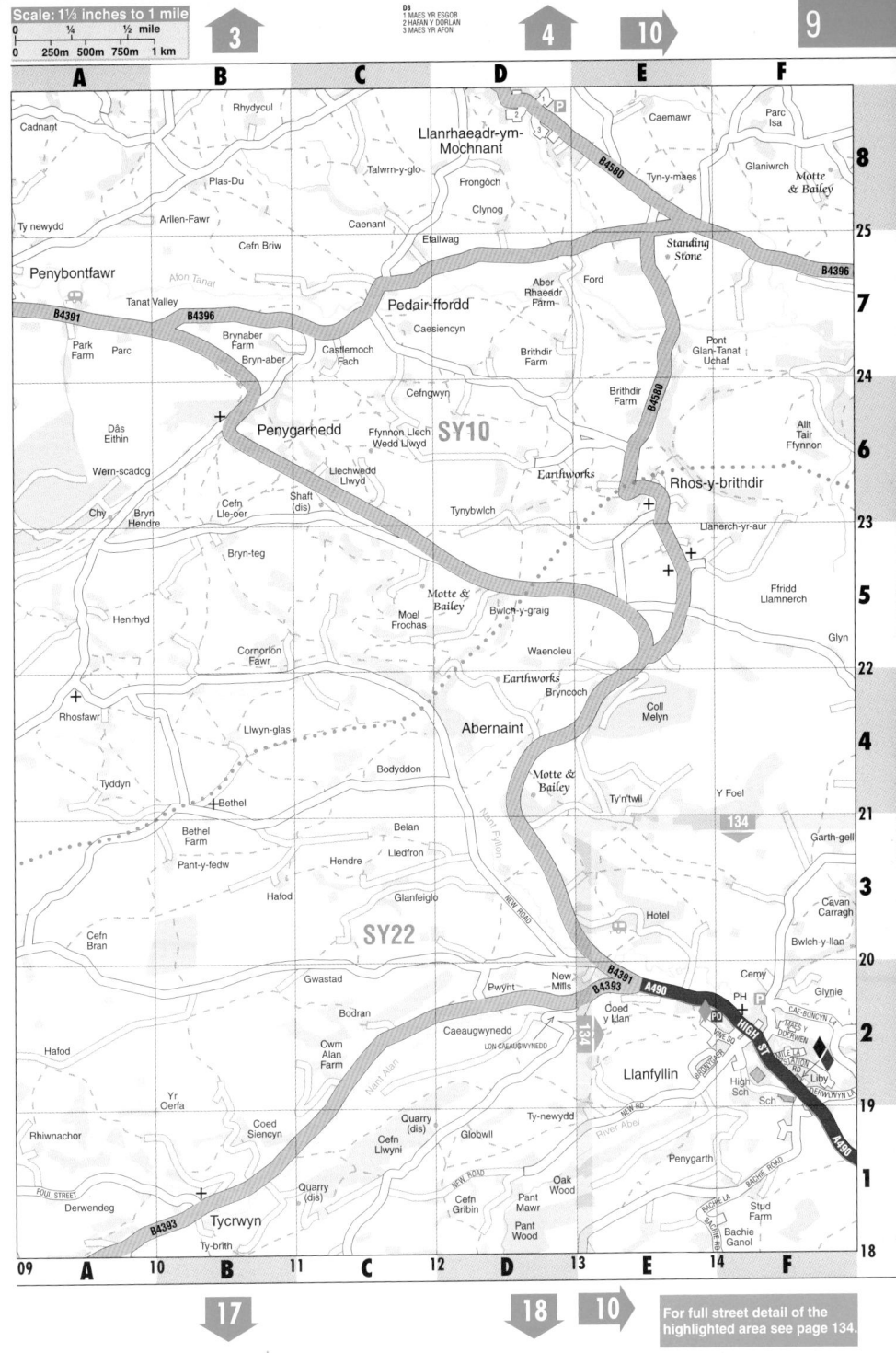

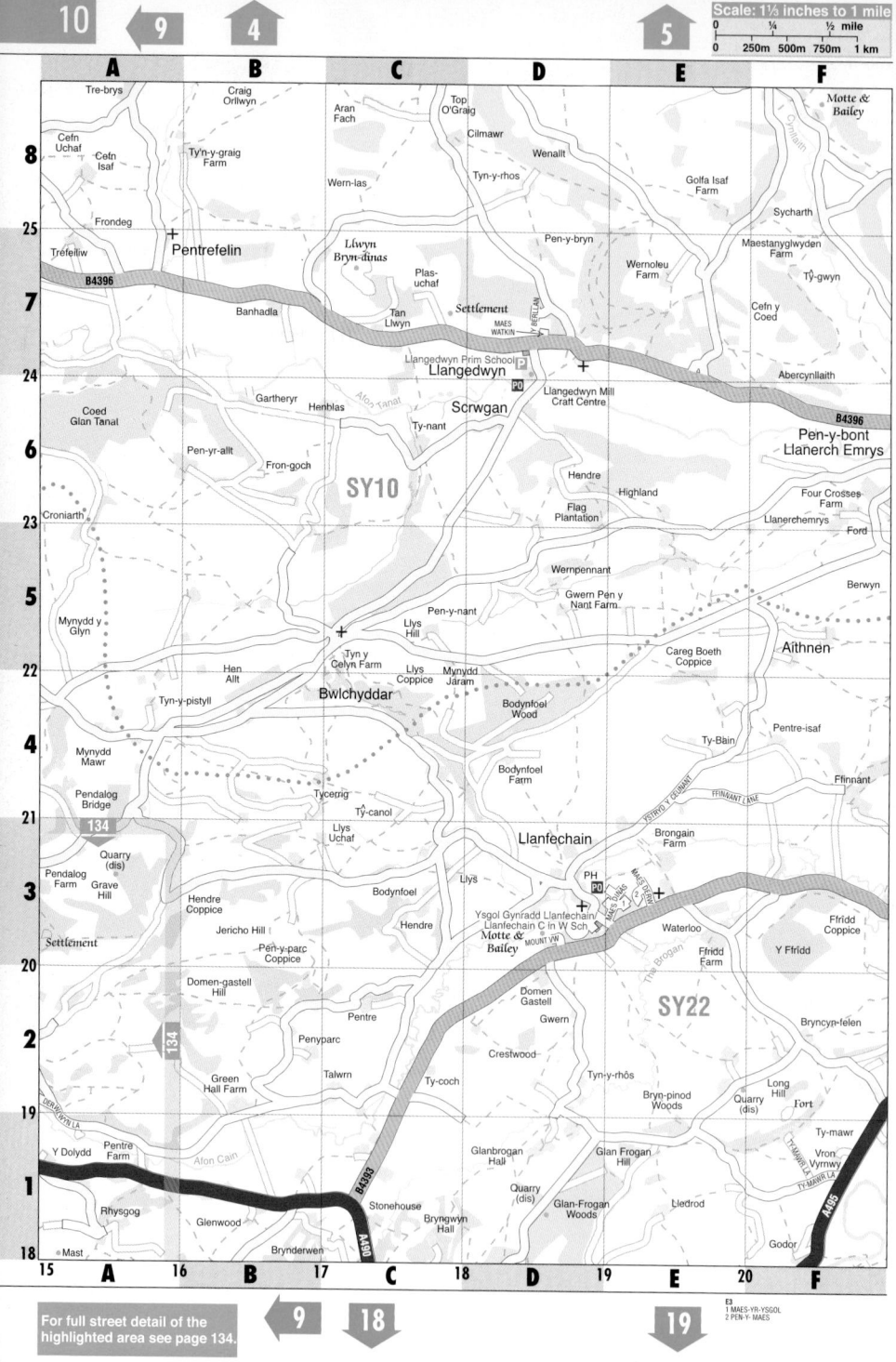

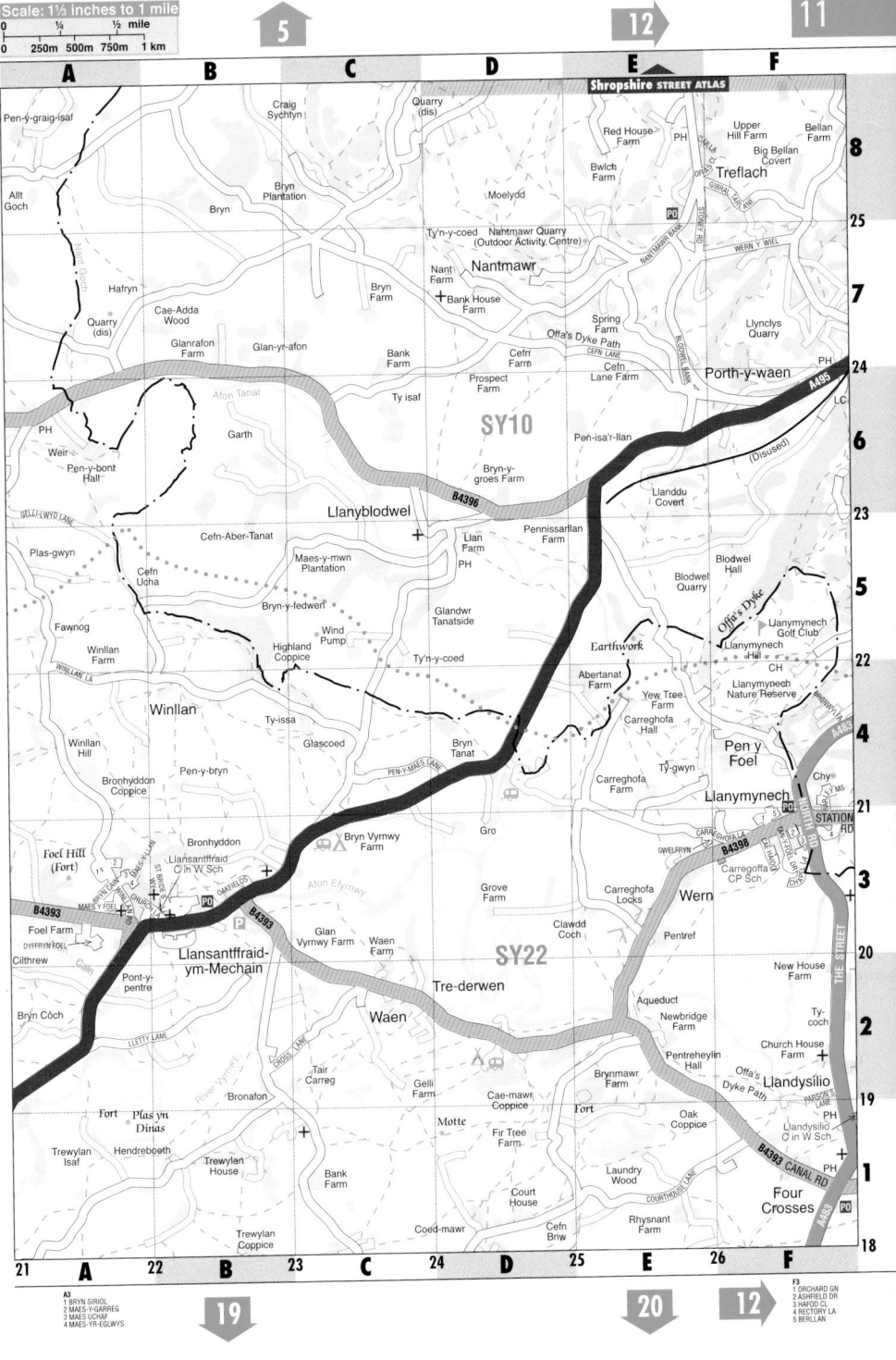

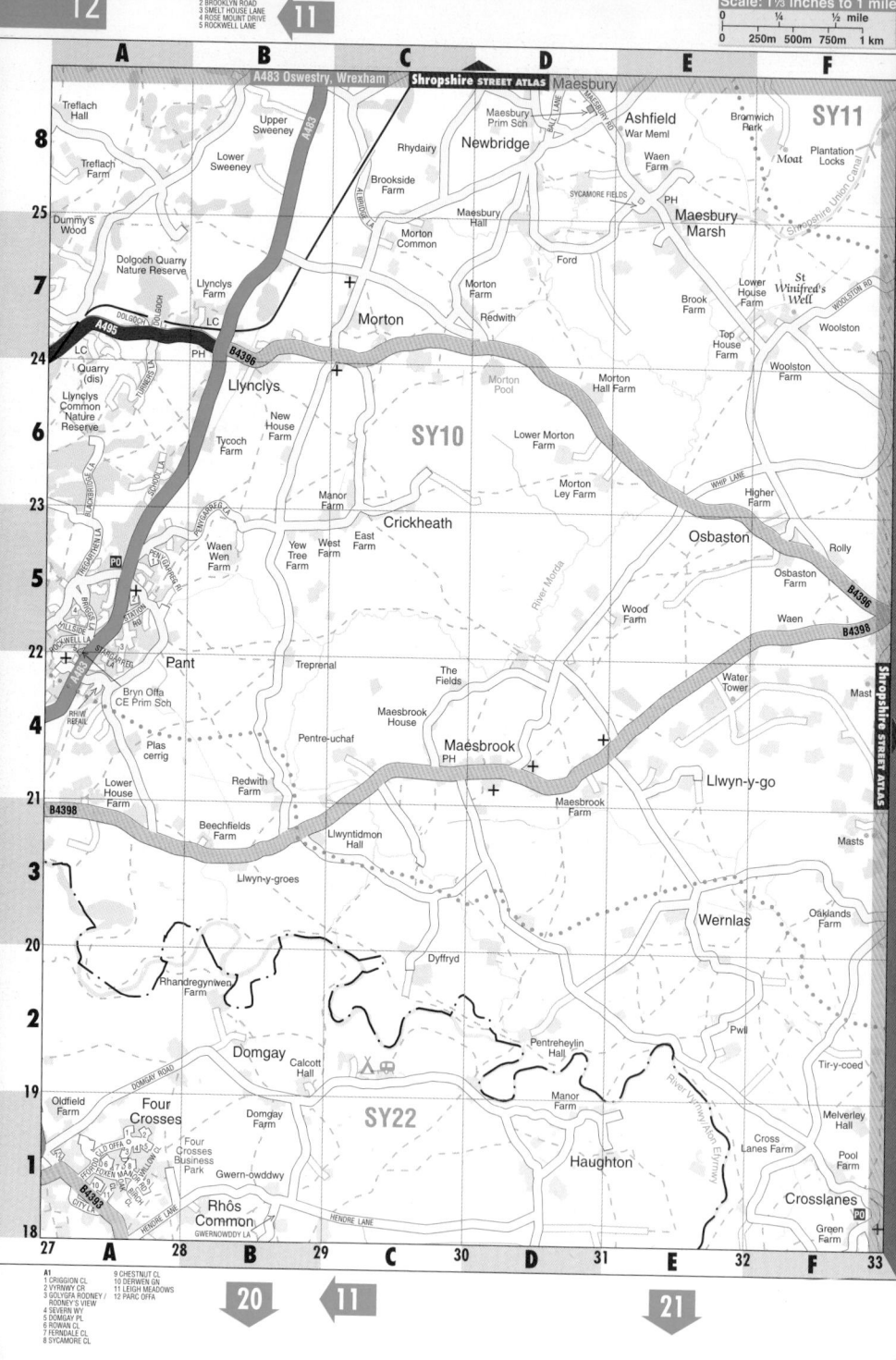

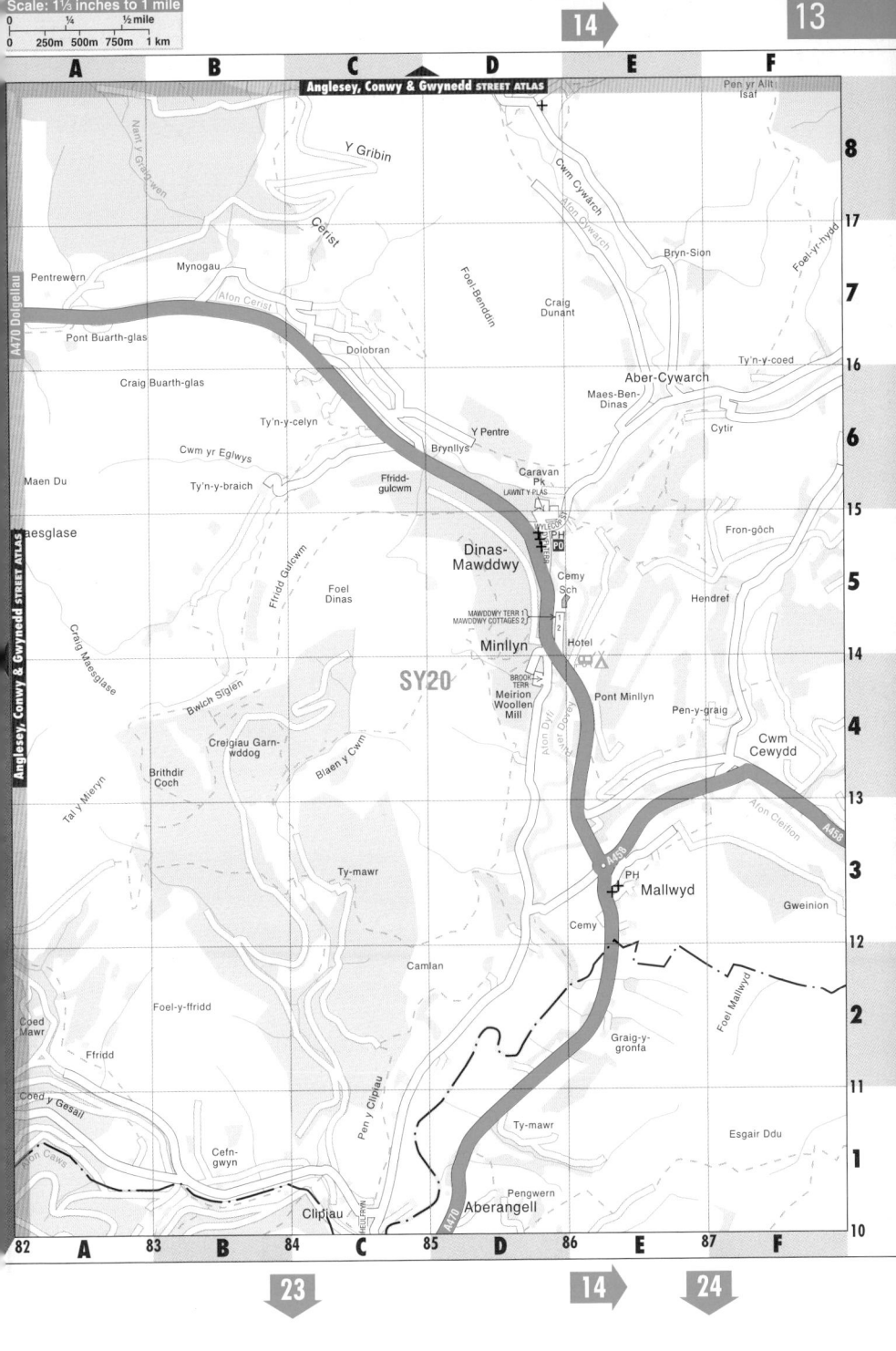

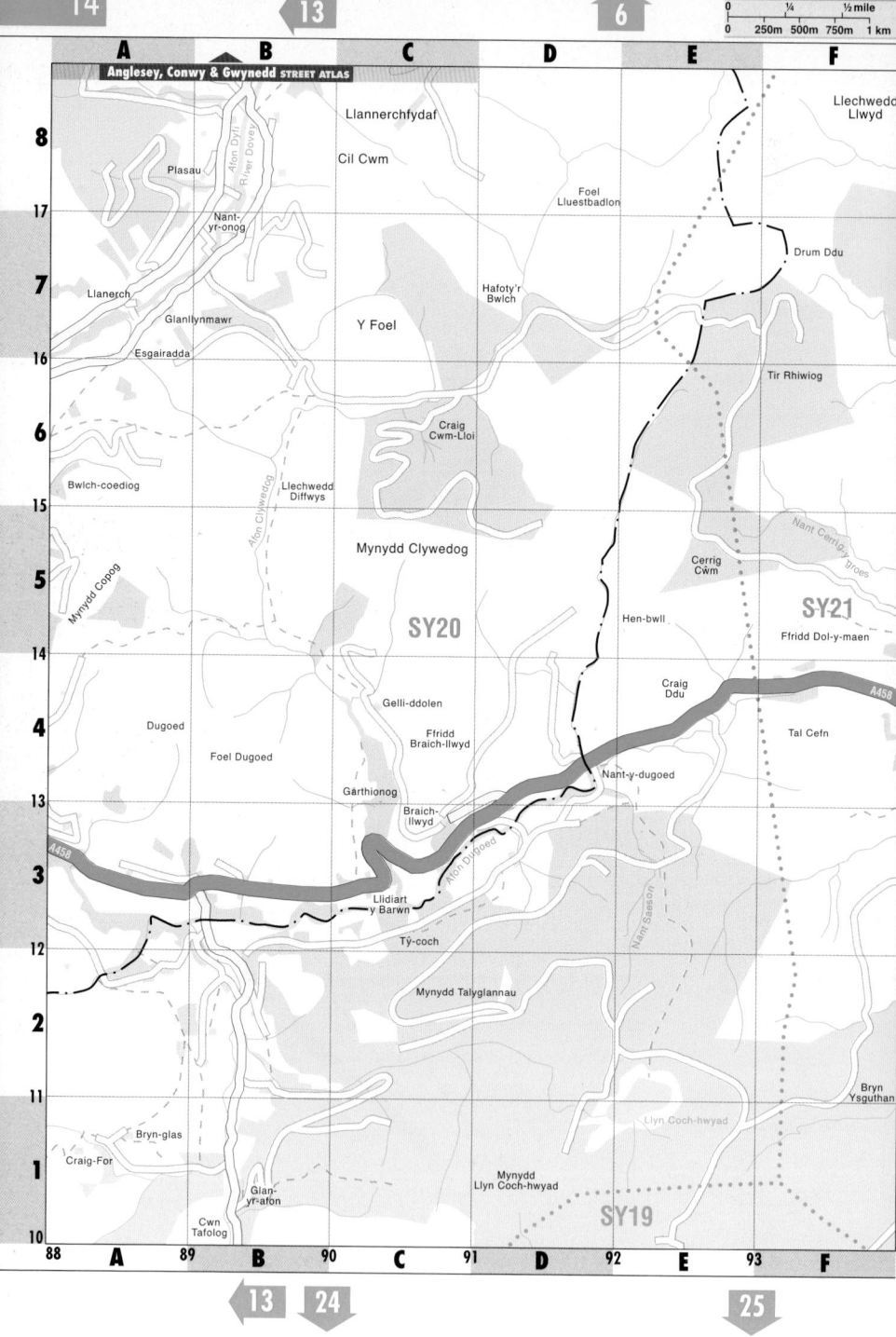

Anglesey, Conwy & Gwynedd STREET ATLAS

Llannerchfydaf

Cil Cwm

Llechwedd Llwyd

Plasau

Afon Dyfi

River Dovey

Nant-yr-ongg

Foel Lluestbadlon

Drum Ddu

Llanerch

Hafoty'r Bwlch

Glanllynmawr

Y Foel

Esgairadda

Tir Rhiwiog

Craig Cwm-Lloi

Bwlch-coediog

Afon Clywedog

Llechwedd Diffwys

Nant Cerrig-y-groes

Mynydd Clywedog

Cerrig Cwm

Mynydd Copog

SY20

SY21

Ffridd Dol-y-maen

Hen-bwll

Gelli-ddolen

Craig Ddu

A458

Dugoed

Ffridd Braich-llwyd

Tal Cefn

Foel Dugoed

Nant-y-dugoed

Garthionog

Braich-llwyd

Afon Dugoed

A458

Llidiart y Barwn

Nant Saeson

Tŷ-coch

Mynydd Talyglannau

Bryn-glas

Bryn Ysguthan

Craig-For

Llyn Coch-hwyad

Glan-yr-afon

Cwn Tafolog

Mynydd Llyn Coch-hwyad

SY19

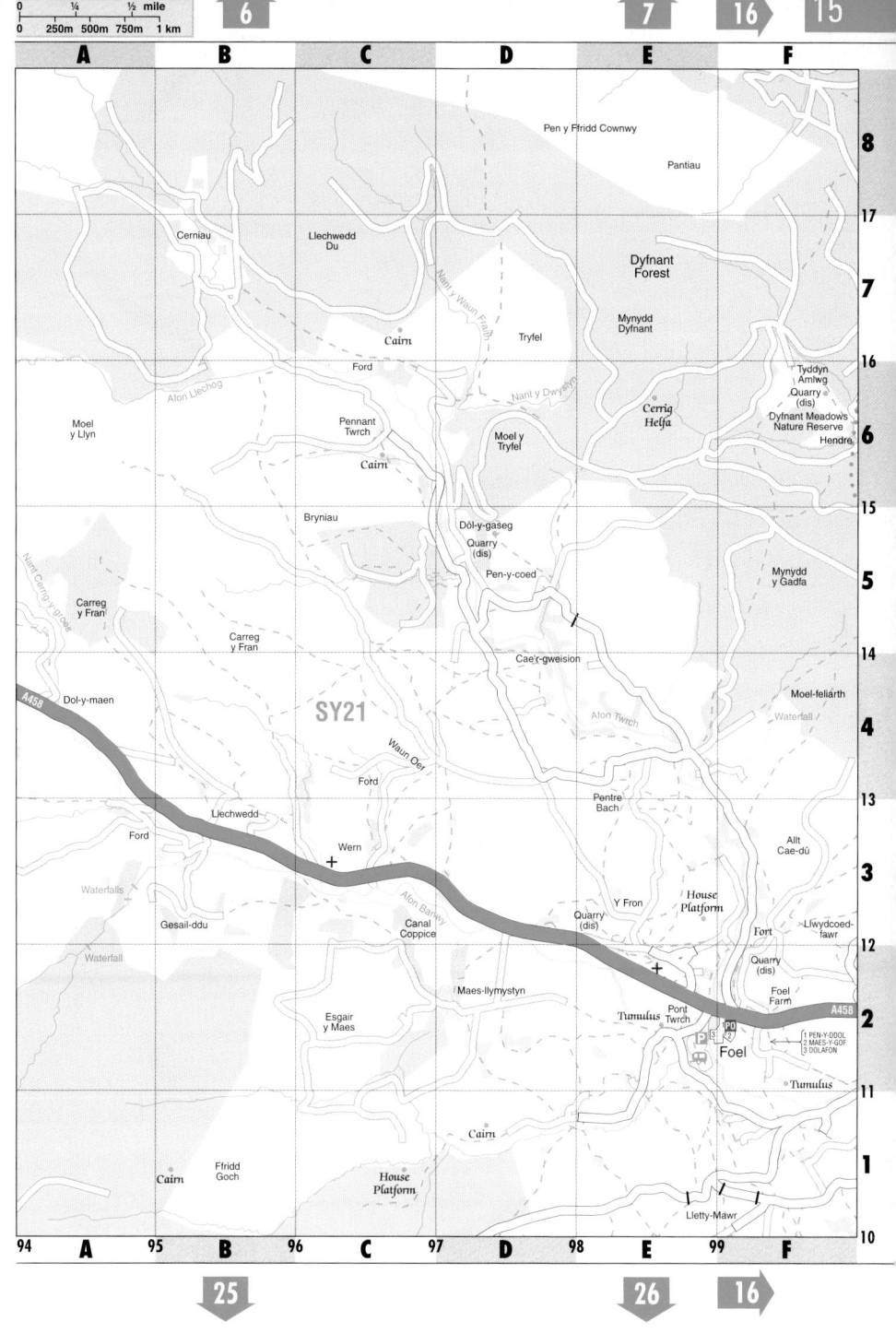

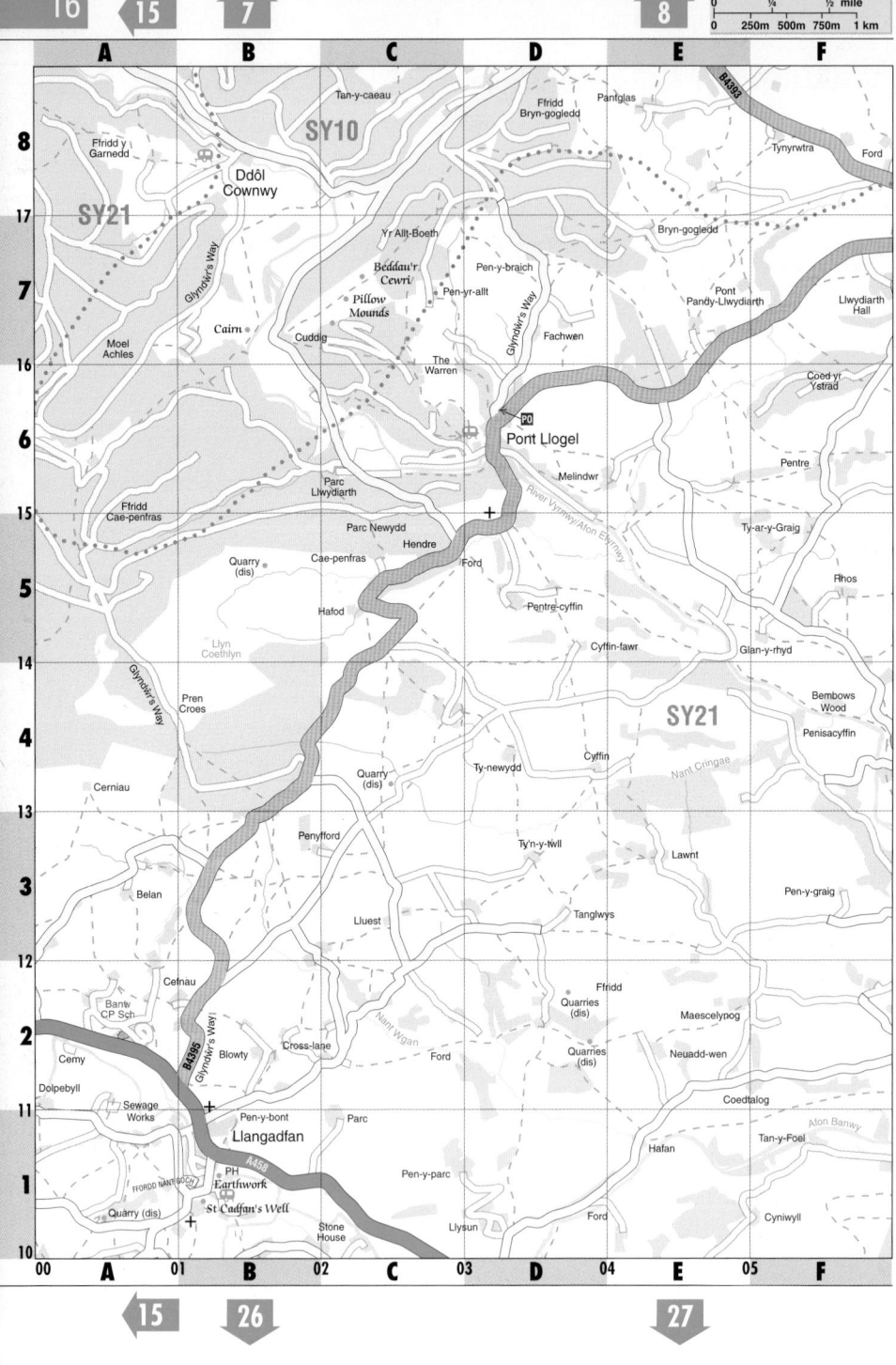

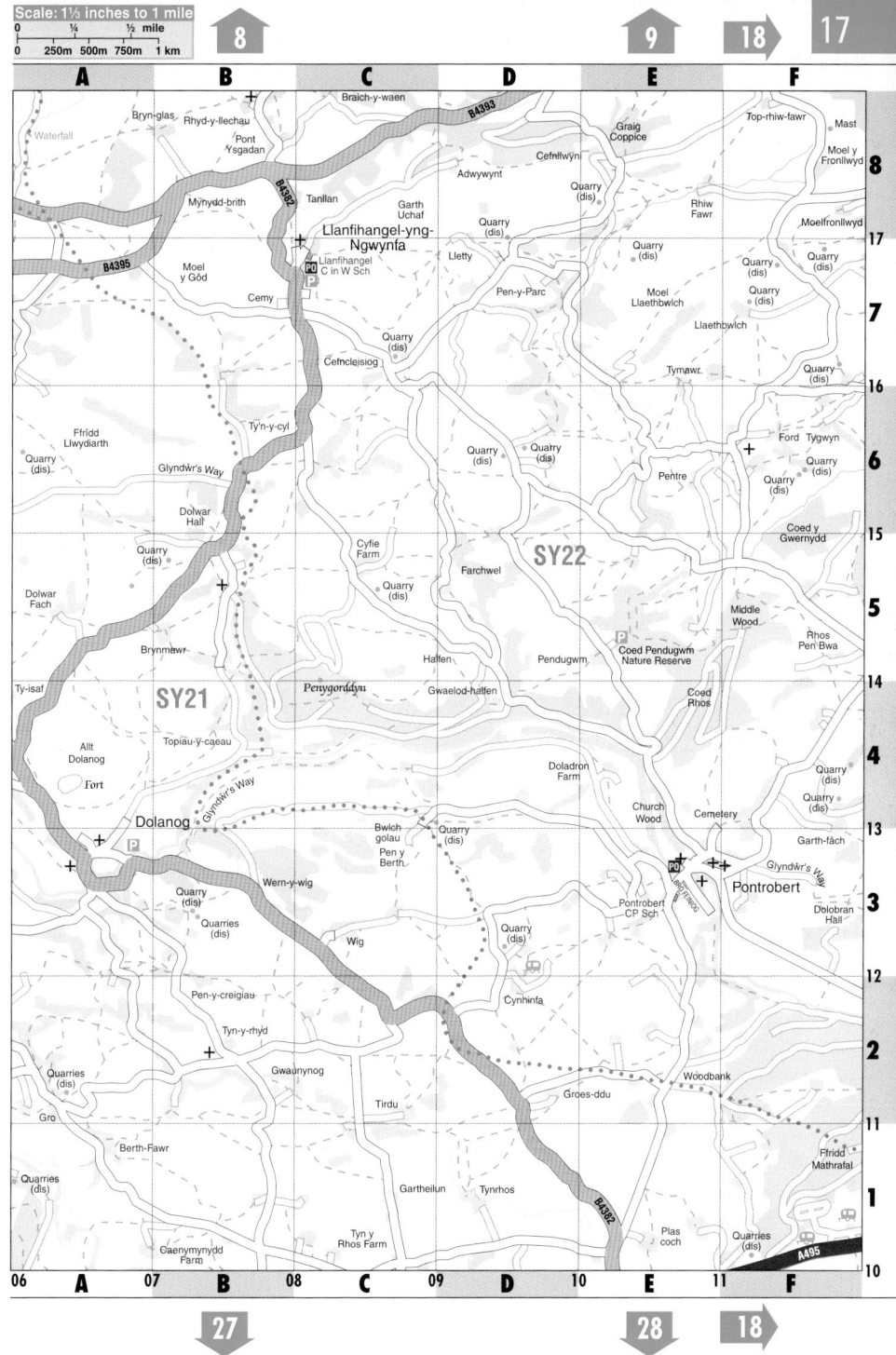

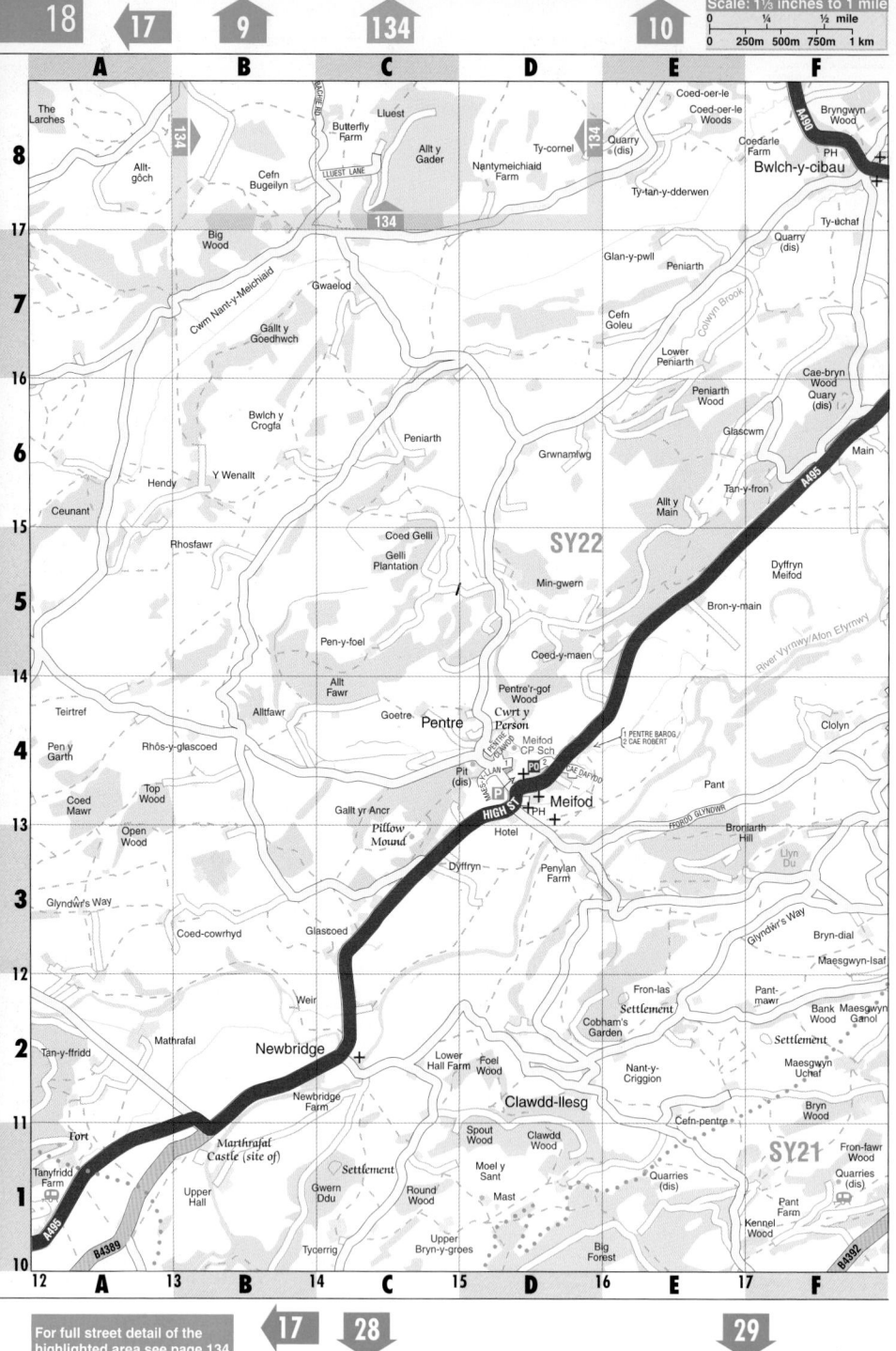

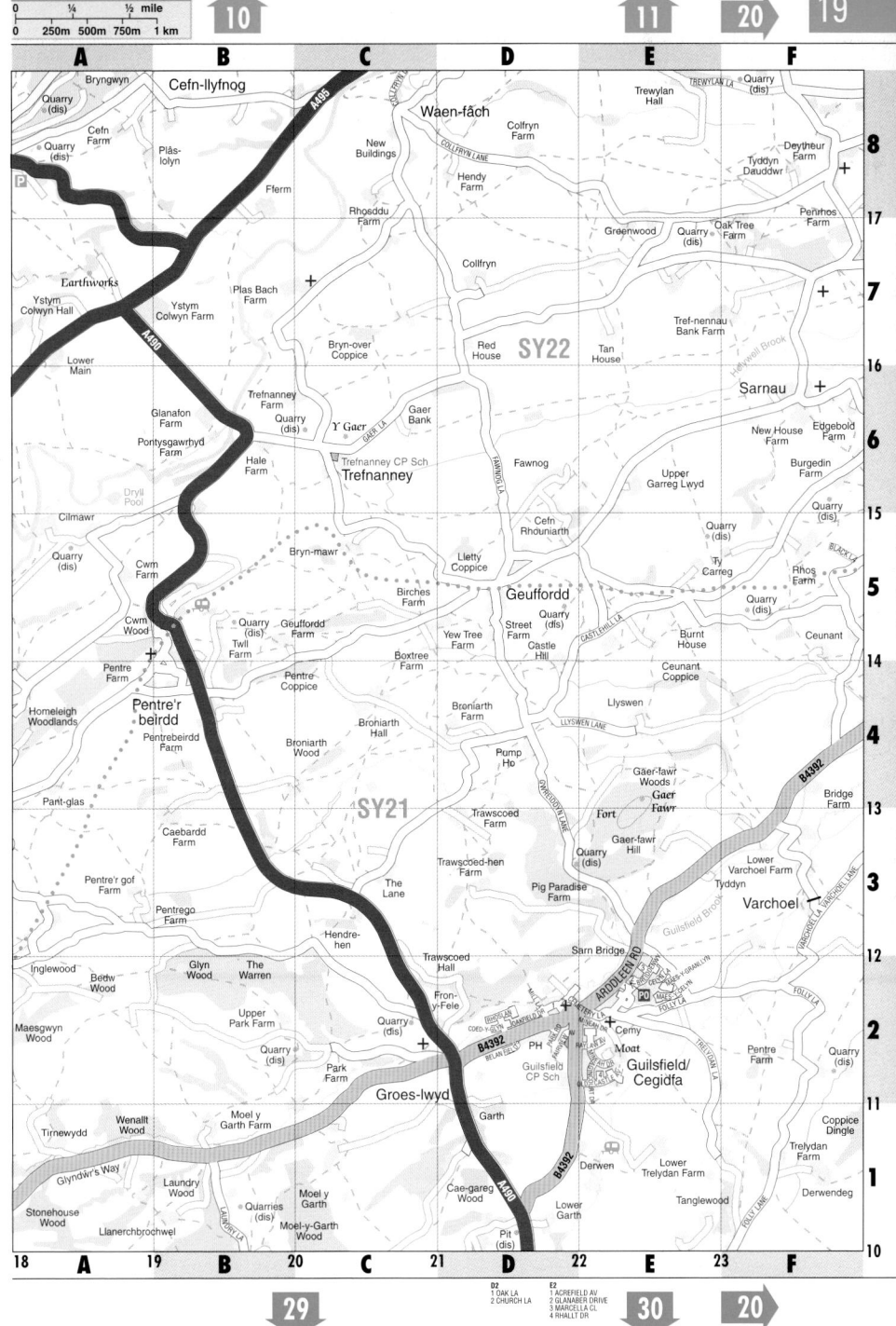

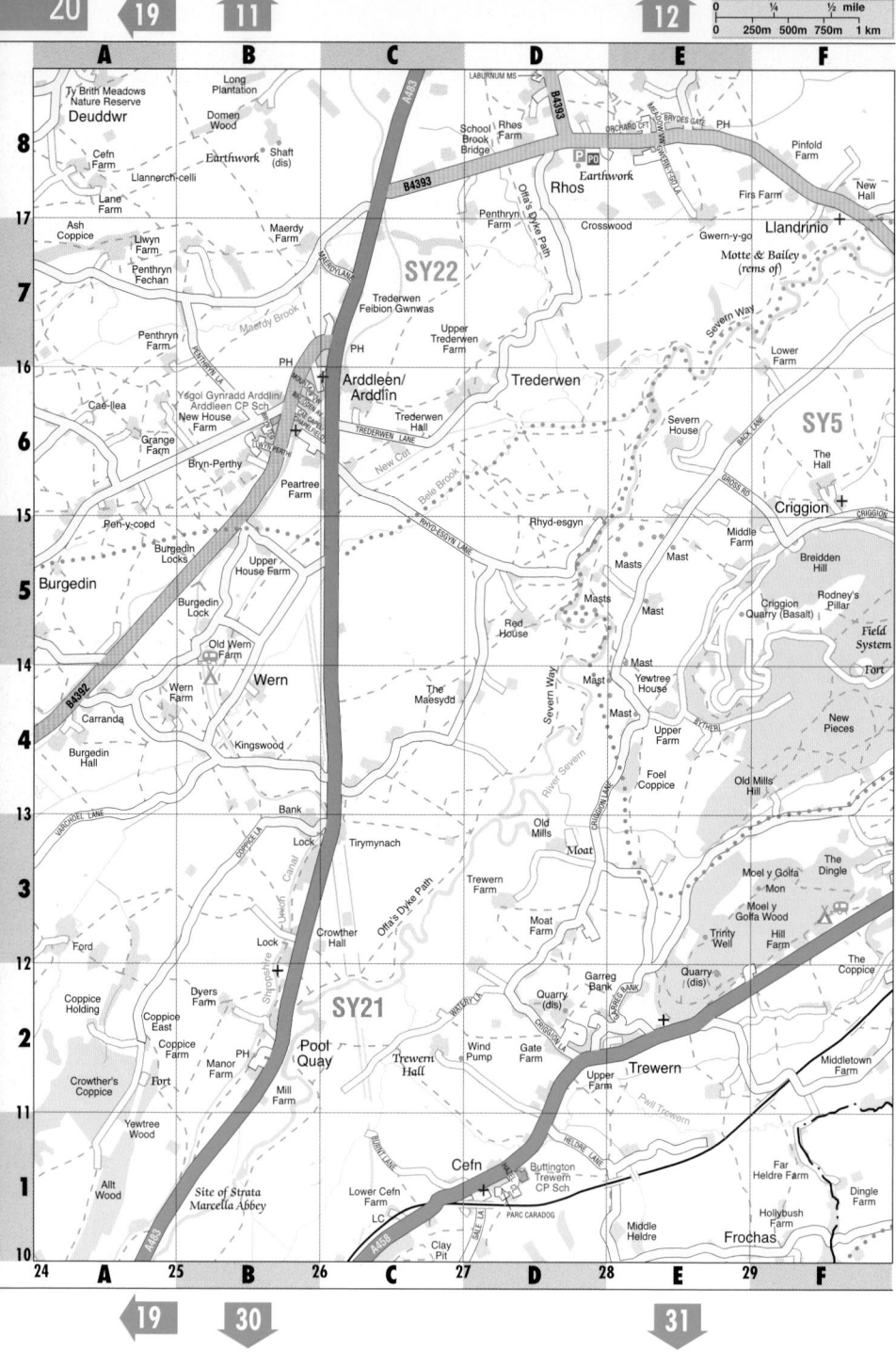

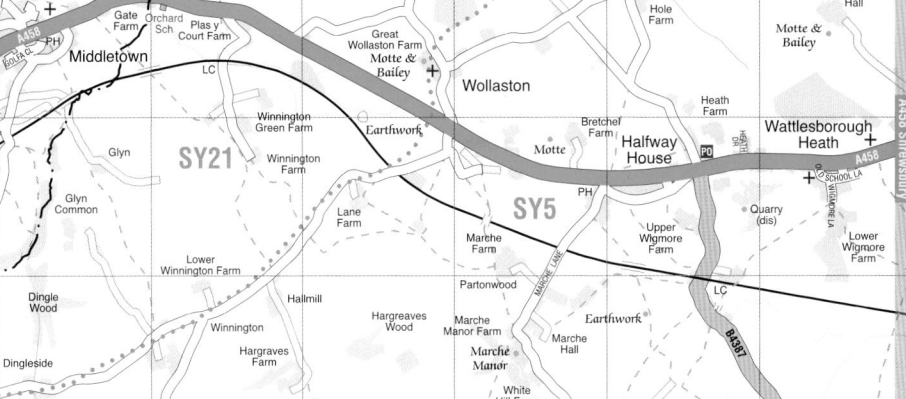

Sychpwll
The Shores
Haughton Farm
Hendre Farm
Hendre
Hendre Villa
Duglands
SY10
Severnside
PH
SY4
8
Bontain Farm
Bank Farm
Pomthen
Oap Howel
Haimwood Farm
SY22
17
Lower House
The Rendezvous
Haimwood
The Haim
Melverley
Melverley Craft Centre PH
CHURCH LA
River Severn
7
Coppice Farm
Severn Way
Lord's Plantation
16
Criggion Bridge
Quarry (dis)
Manor Farm
Bellan House
MAES HAFREN
Brook House Farm
PH
Seven Oaks Farm
Pentre Farm
Upper Hayes Farm
Partner's Coppice
6
Lane Farm
MALT RD
Bryphafren CP Sch
PH
PISLEY VW
PRINCESS CT
Lower Hayes Farm
15
PH
Crewgreen
LA
Bausley Hill Farm
Bausley House
Coedway
Red House Farm
Loton Park
Alberbury Castle
Brimford House
Brimford Wood
Pritchard's Hill
Lower House Farm
Fort
Bausley Hill
SY5
Malt House Farm PH
Prince's Oak
B4393
Shropshire STREET ATLAS
5
Breidden Forest
Belleisle Wood
Brunant Farm
Kempster's Hill
Hill Farm
Braggington Coppice
BRAGGINGTON LANE
Pecknall Farm
Pecknall Plantation
14
Belle Eisle Farm
Bulthy Hill
Bank Farm
Braggington Hall Farm
Shotton Farm
Pecknall Coppice
Deer Park
4
Fort
Quarry (dis)
Shaft (dis)
Bulthy Farm
CH
Bulthy Hill Farm
Ash Coppice
PECKNALL LANE
Windmill Farm
13
Middletown Hill
Welsh Border Golf Club
Stanford Farm
Wattlesborough Plantation
Wattlesborough Hall
Quarry (dis)
Ingleside
Stanford
Hole Farm
Motte & Bailey
3
A458
FOXTA CL
Gate Farm
Orchard Sch
Plas y Court Farm
LC
Great Wollaston Farm
Motte & Bailey
Wollaston
Heath Farm
Wattlesborough Heath
A458 Shrewsbury
Middletown
Winnington Green Farm
Earthwork
Bretchel Farm
Motte
Halfway House
PO
SCHOOL LA
WIGMORE LA
12
Glyn
SY21
Winnington Farm
PH
SY5
Upper Wigmore Farm
Quarry (dis)
Lower Wigmore Farm
2
Glyn Common
Lane Farm
MARCHE LANE
11
Lower Winnington Farm
Hallmill
Partonwood
LC
B4387
Dingle Wood
Winnington
Hargreaves Wood
Marche Manor Farm
Earthwork
Dingleside
Hargraves Farm
Marche Manor
Marche Hall
1
Trefnant Hall Farm
White Hill Farm

Scale: 1½ inches to 1 mile

0   ¼   ½ mile
0   250m 500m 750m 1 km

Ceredigion & S.Gwynedd STREET ATLAS

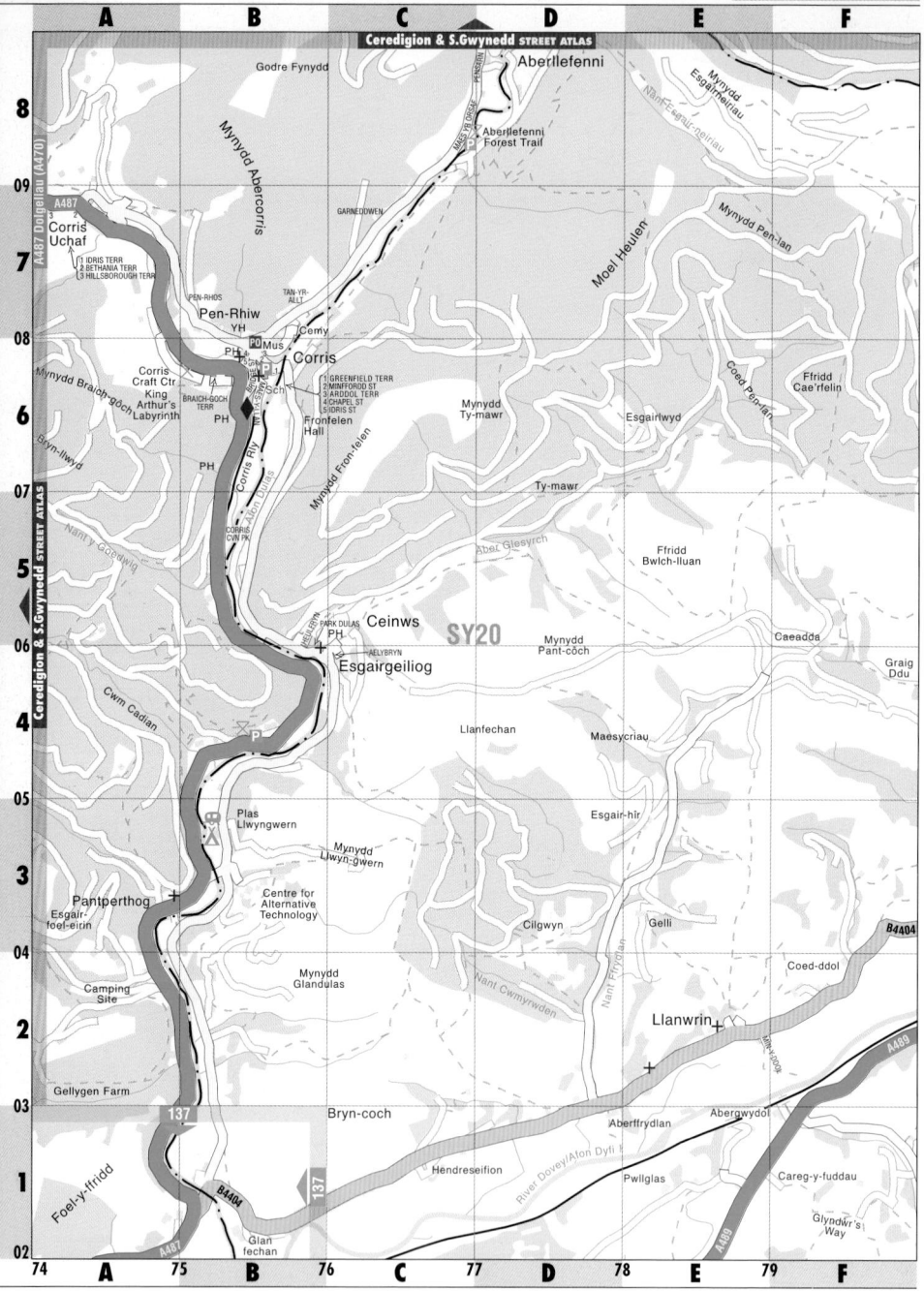

For full street detail of the highlighted area see page 137.

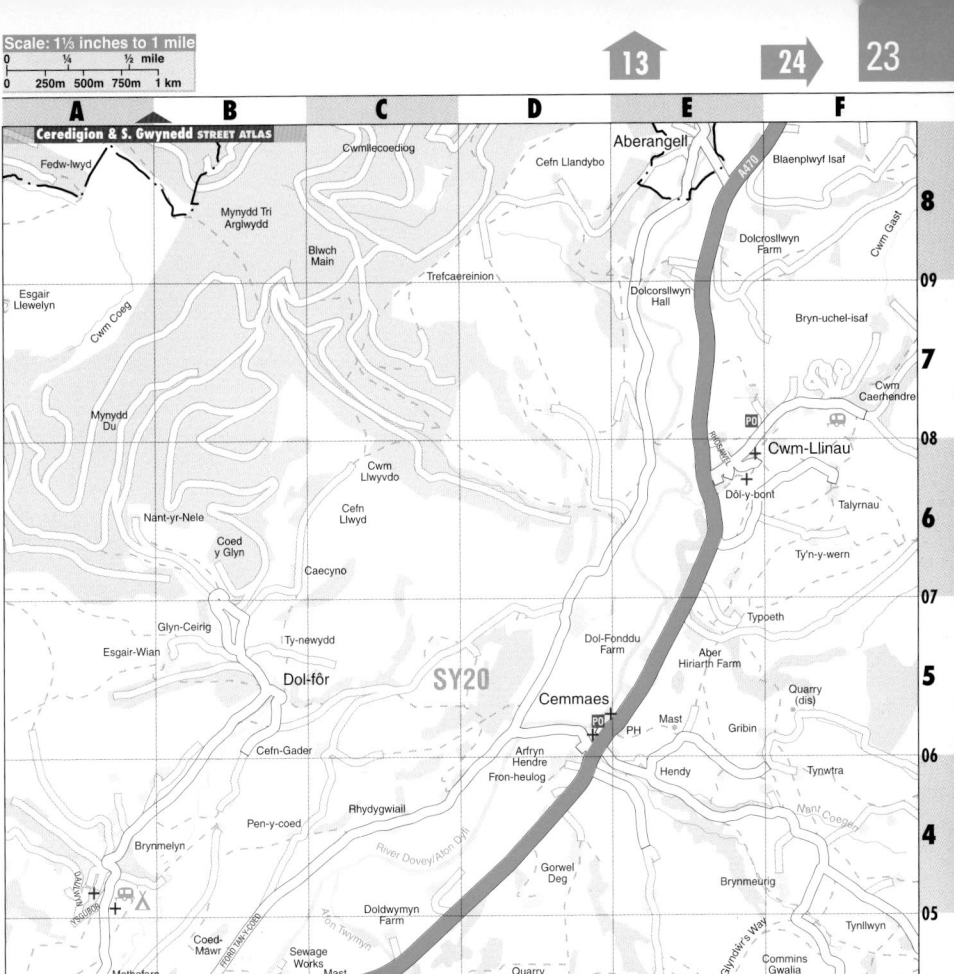

Ceredigion & S. Gwynedd STREET ATLAS

Fedw-lwyd

Esgair Llewelyn

Cwm Coeg

Mynydd Tri Arglwydd

Blwch Main

Cwmllecoediog

Trefcaereinion

Cefn Llandybo

Aberangell

Blaenplwyf Isaf

Cwm Gast

Dolcroslliwyn Farm

Dolcorsllwyn Hall

Bryn-uchel-isaf

Mynydd Du

Cwm Llwyvdo

Cefn Llwyd

Nant-yr-Nele

Coed y Glyn

Caecyno

Glyn-Ceirig

Esgair-Wian

Ty-newydd

Dol-fôr

SY20

Cwm Caerhendre

Cwm-Llinau

Dôl-y-bont

Talyrnau

Ty'n-y-wern

Typoeth

Dol-Fonddu Farm

Aber Hiriarth Farm

Cemmaes

PH Mast

Gribin

Quarry (dis)

Cefn-Gader

Arfryn Hendre Fron-heulog

Hendy

Tynwtra

Rhydygwiail

Pen-y-coed

River Dovey/Afon Dyfi

Nant Coegen

Brynmelyn

Gorwel Deg

Brynmeurig

Tynllwyn

Mathafarn

Coed-Mawr

Gwastadcoed Farm

Sewage Works

Mast

Doldwymyn Farm

Afon Twymyn

Ysgol Glantwymyn

Quarry (dis)

Quarry (dis)

Glyndŵr's Way

Commins Gwalia

Gwerny-bwlch

Bryn-moel

B4404

Grofft Farm

Poisnant Farm

PH PO

Cemmaes Road / Glantwymyn

Pit (dis)

Quarry (dis)

Glyntwymyn

Cae Gidog Farm

Waun

Ffridd Fawr Farm

A489

Comins Bach

Mast

Cefncoch-gwyllt

Cefn Côch

Maen Lywyd

Ty Cerrig Farm

Tip and Quarry (dis)

Commins Coch

A470

Cwm-bychan-bâch

Glyndŵr's Way

Cairn

Cwm-Llywy-uchaf

Cefn Côch

Berllan-dêg

Ty Cerrig Uchaf Farm

Ty Nant Farm

Gwernbere Farm

Briwriant

Cwm Bustach

Rhôs y Silio

Tyn Llwyn Farm

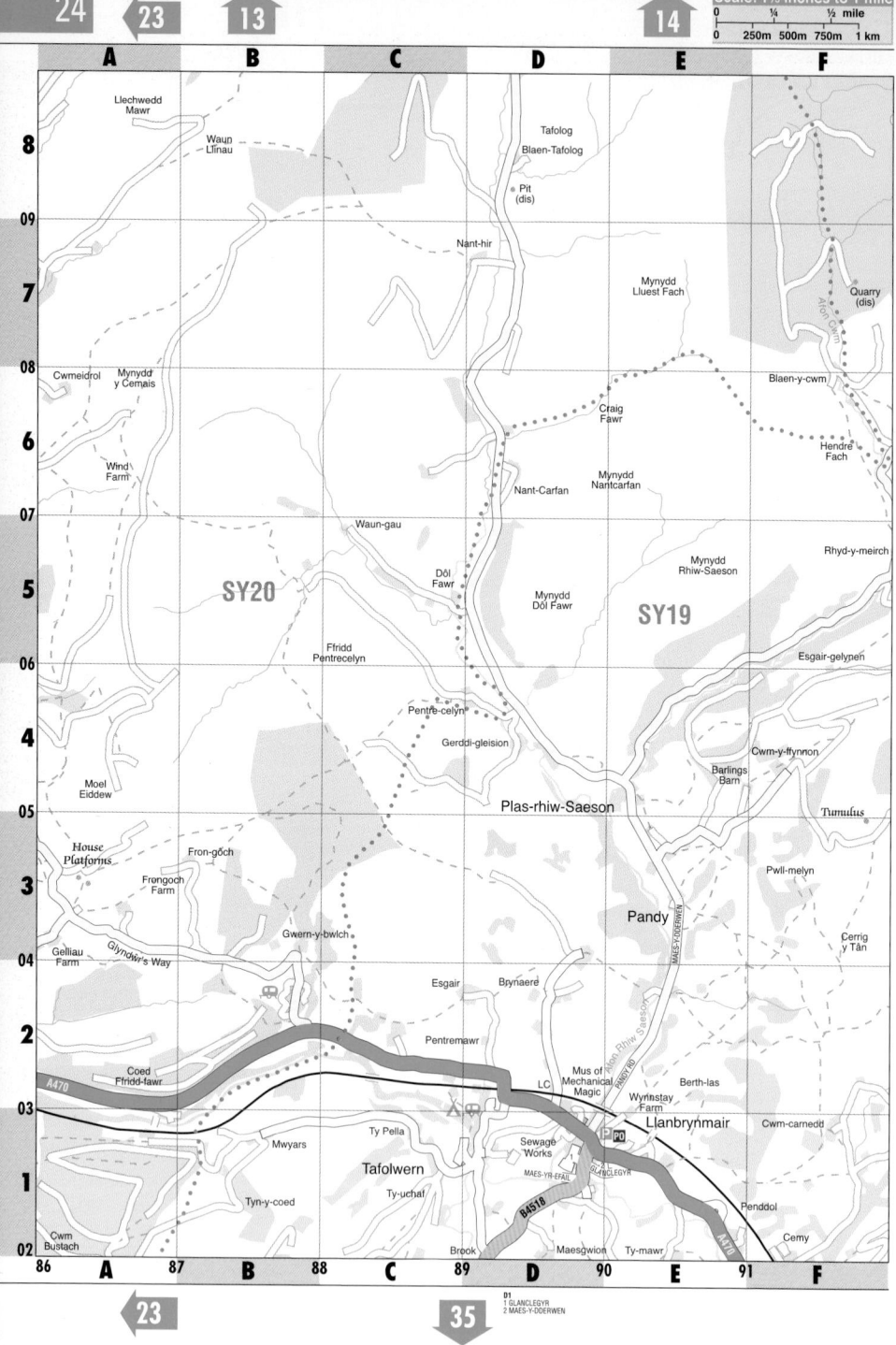

Scale: 1⅓ inches to 1 mile

0   ¼   ½   mile
0   250m 500m 750m 1 km

Llechwedd Mawr

Waun Llinau

Tafolog
Blaen-Tafolog
Pit (dis)

Nant-hir

Cwmeidrol
Mynydd y Cemais

Mynydd Lluest Fach

Quarry (dis)

Afon Cwm

Blaen-y-cwm

Craig Fawr

Hendre Fach

Wind Farm

Nant-Carfan

Mynydd Nantcarfan

Waun-gau

SY20

Dôl Fawr

Mynydd Dôl Fawr

Mynydd Rhiw-Saeson

Rhyd-y-meirch

SY19

Ffridd Pentrecelyn

Esgair-gelypen

Pentre-celyn

Gerddi-gleision

Plas-rhiw-Saeson

Barlings Barn

Cwm-y-ffynnon

Tumulus

Moel Eiddew

House Platforms

Fron-goch

Frongoch Farm

Pwll-melyn

Pandy

Gwern-y-bwlch

Cerrig y Tân

Gelliau Farm

Glyndŵr's Way

MAES-Y-ODERWEN

Afon Rhiw Saeson

Esgair

Brynaere

Coed Ffridd-fawr

A470

Pentremawr

Mus of Mechanical Magic

LC

Berth-las

Wynnstay Farm

Llanbrynmair

Cwm-carnedd

Ty Pella

Sewage Works

PO

GLANCLEGYR

Mwyars

Tafolwern

Ty-uchaf

MAES-YR-EFAIL

Penddol

Tyn-y-coed

B4518

Cemy

A470

Cwm Bustach

Brook

Maesgwion

Ty-mawr

D1
1 GLANCLEGYR
2 MAES-Y-ODDERWEN

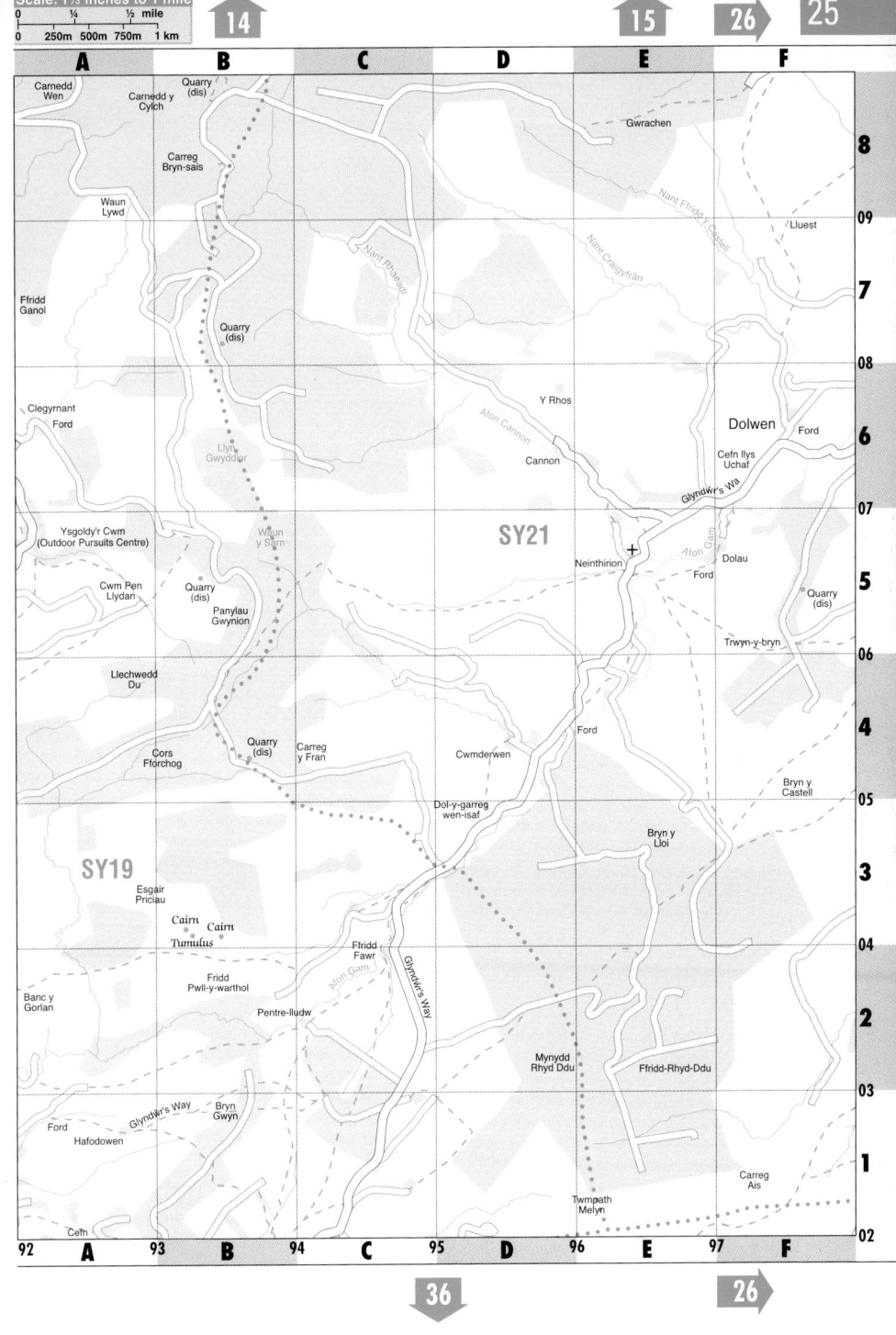

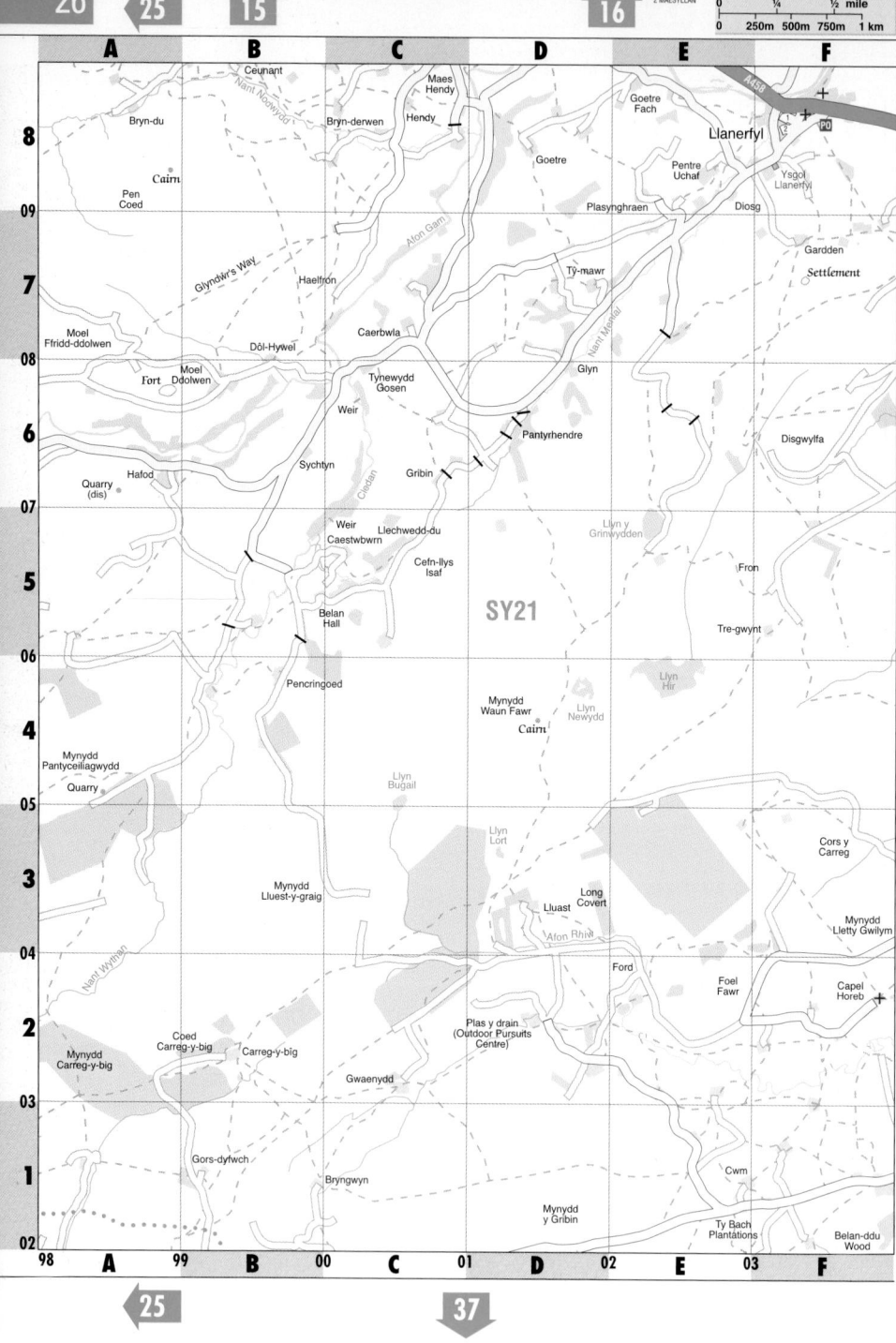

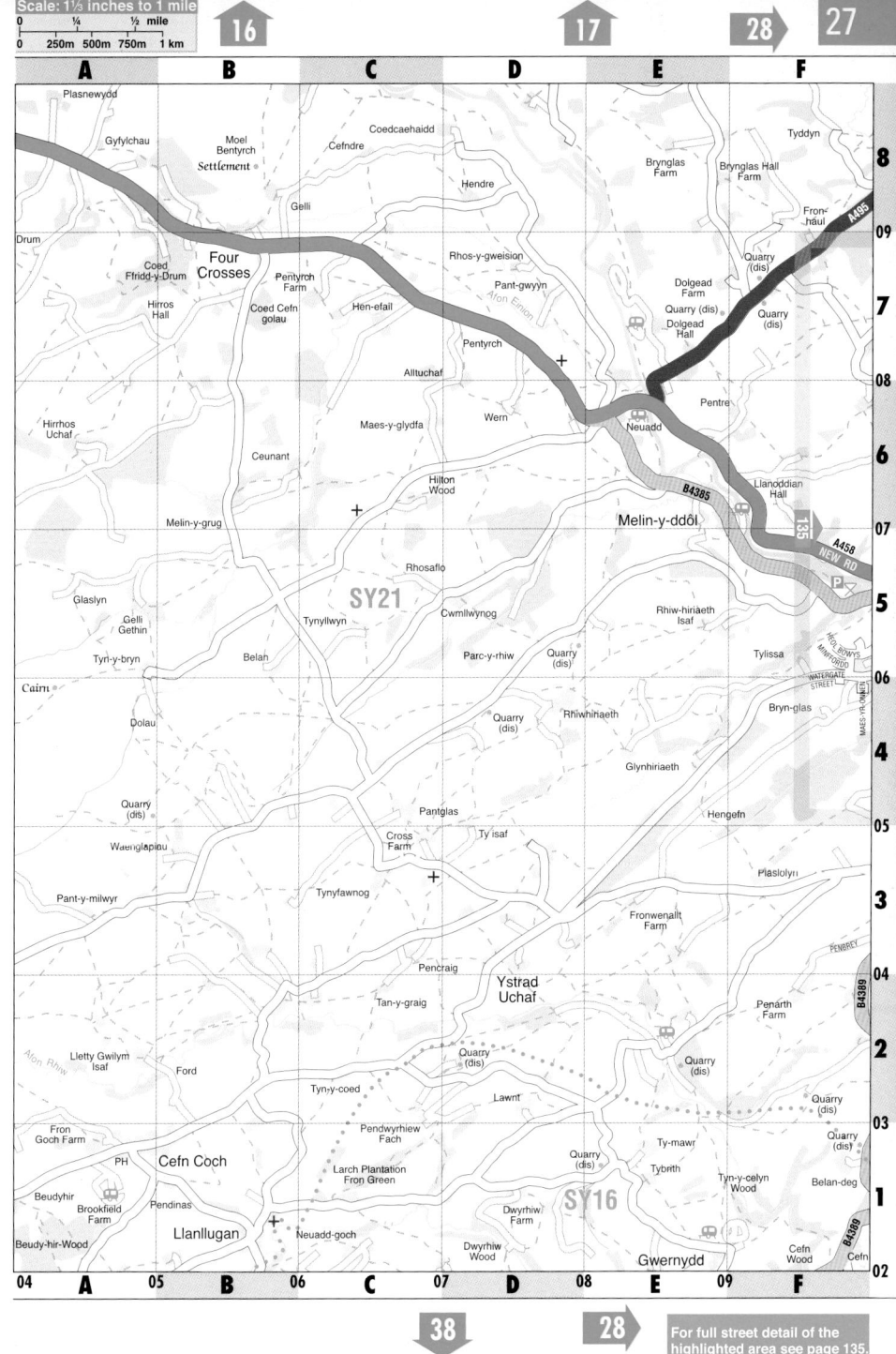

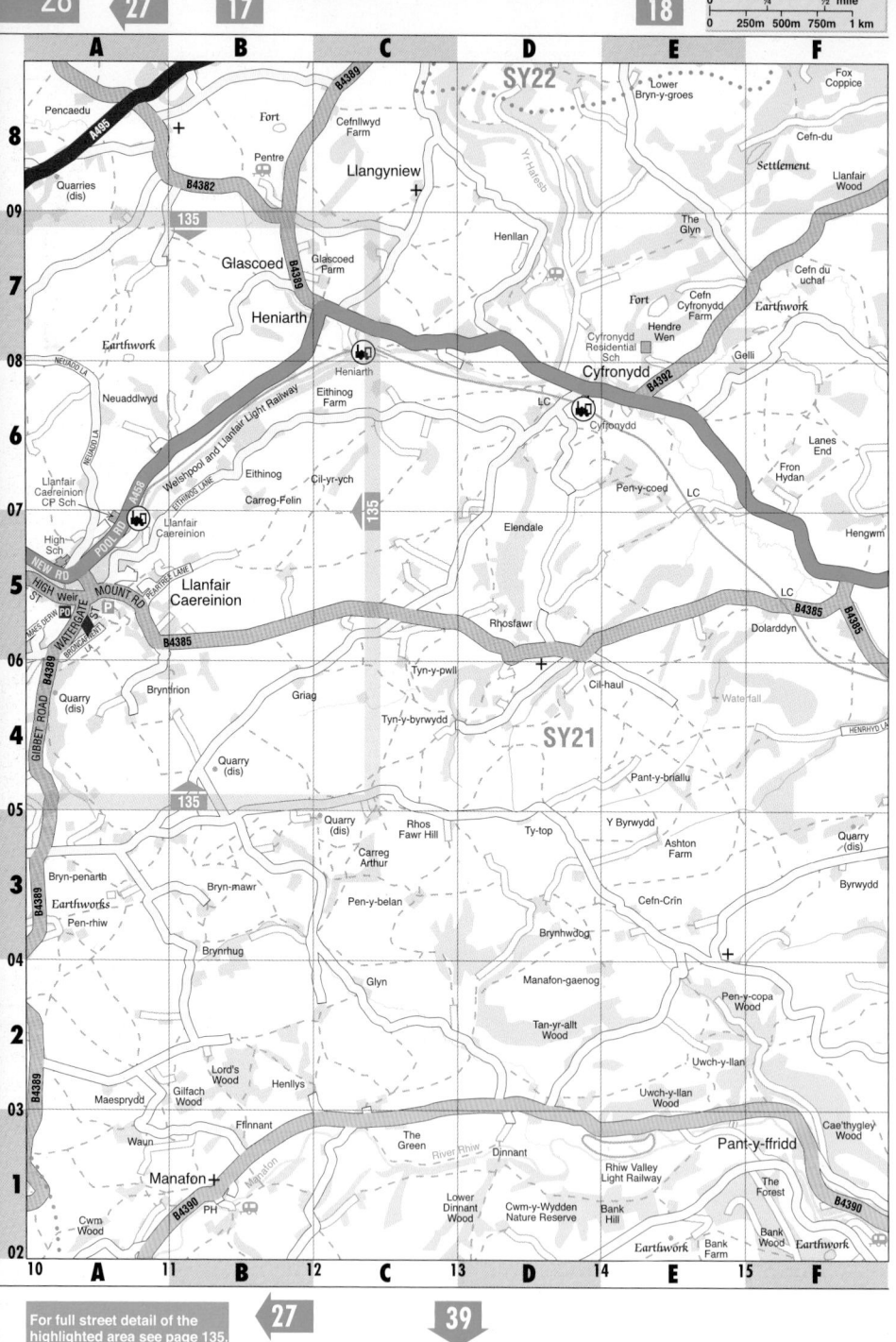

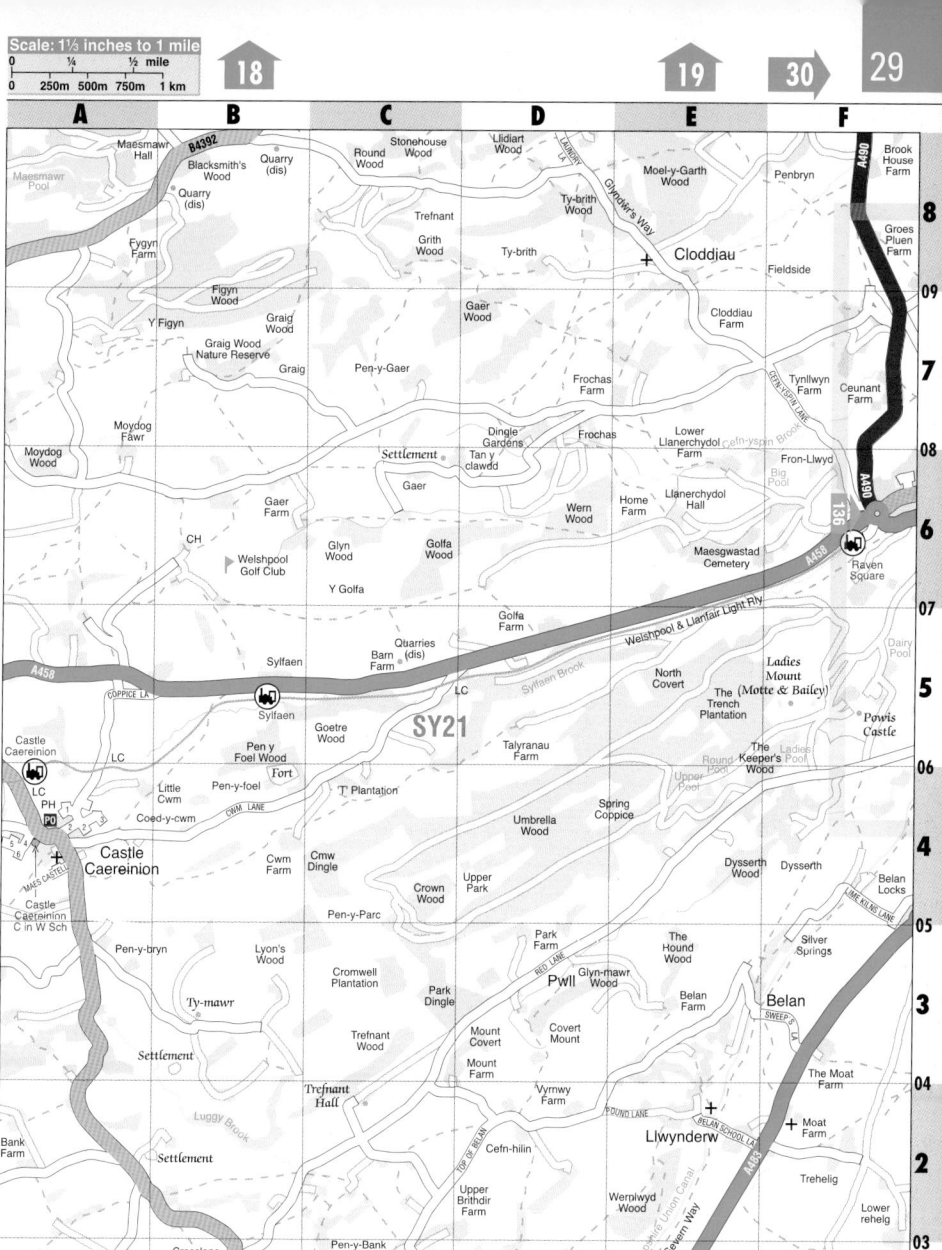

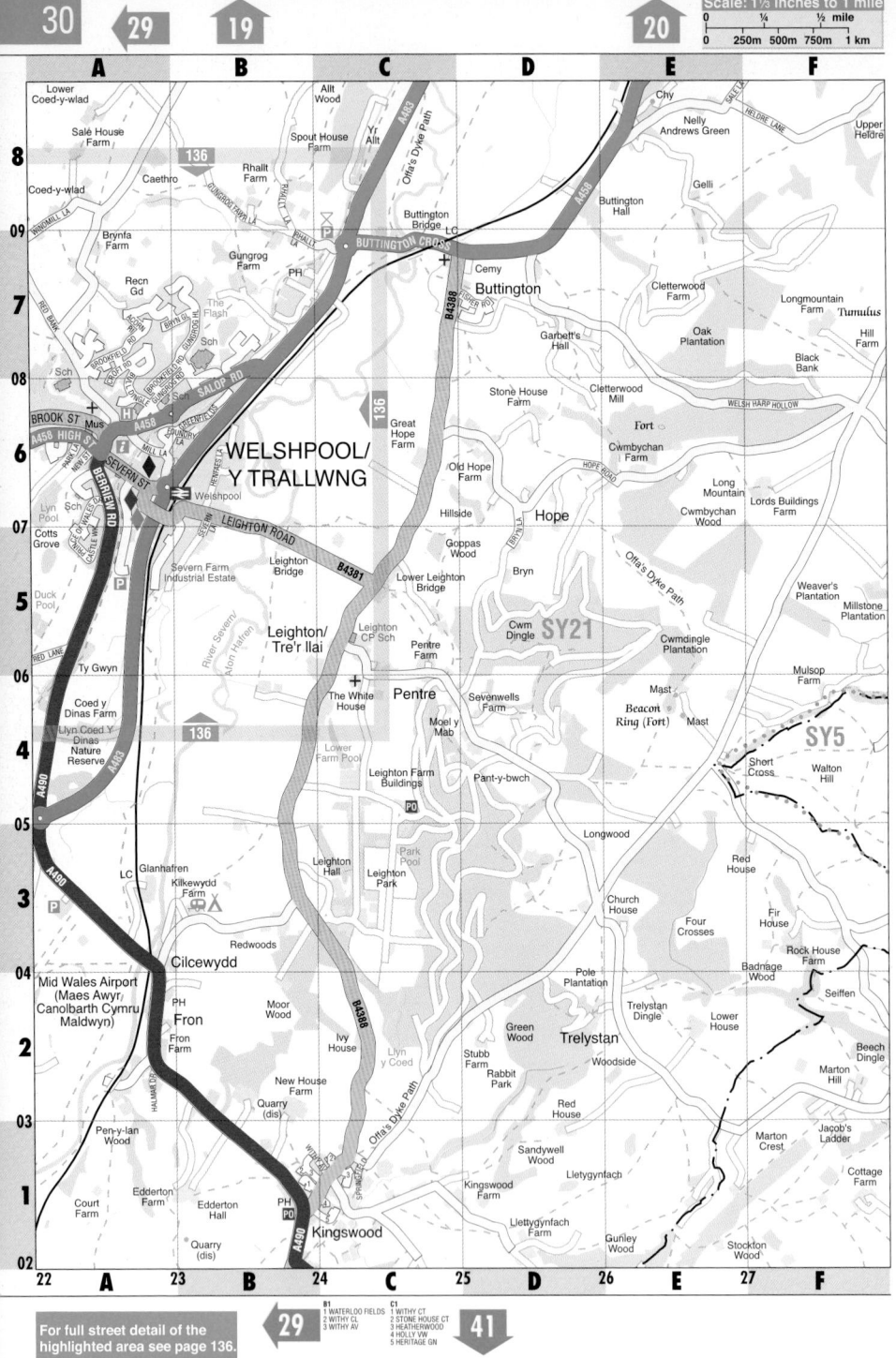

A B C D E F

Lower Coed-y-wlad
Allt Wood
Chy
Upper Heldre

Sale House Farm
136
Spout House Farm
Yr Allt
Nelly Andrews Green

8

Rhalt Farm
Gelli

Coed-y-wlad
Caethro
Buttington Hall
A458

09
Brynfa Farm
Gungrog Farm
Buttington Bridge
BUTTINGTON CROSS
LC

Recn Gd
PH
B4388
Cemy
Buttington
Cletterwood Farm
Longmountain Farm
Tumulus

7
The Flash
Sch
Garbett's Hall
Oak Plantation
Hill Farm

Sch
BROOK ST Mus
SALOP RD
A458
Stone House Farm
Cletterwood Mill
Black Bank

08
A458 HIGH
136
Great Hope Farm
Fort
WELSH HARP HOLLOW

6
WELSHPOOL/ Y TRALLWNG
Welshpool
Old Hope Farm
Cwmbychan Farm
Long Mountain
Lords Buildings Farm

Lyn Pool
Sch
SEVERN ST
LEIGHTON ROAD
Hillside
Hope
HOPE ROAD
Cwmbychan Wood

07
Cotts Grove
BERRIEW RD
Severn Farm Industrial Estate
Leighton Bridge
B4381
Goppas Wood
Bryn
Offa's Dyke Path
Weaver's Plantation
Millstone Plantation

Duck Pool
RED LANE
Ty Gwyn
Leighton/ Tre'r llai
Lower Leighton Bridge
Cwm Dingle
SY21
Cwmdingle Plantation

5
River Severn / Afon Hafren
Leighton CP Sch
Pentre Farm

06
Coed y Dinas Farm
The White House
Pentre
Sevenwells Farm
Mast
Beacon Ring (Fort)
Mast
Mulsop Farm

A490
Llyn Coed Y Dinas Nature Reserve
136
Moel y Mab
SY5

4
A483
Lower Farm Pool
Leighton Farm Buildings
Pant-y-bwch
Short Cross
Walton Hill

05
PO
Longwood
Red House
Fir House

3
A490
LC
Glanhafren
Kilkewydd Farm
Leighton Hall
Park Pool
Leighton Park
Church House
Four Crosses
Rock House Farm
Seiffen

04
Mid Wales Airport (Maes Awyr Canolbarth Cymru Maldwyn)
Redwoods
Cilcewydd
Pole Plantation
Trelystan Dingle
Lower House
Beech Dingle

2
PH
Fron
Fron Farm
Moor Wood
B4388
Ivy House
Green Wood
Trelystan
Woodside
Marton Hill

03
Pen-y-lan Wood
New House Farm Quarry (dis)
Llyn y Coed
Offa's Dyke Path
Stubb Farm
Rabbit Park
Red House
Sandywell Wood
Llettygynfach
Marton Crest
Jacob's Ladder

1
Court Farm
Edderton Farm
Edderton Hall
Quarry (dis)
PH PO
A490
Kingswood
Kingswood Farm
Llettygynfach Farm
Gunley Wood
Stockton Wood
Cottage Farm

02
22 A 23 B 24 C 25 D 26 E 27 F

For full street detail of the highlighted area see page 136.

29
41

B1
1 WATERLOO FIELDS
2 WITHY CL
3 WITHY AV

C1
1 WITHY CT
2 STONE HOUSE CT
3 HEATHERWOOD
4 HOLLY VW
5 HERITAGE GN

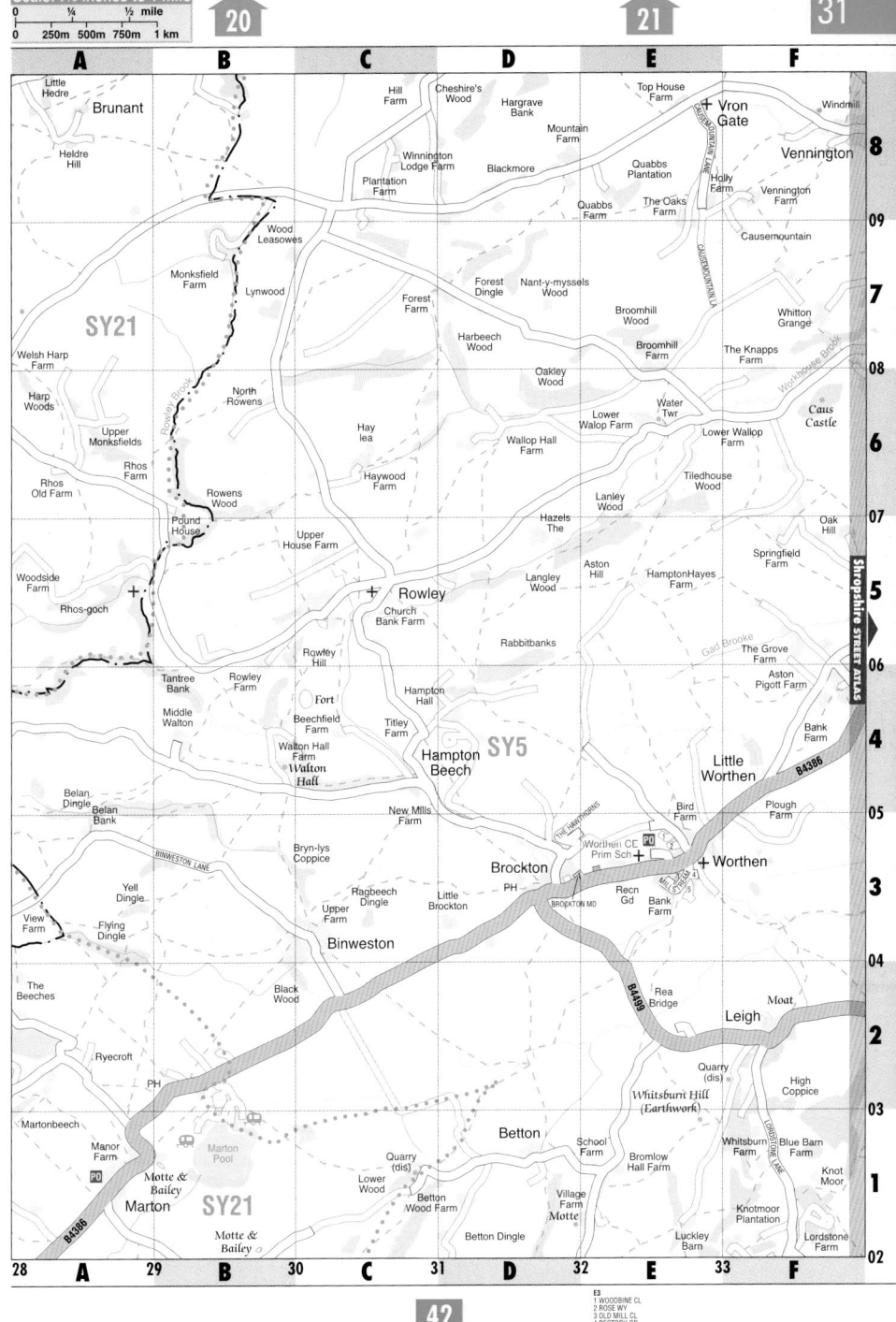

A   B   C   D   E   F

Little Hedre
Brunant
Heldre Hill
Welsh Harp Farm
Harp Woods
Upper Monksfields
Rhos Farm
Rhos Old Farm
Woodside Farm
Rhos-goch

SY21
Monksfield Farm
Lynwood
North Rowens
Rowens Wood
Pound House
Tantree Bank
Middle Walton

Hill Farm
Plantation Farm
Forest Farm
Hay lea
Haywood Farm
Upper House Farm
Rowley Hill
Rowley Farm
Fort
Beechfield Farm
Walton Hall Farm
Walton Hall

Cheshire's Wood
Winnington Lodge Farm
Blackmore
Forest Dingle
Harbeech Wood
Wallop Hall Farm
Rowley
Church Bank Farm
Rabbitbanks
Hampton Hall
Titley Farm
Hampton Beech

Hargrave Bank
Mountain Farm
Nant-y-myssels Wood
Oakley Wood
Langley Wood
Hazels The
Aston Hill
Langley Wood

Top House Farm
Vron Gate
Quabbs Plantation
Quabbs Farm
The Oaks Farm
Broomhill Wood
Broomhill Farm
Lower Walop Farm
Water Twr
Lower Walop Farm
Tiledhouse Wood
Lanley Wood
HamptonHayes Farm
SY5

Windmill
Vennington
Holly Farm
Vennington Farm
Causemountain
CAUSEMOUNTAIN LA
Whitton Grange
The Knapps Farm
Worthouse Brook
Caus Castle
Oak Hill
Springfield Farm
The Grove Farm
Aston Pigott Farm
Bank Farm
Little Worthen
B4386

Belan Dingle
Belan Bank
Yell Dingle
Flying Dingle
View Farm
The Beeches
Ryecroft
Martonbeech
Manor Farm
Marton

BINWESTON LANE
Bryn-lys Coppice
Ragbeech Dingle
Upper Farm
Black Wood

Binweston

New Mills Farm
Little Brockton
PH
Brockton
BROCKTON MD

THE HAWTHORNS
Worthen CE Prim Sch
Bird Farm
Recn Gd
Bank Farm
MILL STREAM
Worthen
Plough Farm
Rea Bridge
Leigh
Moat
Quarry (dis)
High Coppice
Whitsburn Hill (Earthwork)
Whitsburn Farm
Blue Barn Farm
Knot Moor
Knotmoor Plantation
Lordstone Farm

PH
Motte & Bailey
Marton
SY21
Motte & Bailey

Quarry (dis)
Lower Wood
Betton Wood Farm
Betton Dingle

Betton
School Farm
Bromlow Hall Farm
Village Farm Motte
Luckley Barn

Marton Pool

Shropshire STREET ATLAS

E3
1 WOODBINE CL
2 ROSE WY
3 OLD MILL CL
4 RECTORY GD
5 BROOKSIDE

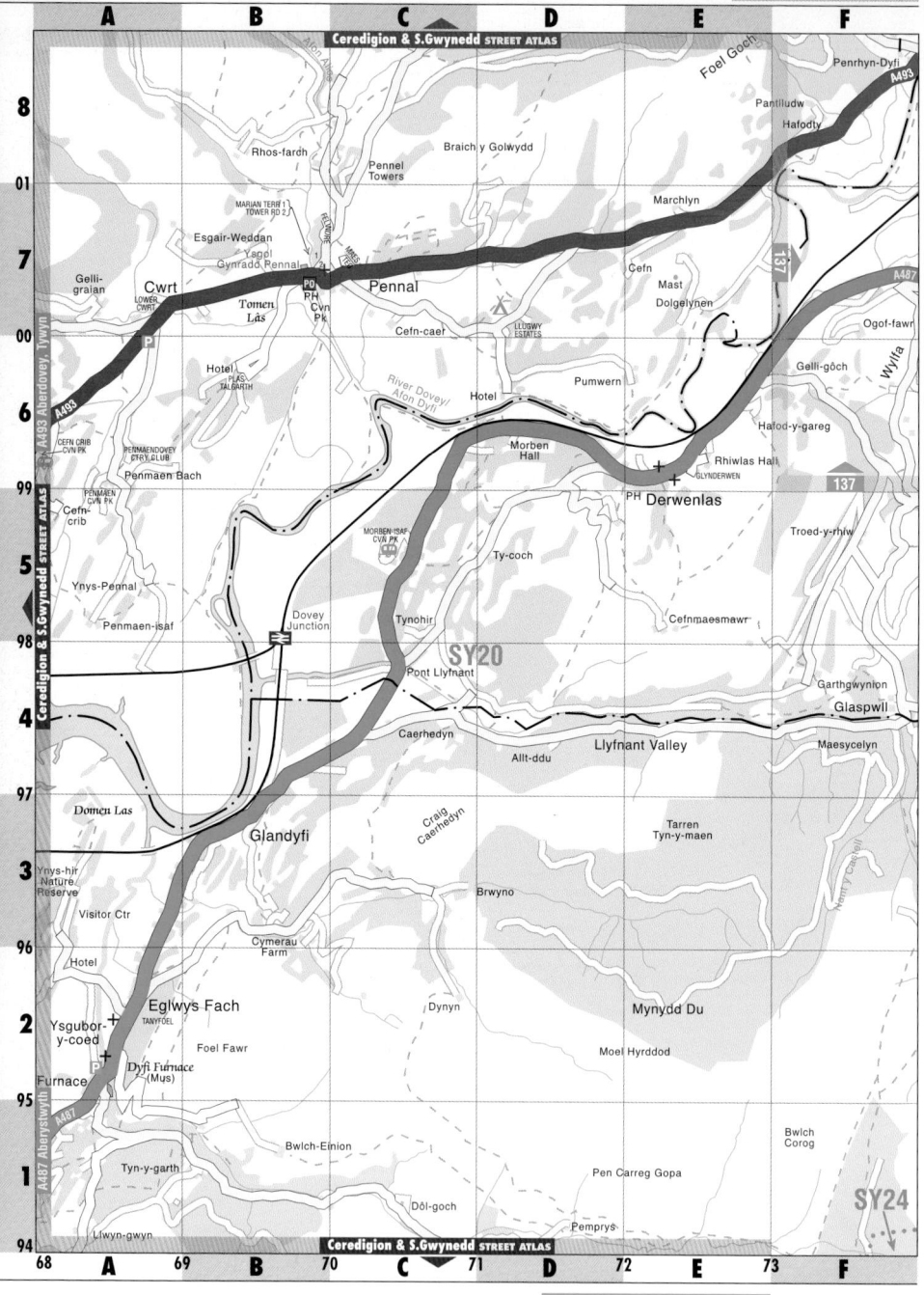

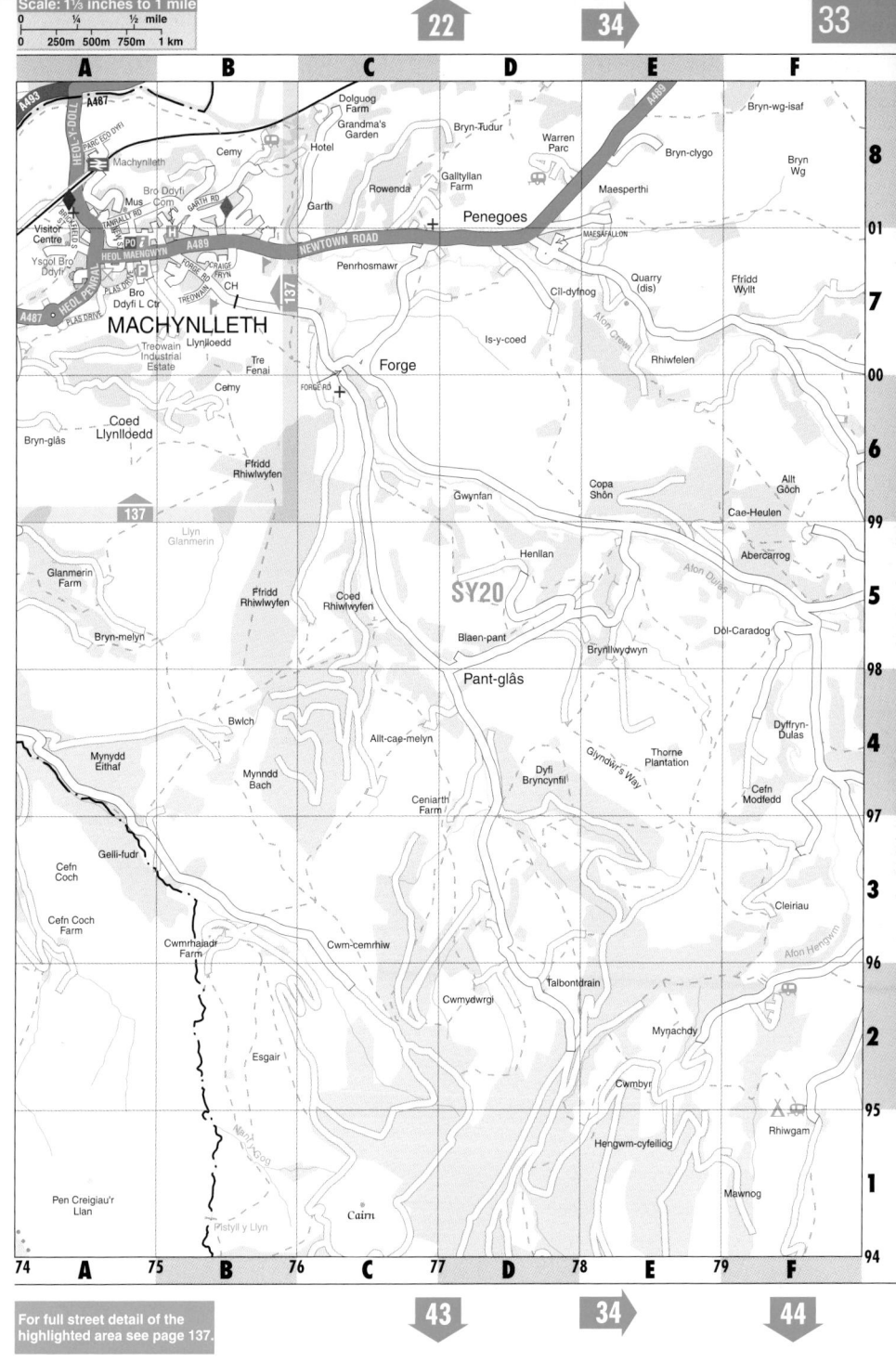

8
01
7
00
6
99
5
98
4
97
3
96
2
95
1
94

A   B   C   D   E   F

A483
A487
HEOL-Y-DOLI
PARC EÓ DYFI
Machynlleth
Mus
Com
Bro Ddyfi
GARTH RD
Cemy
TABERNACLE RD
Visitor
Centre
Ysgol Bro
Ddyfi
PO
HEOL MAENGWYN
A489
PLAS DRIVE
PLAS UST CR
CRAIGE
FRYN
FORGE RD
TREOWAIN
CH
HEOL PENRAL
A487
PLAS DRIVE

Dolguog
Farm
Grandma's
Garden
Hotel
Bryn-Tudur
Cerny
Rowenda
Garth
Galltyllan
Farm
Warren
Parc
Bryn-wg-isaf
Bryn-clygo
Maesperthi
Bryn
Wg
Penrhosmawr
NEWTOWN ROAD
Penegoes
MAESAFALLON
137
Cil-dyfnog
Quarry
(dis)
Ffridd
Wyllt
MACHYNLLETH
Treowain
Industrial
Estate
Llynlloedd
Cerny
Tre
Fenai
FORGE RD
Forge
Is-y-coed
Afon Crewi
Rhiwfelen
Bryn-glâs
Coed
Llynlloedd
Bryn-glâs
Ffridd
Rhiwlwyfen
Gwynfan
Copa
Shôn
Allt
Gôch
Cae-Heulen
Abercarrog
137
Llyn
Glanmerin
Glanmerin
Farm
Ffridd
Rhiwlwyfen
Coed
Rhiwlwyfen
Henilan
SY20
Afon Dulas
Bryn-melyn
Blaen-pant
Brynllwydwyn
Dôl-Caradog
Pant-glâs
Bwlch
Dyffryn-
Dulas
Mynydd
Eithaf
Mynndd
Bach
Allt-cae-melyn
Dyfi
Bryncynfil
Glyndŵr's Way
Thorne
Plantation
Cefn
Modfedd
Ceniarth
Farm
Cefn
Coch
Gelli-fudr
Cleiriau
Cefn Coch
Farm
Cwmrhaiadr
Farm
Cwm-cemrhiw
Afon Hengwm
Talbontdrain
Cwmydwrgi
Mynachdy
Esgair
Cwmbyr
Nant Moog
Rhiwgam
Pen Creigiau'r
Llan
Pistyll y Llyn
Cairn
Hengwm-cyfeiliog
Mawnog

74   A   75   B   76   C   77   D   78   E   79   F

43   34   44

For full street detail of the
highlighted area see page 137.

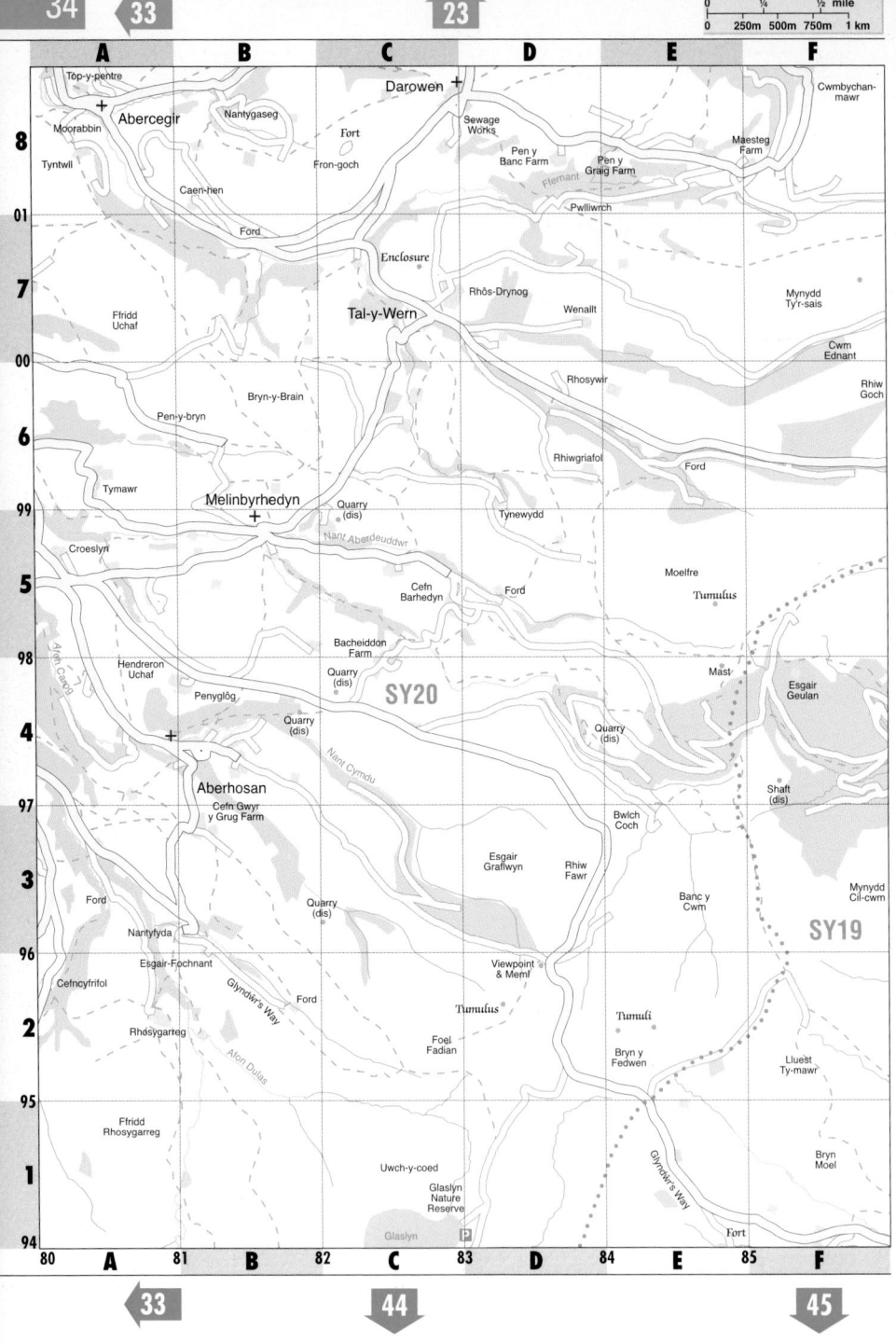

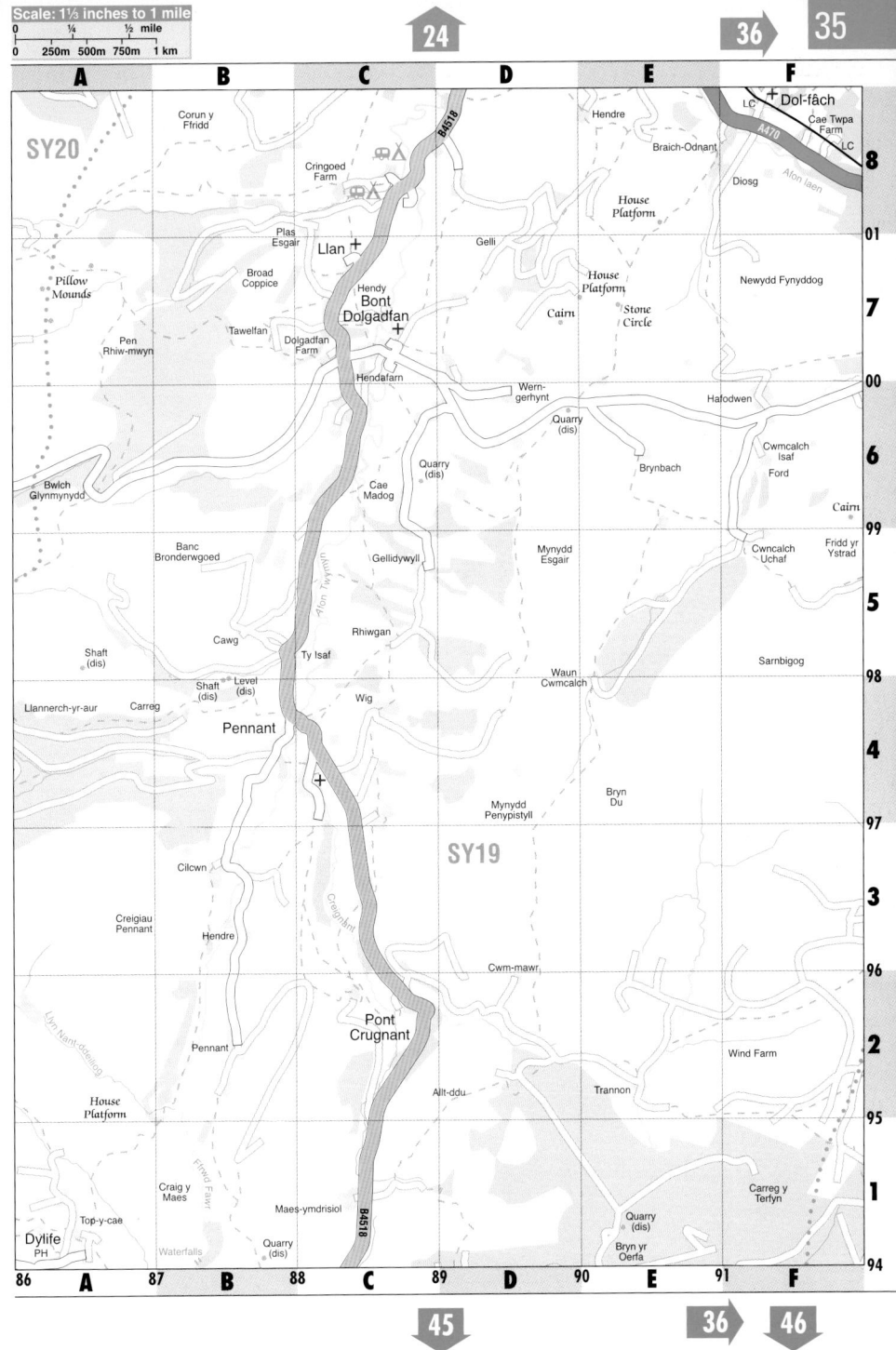

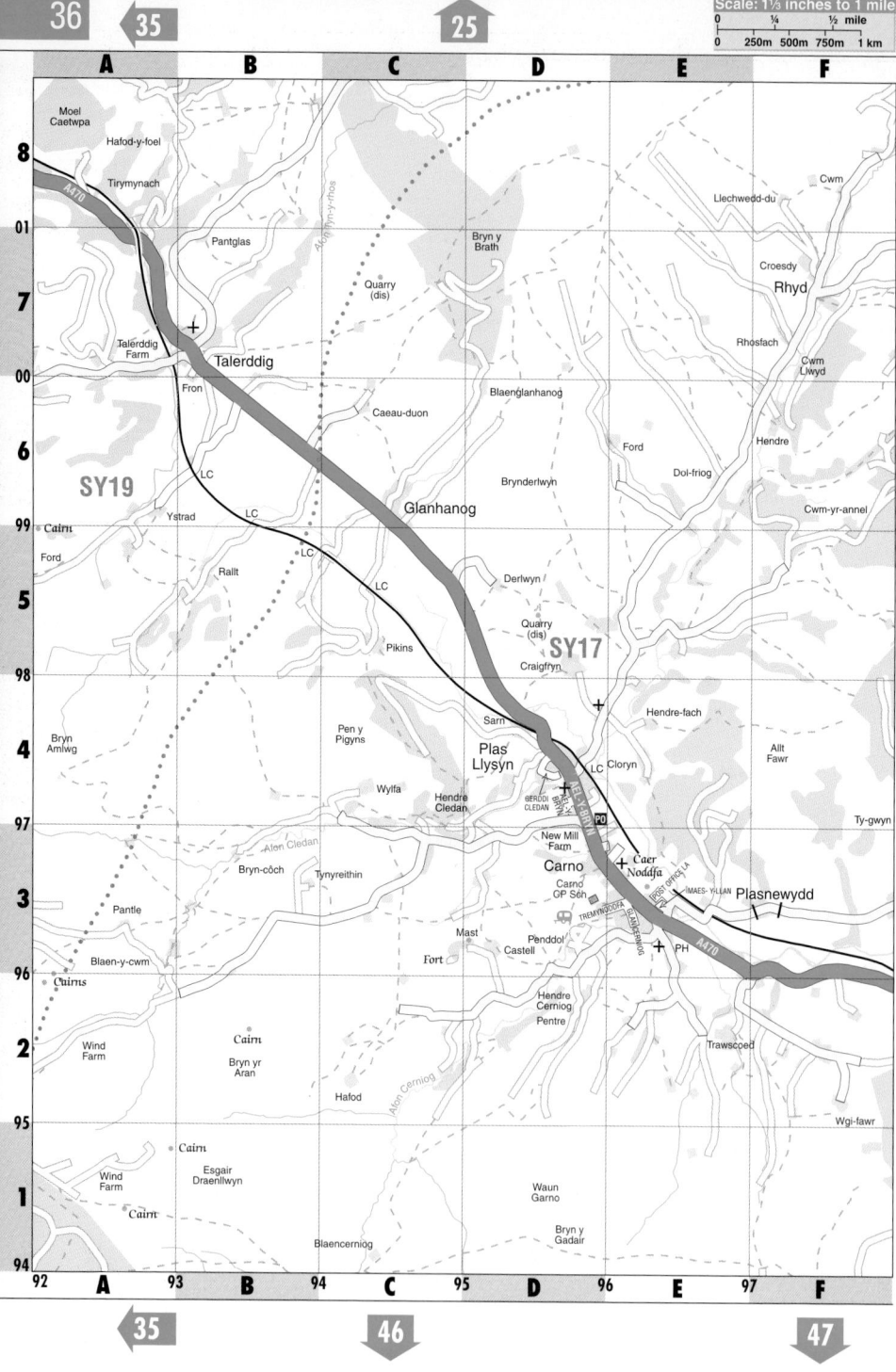

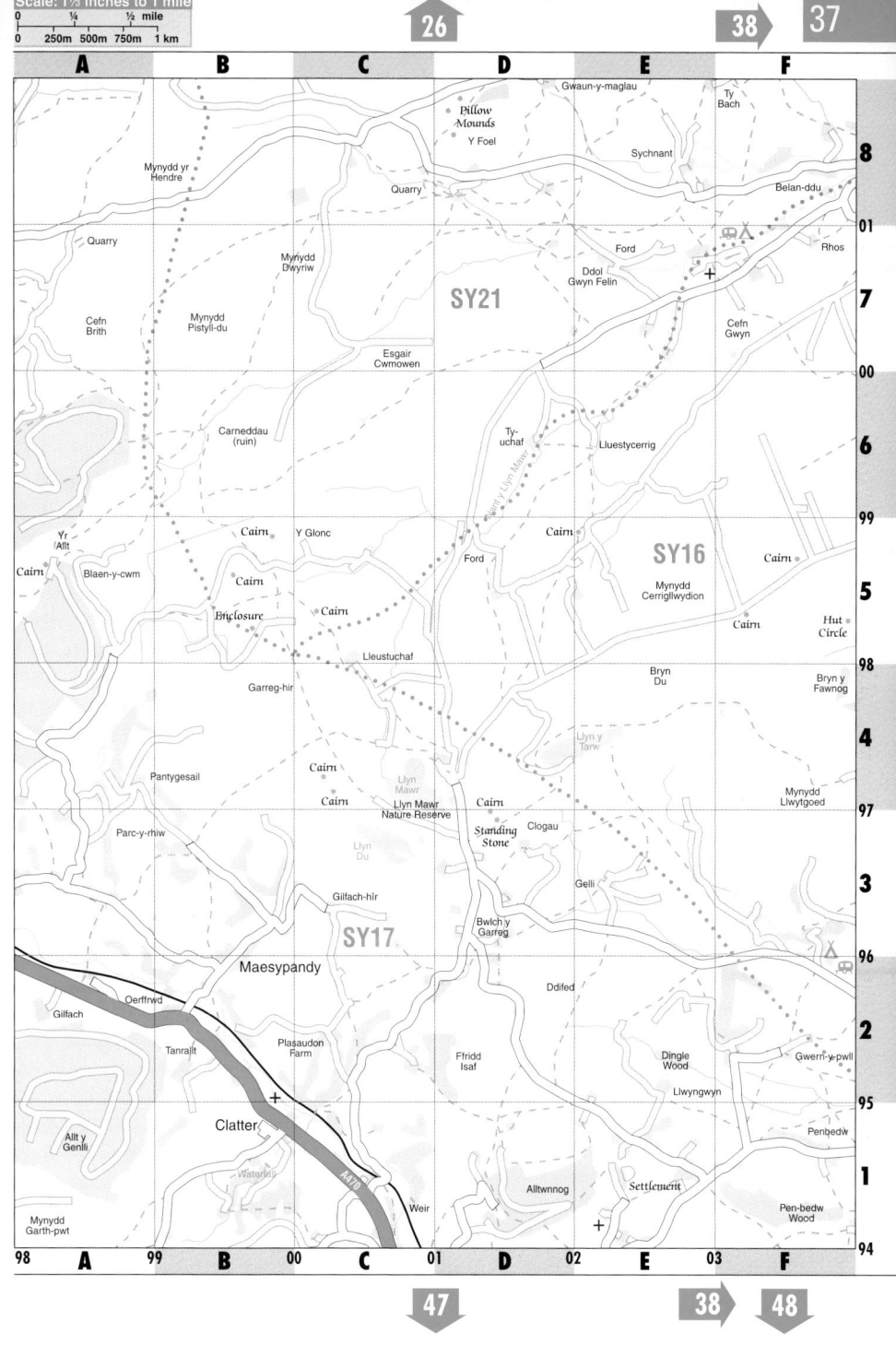

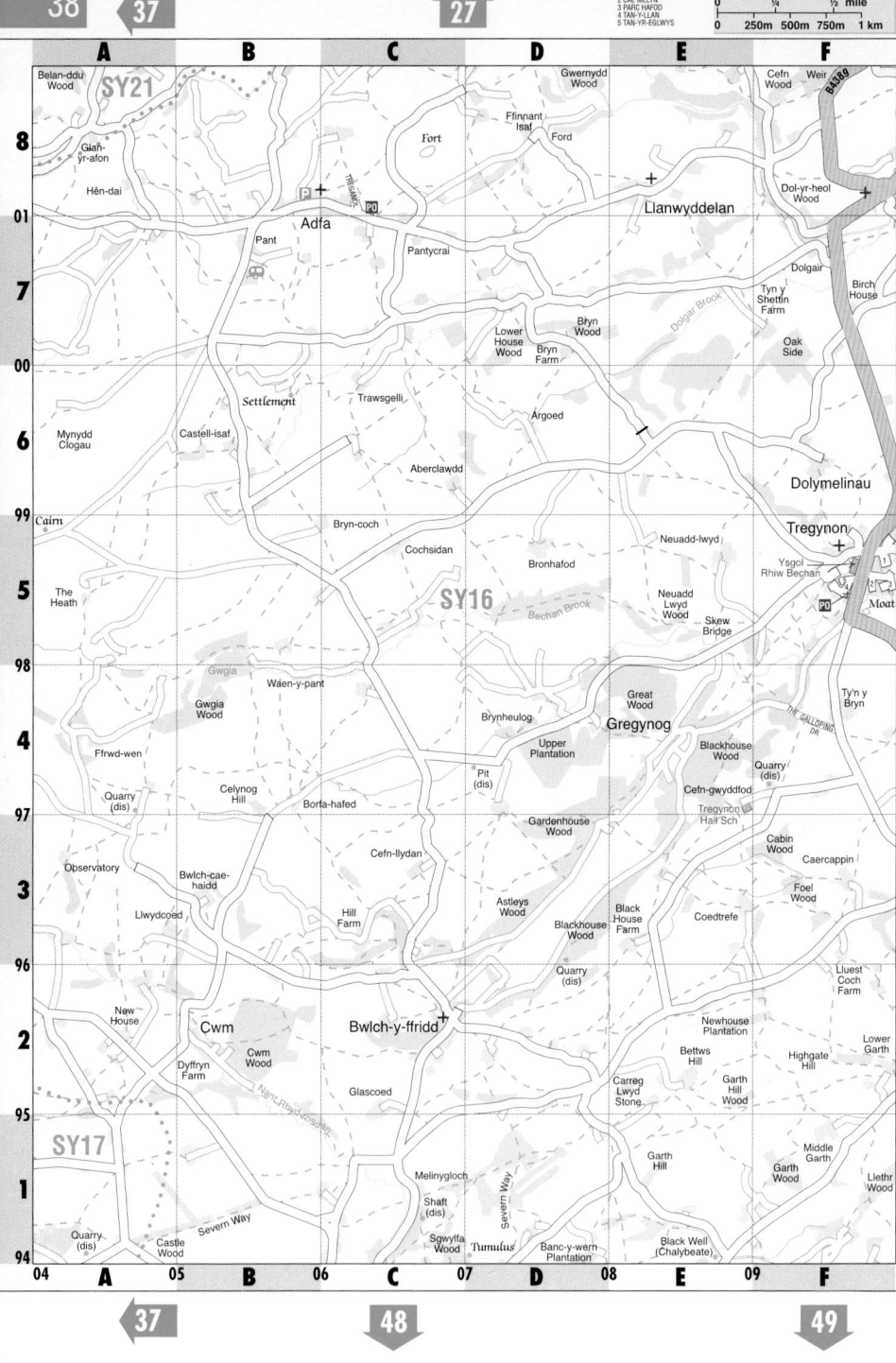

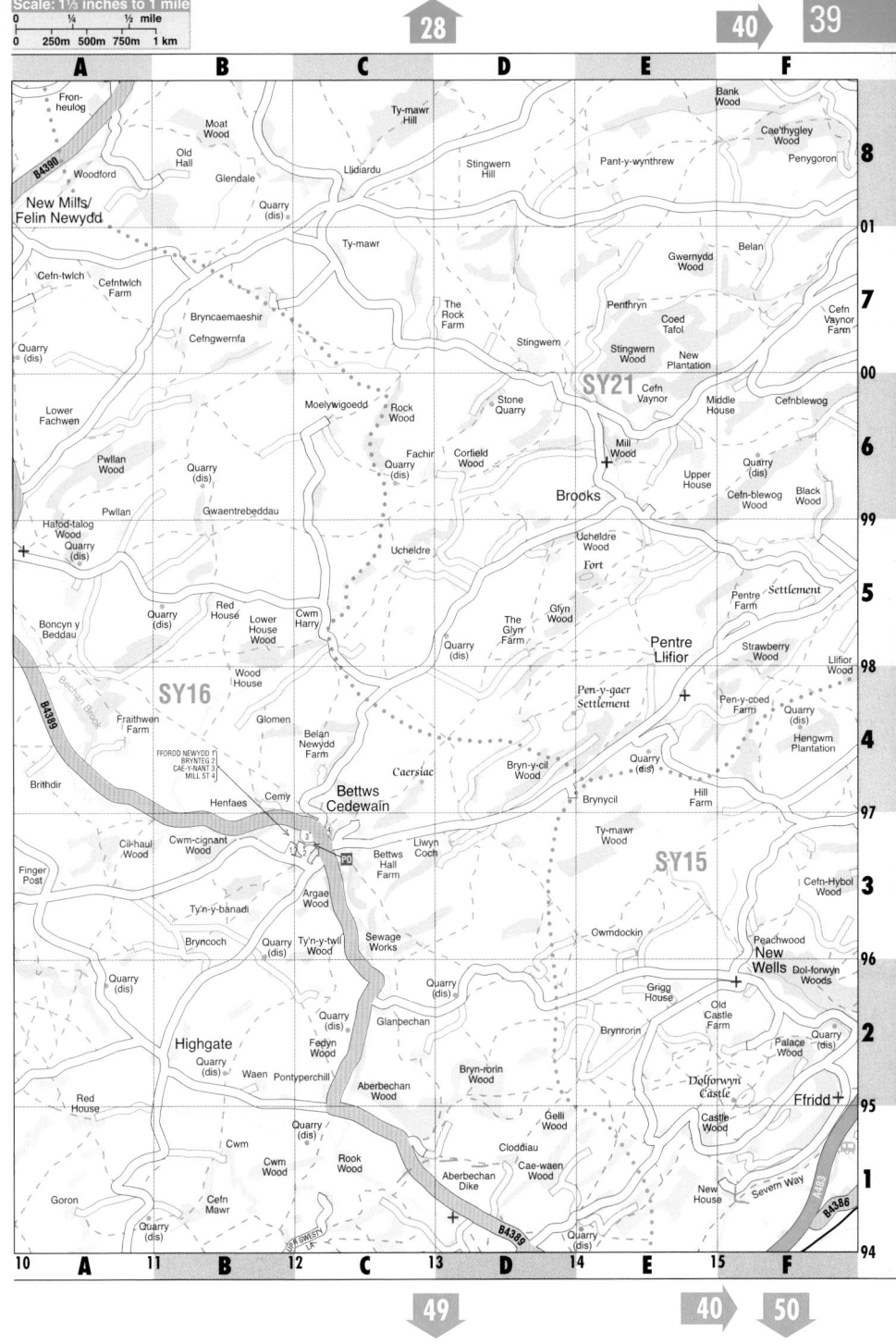

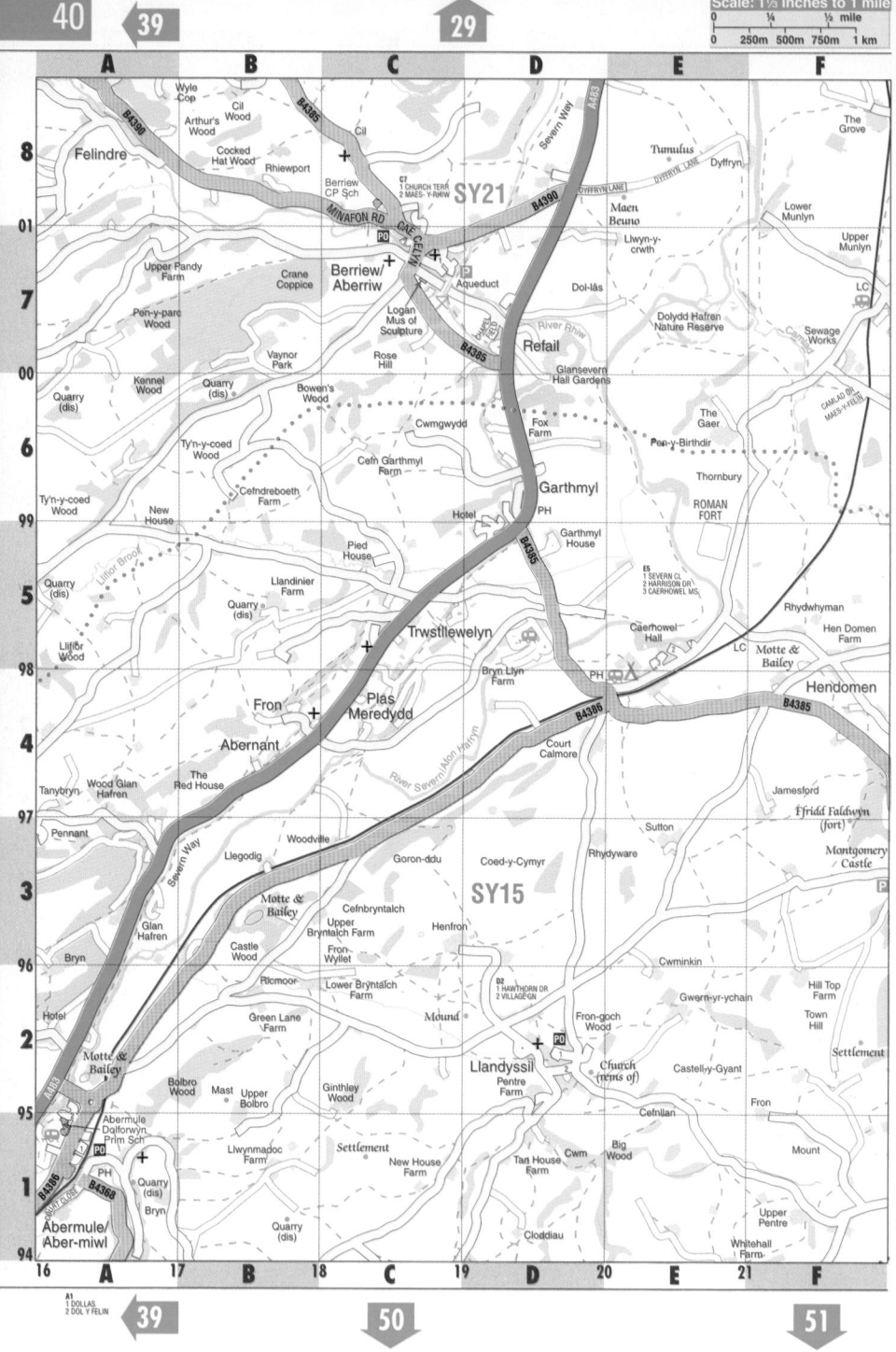

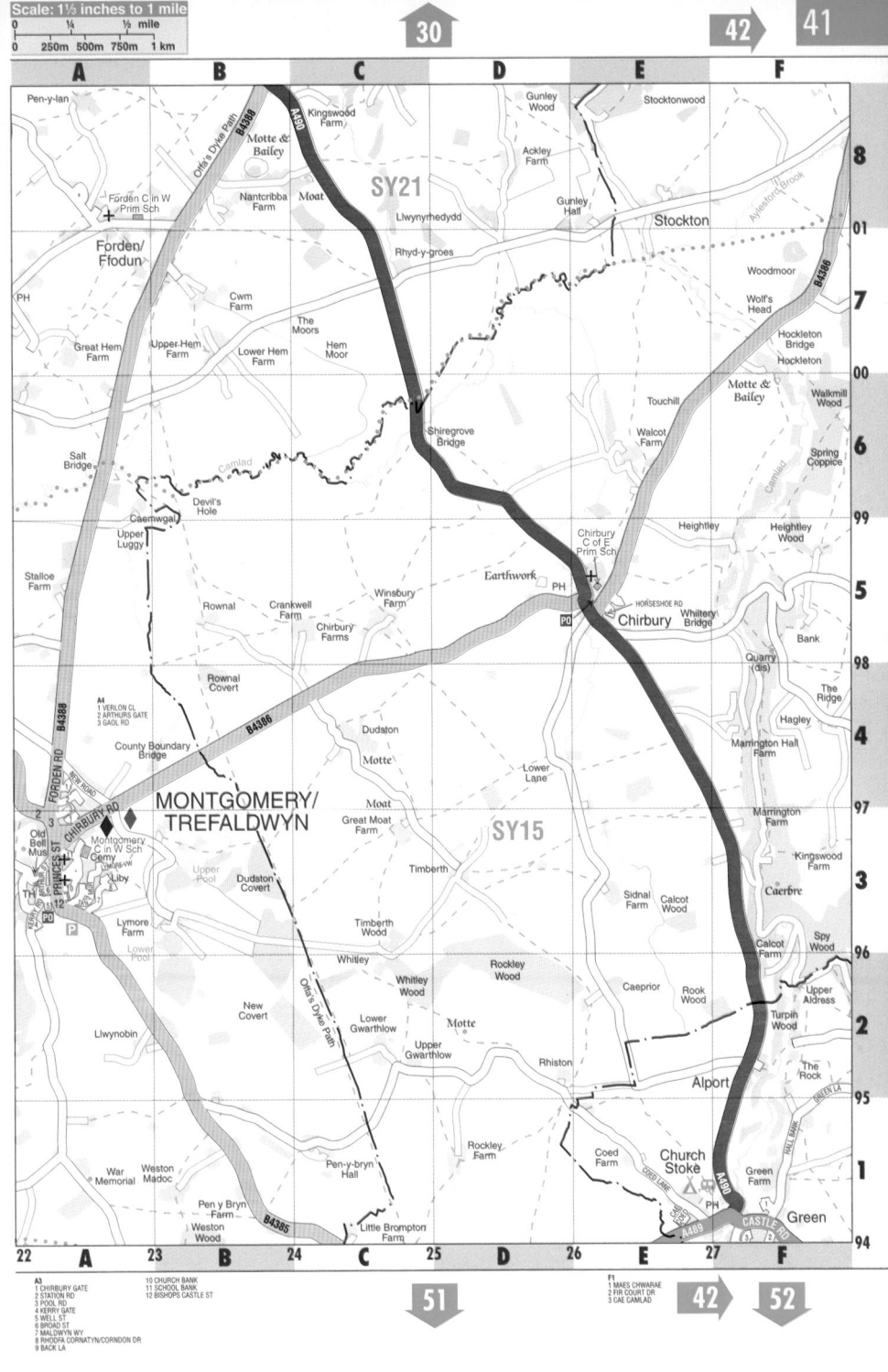

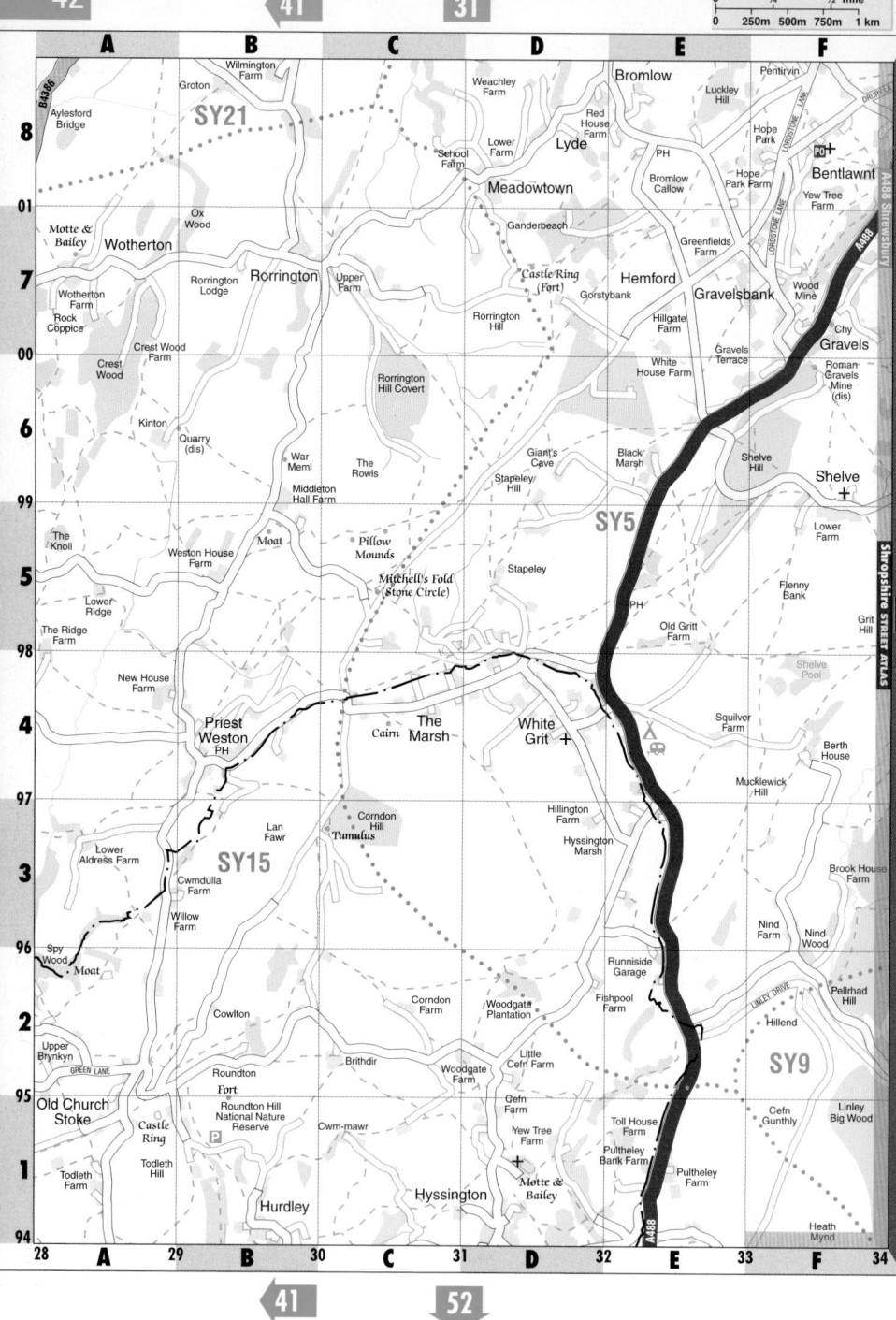

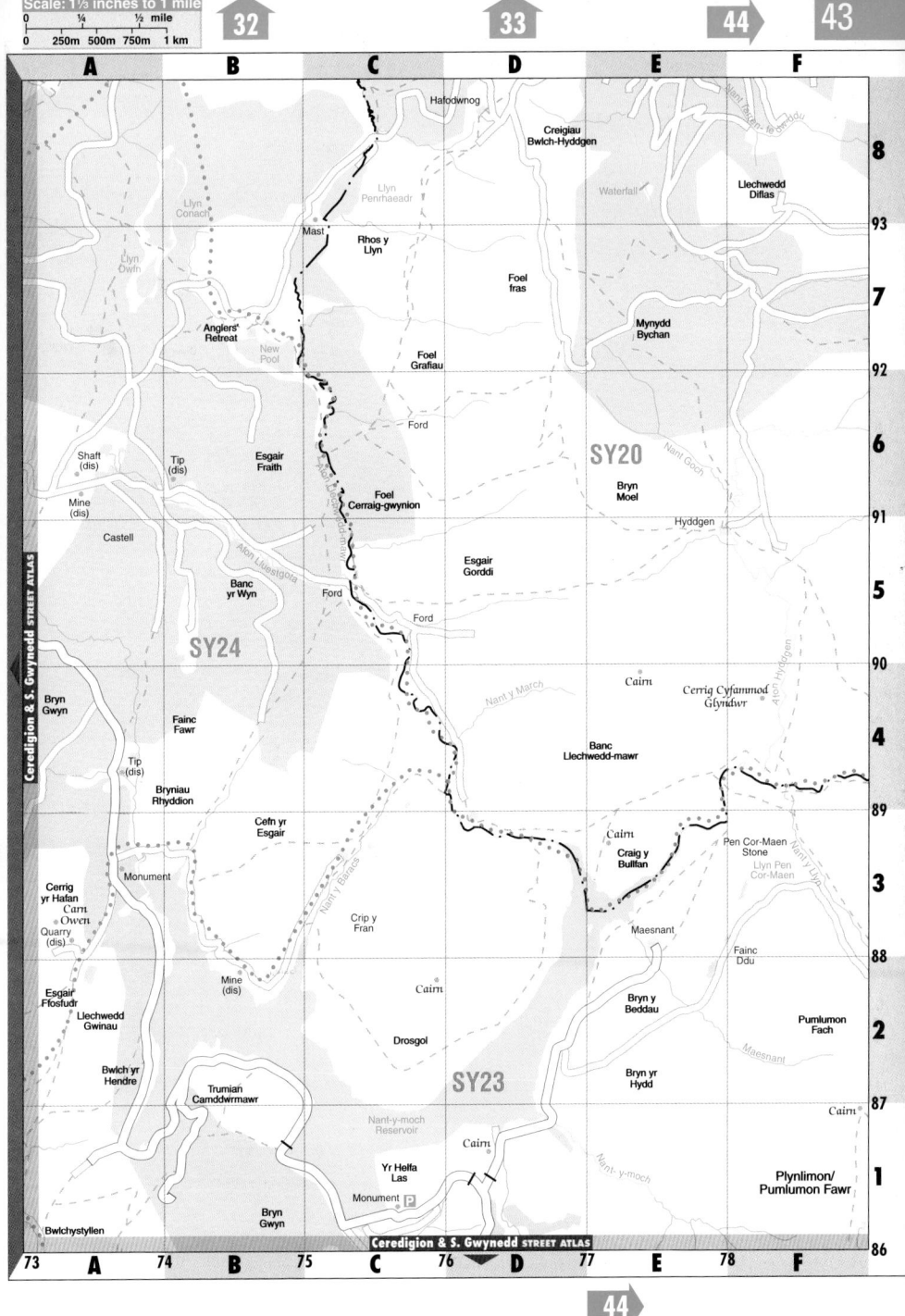

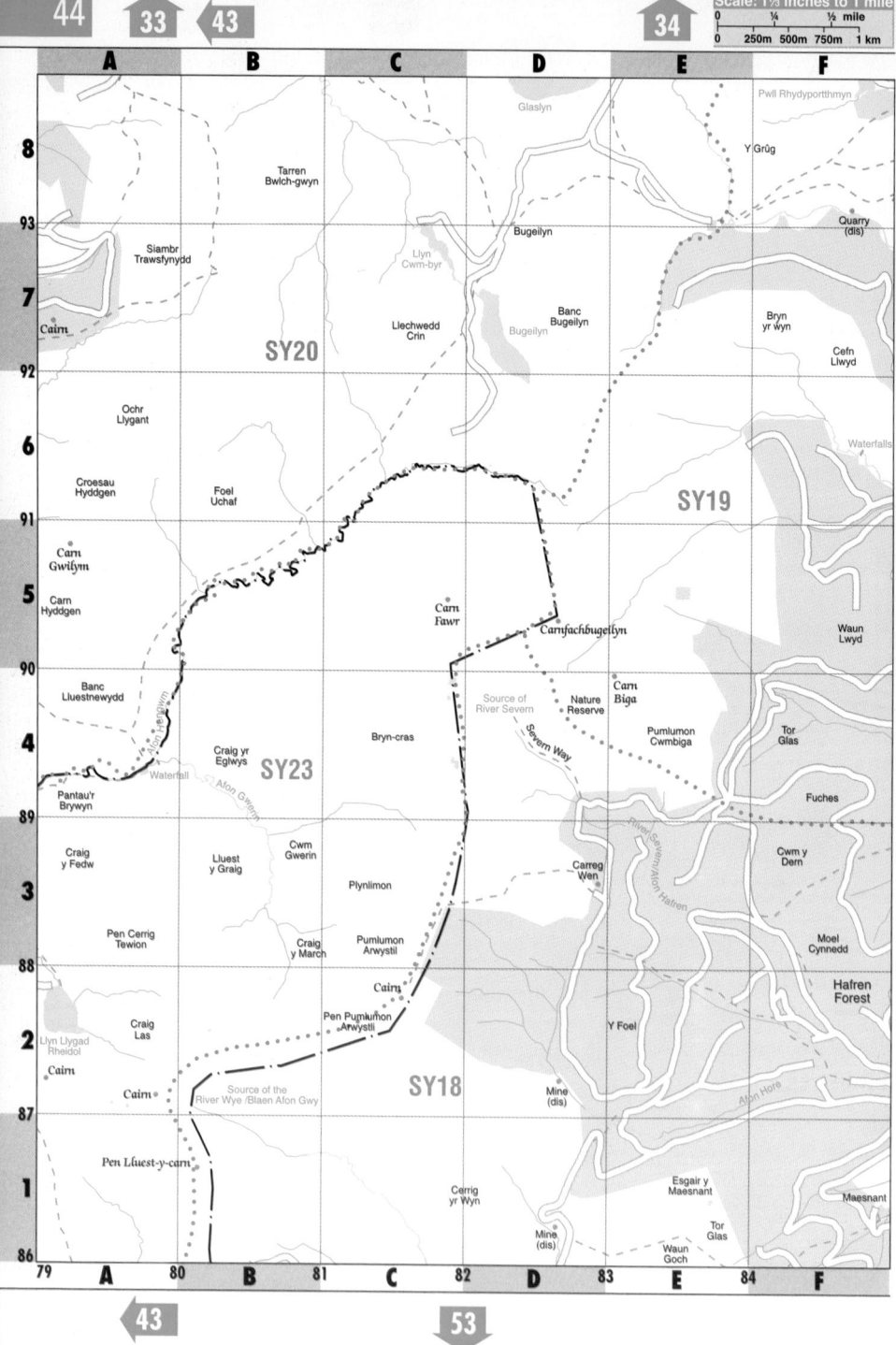

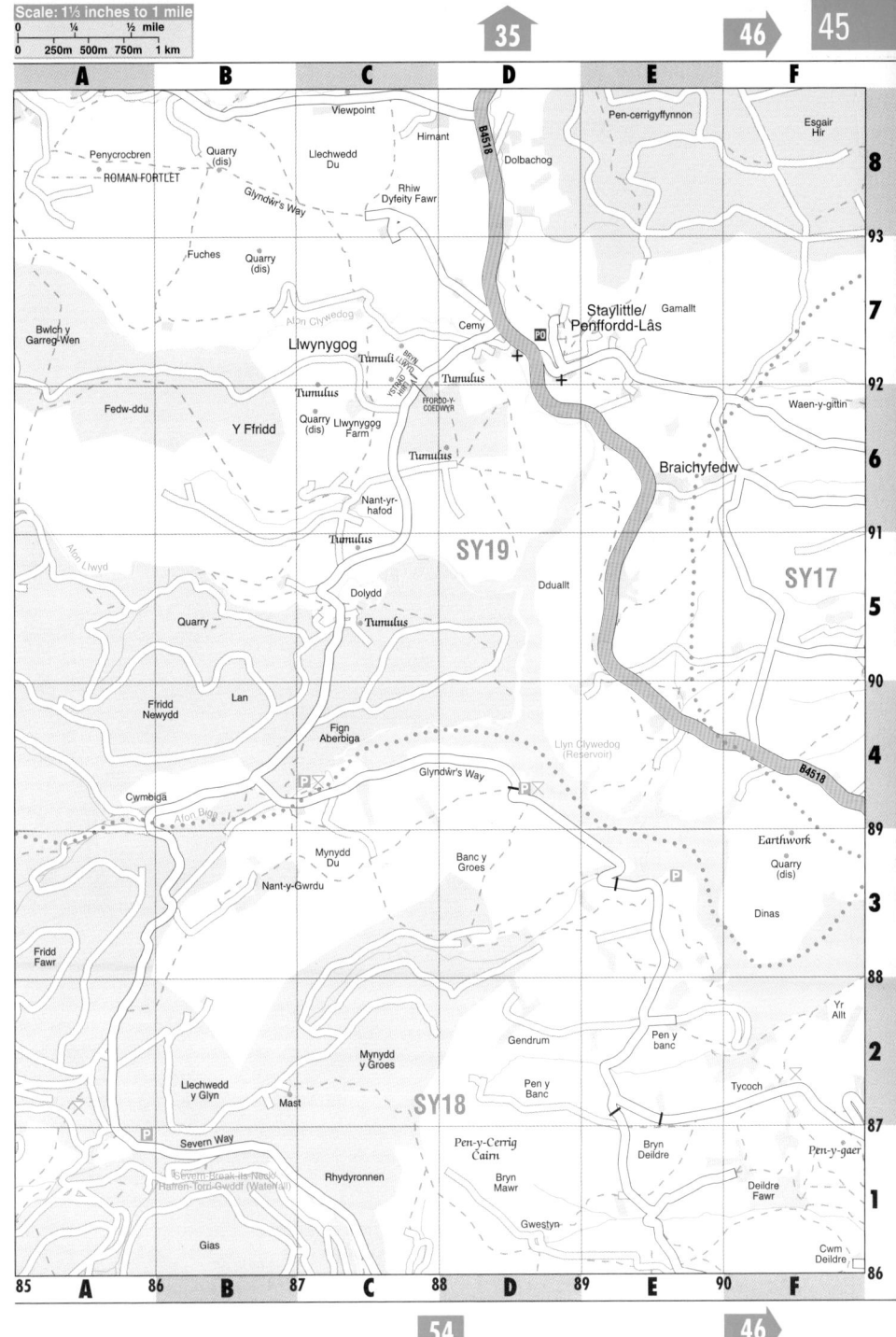

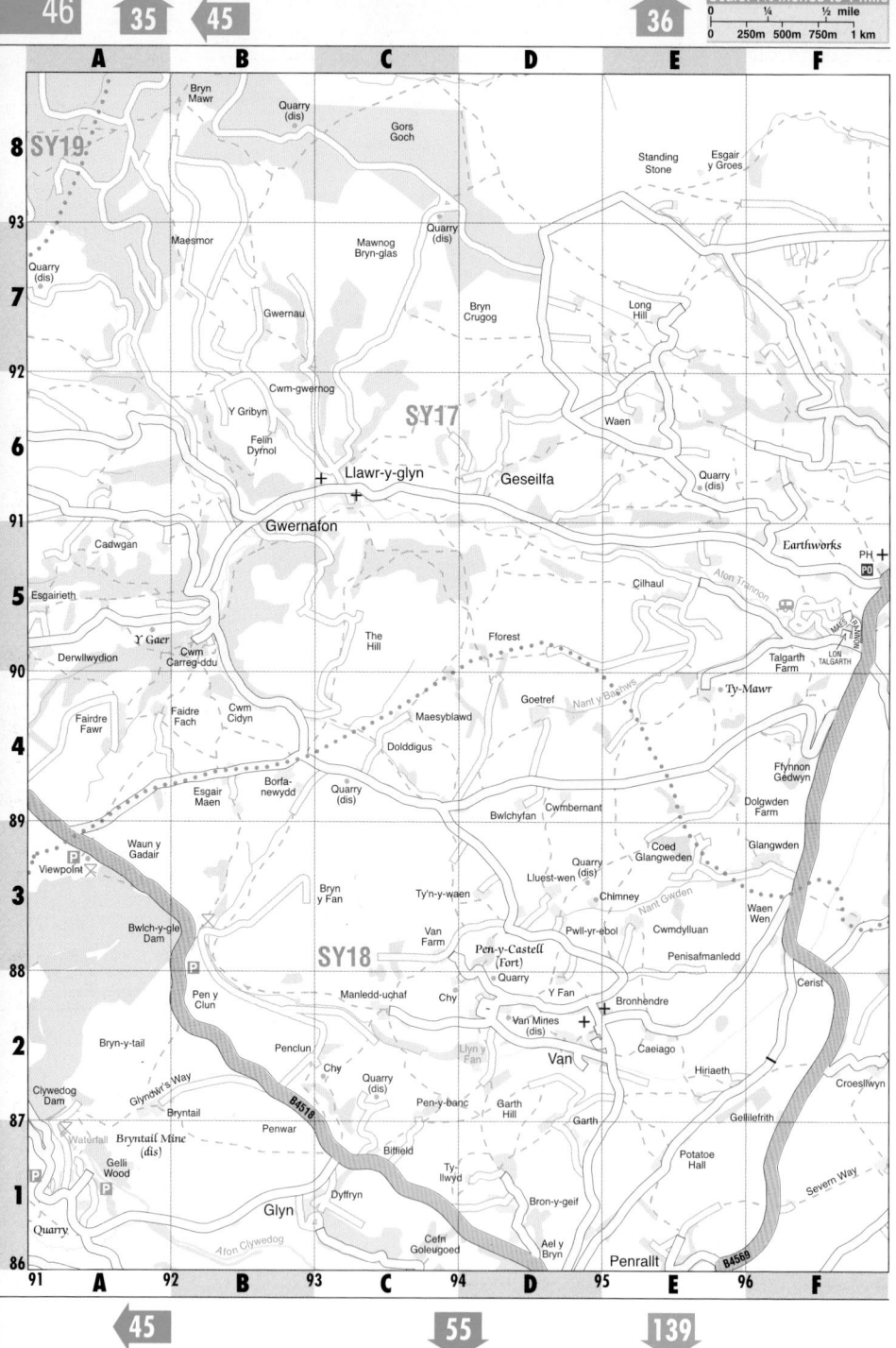

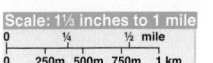

Scale: 1½ inches to 1 mile

0   ¼   ½   mile
0   250m 500m 750m 1 km

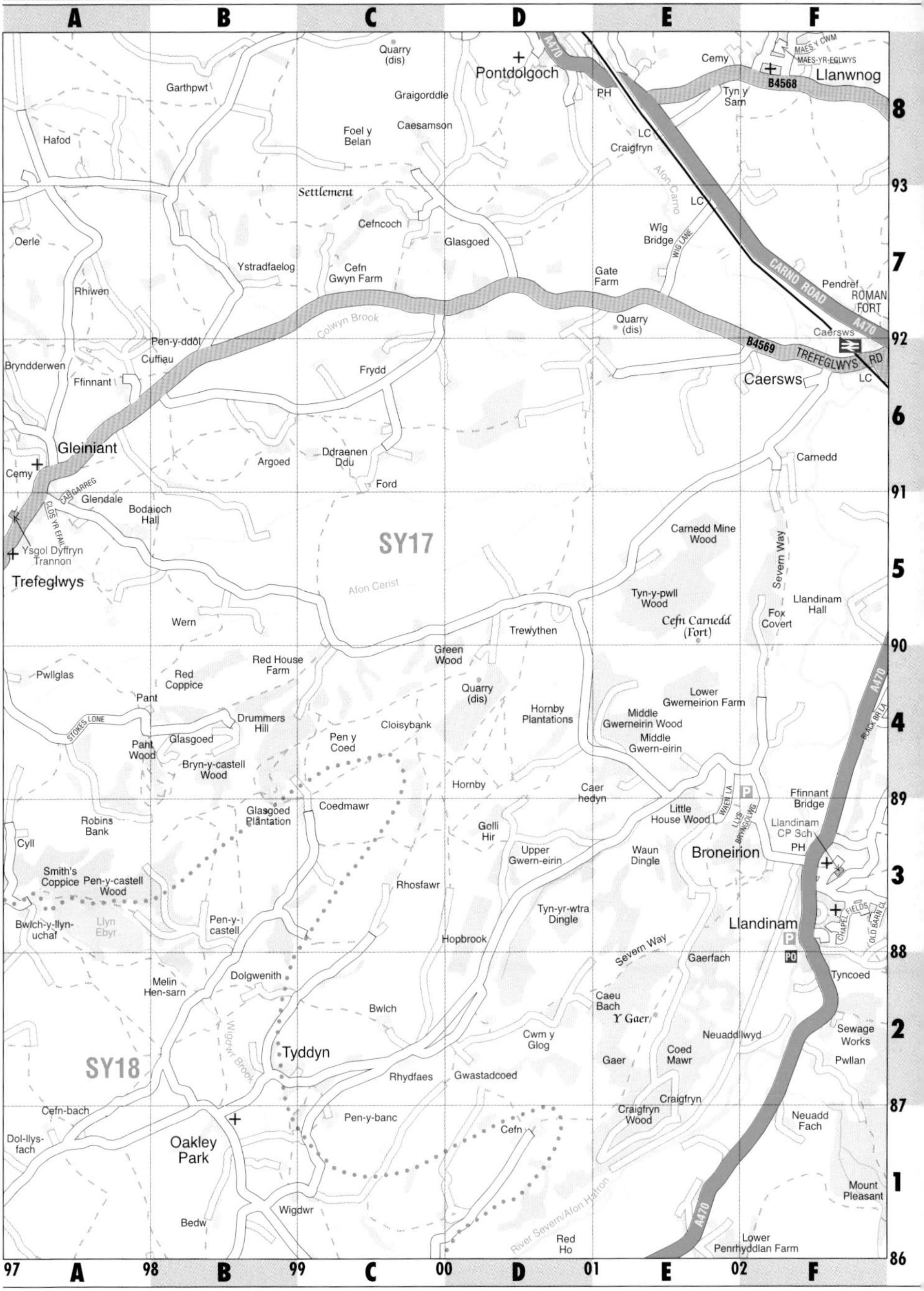

37   48   47

A   B   C   D   E   F

Quarry (dis)
Pontdolgoch
Garthpwt
Graigorddle
Caesamson
Foel y Belan
Cemy
MAES Y CWM
MAES-YR-EGLWYS
Llanwnog
B4568
Tyn y Sarn
PH
LC
Craigfryn
8

Hafod
Settlement
Cefncoch
Glasgoed
Wig Bridge
LC
93

Oerle
Ystradfaelog
Cefn Gwyn Farm
Gate Farm
7

Rhiwen
Colwyn Brook
Quarry (dis)
CARNO ROAD
Pendref
ROMAN FORT
92

Pen-y-ddôl
Cuffiau
Frydd
B4569
TREFEGLWYS RD
Caersws
A470
Bryndderwen
Ffinnant
Caersws
LC

Gleiniant
Argoed
Ddraenen Ddu
Ford
Carnedd
6

Cemy
Glendale
Bodaioch Hall
SY17
91

Ysgol Dyffryn Trannon
Carnedd Mine Wood
Severn Way
5

Trefeglwys
Wern
Afon Cerist
Tyn-y-pwll Wood
Cefn Carnedd (Fort)
Llandinam Hall
Fox Covert

Trewythen
90

Pwllglas
Red Coppice
Red House Farm
Green Wood
Quarry (dis)
Hornby Plantations
Lower Gwerneirion Farm
A470
4

Pant
Drummers Hill
Pen y Coed
Cloisybank
Middle Gwerneirin Wood
Middle Gwern-eirin
Ffinnant Bridge

Pant Wood
Glasgoed
Bryn-y-castell Wood
Coedmawr
Hornby
Caer hedyn
Little House Wood
Llandinam CP Sch
89
3

Robins Bank
Glasgoed Plantation
Gelli Hir
Waun Dingle
Broneirion
PH

Cyll
Smith's Coppice
Pen-y-castell Wood
Rhosfawr
Upper Gwern-eirin
Tyn-yr-wtra Dingle
Llandinam

Bwlch-y-llyn-uchaf
Llyn Ebyr
Pen-y-castell
Hopbrook
Severn Way
Gaerfach
PO
88

Melin Hen-sarn
Dolgwenith
Bwlch
Caeu Bach Y Gaer
Neuaddllwyd
Tyncoed
2

SY18
Tyddyn
Rhydfaes
Gwastadcoed
Cwm y Glog
Gaer
Coed Mawr
Sewage Works
Pwllan

Cefn-bach
Pen-y-banc
Cefn
Craigfryn Wood
Craigfryn
Neuadd Fach
87

Dol-llys-fach
Oakley Park
Cefn
1

Bedw
Wigdwr
River Severn/Afon Hafren
Red Ho
Lower Penrhyddlan Farm
Mount Pleasant
86

97   A   98   B   99   C   00   D   01   E   02   F

56   48

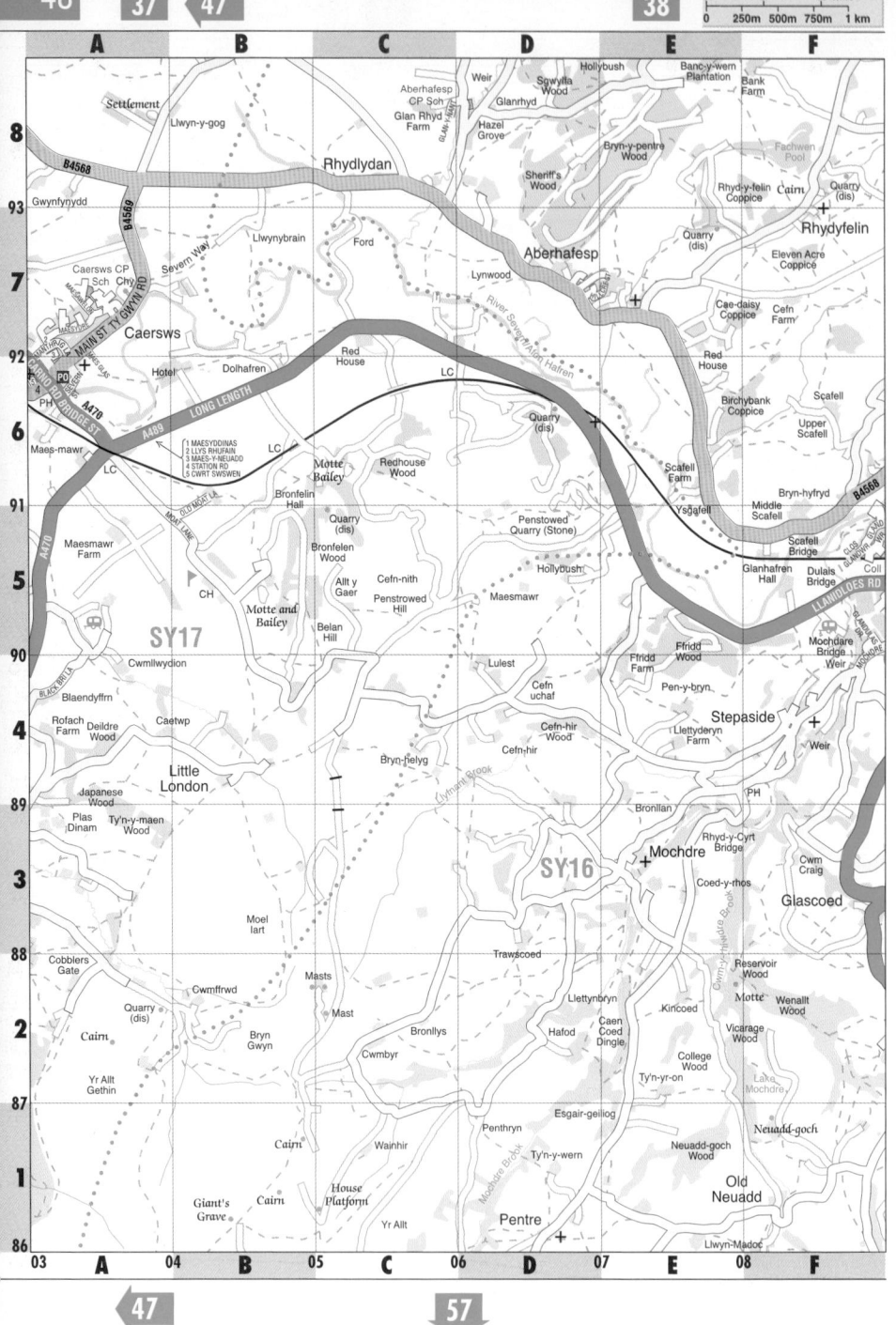

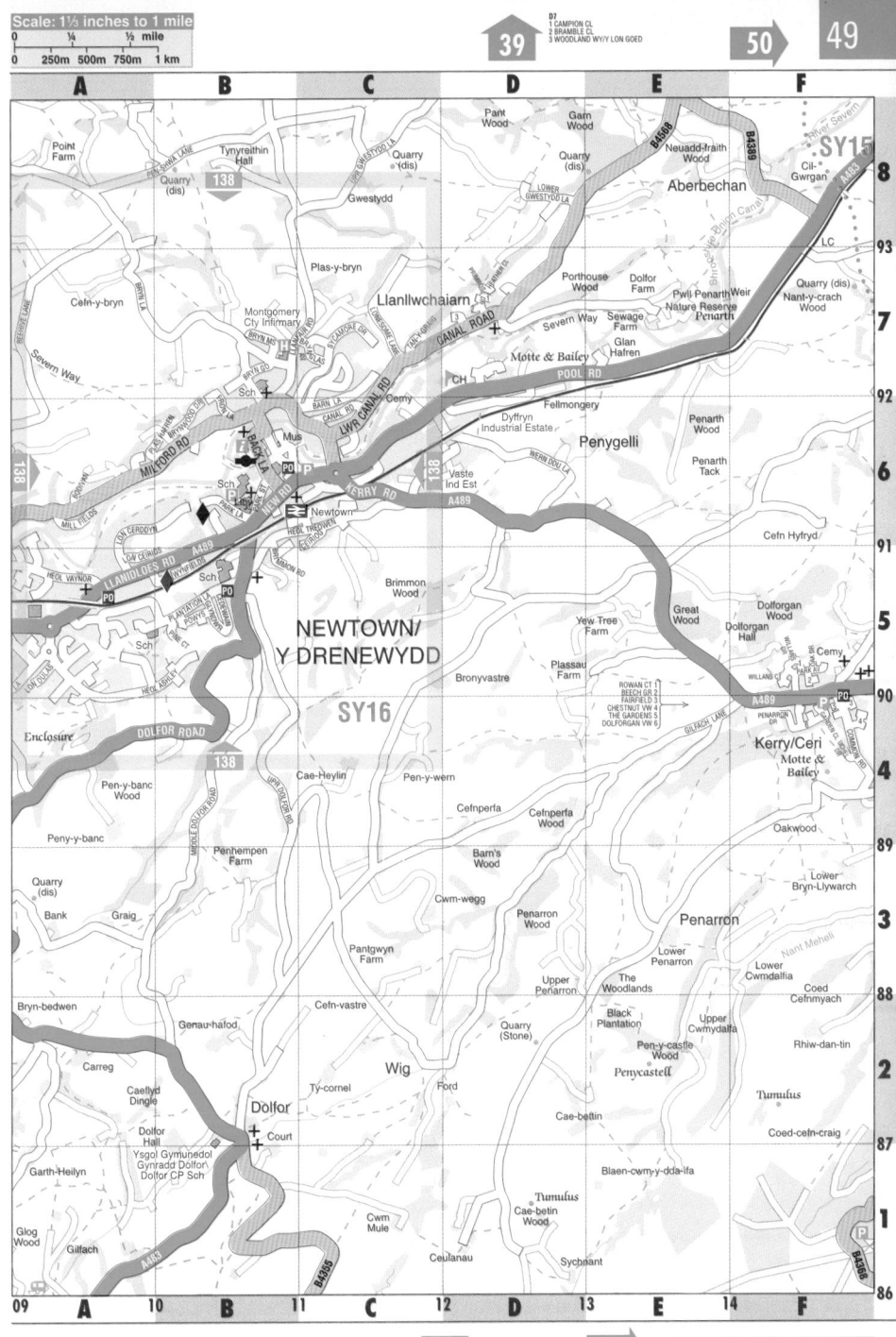

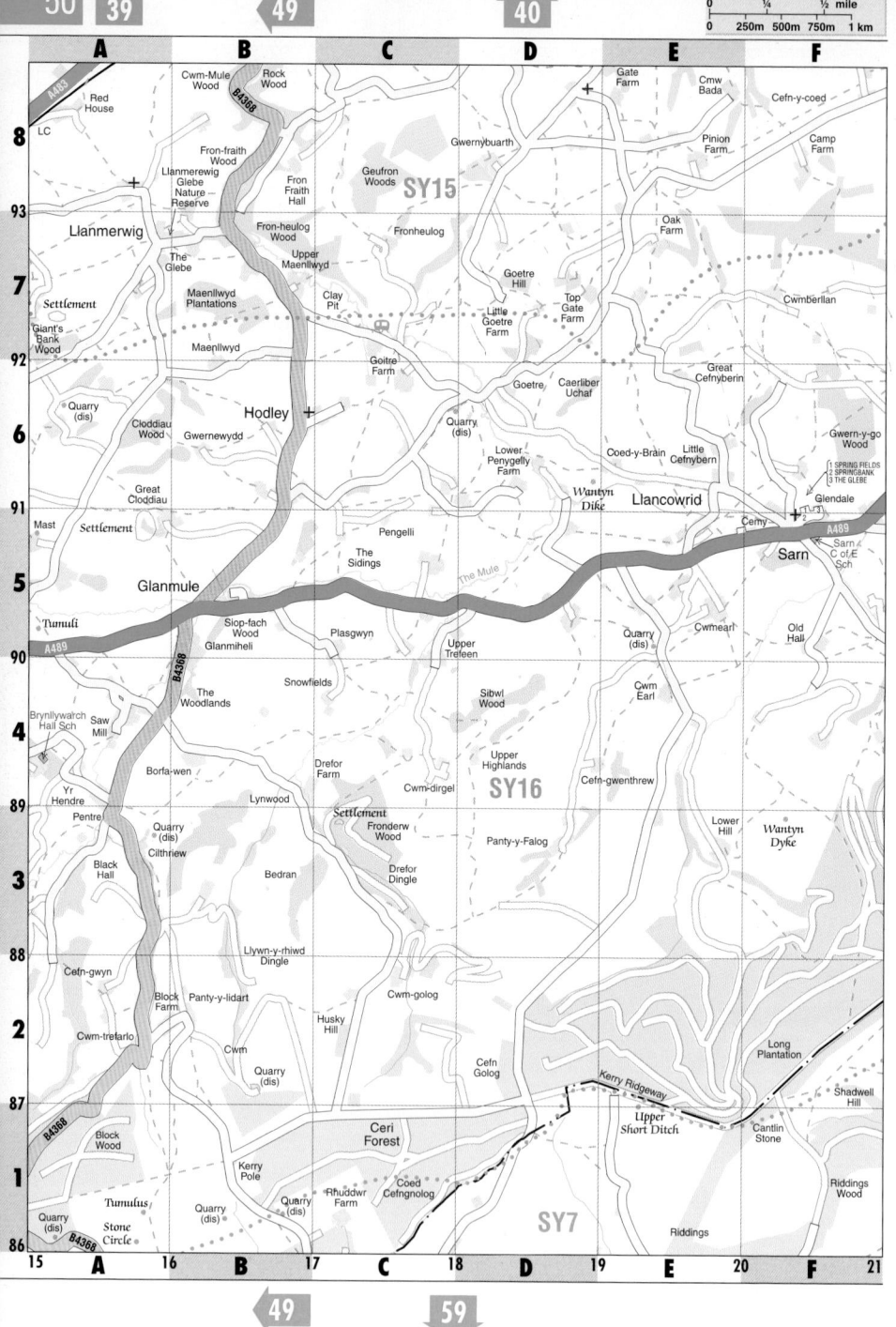

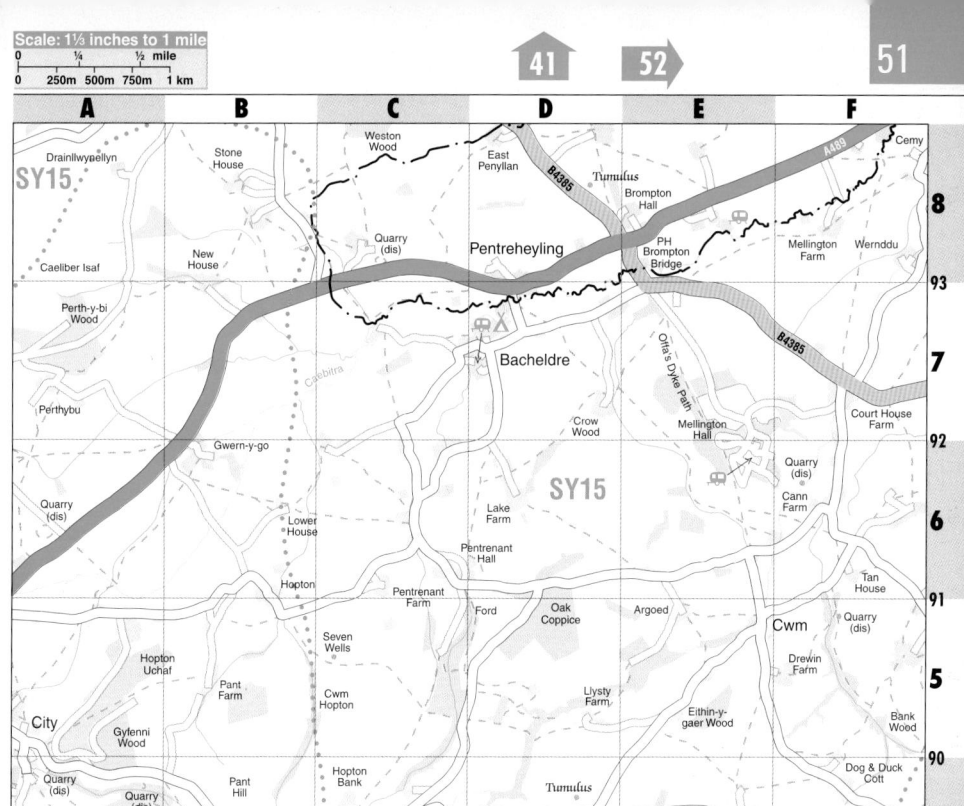

A   B   C   D   E   F

Drainllwynellyn

SY15

Caeliber Isaf

Stone House

New House

Perth-y-bi Wood

Perthybu

Gwern-y-go

Quarry (dis)

Caebitra

Weston Wood

Quarry (dis)

East Penyllan

Pentreheyling

Bacheldre

Crow Wood

B4385

Tumulus

Brompton Hall

PH Brompton Bridge

Cemy

A489

Mellington Farm

Wernddu

8

93

7

B4385

Offa's Dyke Path

Mellington Hall

Court House Farm

92

SY15

Quarry (dis)

Cann Farm

Lower House

Hopton

Lake Farm

Pentrenant Hall

Pentrenant Farm

Ford

Oak Coppice

Argoed

Cwm

Drewin Farm

Tan House

6

91

Hopton Uchaf

Pant Farm

Seven Wells

Cwm Hopton

Llysty Farm

Eithin-y-gaer Wood

Bank Wood

Quarry (dis)

5

City

Gyfenni Wood

Pant Hill

Hopton Bank

Tumulus

Dog & Duck Cott

90

Quarry (dis)

Quarry (dis)

Quarry (dis)

Ford

SY16

Pantglas

Kerry Ridgeway/Cefnffordd Ceri

Nut Wood

Buston Wood

4

89

Round Bank

Turbury Plantation

Kerry Ridgeway/Cefnffordd Ceri

Tumulus

Lower Dolfawr

3

Lower Short Ditch

Quarry (dis)

Quarry (dis)

Long Plantation

Quarries (dis)

Reservoir

Weir

Round Bank

Edenhope Hill

Offa's Dyke Path

SY9

Churchtown

Churchtown Plantation

2

88

Ditch Dingle

Mason's Bank

Round Bank Plantation

Churchtown Hill

Churchtown Wood

87

Long Pike Hollow

Cwm Ffrydd

Barretts

SY7

Birches Wood

Knuck Bank

Settlement

Middle Knuck

1

Clun Forest

Shropshire STREET ATLAS

86

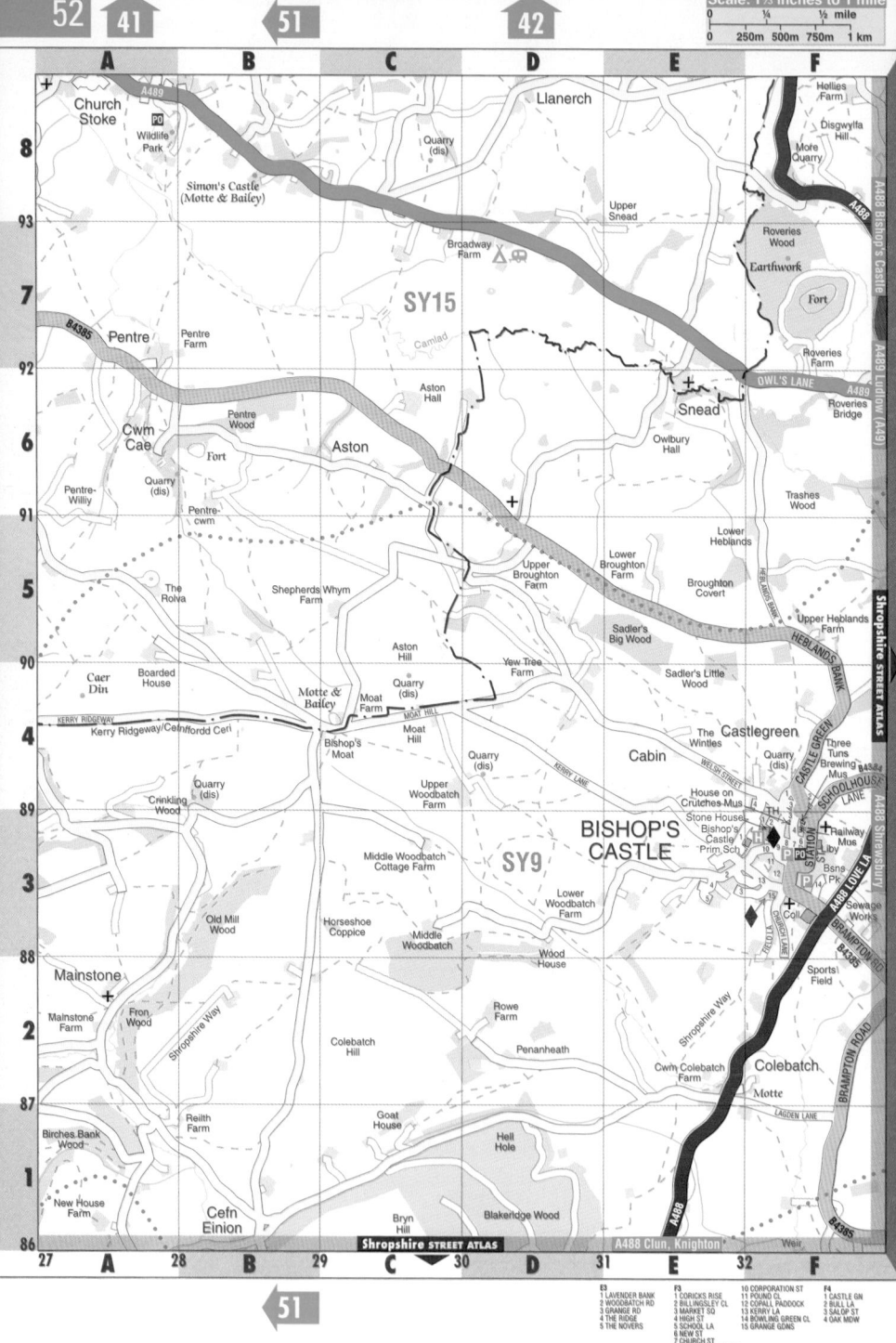

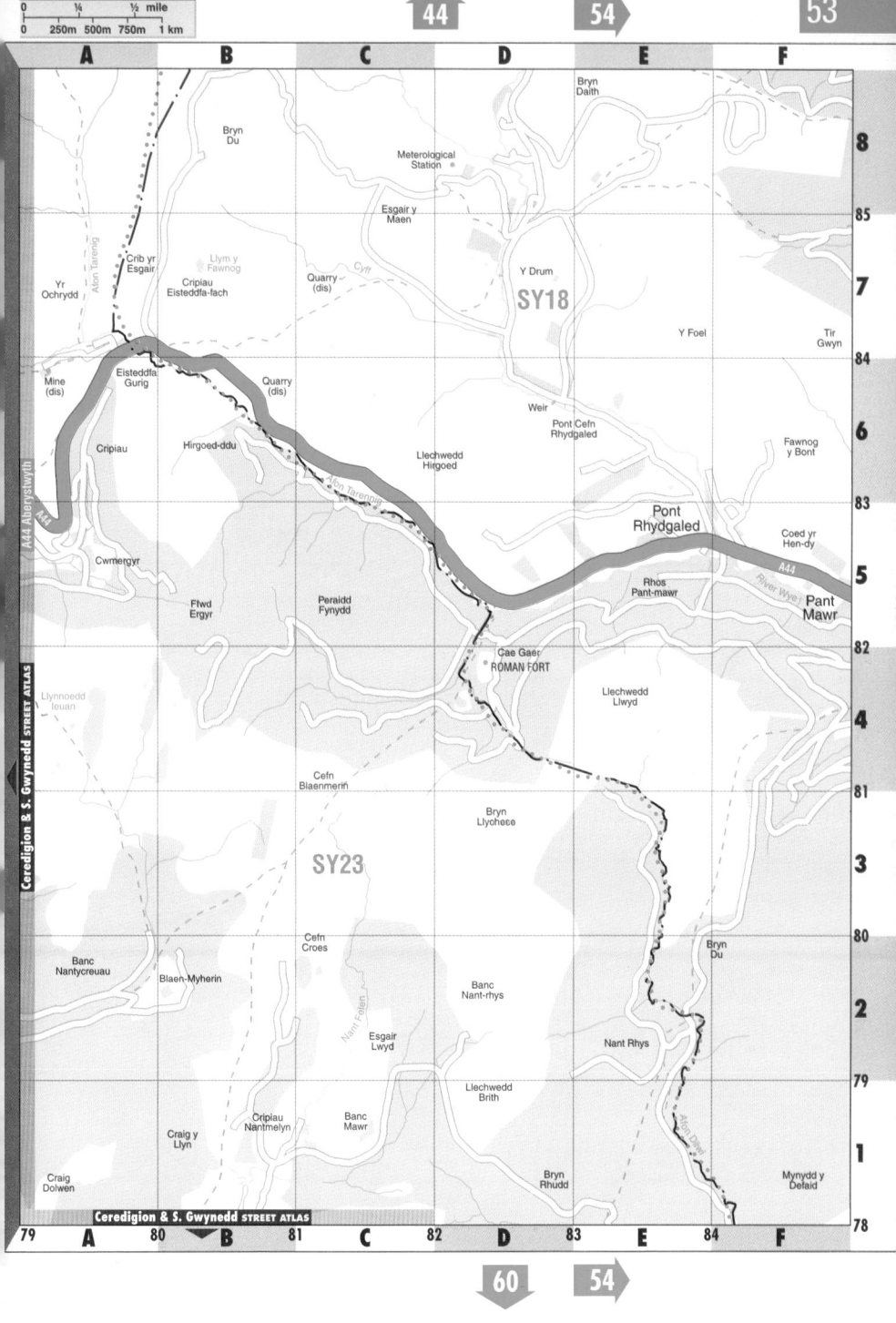

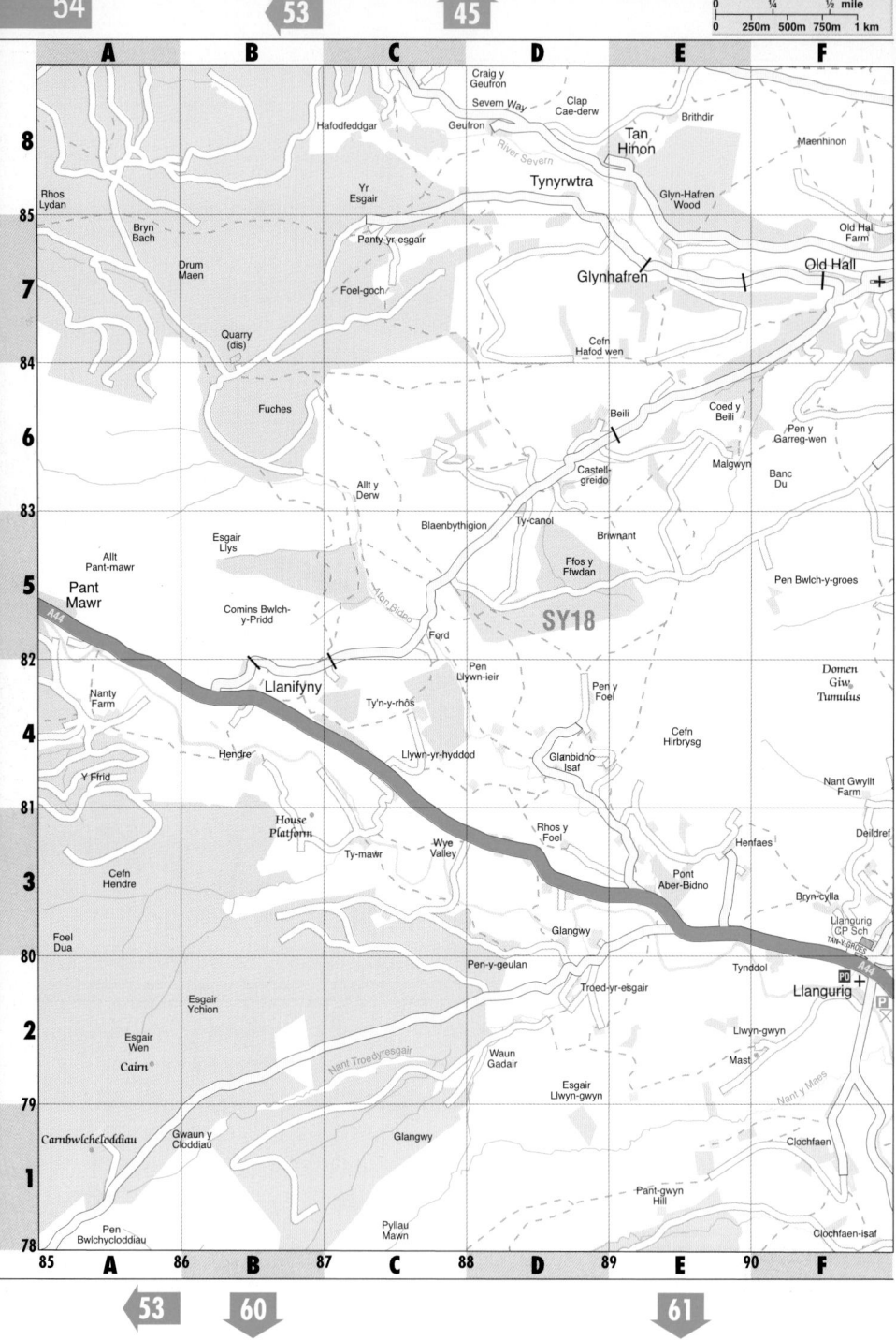

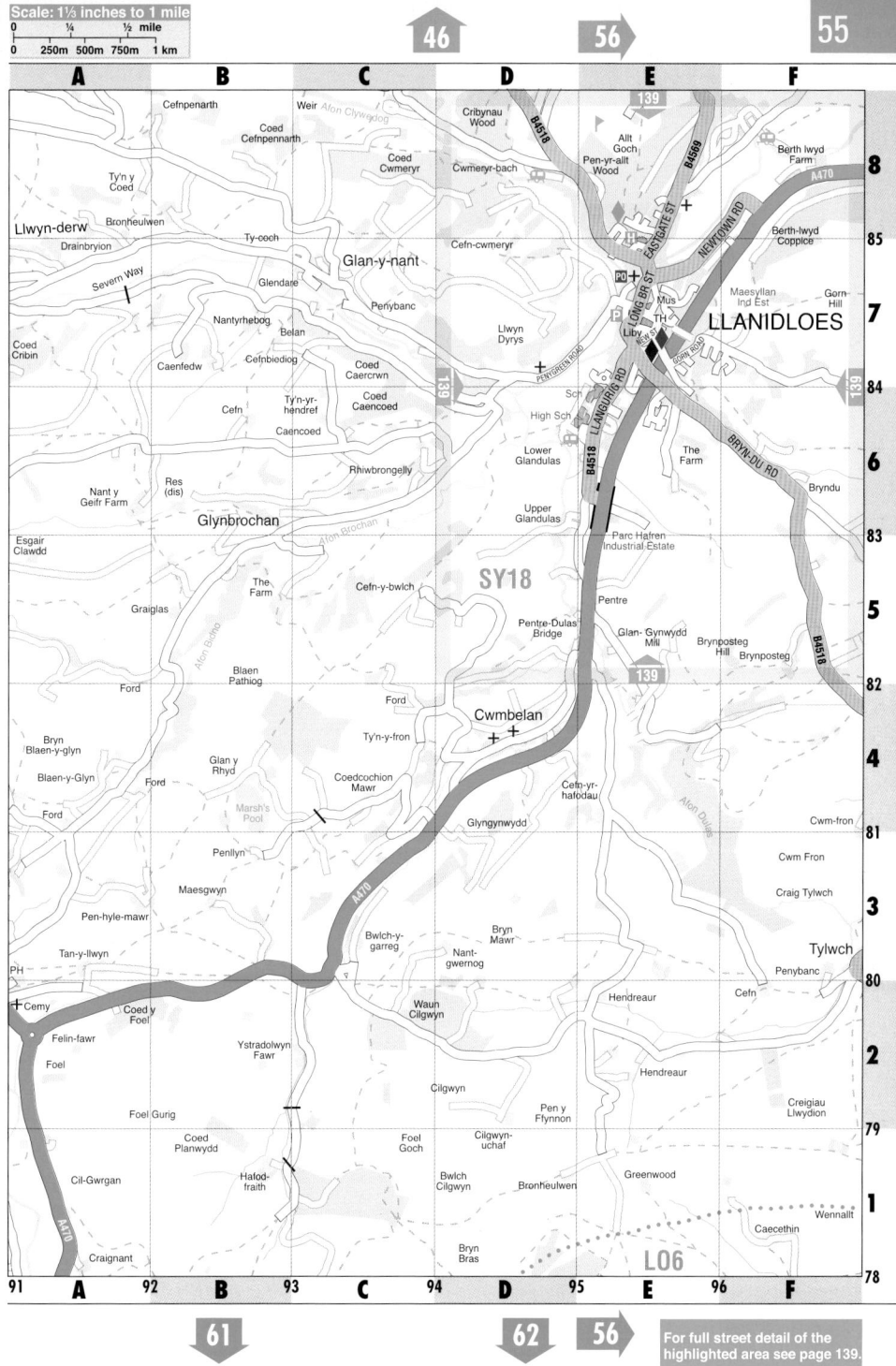

A B C D E F

Cefnpenarth
Coed Cefnpennarth
Weir Afon Clywedog
Coed Cwmeryr
Cribynau Wood
Cwmeryr-bach
Allt Goch Pen-yr-allt Wood
139
Berth lwyd Farm
A470
Ty'n y Coed
Llwyn-derw
Bronheulwen
Ty-coch
EASTGATE ST
Berth-lwyd Coppice
Drainbryion
Cefn-cwmeryr
85
Severn Way
Glan-y-nant
LONG BR ST
Maesyllan Ind Est
Gorn Hill
Glendare
Penybanc
PO
Mus
LLANIDLOES 7
Nantyrhebog
Belan
Llwyn Dyrys
Lib TH
Coed Cribin
Caenfedw
Cefnbiediog
PENTGREEN ROAD
139 84
Cefn
Ty'n-yr-hendref
Coed Caercrwn
Coed Caencoed
High Sch
Caencoed
Rhiwbrongelly
Lower Glandulas
The Farm
BRYN-DU RD
6
Nant y Geifr Farm
Res (dis)
Glynbrochan
Afon Brochan
Upper Glandulas
Bryndu
Esgair Clawdd
Parc Hafren Industrial Estate
83
Graiglas
The Farm
Cefn-y-bwlch
SY18
Pentre
Blaen Pathiog
Afon Biidno
Pentre-Dulas Bridge
Glan- Gynwydd Mill
Brynposteg Hill
Brynposteg 5
Ford
Ford
139 82
Bryn Blaen-y-glyn
Glan y Rhyd
Ty'n-y-fron
Cwmbelan
Cefn-yr-hafodau
B4518
Blaen-y-Glyn
Coedcochion Mawr
Cwm-fron
Ford
Marsh's Pool
Glyngynwydd
81
Penllyn
Cwm Fron
Maesgwyn
A470
Craig Tylwch 3
Pen-hyle-mawr
Bryn Mawr
Tan-y-llwyn
Bwlch-y-garreg
Nant-gwernog
Tylwch
PH
Hendreaur
Cefn
Penybanc
80
Cemy
Coed y Foel
Waun Cilgwyn
Felin-fawr
Foel
Hendreaur 2
Ystradolwyn Fawr
Foel Gurig
Cilgwyn
Pen y Ffynnon
Creigiau Llwydion
79
Coed Planwydd
Foel Goch
Cilgwyn-uchaf
Cil-Gwrgan
Hafod-fraith
Bwlch Cilgwyn
Bronheulwen
Greenwood
Wennallt 1
A470
Caecethin
Craignant
Bryn Bras
L06
78

91 A 92 B 93 C 94 D 95 E 96 F

For full street detail of the highlighted area see page 139.

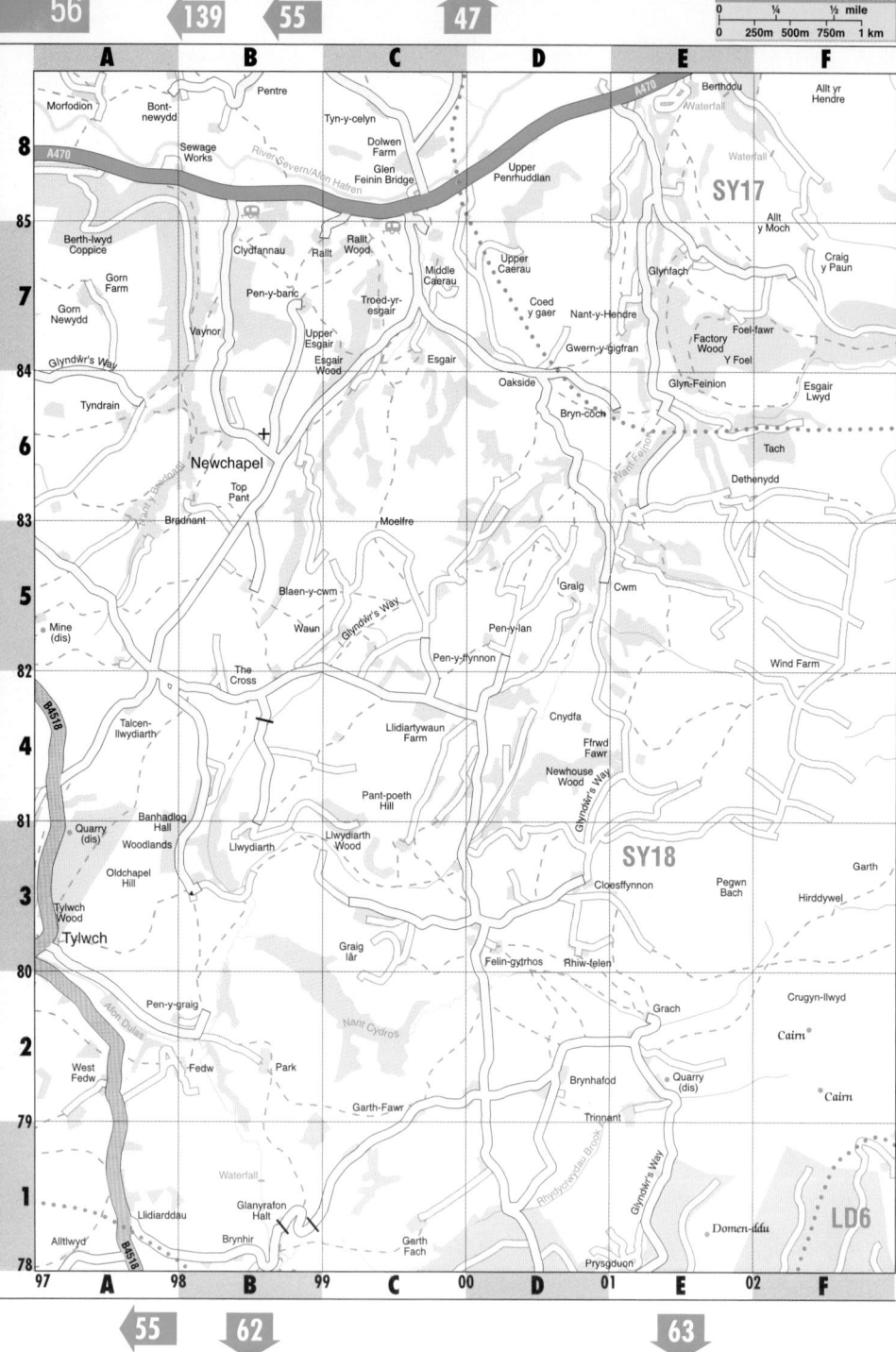

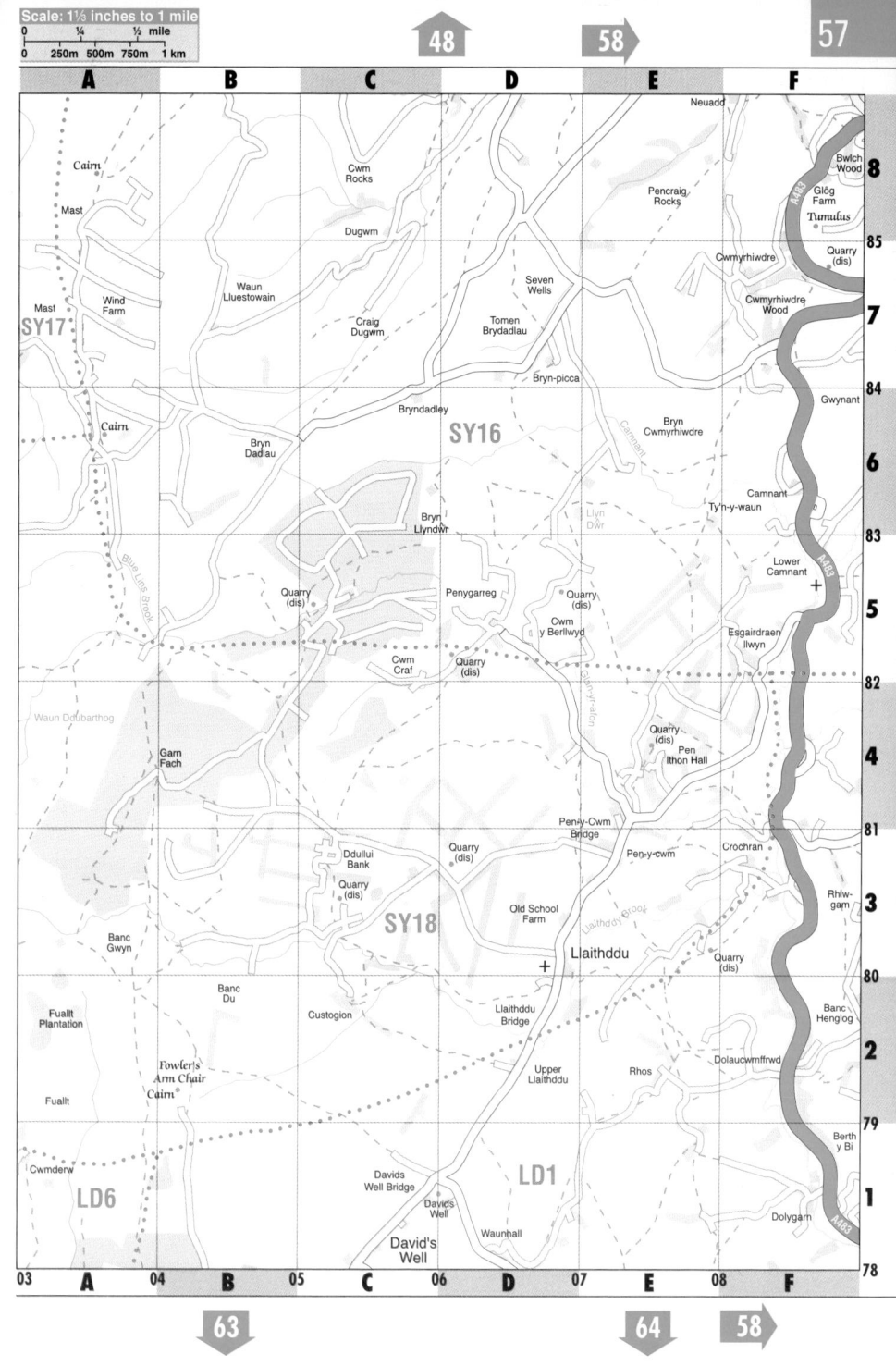

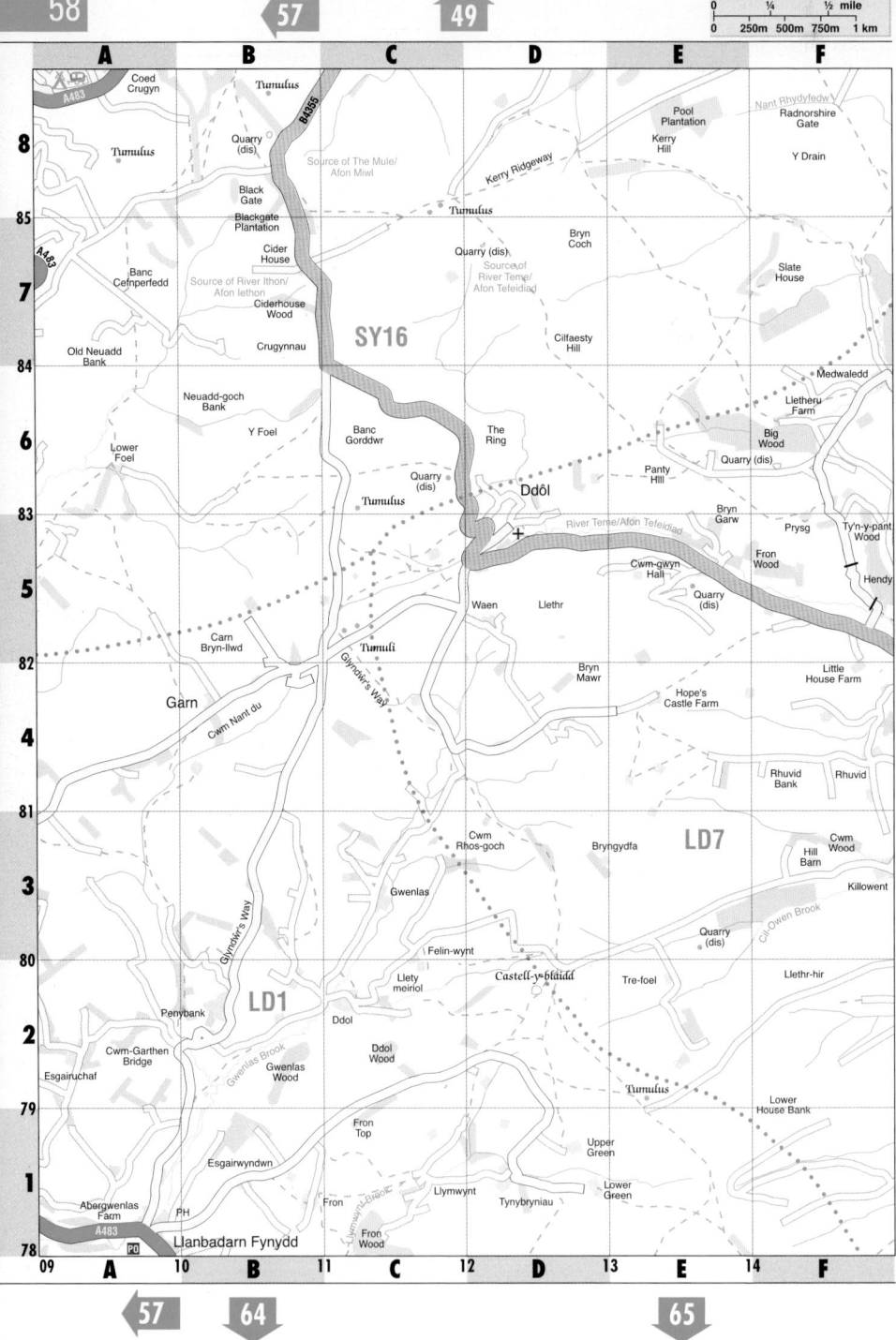

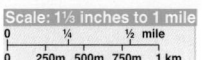

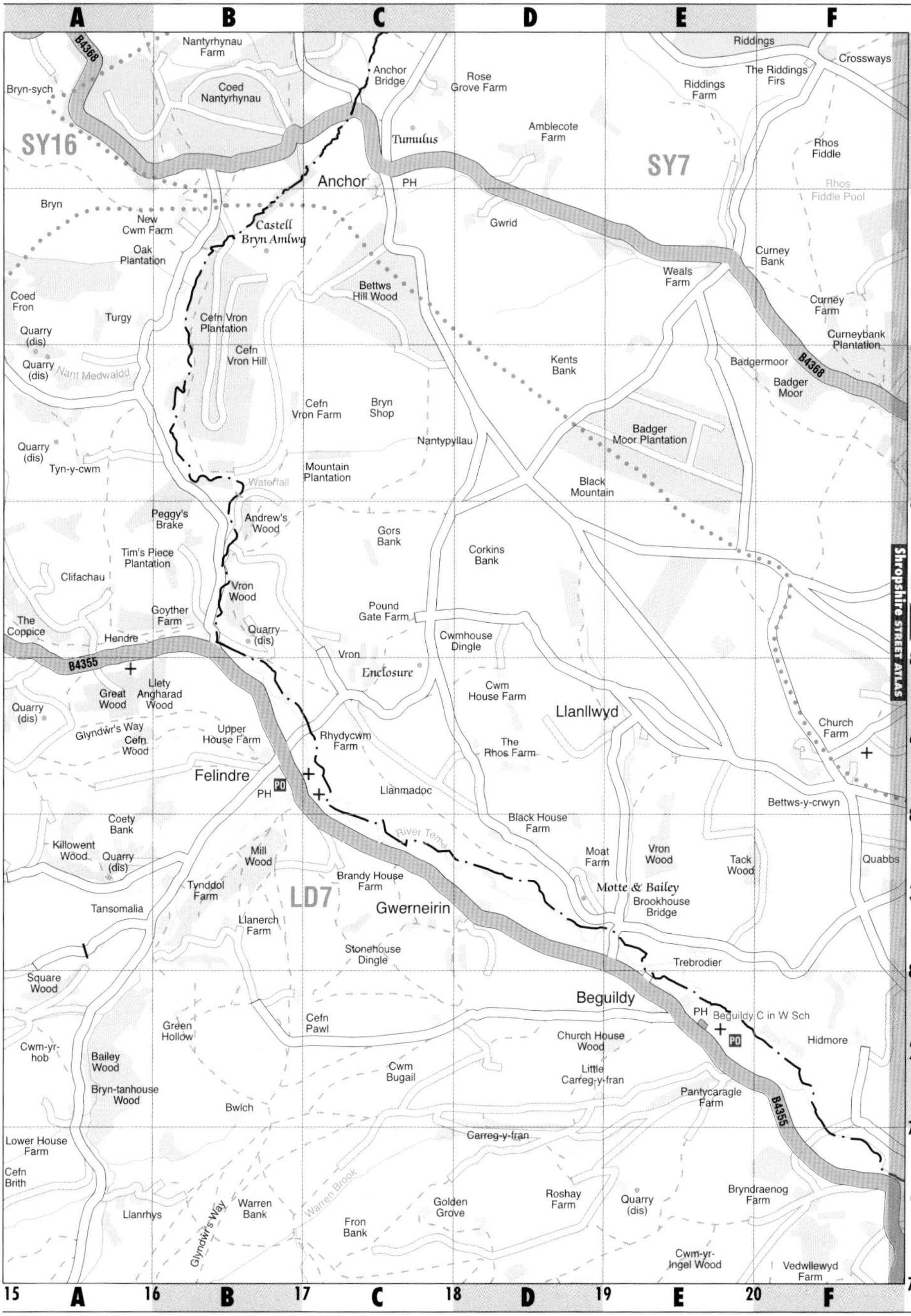

Scale: 1½ inches to 1 mile

0   ¼   ½   mile
0   250m 500m 750m 1 km

A   B   C   D   E   F

B4368

Bryn-sych

Nantyrhynau Farm

Coed Nantyrhynau

Anchor Bridge

Rose Grove Farm

Riddings

The Riddings Firs

Crossways

SY16

Tumulus

Ambiecote Farm

Riddings Farm

Rhos Fiddle

8

Anchor

PH

SY7

Rhos Fiddle Pool

85

Bryn

New Cwm Farm

Castell Bryn Amlwg

Gwrid

Curney Bank

Oak Plantation

Bettws Hill Wood

Weals Farm

Curney Farm

7

Coed Fron

Turgy

Cefn Vron Plantation

Curneybank Plantation

Quarry (dis)

Cefn Vron Hill

Nant Medwaldd

Kents Bank

Badgermoor

Badger Moor

84

Quarry (dis)

Cefn Vron Farm

Bryn Shop

Nantypyllau

Badger Moor Plantation

B4368

6

Quarry (dis)

Tyn-y-cwm

Mountain Plantation

Black Mountain

83

Waterfall

Peggy's Brake

Andrew's Wood

Gors Bank

Corkins Bank

Tim's Piece Plantation

Clifachau

Vron Wood

Pound Gate Farm

Cwmhouse Dingle

Shropshire STREET ATLAS

5

The Coppice

Goyther Farm

Hendre

Quarry (dis)

Vron

Enclosure

Cwm House Farm

Llanllwyd

Church Farm

82

B4355

Great Wood

Llety Angharad Wood

Upper House Farm

Rhydycwm Farm

The Rhos Farm

4

Quarry (dis)

Glyndwr's Way

Cefn Wood

Felindre

PH   PO

Llanmadoc

Black House Farm

Bettws-y-crwyn

81

Coety Bank

Mill Wood

River Teme

Moat Farm

Vron Wood

Tack Wood

Quabbs

Killowent Wood

Quarry (dis)

Tynddol Farm

Brandy House Farm

Motte & Bailey

Brookhouse Bridge

3

Tansomalia

Llanerch Farm

LD7

Gwerneirin

Stonehouse Dingle

Trebrodier

80

Square Wood

Green Hollow

Cefn Pawl

Beguildy

PH   Beguildy C in W Sch

PO   Hidmore

2

Cwm-yr-hob

Bailey Wood

Cwm Bugail

Church House Wood

Pantycaragle Farm

Bryn-tanhouse Wood

Bwlch

Little Carreg-y-fran

B4355

Lower House Farm

Carreg-y-fran

Bryndraenog Farm

79

Cefn Brith

Llanrhys

Glyndwr's Way

Warren Bank

Fron Bank

Warren Brook

Golden Grove

Roshay Farm

Quarry (dis)

Cwm-yr-ingel Wood

Vedwllewyd Farm

1

78

15   A   16   B   17   C   18   D   19   E   20   F

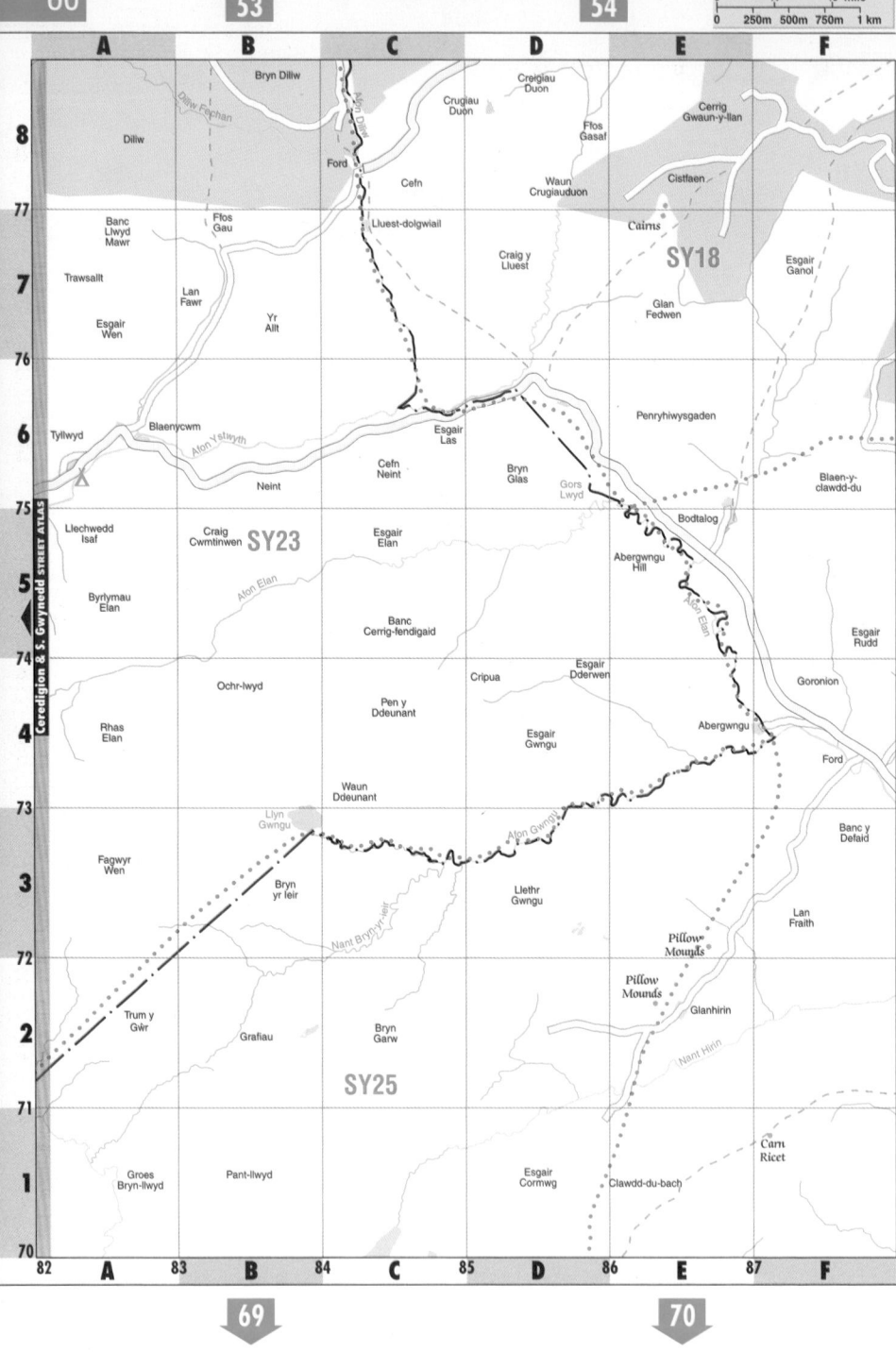

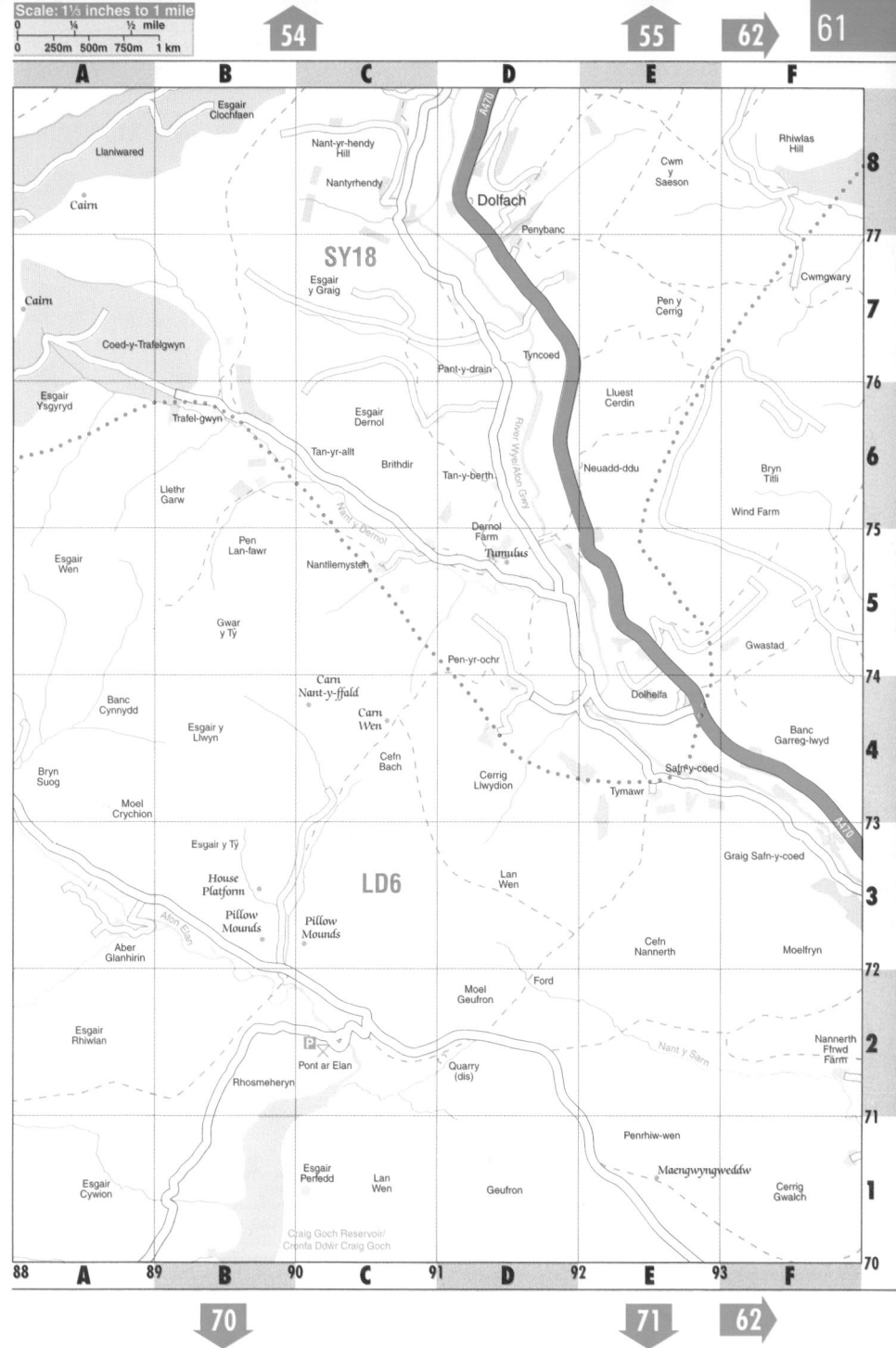

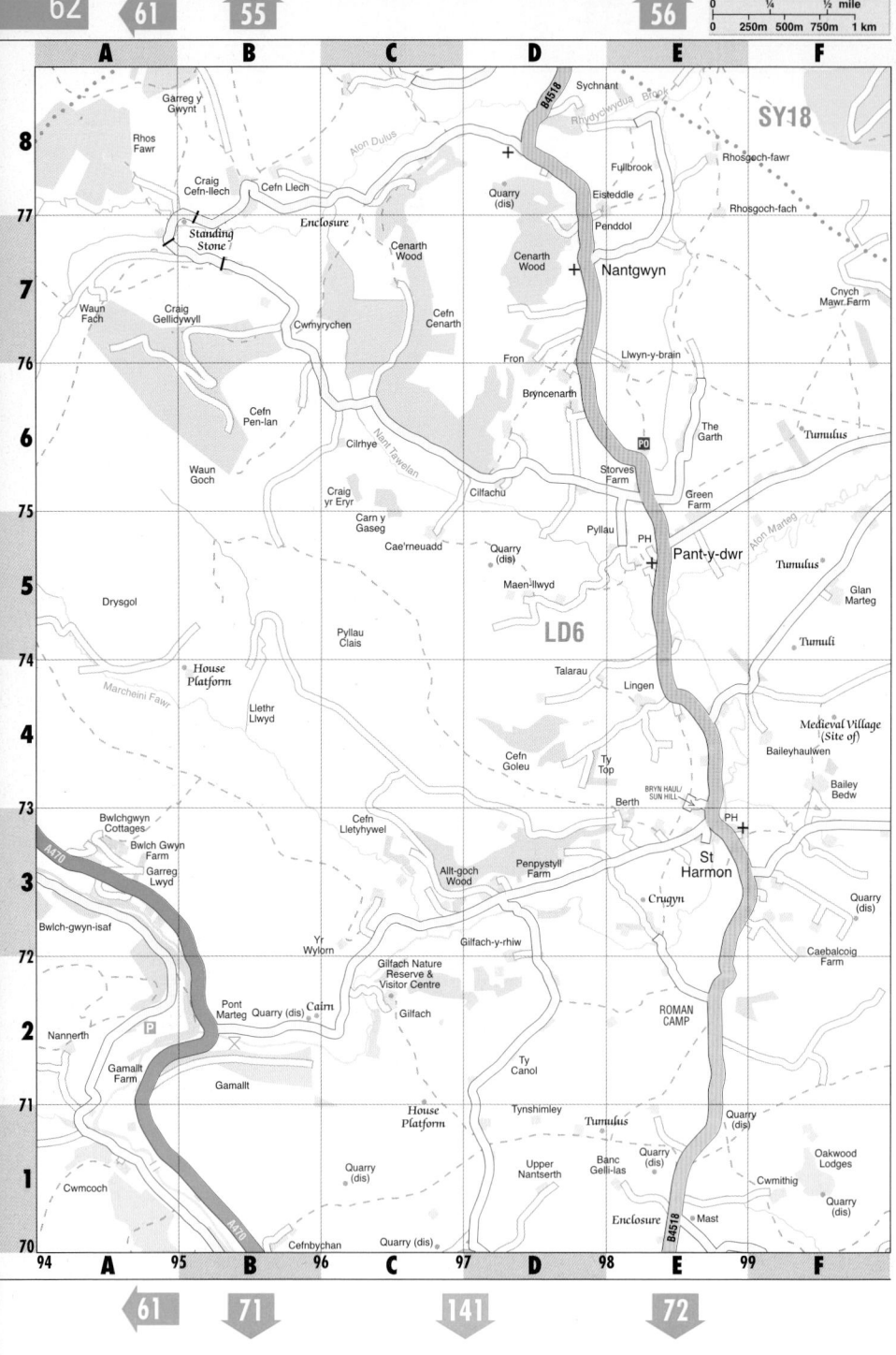

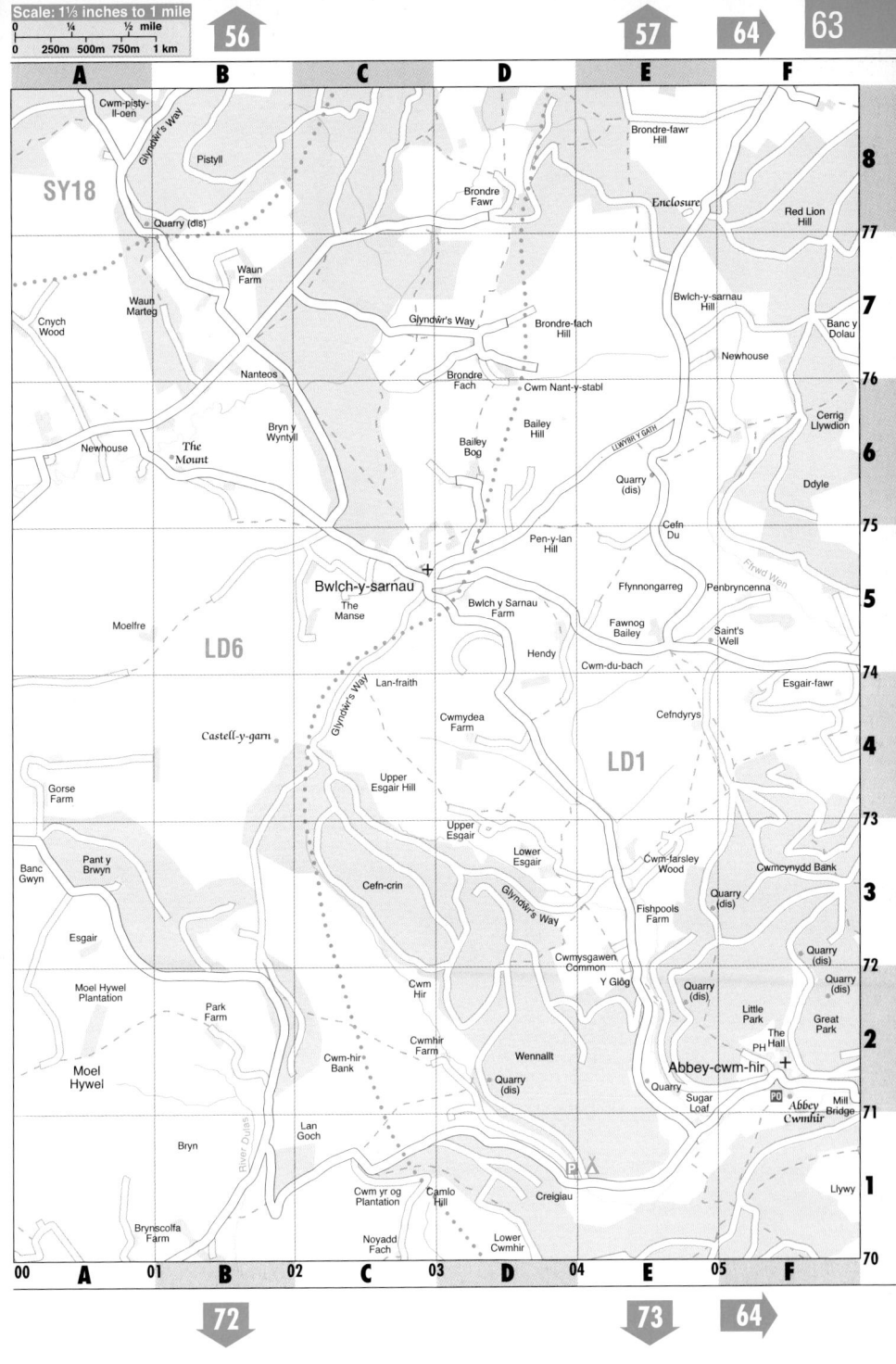

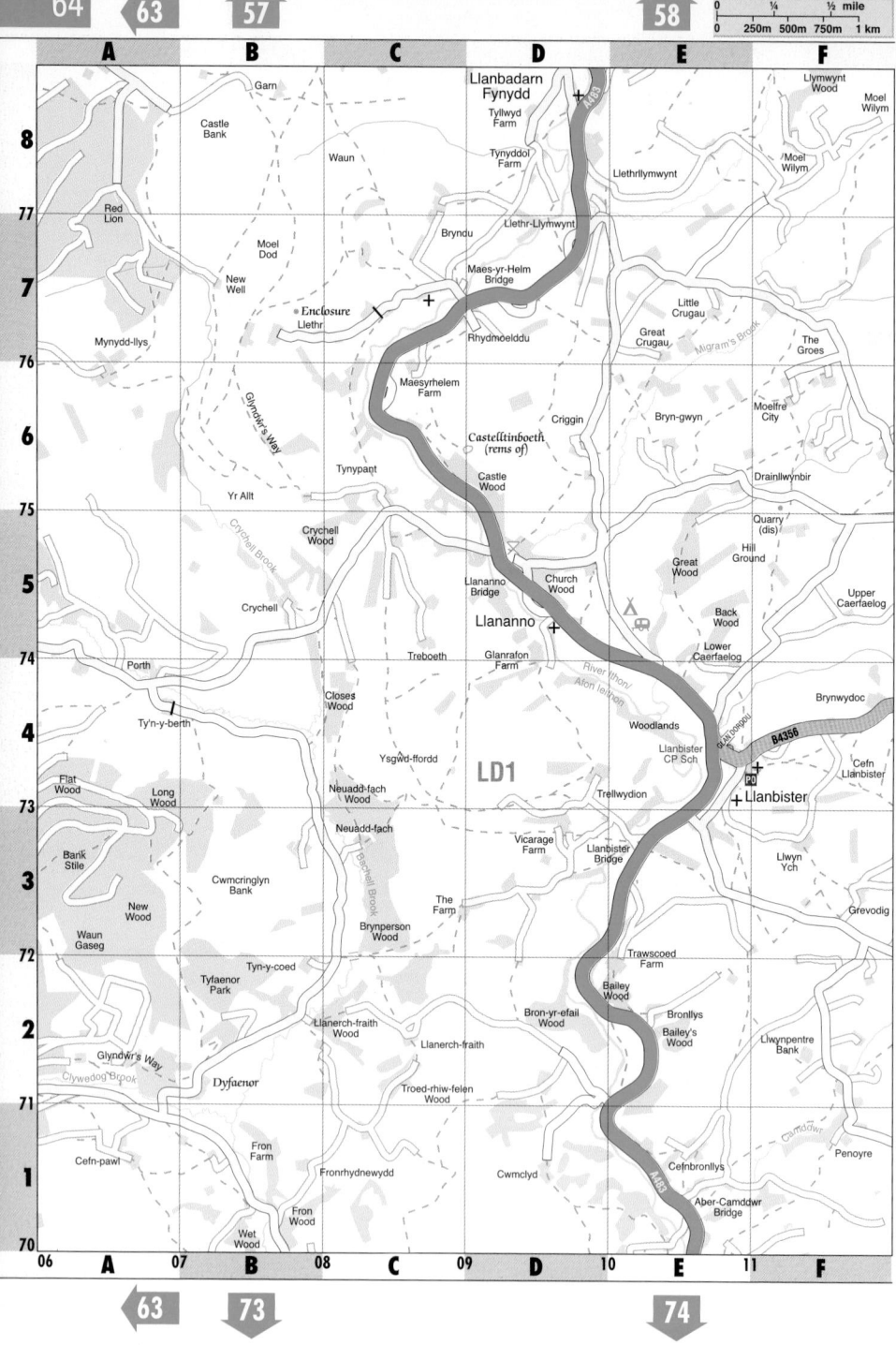

Scale: 1½ inches to 1 mile

0 ¼ ½ mile
0 250m 500m 750m 1 km

| | A | B | C | D | E | F |

Llanbadarn Fynydd

Garn

Castle Bank

Waun

Red Lion

Tyllwyd Farm

Tynyddol Farm

Bryndu

Llethr-Llywmynt

Llethrllymwynt

Llymwynt Wood

Moel Wilym

Moel Wilym

Moel Dod

New Well

Maes-yr-Helm Bridge

Maesyrhelem Farm

Enclosure Llethr

Rhydmoelddu

Little Crugau

Great Crugau

The Groes

Mynydd-llys

Glyndwr's Way

Castelltinboeth (rems of)

Criggin

Bryn-gwyn

Moelfre City

Tynypant

Castle Wood

Drainllwynbir

Yr Allt

Crychell Brook

Crychell Wood

Llananno Bridge

Church Wood

Great Wood

Hill Ground

Quarry (dis)

Upper Caerfaelog

Crychell

Llananno

Back Wood

Porth

Treboeth

Glanrafon Farm

River Ithon/ Afon Ieithon

Lower Caerfaelog

Closes Wood

Ty'n-y-berth

Woodlands

GLYNDWODWL

Brynwydoc

Flat Wood

Long Wood

Ysgwd-ffordd

Neuadd-fach Wood

LD1

Llanbister CP Sch

B4356

Cefn Llanbister

Bank Stile

Neuadd-fach

Llanbister Bridge

PO

Llanbister

New Wood

Cwmcringlyn Bank

Vicarage Farm

Llwyn Ych

Waun Gaseg

Tyn-y-coed

The Farm

Trellwydion

Grevodig

Tyfaenor Park

Brynperson Wood

Trawscoed Farm

Glyndwr's Way

Llanerch-fraith Wood

Llanerch-fraith

Bron-yr-efail Wood

Bailey Wood

Bronllys

Bailey's Wood

Llwynpentre Bank

Clywedog Brook

Dyfaenor

Troed-rhiw-felen Wood

Camddwr

Cefn-pawl

Fron Farm

Fronrhydnewydd

Cwmclyd

Cefnbronllys

Penoyre

Fron Wood

Wet Wood

Aber-Camddwr Bridge

| 06 | A | 07 | B | 08 | C | 09 | D | 10 | E | 11 | F |

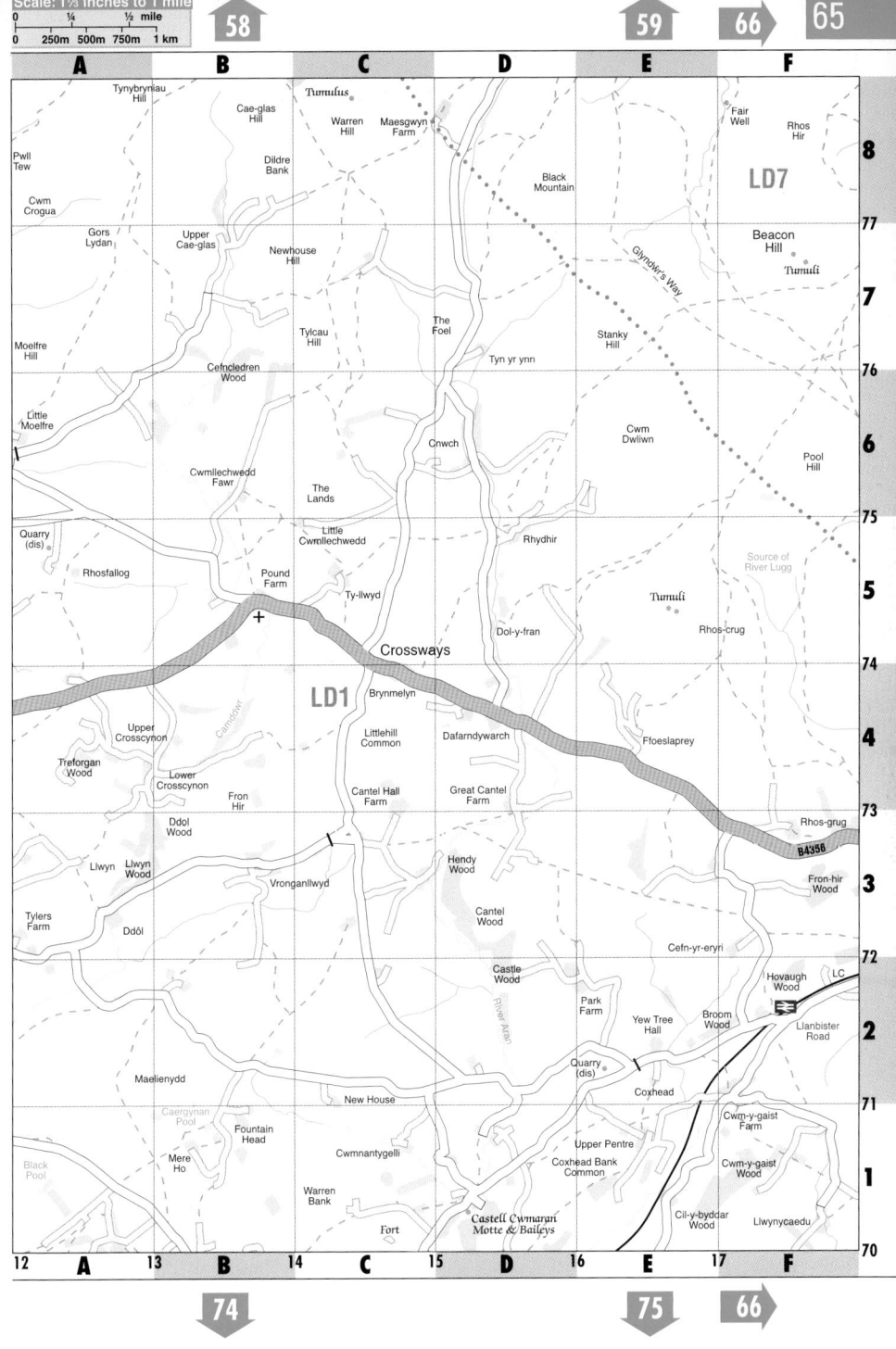

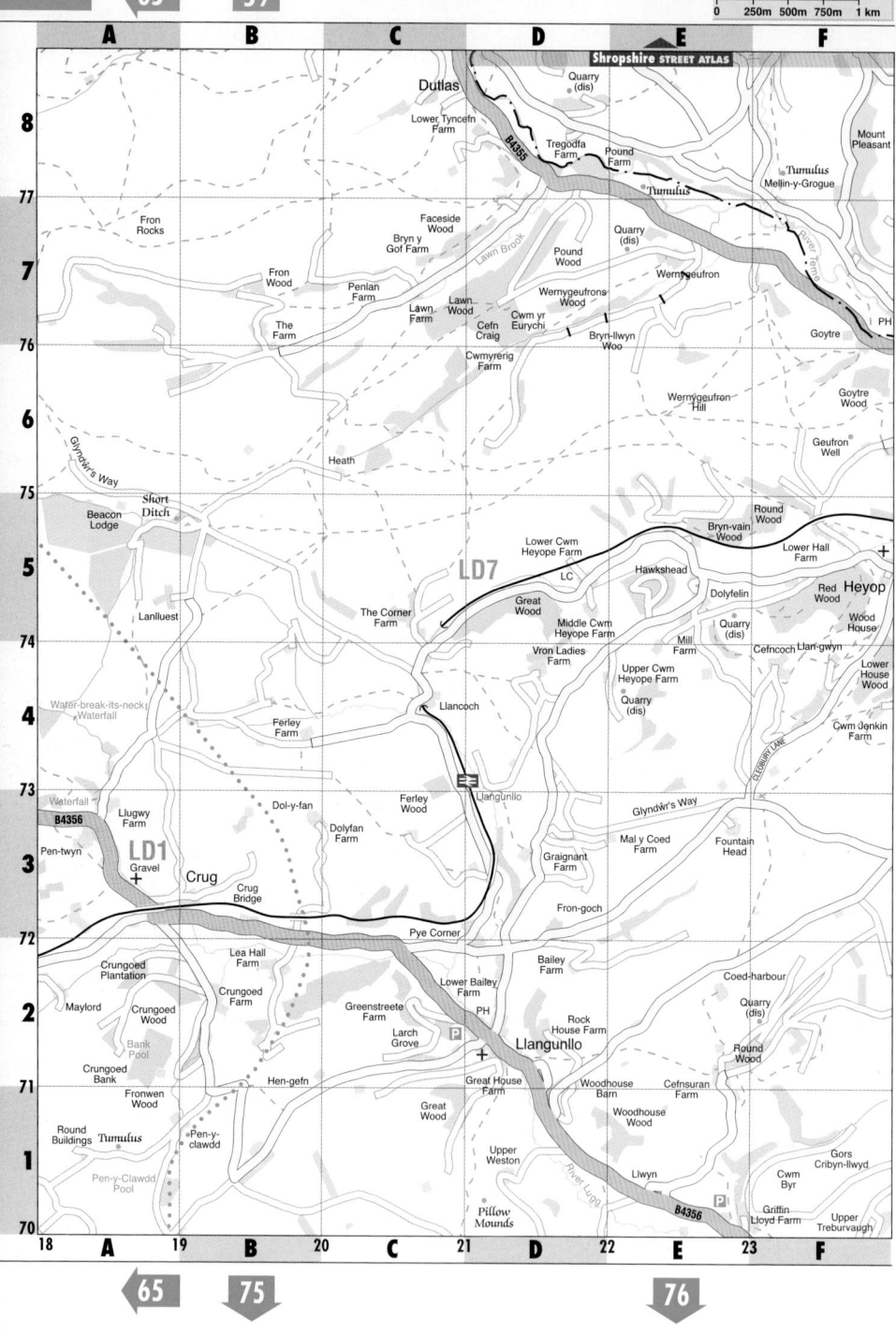

Scale: 1½ inches to 1 mile

Shropshire STREET ATLAS

Dutlas
Quarry (dis)
Lower Tyncefn Farm
Tregodfa Farm
Pound Farm
Tumulus
Mellin-y-Grogue
Mount Pleasant
Fron Rocks
Faceside Wood
Bryn y Gof Farm
Lawn Brook
Quarry (dis)
Pound Wood
Wernygeufron
River Teme
Fron Wood
Penlan Farm
Lawn Wood
Lawn Farm
Wernygeufrons Wood
Cefn Craig
Cwm yr Eurychi
The Farm
Bryn-llwyn Woo
Goytre
PH
Cwmyrerig Farm
Wernygeufron Hill
Goytre Wood
Heath
Geufron Well
Glyndwr's Way
Short Ditch
Round Wood
Bryn-vain Wood
Beacon Lodge
Lower Cwm Heyope Farm
Lower Hall Farm
LD7
LC
Hawkshead
Red Wood
Heyop
Lanlluest
The Corner Farm
Great Wood
Middle Cwm Heyope Farm
Dolyfelin
Quarry (dis)
Cefncoch
Llan-gwyn
Wood House
Lower House Wood
Vron Ladies Farm
Upper Cwm Heyope Farm
Mill Farm
Water-break-its-neck Waterfall
Ferley Farm
Llancoch
Quarry (dis)
Cwm Jenkin Farm
Waterfall
Dol-y-fan
Ferley Wood
Llangunllo
Glyndwr's Way
CLEGNURY LANE
B4356
Llugwy Farm
Dolyfan Farm
Mal y Coed Farm
Fountain Head
Pen-twyn
LD1
Gravel
Crug
Crug Bridge
Graignant Farm
Pye Corner
Fron-goch
Crungoed Plantation
Lea Hall Farm
Crungoed Farm
Lower Bailey Farm
Bailey Farm
Coed-harbour
Maylord
Crungoed Wood
Greenstreete Farm
PH
Larch Grove
Rock House Farm
Quarry (dis)
Bank Pool
Llangunllo
Round Wood
Crungoed Bank
Hen-gefn
Great House Farm
Woodhouse Barn
Cefnsuran Farm
Fronwen Wood
Great Wood
Woodhouse Wood
Round Buildings
Tumulus
Pen-y-clawdd
Llwyn
Cwm Byr
Gors Cribyn-llwyd
Pen-y-Clawdd Pool
Upper Weston
River Lugg
Griffin Lloyd Farm
Upper Treburvaigh
Pillow Mounds
B4356

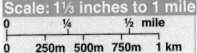

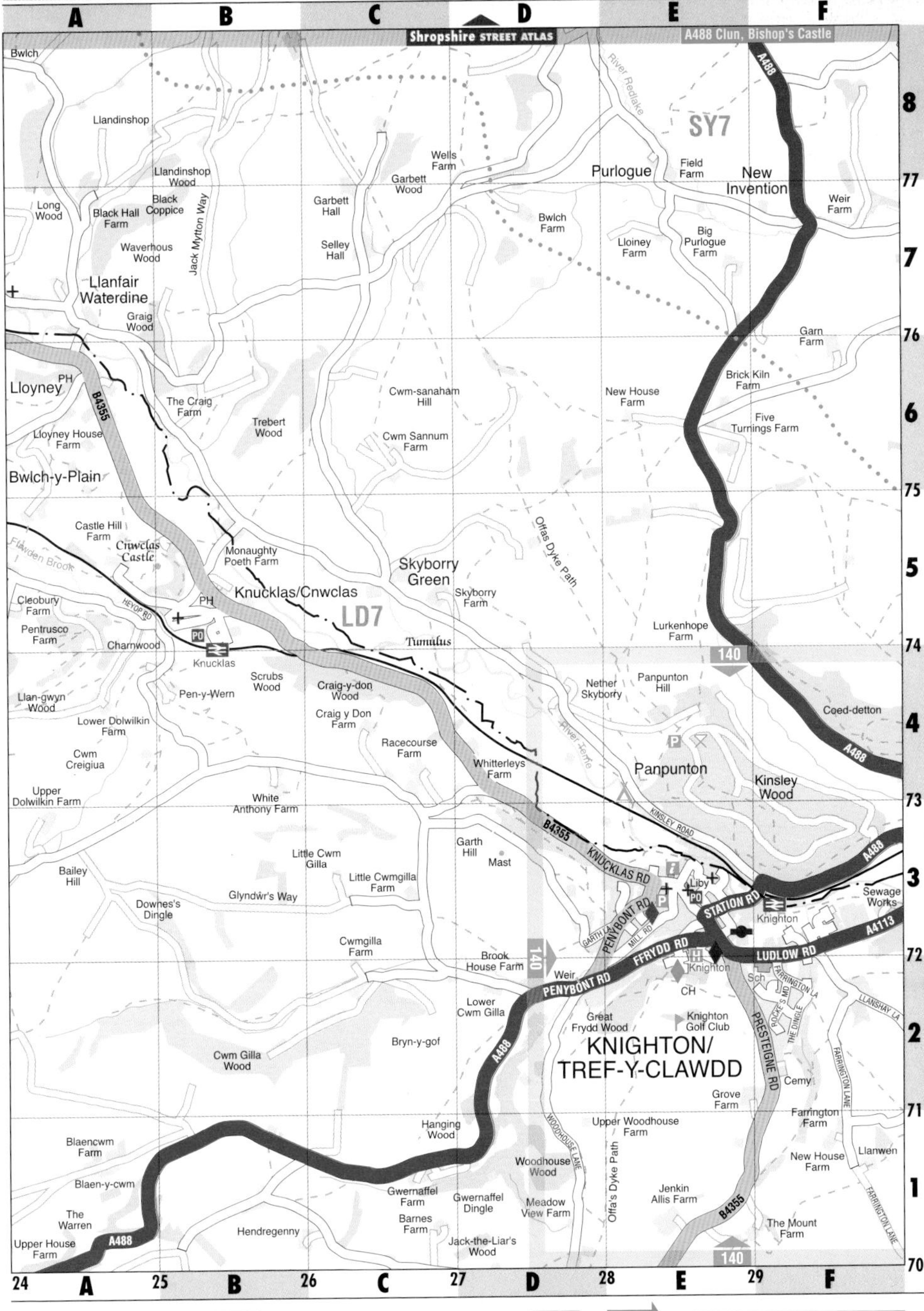

Shropshire STREET ATLAS

A488 Clun, Bishop's Castle

Bwlch

Llandinshop

Llandinshop Wood

Wells Farm

Garbett Wood

Garbett Hall

SY7

Purlogue

Field Farm

New Invention

Weir Farm

Long Wood

Black Hall Farm

Black Coppice

Jack Mytton Way

Selley Hall

Bwlch Farm

Lloiney Farm

Big Purlogue Farm

7

Waverhous Wood

Llanfair Waterdine

Graig Wood

76

Garn Farm

Lloyney

PH

B4355

The Craig Farm

Trebert Wood

Cwm-sanaham Hill

New House Farm

Brick Kiln Farm

6

Lloyney House Farm

Five Turnings Farm

Bwlch-y-Plain

Cwm Sannum Farm

75

Castle Hill Farm

Flanden Brook

Cnwclas Castle

Monaughty Poeth Farm

Skyborry Green

Offa's Dyke Path

5

Cleobury Farm

HEYOP RD

PH

Knucklas/Cnwclas

LD7

Skyborry Farm

Lurkenhope Farm

74

Pentrusco Farm

Charnwood

PO

Knucklas

Tumulus

140

Llan-gwyn Wood

Pen-y-Wern

Scrubs Wood

Craig-y-don Wood

Nether Skyborry

Panpunton Hill

Coed-detton

4

Lower Dolwilkin Farm

Craig y Don Farm

Racecourse Farm

P

Panpunton

73

Cwm Creigiua

Whitterleys Farm

B4355

KINSLEY ROAD

Kinsley Wood

A488

Upper Dolwilkin Farm

White Anthony Farm

Little Cwm Gilla

Garth Hill

Mast

KNUCKLAS RD

Liby PO

Kinsley Wood

3

Bailey Hill

Little Cwmgilla Farm

STATION RD

Knighton

Sewage Works

A4113

Dowhes's Dingle

Glyndwr's Way

PENYBONT RD

FFRYDD RD

LUDLOW RD

72

Cwmgilla Farm

Brook House Farm

140

Weir

Knighton

CH

LLANSHAY LA

Lower Cwm Gilla

A488

PENYBONT RD

Great Frydd Wood

Knighton Golf Club

PRESTEIGNE RD

Cemy

FARRINGTON LANE

2

Cwm Gilla Wood

Bryn-y-gof

Grove Farm

Farrington Farm

Blaencwm Farm

Hanging Wood

Upper Woodhouse Farm

New House Farm

Llanwen

71

Blaen-y-cwm

WOODHOUSE LANE

Woodhouse Wood

Offa's Dyke Path

Jenkin Allis Farm

The Mount Farm

The Warren

A488

Gwernaffel Farm

Gwernaffel Dingle

Meadow View Farm

B4355

1

Upper House Farm

Hendregenny

Barnes Farm

Jack-the-Liar's Wood

140

KNIGHTON/ TREF-Y-CLAWDD

76 77 68

For full street detail of the highlighted area see page 140.

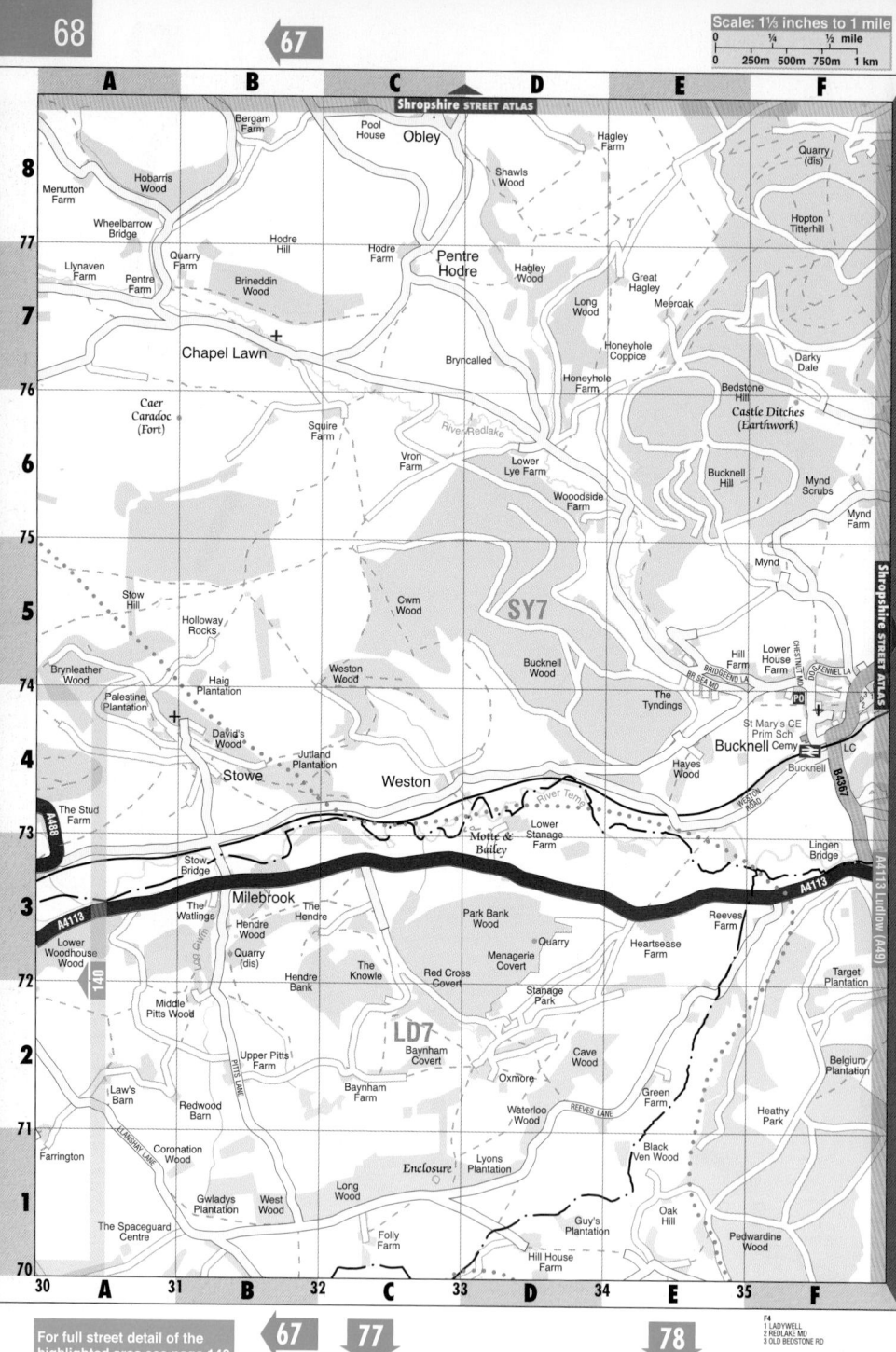

Shropshire STREET ATLAS

68 **67**

8
Menutton Farm
Hobarris Wood
Bergam Farm
Pool House
Obley
Shawls Wood
Hagley Farm
Quarry (dis)

77
Wheelbarrow Bridge
Hodre Hill
Hodre Farm
Pentre Hodre
Hagley Wood
Hopton Titterhill

Llynaven Farm
Pentre Farm
Quarry Farm
Brineddin Wood
Great Hagley
Meeroak
Darky Dale

7
Chapel Lawn
Bryncalled
Long Wood
Honeyhole Coppice

76
Caer Caradoc (Fort)
Squire Farm
River Redlake
Honeyhole Farm
Bedstone Hill
Castle Ditches (Earthwork)

6
Vron Farm
Lower Lye Farm
Wooodside Farm
Bucknell Hill
Mynd Scrubs
Mynd Farm

75
Stow Hill
Holloway Rocks
Cwm Wood
SY7
Mynd

5
Brynleather Wood
Haig Plantation
Weston Wood
Bucknell Wood
Hill Farm
BRIDGEEND LA
BR SEA MD
Lower House Farm
CHESTNUT LA
CHANNEL LA
PO

74
Palestine Plantation
David's Wood
Jutland Plantation
The Tyndings
St Mary's CE Prim Sch
Bucknell
Cemy
LC

4
Stowe
Weston
Hayes Wood
WESTON COLD
Bucknell
B4367

73
The Stud Farm
A488
Stow Bridge
Motte & Bailey
Lower Stanage Farm
River Teme
Lingen Bridge
A4113 Ludlow (A49)

3
A4113
Milebrook
The Hendre
The Watlings
Park Bank Wood
A4113
Reeves Farm

72
Lower Woodhouse Wood
140
Hendre Wood
Quarry (dis)
Hendre Bank
The Knowle
Red Cross Covert
Menagerie Covert
Quarry
Stanage Park
Heartsease Farm
Target Plantation

2
Middle Pitts Wood
Upper Pitts Farm
LD7
Baynham Covert
Oxmore
Cave Wood
Green Farm
Heathy Park
Belgium Plantation

71
Law's Barn
Redwood Barn
Baynham Farm
Waterloo Wood
REEVES LANE
Black Ven Wood

Farrington
Coronation Wood
PITTS LANE
ELANSARY LANE
Lyons Plantation
Guy's Plantation
Oak Hill
Pedwardine Wood

1
The Spaceguard Centre
Gwladys Plantation
West Wood
Long Wood
Enclosure

70
Folly Farm
Hill House Farm

30 A 31 B 32 C 33 D 34 E 35 F

Shropshire STREET ATLAS

For full street detail of the highlighted area see page 140.

67 77 78

F4
1 LADYWELL
2 REDLAKE MD
3 OLD BEDSTONE RD

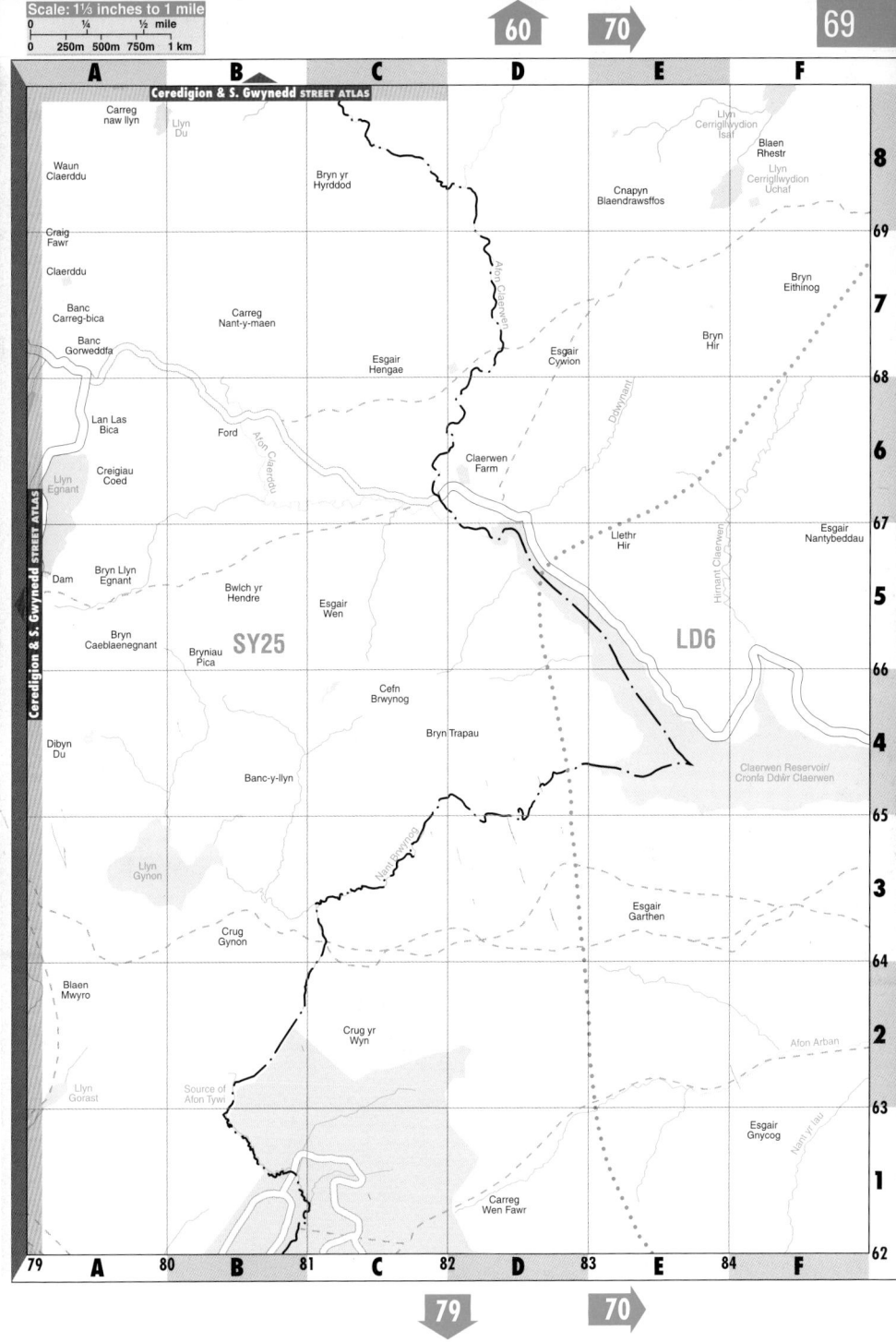

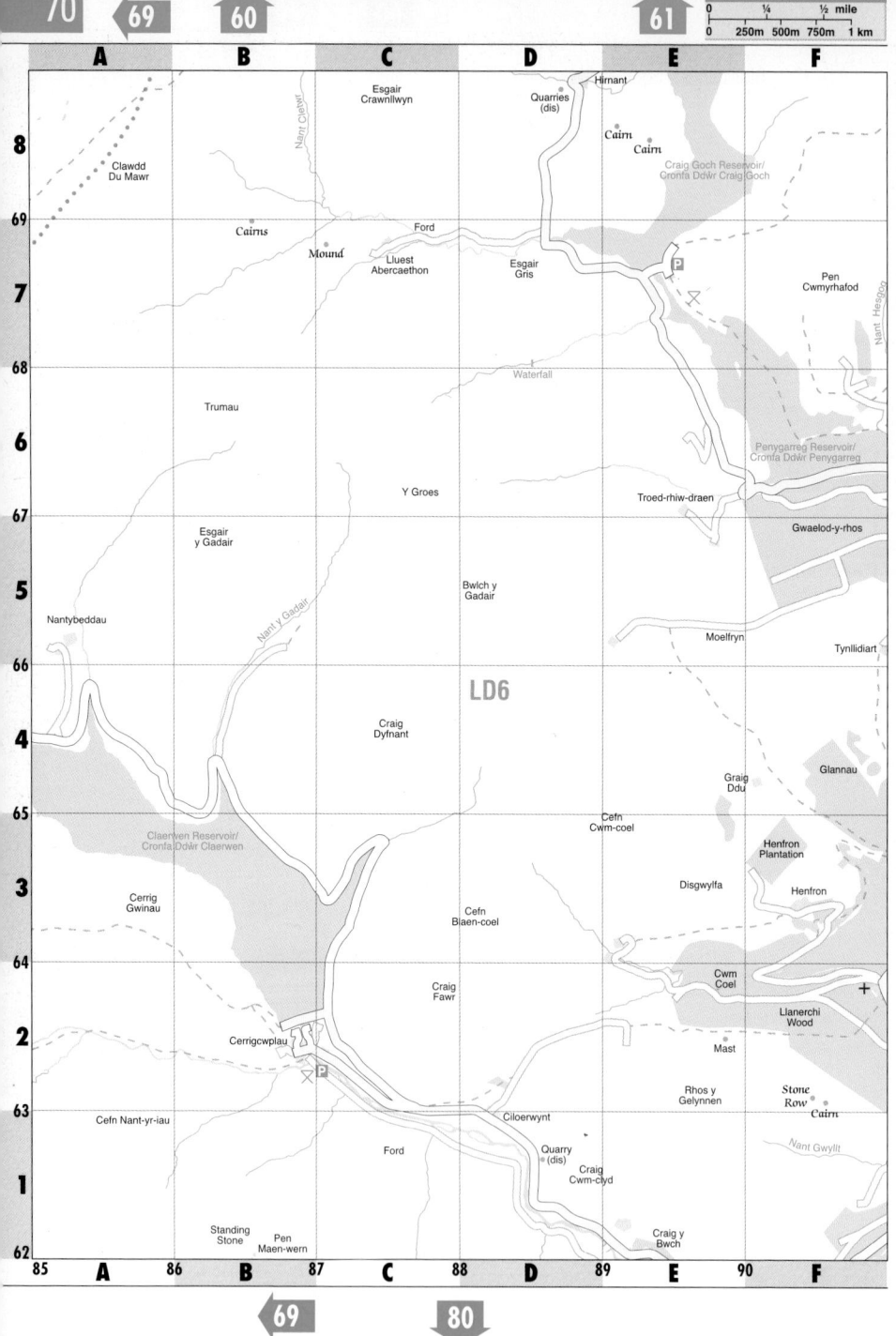

Scale: 1½ inches to 1 mile

| 0 | ¼ | ½ mile |
| 0 | 250m | 500m | 750m | 1 km |

A B C D E F

8

Clawdd
Du Mawr

Esgair
Crawnllwyn

Quarries
(dis)

Hirnant

Cairn

Cairn

Craig Goch Reservoir/
Cronfa Ddwr Craig Goch

69

Cairns

Mound

Ford

Lluest
Abercaethon

Esgair
Gris

P

Pen
Cwmyrhafod

Nant Hesgog

7

68

Waterfall

Trumau

Penygarreg Reservoir/
Cronfa Ddwr Penygarreg

6

Y Groes

Troed-rhiw-draen

67

Esgair
y Gadair

Gwaelod-y-rhos

5

Nantybeddau

Nant y Gadair

Bwlch y
Gadair

Moelfryn

Tynllidiart

66

LD6

4

Craig
Dyfnant

Graig
Ddu

Glannau

65

Claerwen Reservoir/
Cronfa Ddwr Claerwen

Cefn
Cwm-coel

Henfron
Plantation

3

Cerrig
Gwinau

Cefn
Blaen-coel

Disgwylfa

Henfron

64

Craig
Fawr

Cwm
Coel

Llanerchi
Wood

2

Cerrigcwplau

P

Mast

Rhos y
Gelynnen

Stone
Row

Cairn

63

Cefn Nant-yr-iau

Ford

Ciloerwynt

Quarry
(dis)

Craig
Cwm-clyd

Nant Gwyllt

1

Standing
Stone

Pen
Maen-wern

Craig y
Bwch

62

A 86 B 87 C 88 D 89 E 90 F

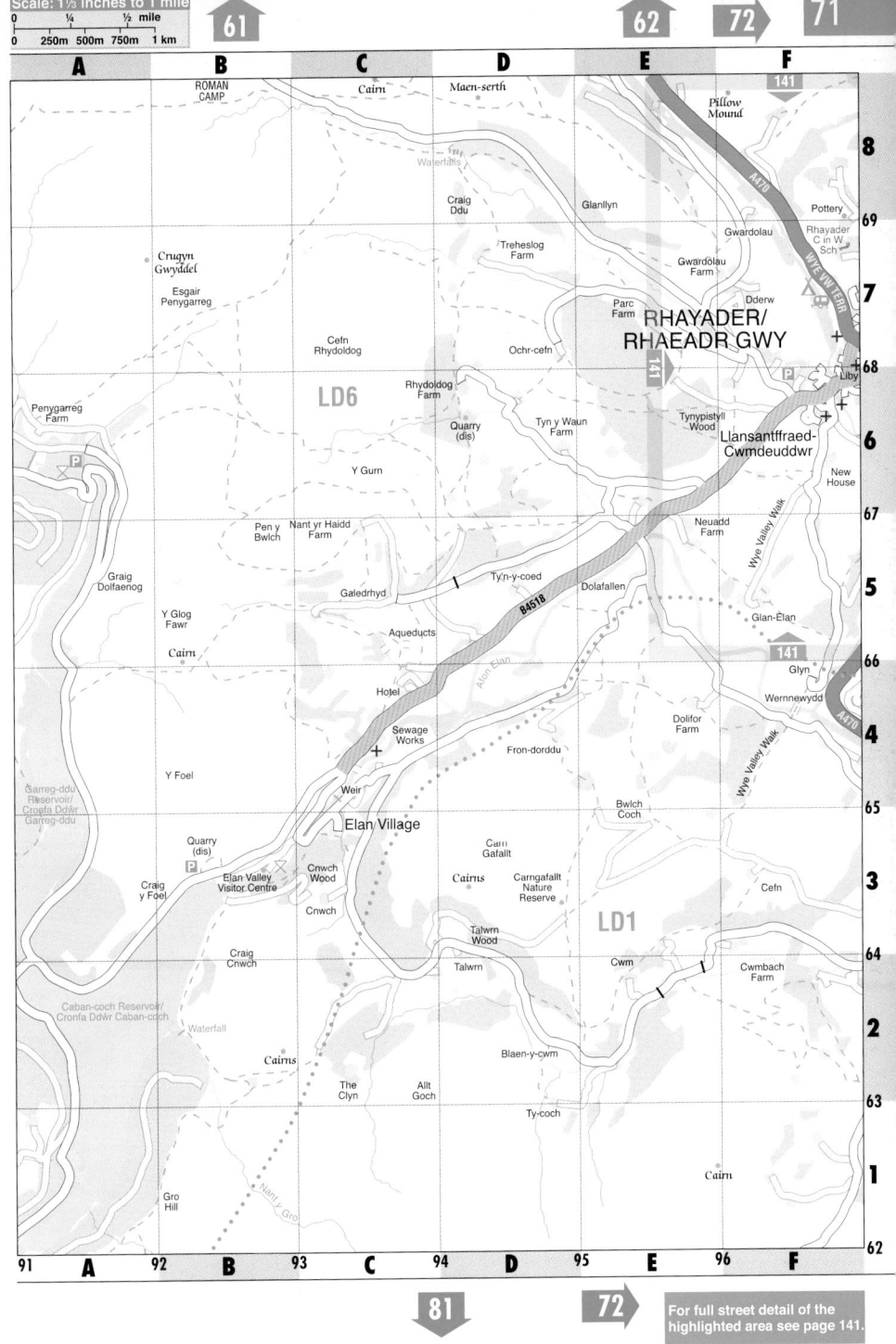

0 ¼ ½ mile
0 250m 500m 750m 1 km

A   B   C   D   E   F

ROMAN CAMP
Cairn
Maen-serth
141
Pillow Mound

Waterfalls
8

Craig Ddu
Glanllyn
Pottery
Rhayader C in W Sch
69

Crugyn Gwyddel
Treheslog Farm
Gwardolau
Esgair Penygarreg
Gwardolau Farm
Dderw
7

Parc Farm
RHAYADER/ RHAEADR GWY

Cefn Rhydolog
Ochr-cefn
141
Liby
68

Penygarreg Farm
LD6
Rhydoldog Farm
Tyn y Waun Farm
Tynypistyll Wood
Llansantffraed-Cwmdeuddwr
6

Quarry (dis)
New House
Y Gurn
Neuadd Farm
67

Graig Dolfaenog
Pen y Bwlch
Nant yr Haidd Farm
Wye Valley Walk

Y Glog Fawr
Galedrhyd
Ty'n-y-coed
Dolafallen
B4518
5

Cairn
Aqueducts
Glan-Elan
141
66

Hotel
Dolifor Farm
Glyn
Wernnewydd

Y Foel
Sewage Works
Fron-dorddu
4

Weir
Garreg-ddu Reservoir/ Cronfa Ddwr Garreg-ddu
Bwlch Coch
65

Elan Village
Carn Gafallt
Quarry (dis)
Cairns
Carngafallt Nature Reserve
Cefn
3

Craig y Foel
Elan Valley Visitor Centre
Cnwch Wood
LD1
Cnwch
Talwrn Wood
Cwm
Cwmbach Farm
64

Craig Cnwch
Talwrn
Caban-coch Reservoir/ Cronfa Ddwr Caban-coch
Waterfall
2

Cairns
Blaen-y-cwm
63

The Clyn
Allt Goch
Ty-coch

Gro Hill
Nant y Gro
Cairn
1

62

91   A   92   B   93   C   94   D   95   E   96   F

For full street detail of the highlighted area see page 141.

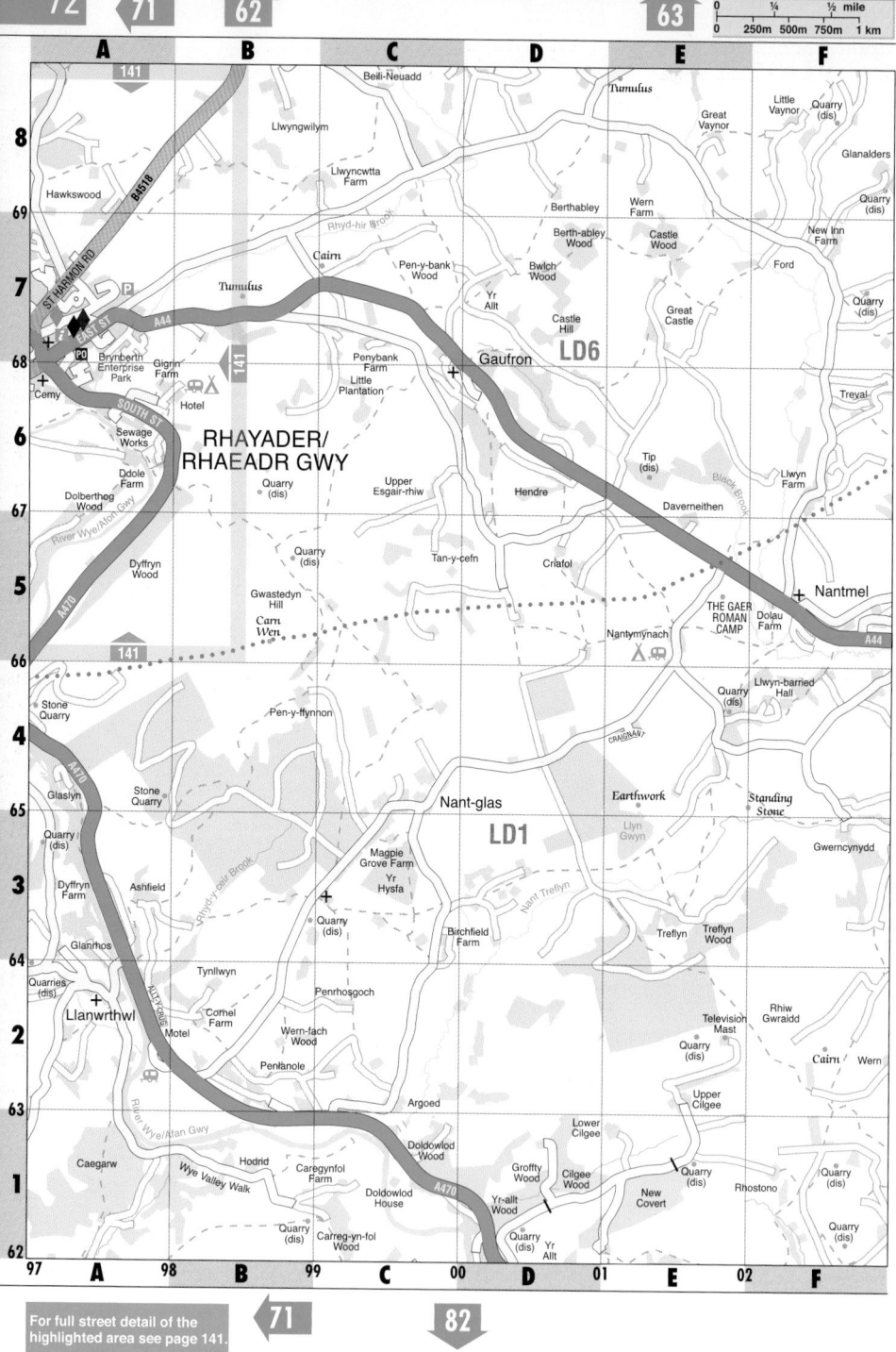

Scale: 1½ inches to 1 mile

¼ ½ mile
250m 500m 750m 1 km

A 141

Beili-Neuadd

Tumulus

Little Vaynor

Quarry (dis)

Llwyngwilym

Great Vaynor

Glanalders

Llwyncwtta Farm

Berthabley

Wern Farm

Quarry (dis)

Hawkswood

B4518

Rhyd-hir Brook

Berth-abley Wood

Castle Wood

New Inn Farm

Cairn

Pen-y-bank Wood

Bwlch Wood

Ford

ST HARMON RD

P

Tumulus

Yr Allt

Great Castle

Quarry (dis)

EAST ST

A44

Castle Hill

Gaufron

LD6

PO

Brynberth Enterprise Park

Penybank Farm

Treval

Cemy

Gigrin Farm

Little Plantation

SOUTH ST

Hotel

RHAYADER/ RHAEADR GWY

Sewage Works

Ddole Farm

Quarry (dis)

Upper Esgair-rhiw

Hendre

Tip (dis)

Llwyn Farm

Dolberthog Wood

River Wye/Afon Gwy

Black Brook

Daverneithen

Dyffryn Wood

Quarry (dis)

Tan-y-cefn

Criafol

Nantmel

A470

Gwastedyn Hill

Carn Wen

THE GAER ROMAN CAMP

Dolau Farm

141

Nantymynach

A44

Stone Quarry

Pen-y-ffynnon

Quarry (dis)

Llwyn-barried Hall

CRAIGNANT

Glaslyn

A470

Stone Quarry

Nant-glas

LD1

Earthwork

Standing Stone

Llyn Gwyn

Gwerncynydd

Quarry (dis)

Dyffryn Farm

Ashfield

Magpie Grove Farm

Yr Hysfa

ALLT GOCH

Llyniau-cwm Brook

Quarry (dis)

Birchfield Farm

Treflyn

Treflyn Wood

Glanrhos

Tynllwyn

Penrhosgoch

Rhiw Gwraidd

Quarries (dis)

Llanwrthwl

Motel

Cornel Farm

Wern-fach Wood

Television Mast

Quarry (dis)

Cairn

Wern

Penfanole

Argoed

Upper Cilgee

Caegarw

Hodrid

River Wye/Afon Gwy

Wye Valley Walk

Caregynfol Farm

Doldowlod Wood

Lower Cilgee

Groffty Wood

Cilgee Wood

Quarry (dis)

Rhostono

Quarry (dis)

A470

Doldowlod House

Yr-allt Wood

New Covert

Quarry (dis)

Quarry (dis)

Quarry (dis)

Carreg-yn-fol Wood

Quarry (dis)

Yr Allt

71 82

For full street detail of the highlighted area see page 141.

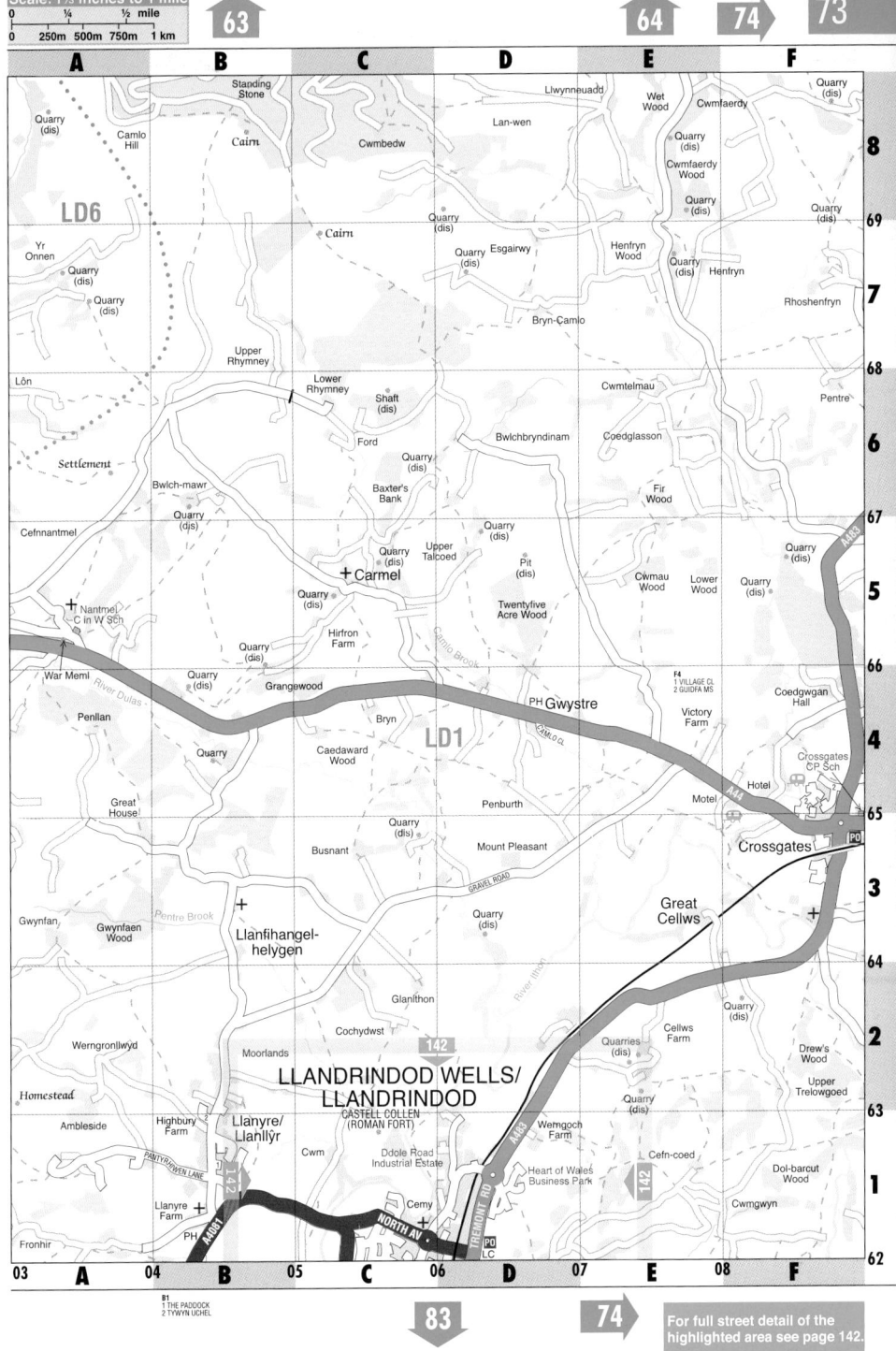

LD6

Quarry (dis)
Camlo Hill
Standing Stone
Cairn
Cwmbedw
Llwynneuadd
Wet Wood
Cwmfaerdy
Quarry (dis)

Lan-wen
Quarry (dis)
Cwmfaerdy Wood

Yr Onnen
Quarry (dis)
Cairn
Quarry (dis)
Esgairwy
Quarry (dis)
Henfryn Wood
Quarry (dis)
Henfryn
Quarry (dis)

Rhoshenfryn

Lôn
Upper Rhymney
Lower Rhymney
Cwmtelmau
Pentre

Settlement
Shaft (dis)
Bwlchbrynidinam
Coedglasson

Ford
Quarry (dis)
Fir Wood

Bwlch-mawr
Baxter's Bank
Upper Talcoed

Cefnnantmel
Quarry (dis)
Quarry (dis)
Quarry (dis)
Pit (dis)
Cwmau Wood
Lower Wood
Quarry (dis)

Nantmel C in W Sch
+ Carmel
Twentyfive Acre Wood

War Meml
Quarry (dis)
Hirfron Farm
Coedgwgan Hall

River Dulas
Quarry (dis)
Grangewood
Camlo Brook
PH Gwystre

Penllan
Bryn
LD1
Victory Farm

Quarry
Caedaward Wood
Motel
Hotel
Crossgates CP Sch

Great House
Busnant
Penburth
Mount Pleasant
Crossgates

Gwynfan
Gwynfaen Wood
Llanfihangel-helygen
GRAVEL ROAD
Quarry (dis)
Great Cellws

Pentre Brook
Glanithon
Quarries (dis)
Cellws Farm
Quarry (dis)
Drew's Wood

Werngronllwyd
Cochydwst
Moorlands
142
Upper Trelowgoed

Homestead
LLANDRINDOD WELLS/ LLANDRINDOD
Quarry (dis)
Cefn-coed

Ambleside
Highbury Farm
Llanyre/ Llanllŷr
CASTELL COLLEN (ROMAN FORT)
Cwm
Ddole Road Industrial Estate
Wernpoch Farm
Dol-barcut Wood

Fronhir
Llanyre Farm
PH
Cemy
NORTH AV
Heart of Wales Business Park
TREMONT RD
142
Cwmgwyn

B1
1 THE PADDOCK
2 TYWYN UCHEL

F4
1 VILLAGE CL
2 GUIDFA MS

For full street detail of the highlighted area see page 142.

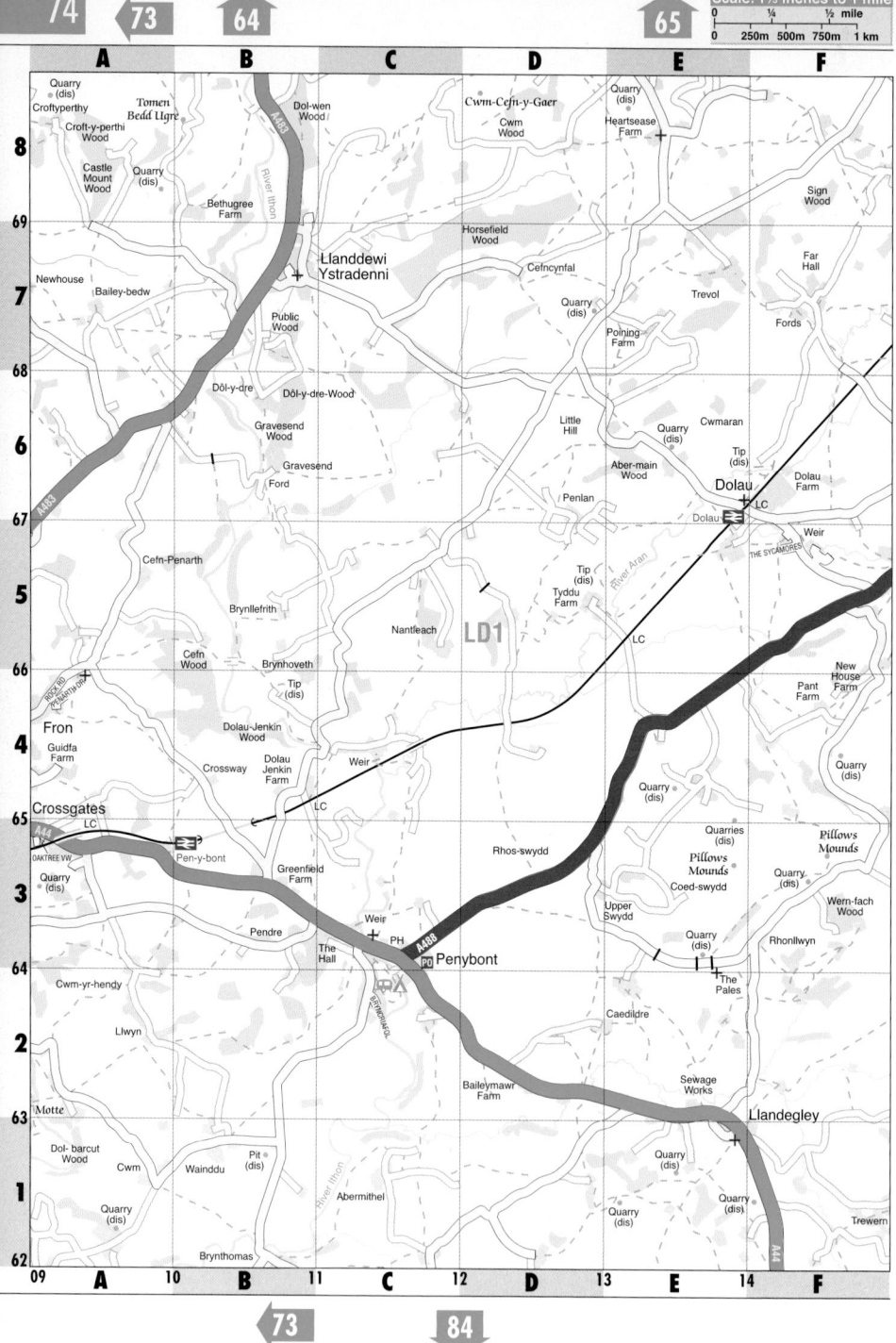

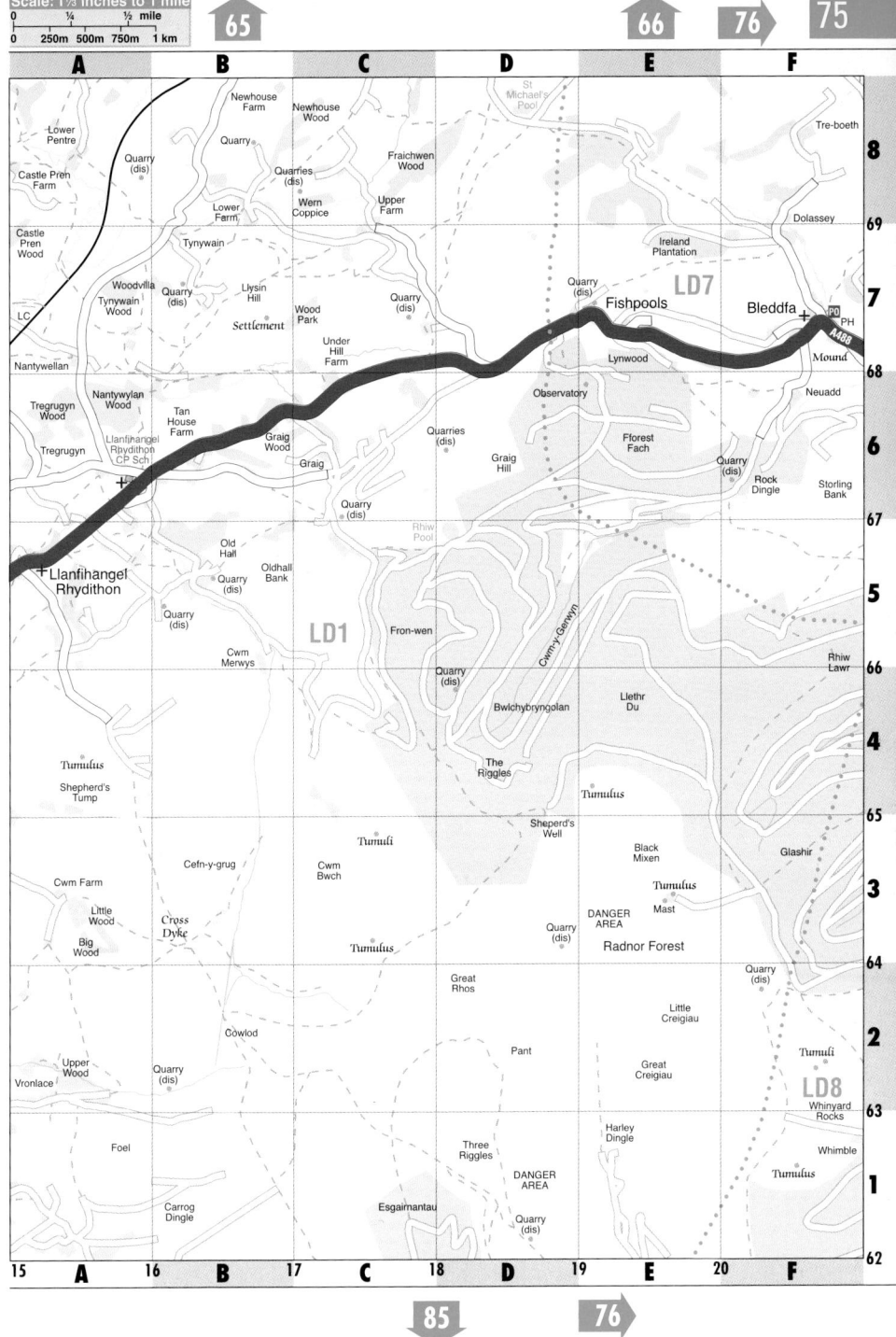

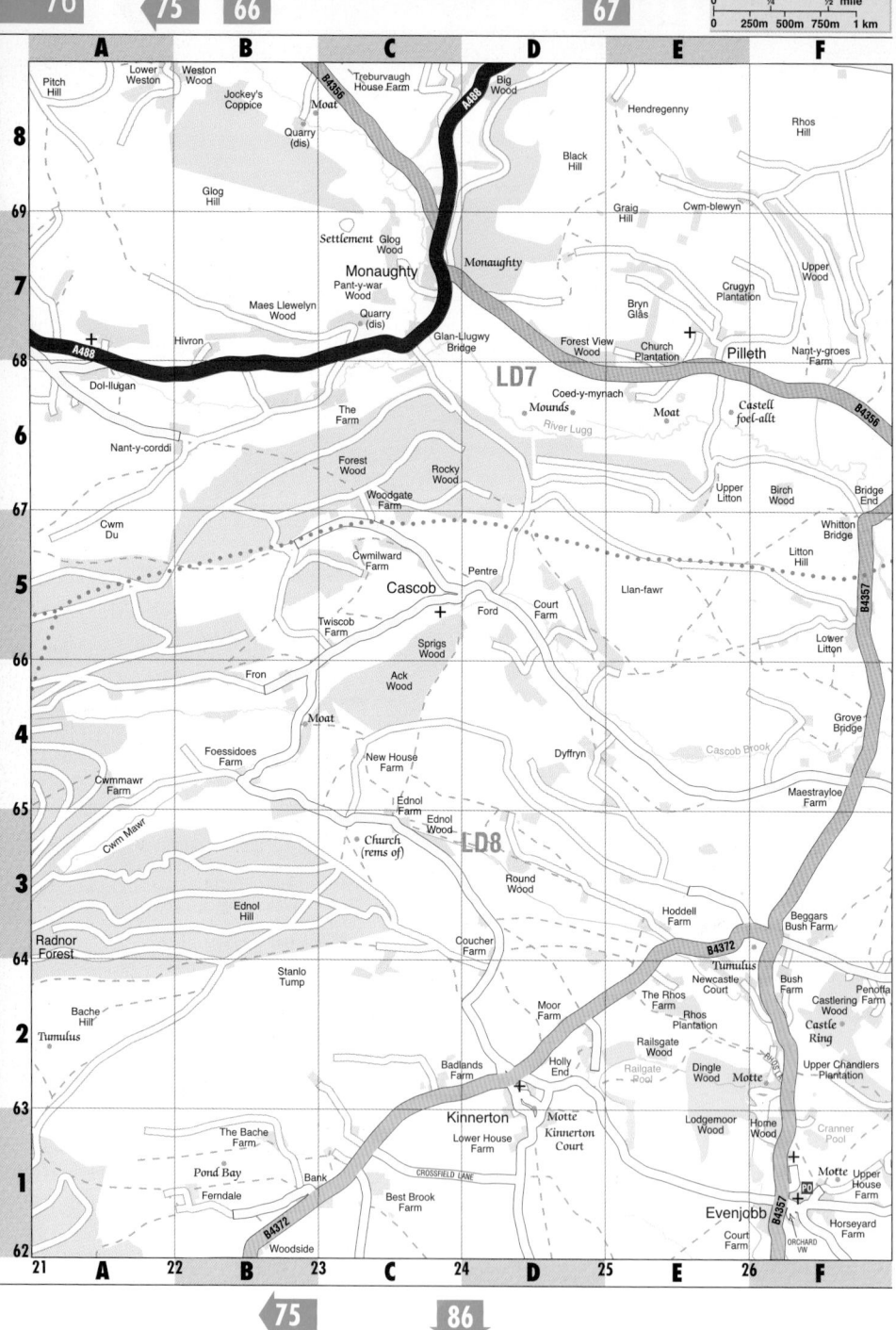

Scale: 1⅓ inches to 1 mile
0   ¼   ½ mile
0   250m 500m 750m 1 km

A B C D E F

8
Pitch Hill
Lower Weston
Weston Wood
Jockey's Coppice
Moat
Treburvaugh House Farm
Big Wood
Hendregenny
Rhos Hill
Quarry (dis)

69
Glog Hill
Settlement
Glog Wood
Graig Hill
Cwm-blewyn
Upper Wood

7
Monaughty
Pant-y-war Wood
Monaughty
Crugyn Plantation
Maes Llewelyn Wood
Quarry (dis)
Bryn Glàs
Church Plantation

68
A488
Hivron
Glan-Llugwy Bridge
Forest View Wood
Pilleth
Nant-y-groes Farm
Dol-llugan
LD7
Coed-y-mynach

6
Nant-y-corddi
The Farm
Mounds
River Lugg
Moat
Castell foel-allt
B4356

Forest Wood
Rocky Wood
Woodgate Farm
Upper Litton
Birch Wood
Bridge End

67
Cwm Du
Cwmilward Farm
Whitton Bridge
Litton Hill
B4357

5
Cascob
Pentre
Ford
Court Farm
Llan-fawr
Twiscob Farm
Sprigs Wood
Lower Litton

66
Fron
Ack Wood

4
Moat
New House Farm
Dyffryn
Cascob Brook
Grove Bridge
Foessidoes Farm

65
Cwmmawr Farm
Ednol Farm
Ednol Wood
Maestrayloe Farm
Cwm Mawr

3
Ednol Hill
Church (rems of)
LD8
Round Wood
Hoddell Farm
Beggars Bush Farm

64
Radnor Forest
Coucher Farm
B4372
Tumulus
Bush Farm
Penoffa
Castling Farm
Stanlo Tump
Newcastle Court
Castlering Wood

2
Bache Hill
Tumulus
Moor Farm
The Rhos Farm
Rhos Plantation
Railsgate Wood
Castle Ring
Upper Chandlers Plantation
Dingle Wood
Motte

63
Badlands Farm
Holly End
Railgate Pool
Lodgemoor Wood
Home Wood
Cranner Pool
The Bache Farm
Kinnerton
Lower House Farm
Motte Kinnerton Court
Motte

1
Pond Bay
Bank
CROSSFIELD LANE
Upper House Farm
Ferndale
Best Brook Farm
Evenjobb
B4357
Horseyard Farm

62
Woodside
Court Farm
ORCHARD VW

21 A 22 B 23 C 24 D 25 E 26 F

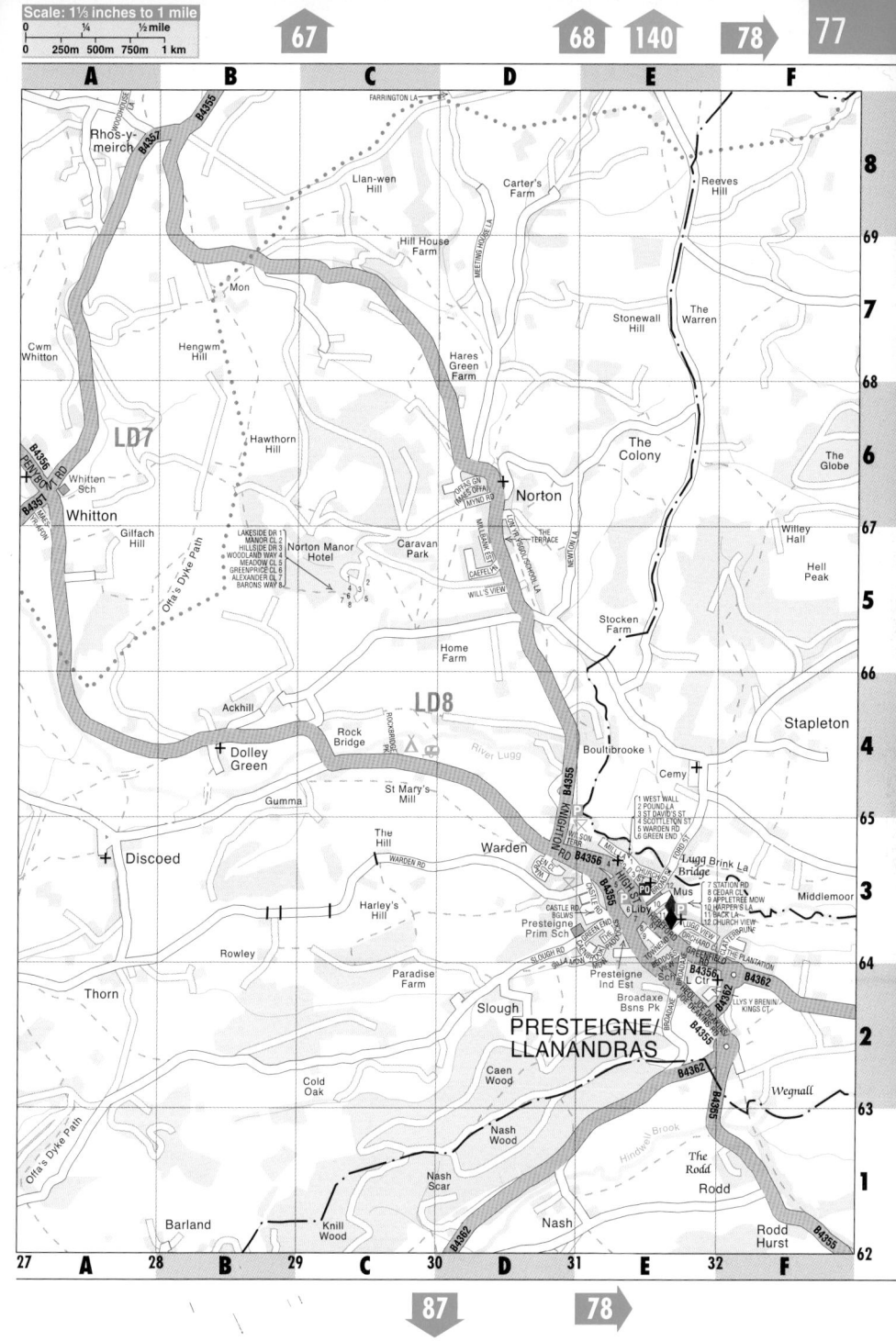

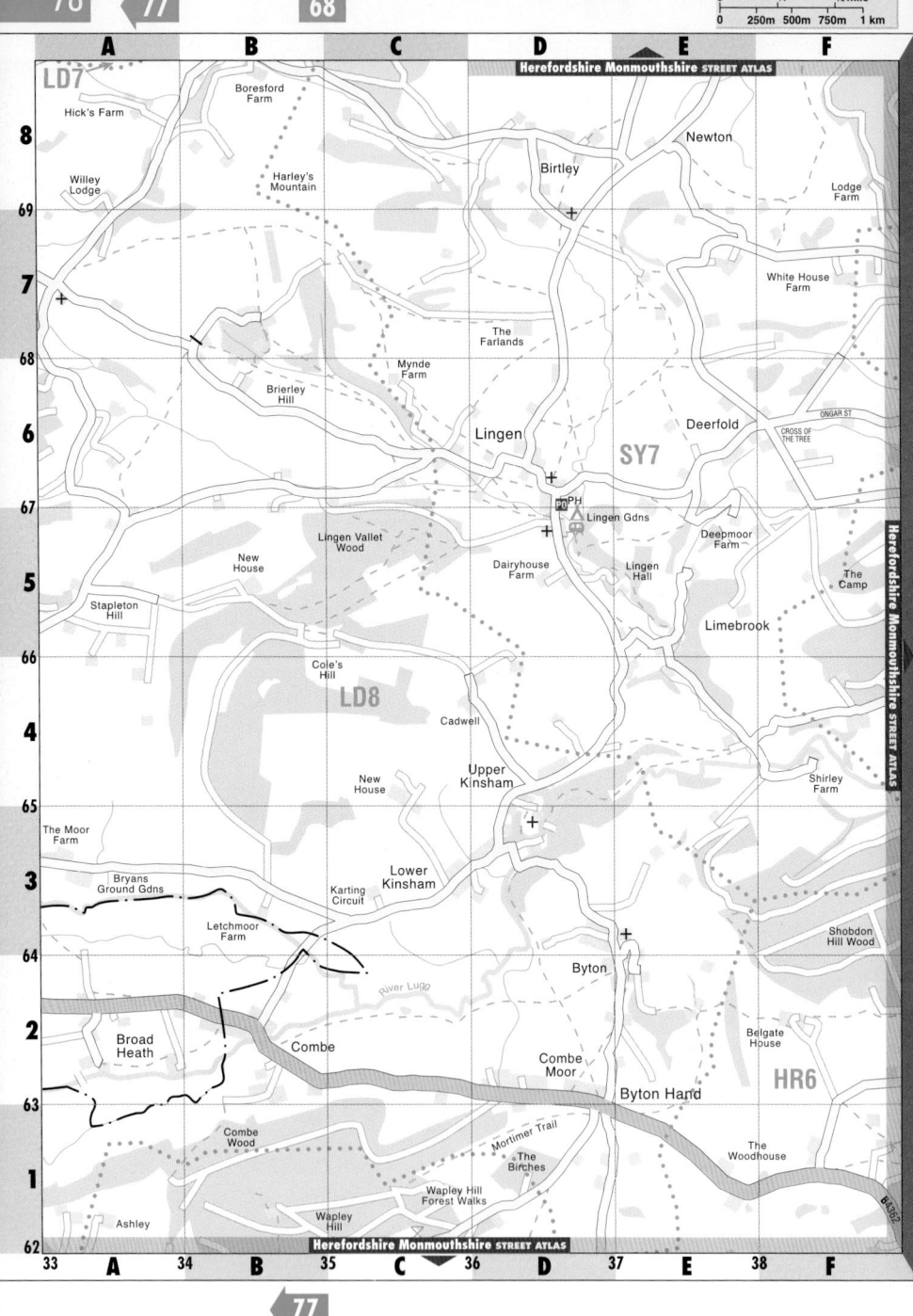

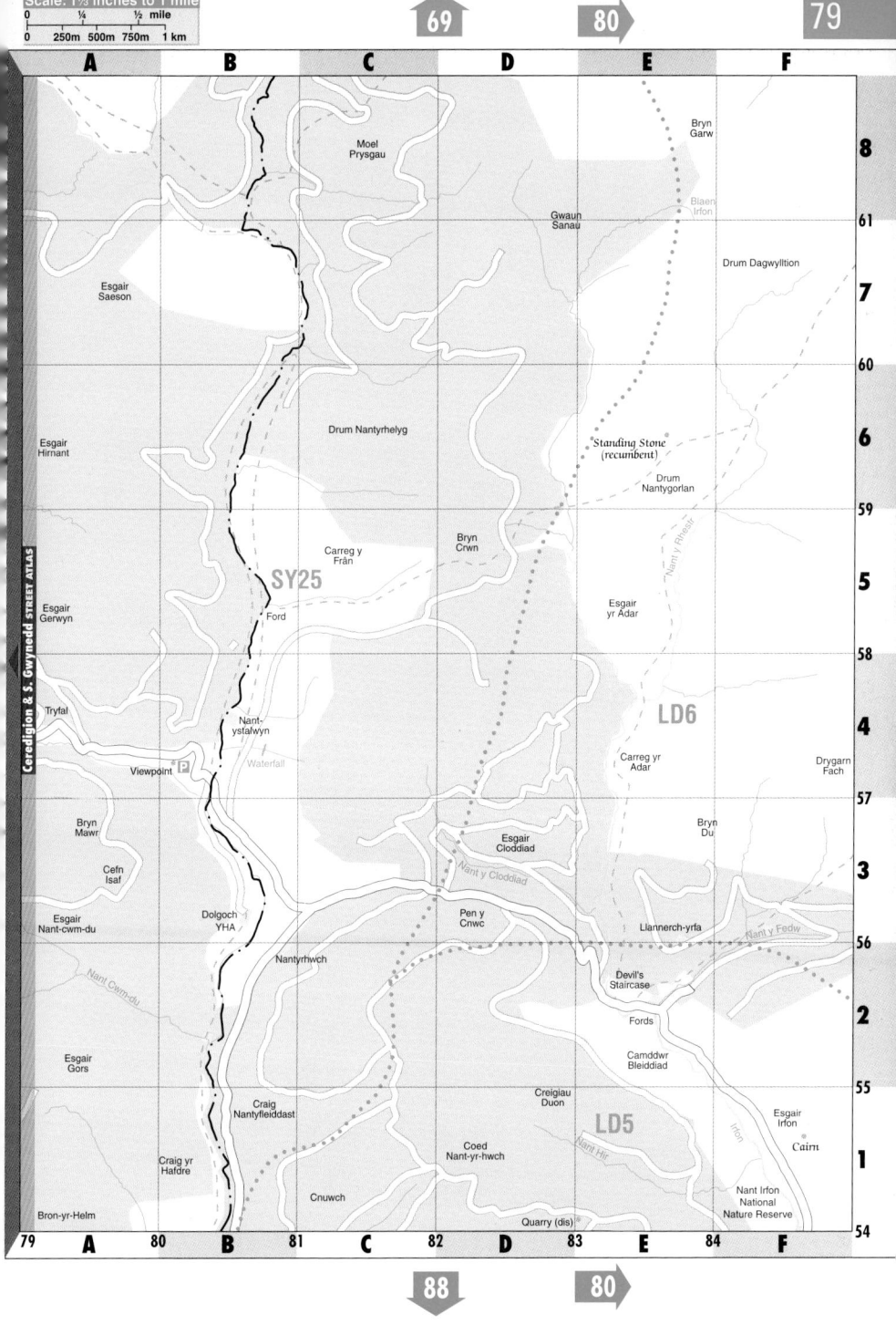

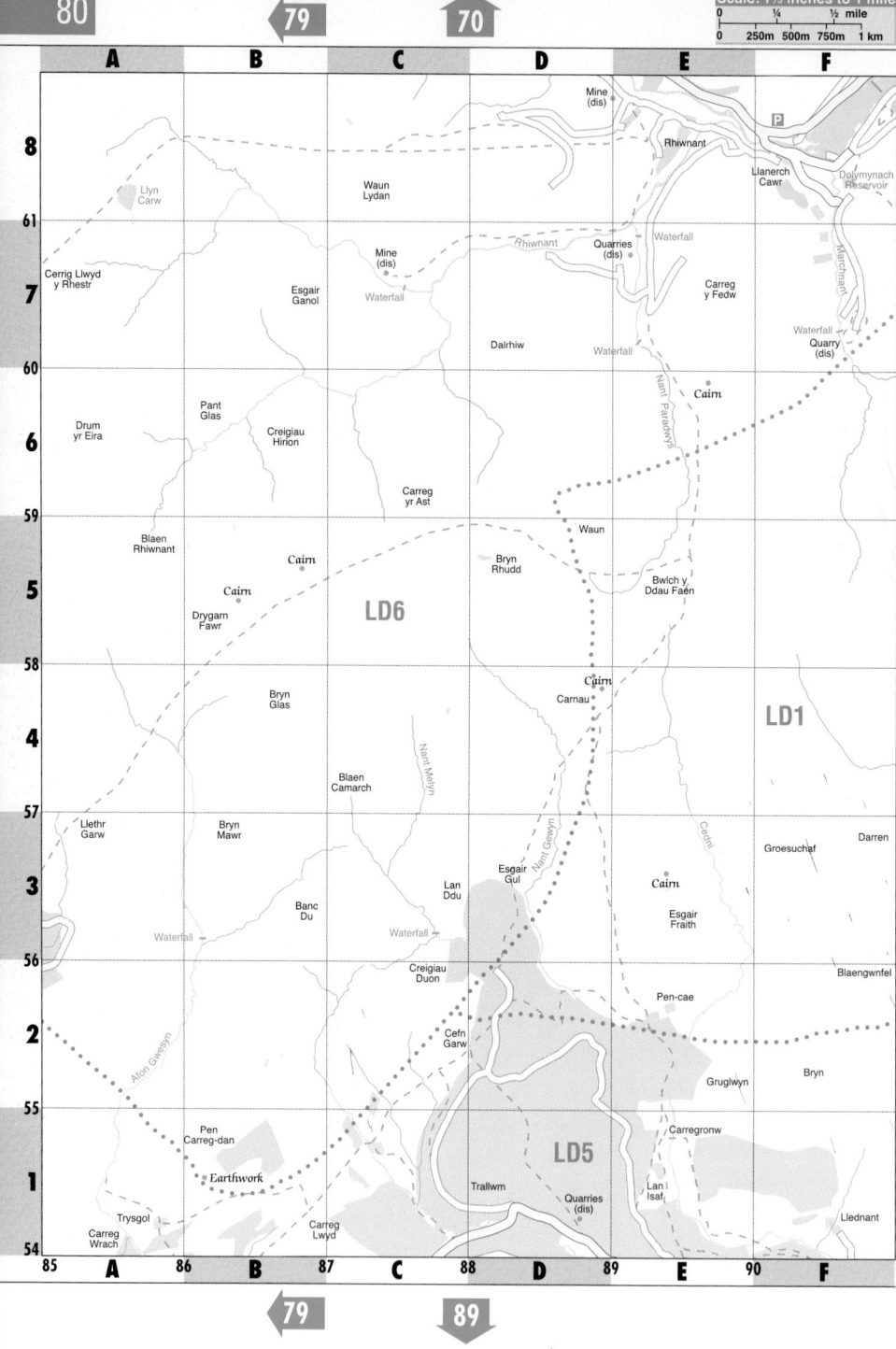

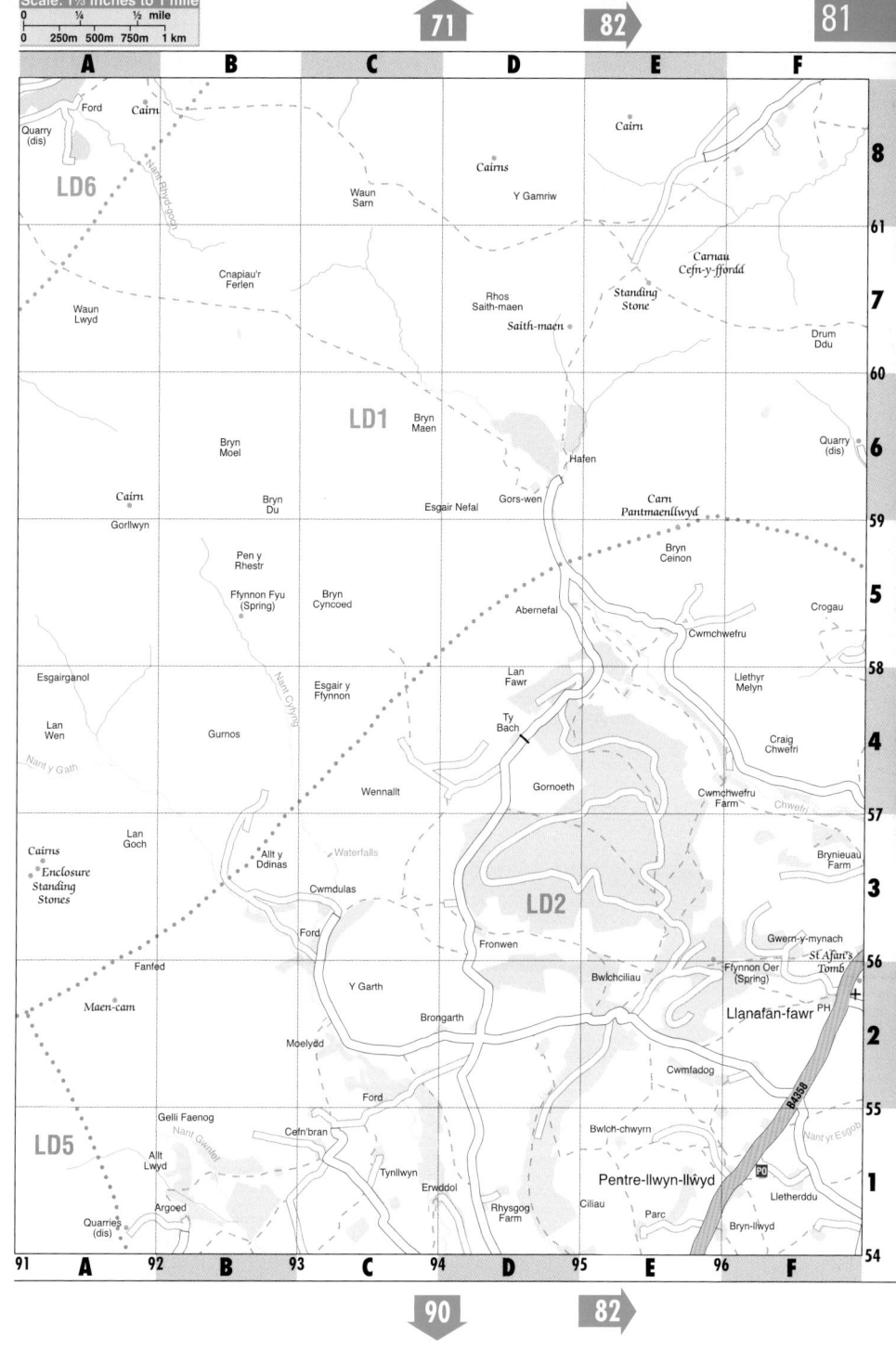

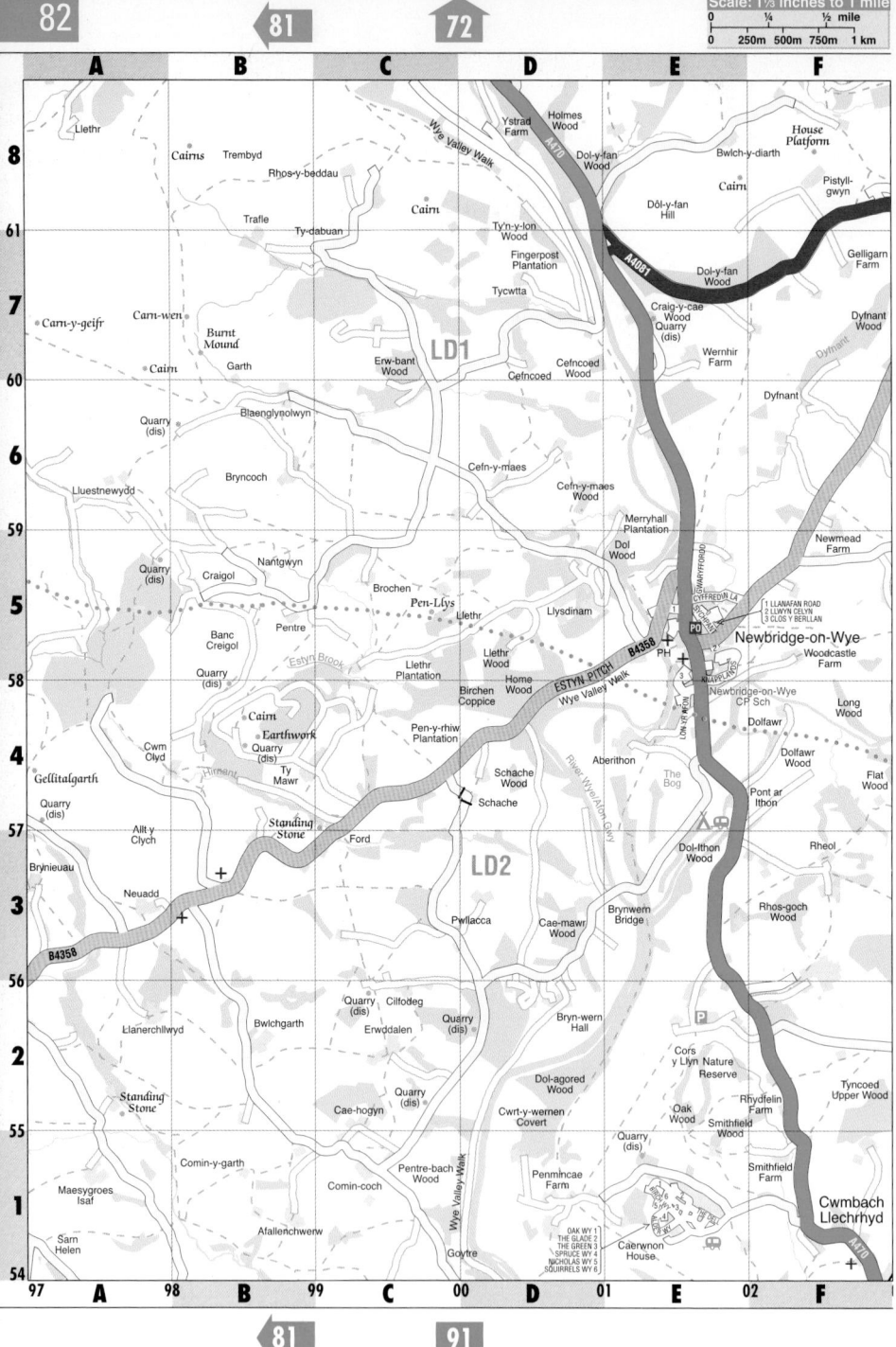

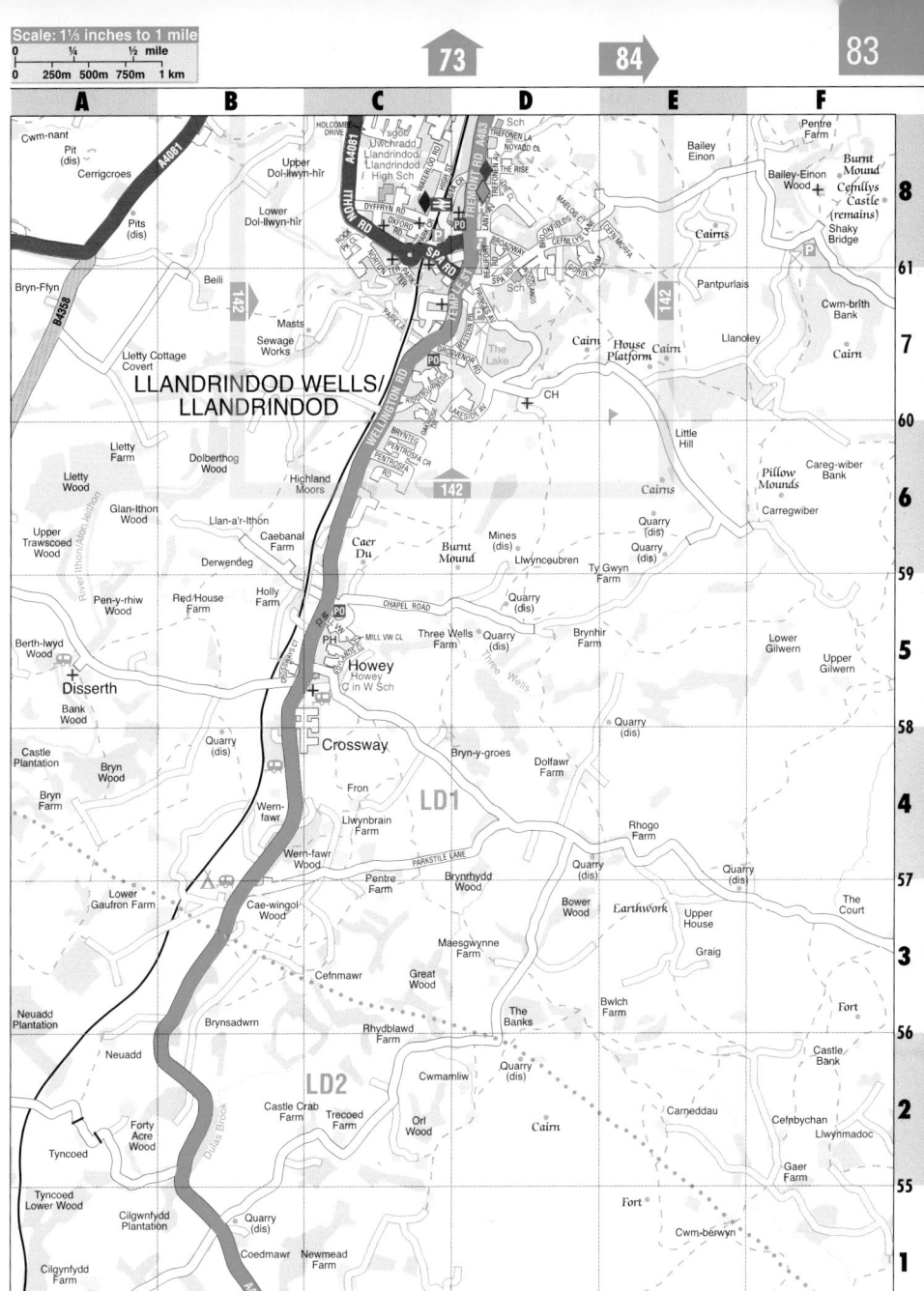

Scale: 1⅓ inches to 1 mile

0 ¼ ½ mile
0 250m 500m 750m 1 km

LLANDRINDOD WELLS/ LLANDRINDOD

For full street detail of the highlighted area see page 142.

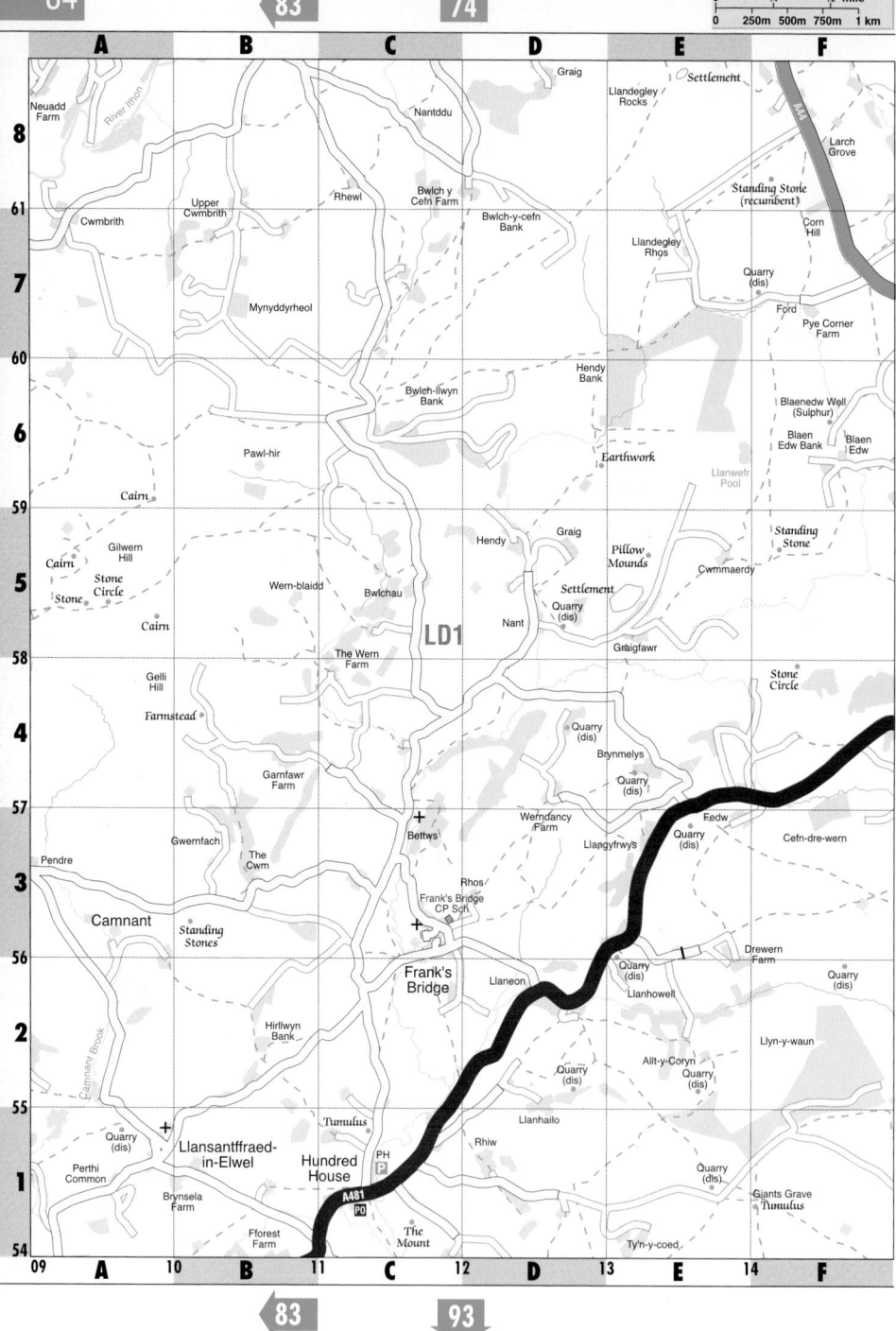

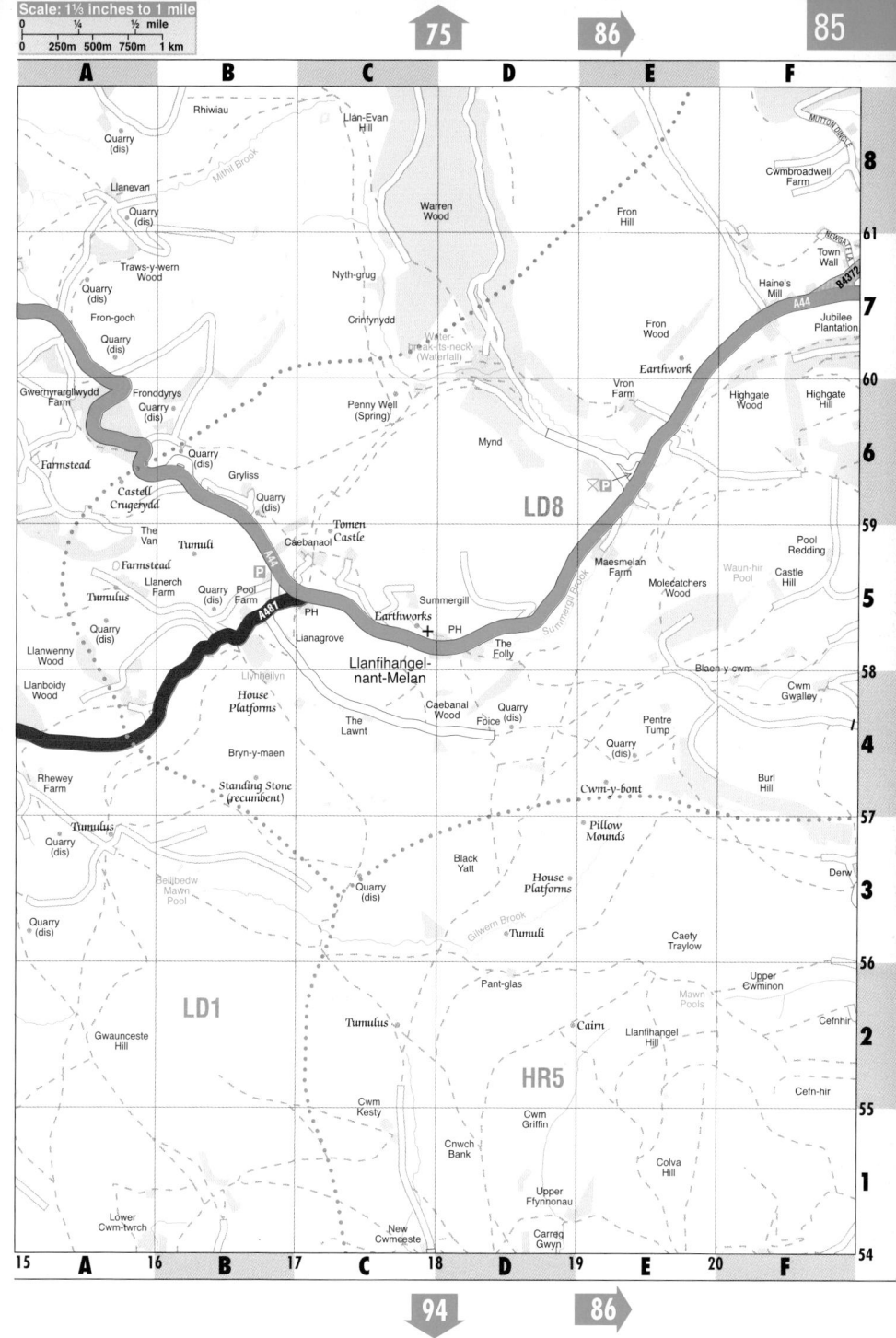

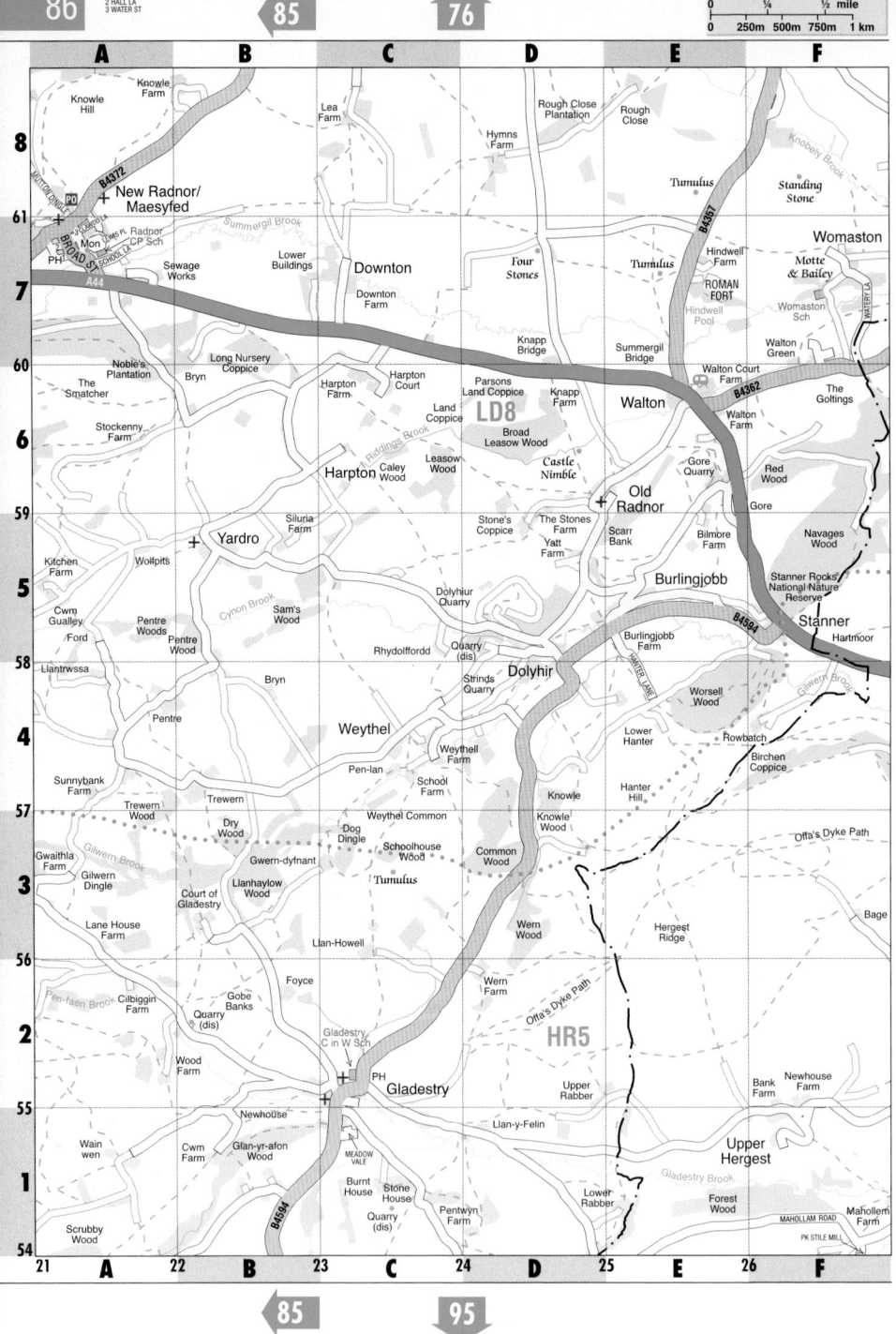

Map labels

A B C D E F

Motte & Bailey
Offa's Dyke Path
Burfa Farm
Middler Wood
Burfa
Hazel Point
Knill Wood
Upper Woodside
B4362
Broadhurst Bridge
Little Brampton
Little Brampton Farm
Rodd Wood
Wychmoor Wood
Mortimer Trail
Green Lane
Green Lane Farm

Tumulus
Motte
Burfa Bank
Fort
Ditchyeld Bridge
Hindwell Brook
Pool Plantation
Knill
Little Brampton Wood
Little Brampton Scar
Stocking Wood
Beech Wood
School Terr

Croft Plantation
Reddings Brook
Weir
Knill Bridge
Knill Court
LD8
Scutchditch Wood
EYWOOD LANE

Lower Harpton Farm
Knill Garraway
Sheepwalk
Kennel Wood
Oakcroft Farm
Cave Wood
Garden Wood
Titley Pool

Herrock Hill
DUNFIELD LANE
Offa's Dyke Path
Rushock Hill
Mortimer Trail
Flintsham Pool
Flintsham
B4355
Offa's Dyke
Garden Pool

Holywell Wood
The Bower
Tinkers Wood
HILL GATE
Pawpitts Farm
Berry's Wood
Titley Mill
Offa's Dyke

Dunfield Farm
Bradnor Hill (NT)
Rackway Farm
The Meads
RUSHOCK
Rushock Farm
Bank Farm
Beech Grove
Offa's Dyke

Kington Golf Club
CH
Bradnor Farm
BRADNOR
Barton Farm
Downfield
River Arrow

Bradnor Wood
Wallstych Farm
Bradnor Green
Floodgates
NEWTON LA
Kington Cottage
BRAMPTON LANE
Sunset Farm
Hatton Gardens Industrial Estate
Waterloo Bridge
Weir
Mill Farm
Lyonshall Park Wood

Vestry Farm
A44
YELD LANE
Yeld Wood
Yeld Farm
MONTPELIER RD
Liby
RIDGEBOURNE ROAD
PO
WATERLOO RD
Heath Coppice
Yaidon Coppice
Tramway Pool

Haywood Farm
Haywood Common
Hill Farm
CUTTERBACH LA
Hergest Croft Gdns
Kington CP Schl
Lady Hawkins Sch
Mus
HEADBROOK
Redhill Farm
Penrhos Farm
A44 Leominster

Park Wood
Weir
The Toll House
Recn Gd
Newburn Farm
KINGTON
Hotel
Ovals Farm
Offa's Dyke

The Grove Farm
Ashmoor
Ashfield Farm
A4111
Penrhos Wood
Garden Wood

Castle Twts Motte & Bailey
UPPER HERGEST
Lower Hergest
HR5
Hergest Court
BREDWARD
Mast
Newlands
Mount Pleasant Farm
Cemy
Rhodds Farm
Rodds Wood
Oxpasture Wood
Green Wood
Lower Lynhales Farm
Lynhales Farm

Hergest Bridge
PICCADILLY
BROAD RD
BRICKYARD ROAD
Woodbrook Farm
Rhodds Farm
JACK'S DITCH LANE
Elston

Sewage Works
River Arrow
Arrow Court Industrial Estate
Arrow Court Farm
Small Breeds Farm Park & Animal Centre
Knapp Coppice
Lilwall Farm
Earthwork

Hergest Farm
Mahollam Bridge
Pound Farm
A4111

A4111 Hereford (A438)
Herefordshire Monmouthshire STREET ATLAS

27 28 29 30 31 32

79

Scale: 1½ inches to 1 mile

0   ¼   ½ mile
0   250m   500m   750m   1 km

A   B   C   D   E   F

8

Bryn Mawr
Tryfal

Esgair Bustach

Cefn Coch

Quarry (dis)

Esgair Bellaf

Irfon

53

SY25

Cwch Rhiwhalog

Cefn Ty'n-y-graig

Tywi Forest

Quarry (dis)

St David's Church (remains of)

7

Ty'n-y-graig

Nant y Fannog

52

Nant-y-Neuadd

Cnuwch

Ty-newydd

Fannog

Cefn Fannog

Craig Carreg-fan

Nant Rhyd-goch

Nant-y-brain

6

Banc Hendre'r-dail

Dyrys Du

P X

Esgair Nant-y-brain

51

Nant y Crafiwyn

LD5

Carreg Clochdy

Nant Cwm-bqs

Pen y Foel

Pen y Garn

5

P

Viewpoint
X P

Mine (dis)

Carreg Wen

50

Llyn Brianne Reservoir

Cairn

Esgair Garn

Cefn Uchaf

Cefn Cwmirfon

4

Allt yr Hwch

Coed Ffos-y-gath

Mynydd Trawsnant

Cefn Blaencwmhenog

49

Weir
P X
Mast

Croes Lwyd Fach

Nant Henog

Cwm Henog

3

Llyne Brianne Visitor Centre

Cwm Henog

Cefn Trybeddgwilym

48

P

Cairn

Cnapau Hafodllywelyn

Cwm Lletgwial

Nant Llergwial

2

SA20

Cefn Ystrad-ffin

Cwm Henog

47

Esgair cynnant

1

Cerrig Cedny

Dolfallt

Waun Coli

Cairn

46

Carn Twrch

Cefn Hafod-y-maen

79   A   80   B   81   C   82   D   83   E   84   F

Ceredigion & S. Gwynedd STREET ATLAS

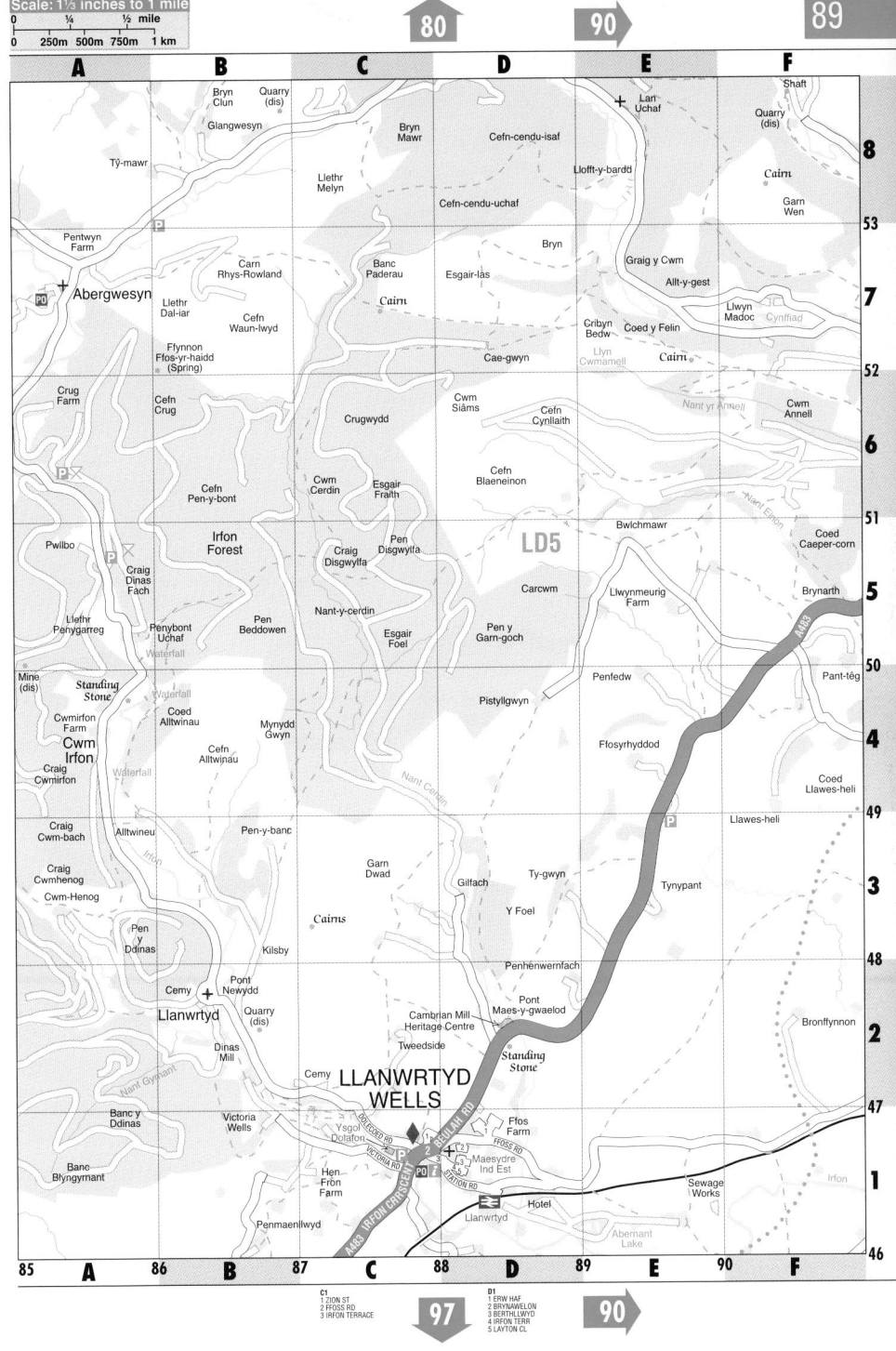

LD5

Bryn Clun
Quarry (dis)
Glangwesyn
Tŷ-mawr
Bryn Mawr
Cefn-cendu-isaf
Llethr Melyn
Llofft-y-bardd
Lan Uchaf
Shaft
Quarry (dis)
Cairn
Garn Wen
Cefn-cendu-uchaf
Pentwyn Farm
Carn Rhys-Rowland
Abergwesyn
Llethr Dal-iar
Cefn Waun-lwyd
Banc Paderau
Bryn
Graig y Cwm
Allt-y-gest
Cairn
Llwyn Madoc
Cynffiad
Flynnon Ffos-yr-haidd (Spring)
Cribyn Bedw
Coed y Felin
Cae-gwyn
Llyn Cwmarell
Cairn
Crug Farm
Cefn Crug
Cairn
Cwm Siâms
Cefn Cynllaith
Nant yr Annell
Cwm Annell
Crugwydd
Cefn Pen-y-bont
Cwm Cerdin
Esgair Fraith
Cefn Blaeneinon
Nant Einon
Pwilbo
Irfon Forest
Craig Disgwylfa
Pen Disgwylfa
Bwlchmawr
Coed Caeper-corn
Craig Dinas Fach
Nant-y-cerdin
Esgair Foel
Pen y Garn-goch
Carcwm
Llwynmeurig Farm
Brynarth
Llethr Penygarreg
Penybont Uchaf
Pen Beddowen
Pant-têg
Waterfall
Mine (dis)
Standing Stone
Waterfall
Coed Alltwinau
Mynydd Gwyn
Pistyllgwyn
Penfedw
Ffosyrhyddod
Cwmirfon Farm
Cwm Irfon
Cefn Alltwinau
Nant Cerdin
Llawes-heli
Coed Llawes-heli
Craig Cwmirfon
Waterfall
Craig Cwm-bach
Alltwineu
Pen-y-banc
Garn Dwad
Tynypant
Craig Cwmhenog
Cwm-Henog
Gilfach
Ty-gwyn
Y Foel
Pen y Ddinas
Cairns
Kilsby
Penhênwernfach
Pont Maes-y-gwaelod
Bronffynnon
Cemy
Pont Newydd
Llanwrtyd
Quarry (dis)
Cambrian Mill Heritage Centre
Tweedside
Standing Stone
Dinas Mill
Cemy
LLANWRTYD WELS
Banc y Ddinas
Victoria Wells
Ysgol Dolafon
Ffos Farm
Banc Blyngyrnant
Hen Fron Farm
Maesydre Ind Est
Hotel
Llanwrtyd
Sewage Works
Irfon
Penmaenllwyd
Abernant Lake

C1
1 ZION ST
2 FFOSS RD
3 IRFON TERRACE

D1
1 ERW HAF
2 BRYNAWELON
3 BERTHLLWYD
4 IRFON TERR
5 LAYTON CL

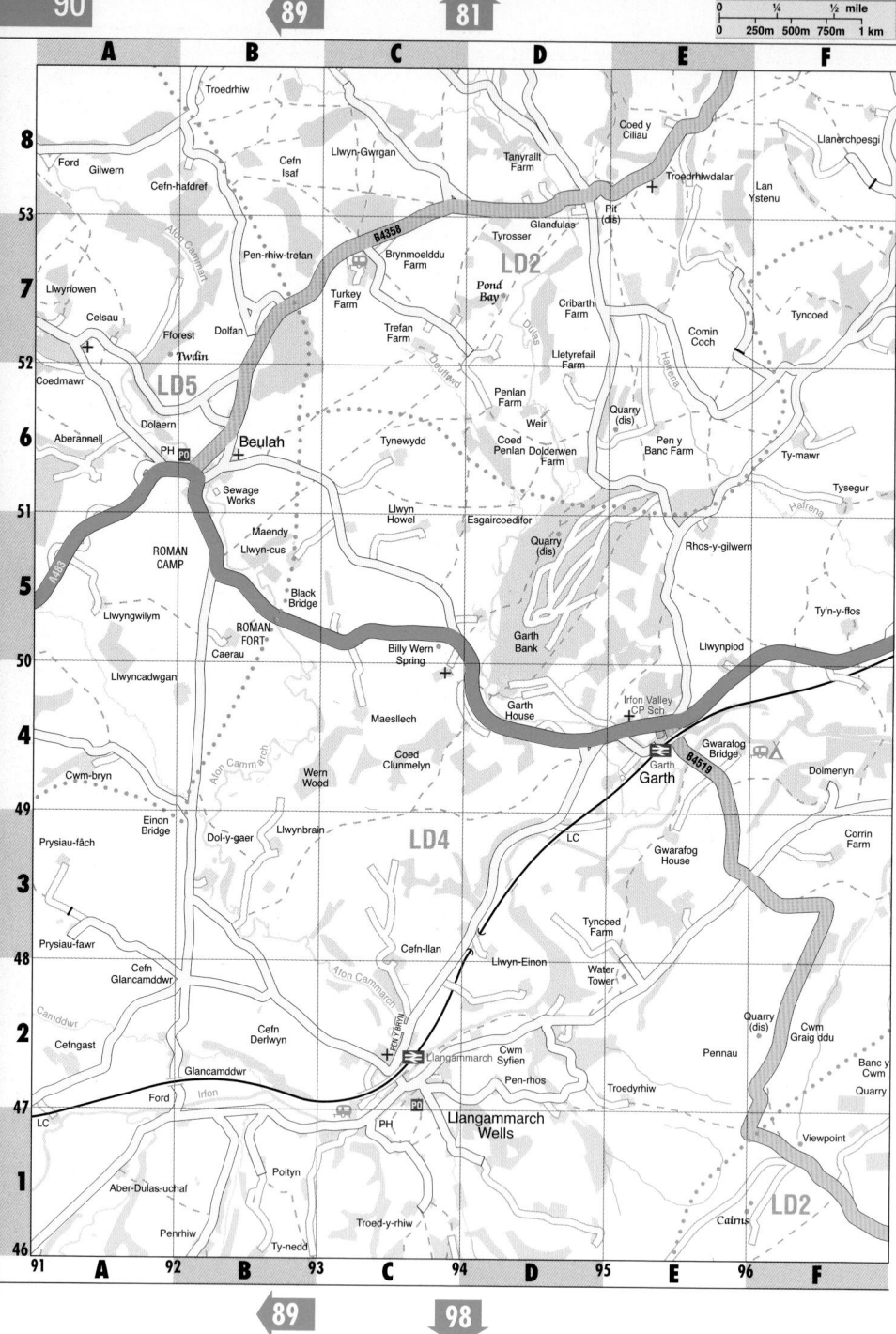

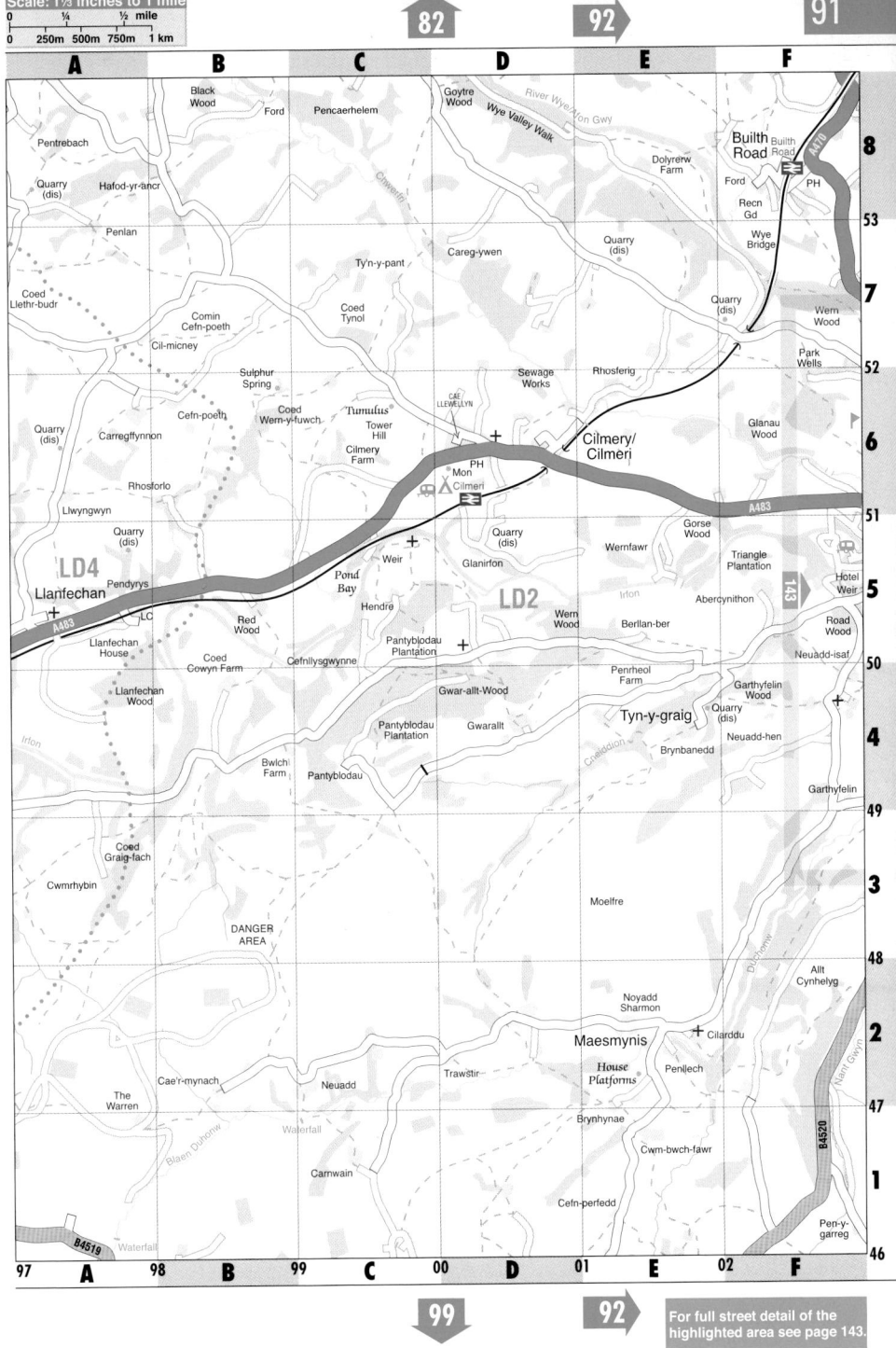

Scale: 1⅓ inches to 1 mile

0 · ¼ · ½ mile
0 · 250m · 500m · 750m · 1 km

91

82 92

For full street detail of the highlighted area see page 143.

99 92

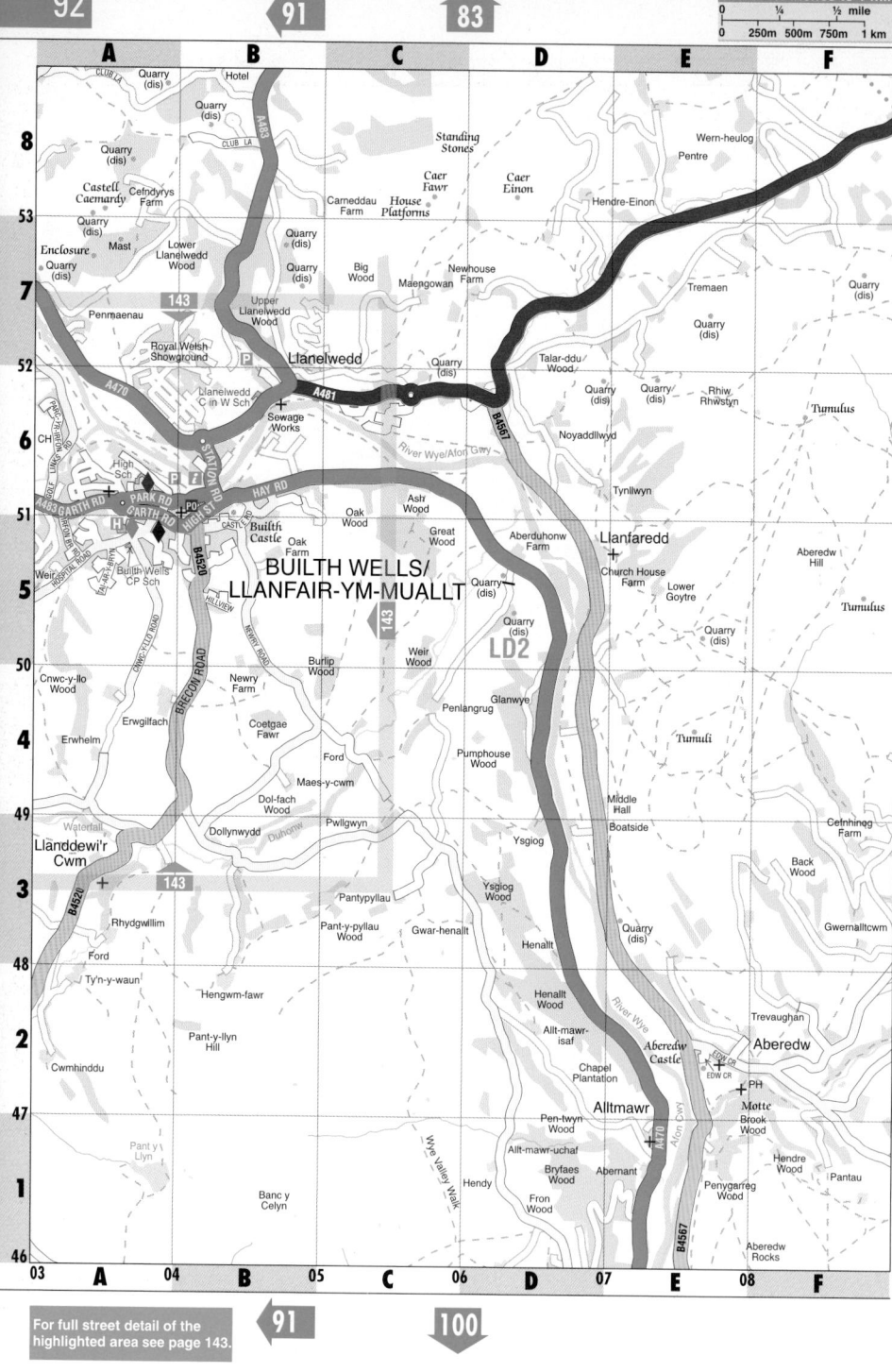

For full street detail of the highlighted area see page 143.

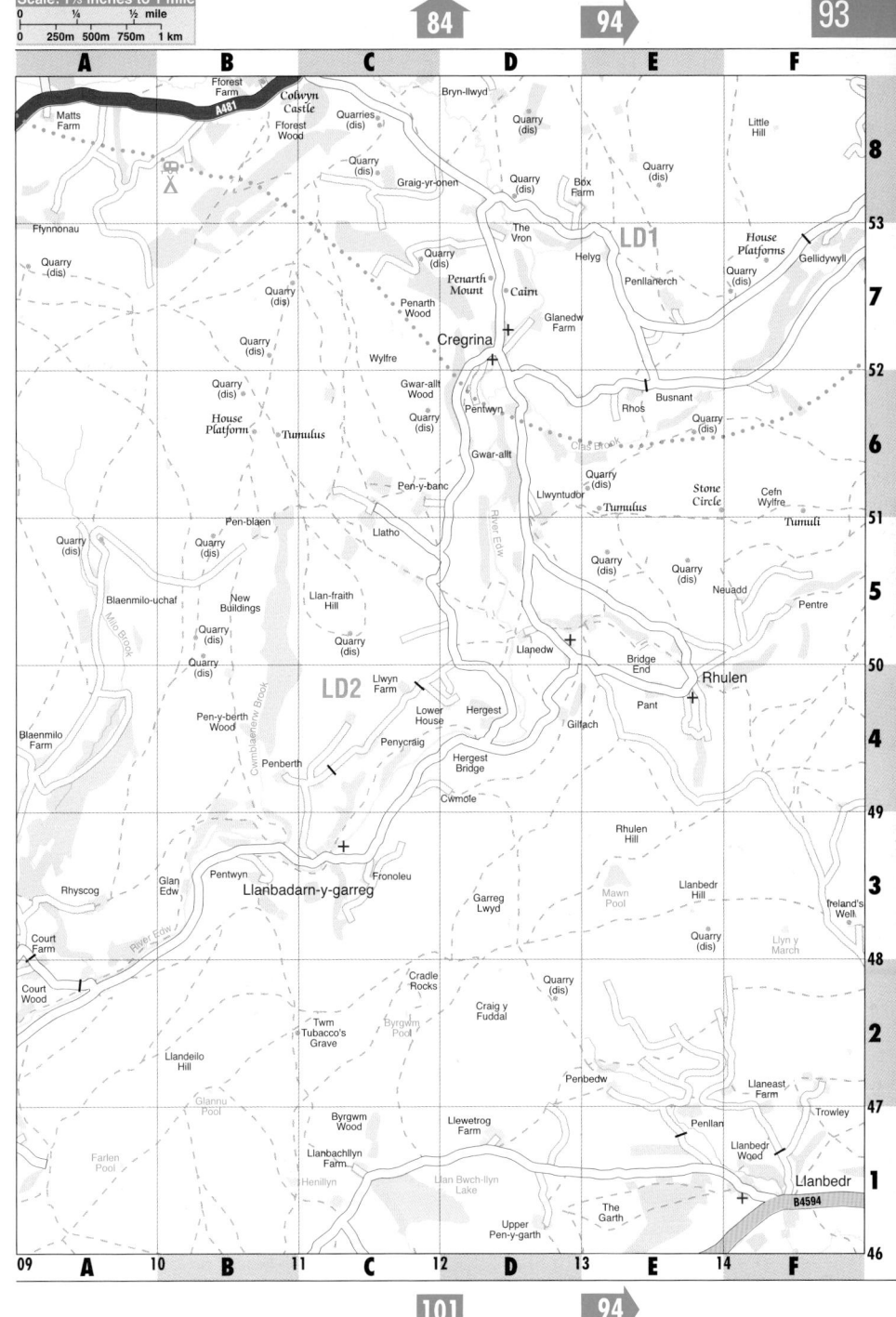

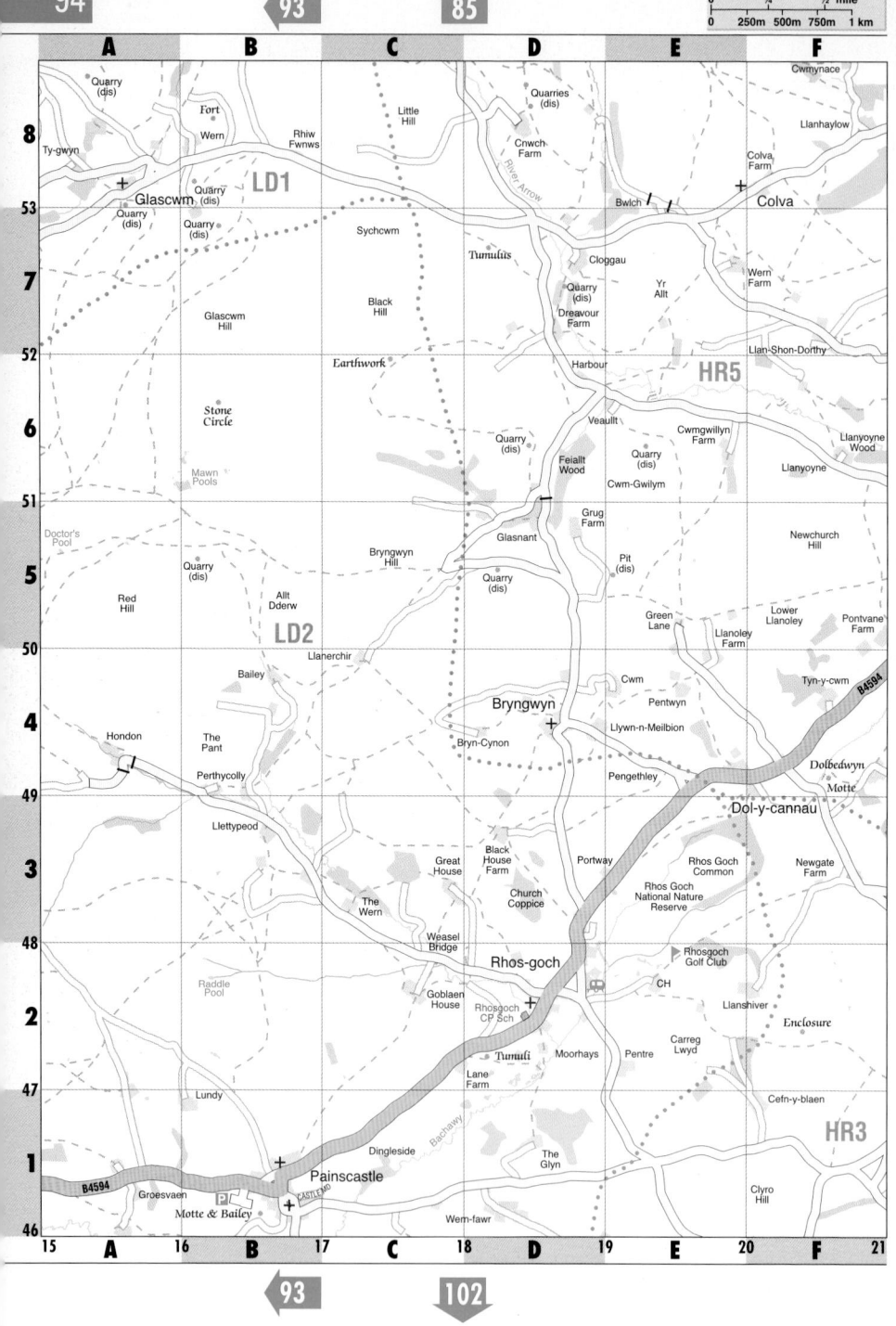

Upper Gwernilla

Hengoed

Fairfields

Llanbella

Huntington
PH
Court

Huntington Park

Lodge Farm

New Barn

Penllan

Grove Farm
GROVE FARM RD

Hill Farm

Llanarrow Cott

River Arrow

Burnt Hengoed
BURNT HENGOED

Quarry Bank

GWERN BRANCH
THE SCHOOL RD
PRE HENGOED

Hengoed

PENLLAN LA

The Wern

Lloyney

Blaencerde

Pentre-draen

Great Gwern-y-bwch

LLAN ARROW

HOSTELES LA
CRABBA RD

Brilley Mountain

Disgwylfa Hill

Baynham Hall

HR5

The Gaer

Newchurch

Milton

Michaelchurch-on-Arrow

High Holborn

HOLBORN LA

Herefordshire Monmouthshire STREET ATLAS

Llan-pica

Church House Farm

Trenewydd

THE REST RD

Gilfach-yr-heol

Milton Hill

BRILLEY CL
THE REST RD

Little Mountain

Redborough

CEFN RD

Brilley CE Prim Sch

B4594

Cefn

Caeau

The Bush

Pentremiley

Pentre GR

Pentregrove

Tan Ho

Brilley Court Farm

PESTLE FARM LA
Brilley

Brilley Green

CHAPEL RD

Crowther's Pool

Pen-Twyn Camp

Pentwyn

Wern

Upper Bridge Court

LOWER BRIDGE CT

Pound Farm

COURT RD

Little Merthyr

THE WOOD RD

PEN-TWYN
CROWTHERS POOL

Pen-Brilley

HR3

Sunny Bank

ROUSE LA

Whitney-on-Wye

Cwmithel

Cae'rneuadd Hill

PH

Rhydspence

River Wye/Afon Gwy

Toll

B4350

Whitney Court

A4350 Hereford

Llwyngwilliam

Chapel Farm

Lower Bettws

PH
THE POUND
CVN PK
WHITNEY VILLAGE RD

Penrhoel

Penycae

Upper Bettws

Cabalva House

Sheepcote Farm

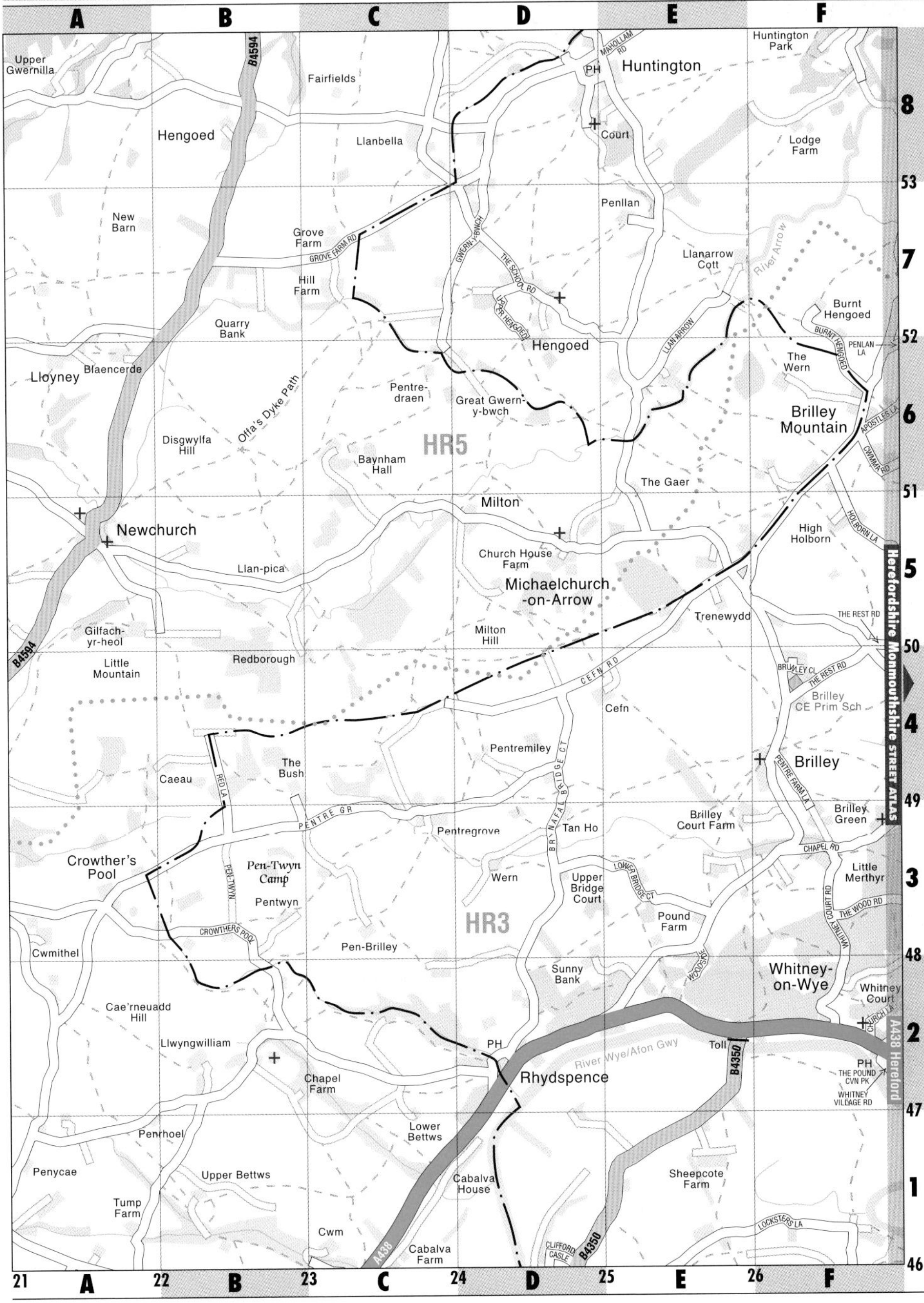

DOCKSTERS LA

Tump Farm

Cwm

Cabalva Farm

A438

CLIFFORD CASTLE

B4350

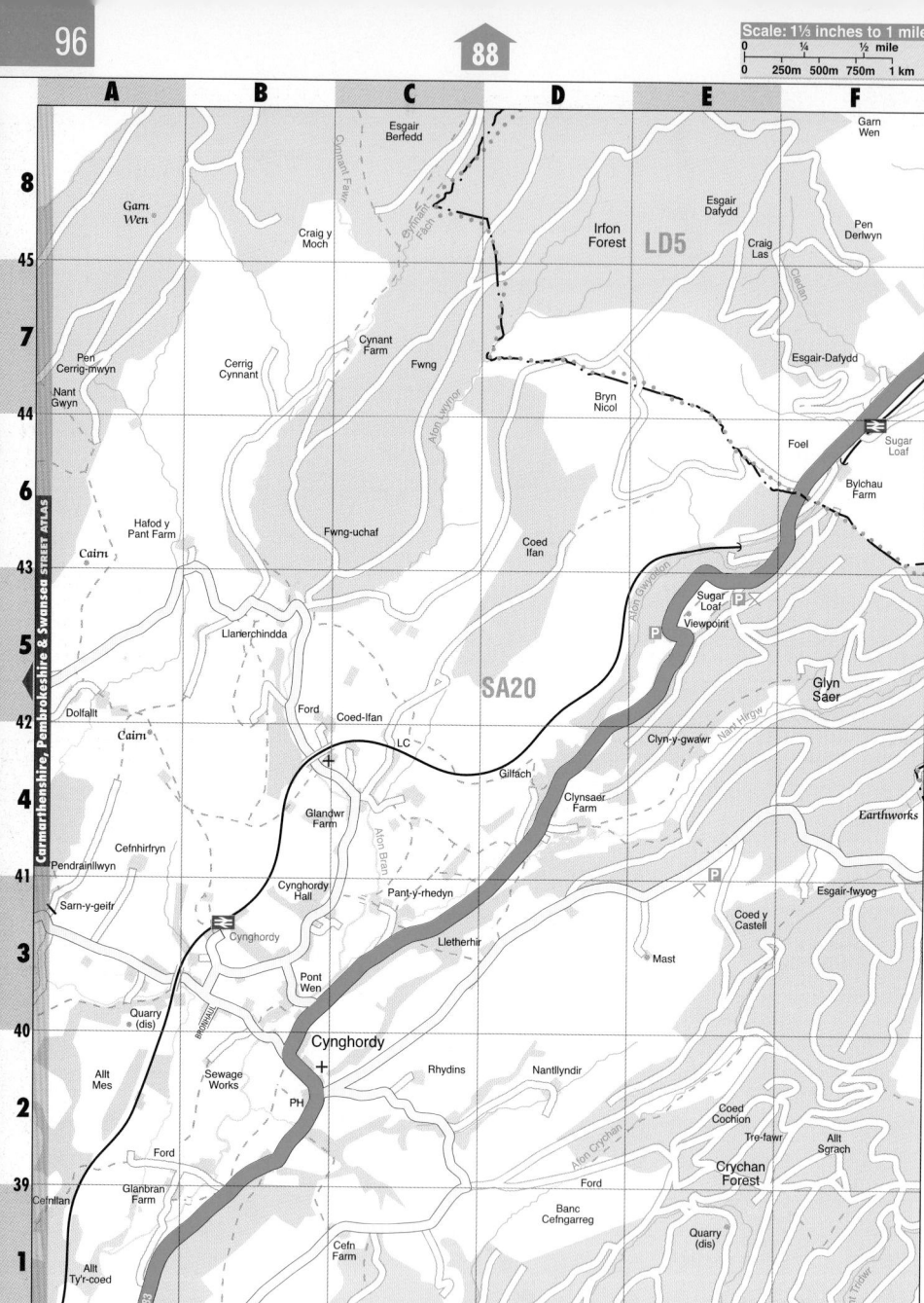

88

Scale: 1⅓ inches to 1 mile

104

STREET ATLAS Carmarthenshire, Pembrokeshire & Swansea

LD5

SA20

Esgair Berfedd

Garn Wen

Garn Wen

Craig y Moch

Irfon Forest

Esgair Dafydd

Pen Derlwyn

Cynant Farm

Fwng

Craig Las

Esgair-Dafydd

Pen Cerrig-mwyn

Cerrig Cynnant

Nant Gwyn

Bryn Nicol

Foel

Sugar Loaf

Bylchau Farm

Hafod y Pant Farm

Cairn

Fwng-uchaf

Coed Ifan

Sugar Loaf
Viewpoint

Glyn Saer

Llanerchindda

Clyn-y-gwawr

Nant Hirgw

Dolfallt

Cairn

Ford

Coed-Ifan

LC

Gilfách

Clynsaer Farm

Earthworks

Glandwr Farm

Aton Bran

Cefnhirfryn

Pendrainllwyn

Cynghordy Hall

Pant-y-rhedyn

Lletherhir

Coed y Castell

Esgair-fwyog

Sarn-y-geifr

Cynghordy

Pont Wen

Mast

Allt Mes

Quarry (dis)

Sewage Works

PH

Cynghordy

Rhydins

Nantllyndir

Coed Cochion

Tre-fawr

Allt Sgrach

Cefnllan

Glanbran Farm

Ford

Ford

Banc Cefngarreg

Crychan Forest

Quarry (dis)

Allt Ty'r-coed

Cefn Farm

Settlement

Aton Crychan

Nant Tridwr

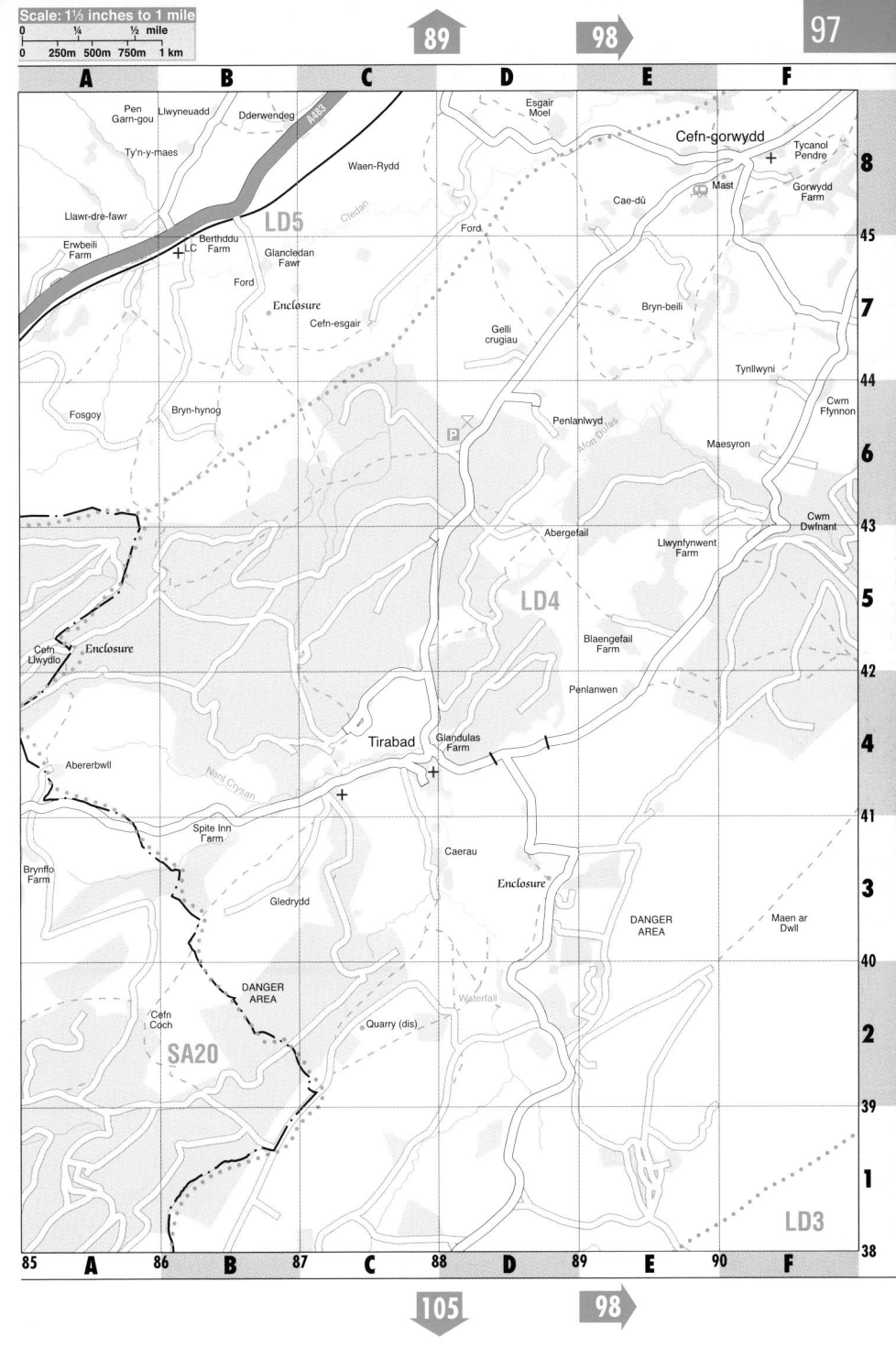

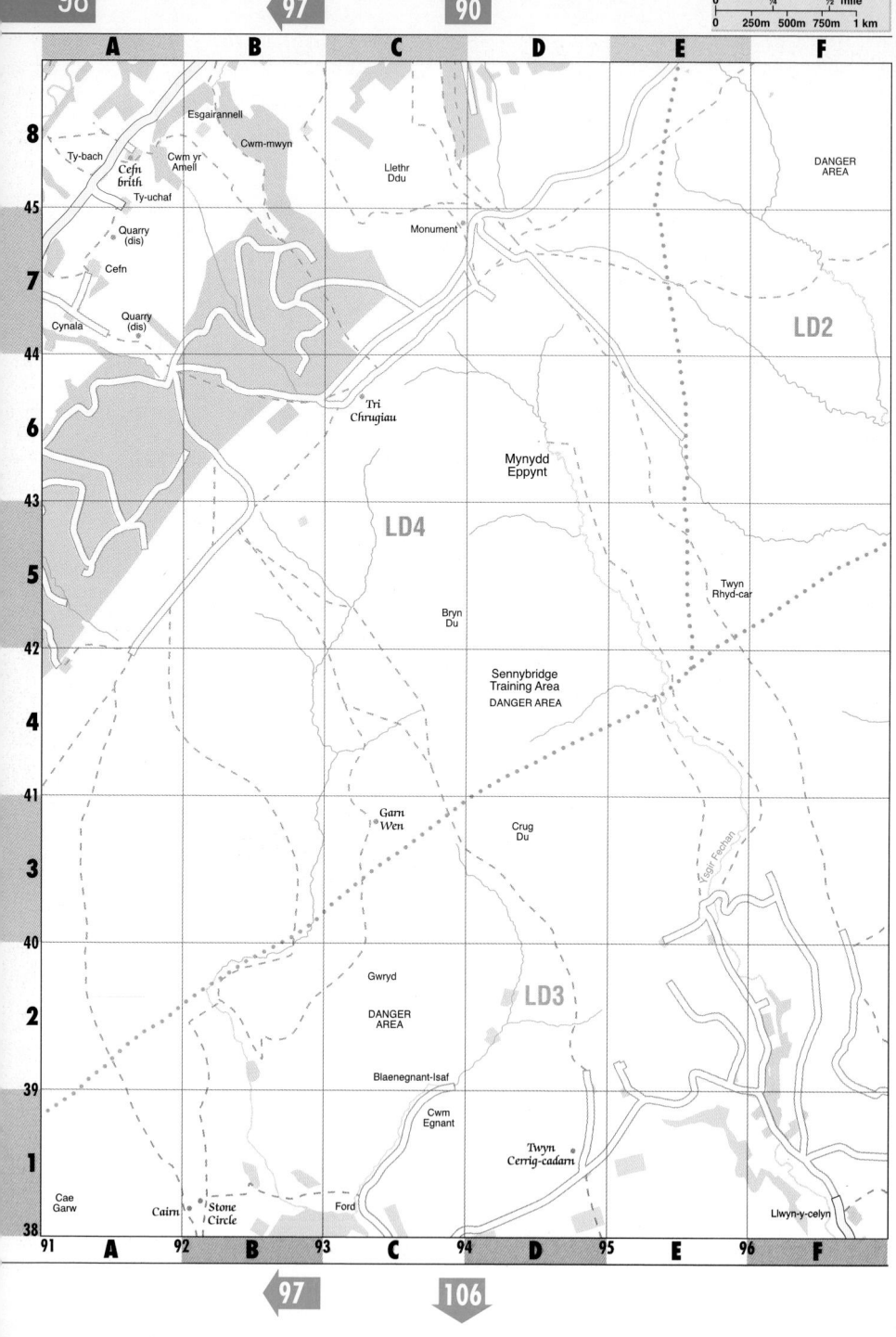

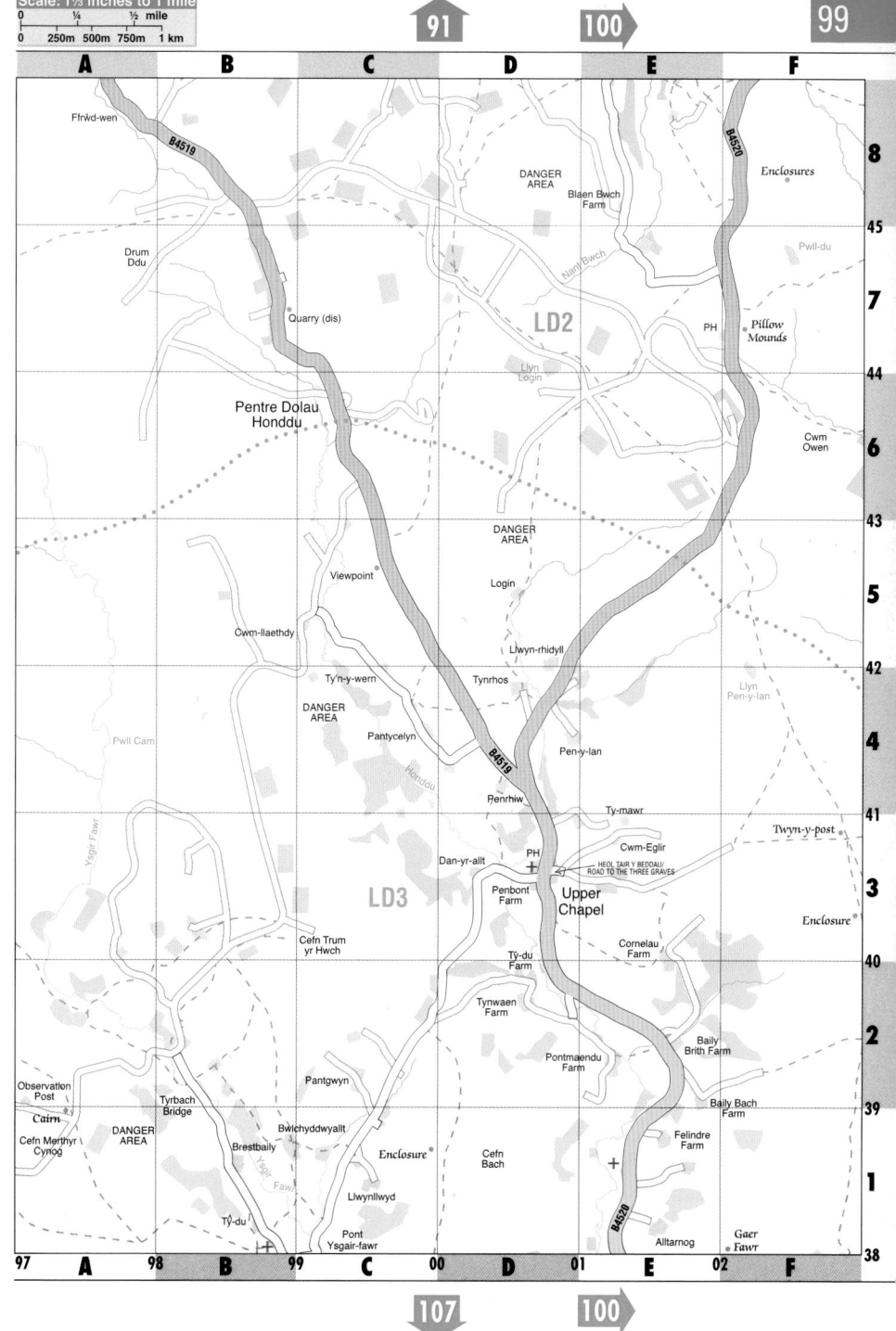

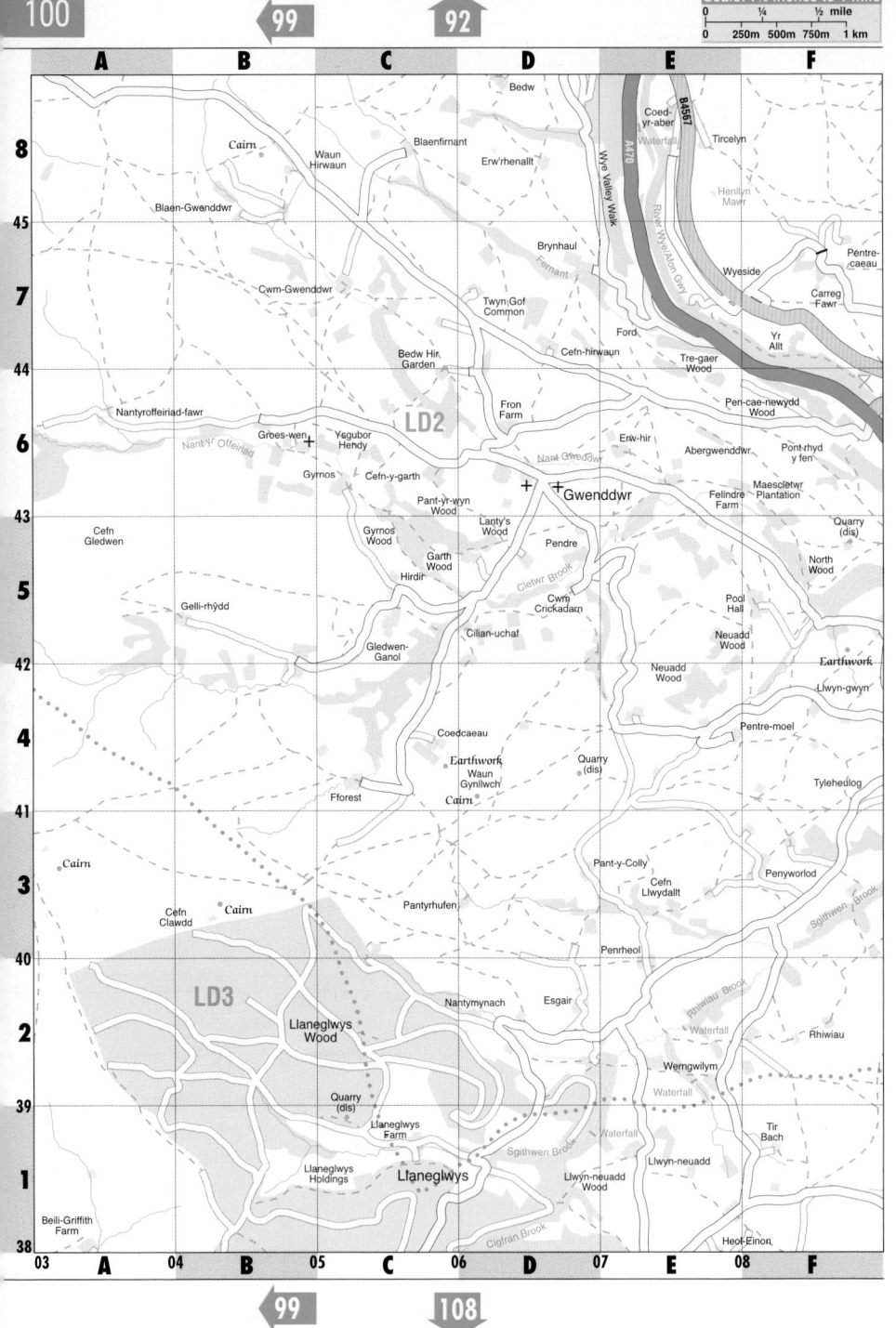

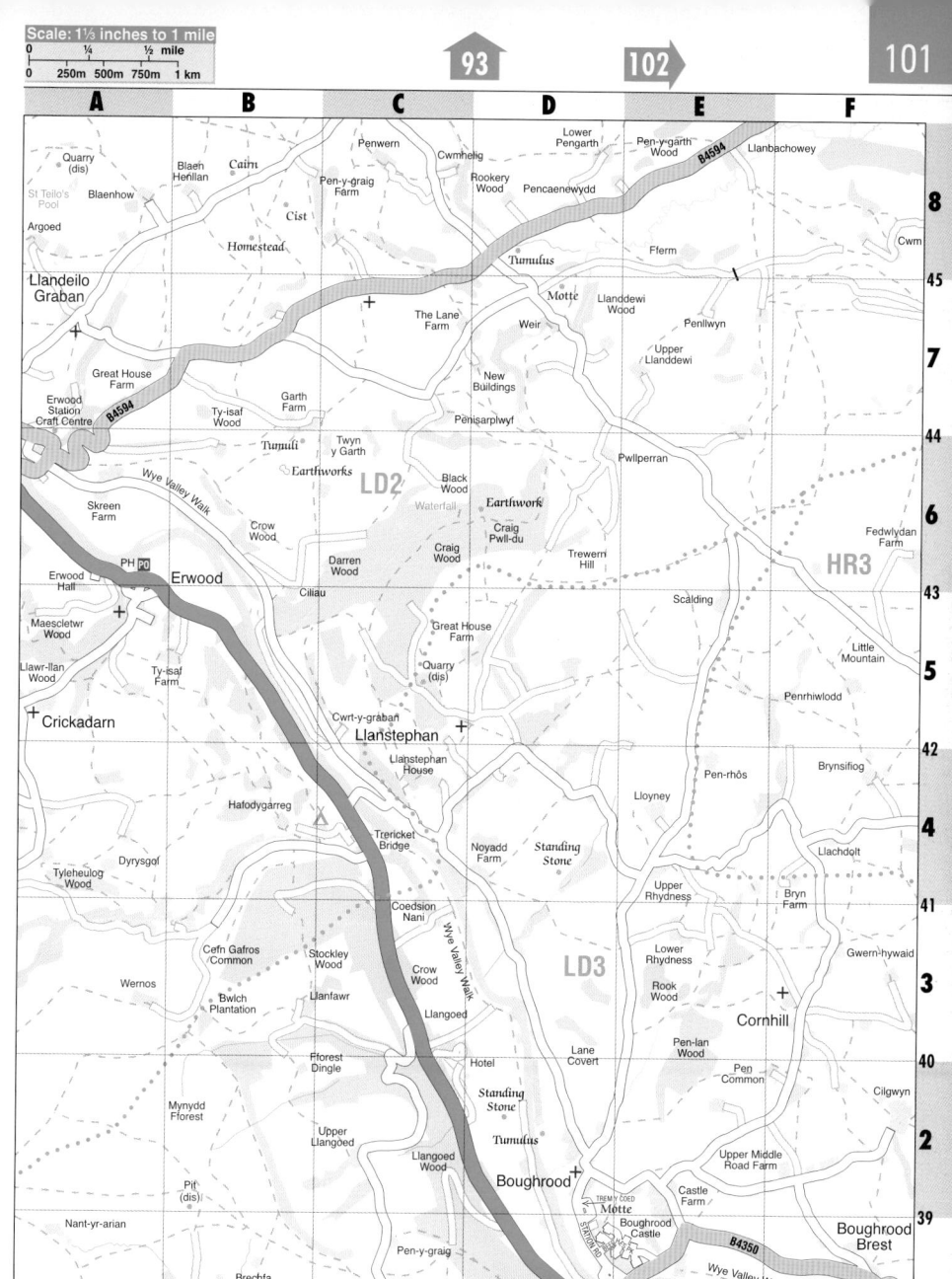

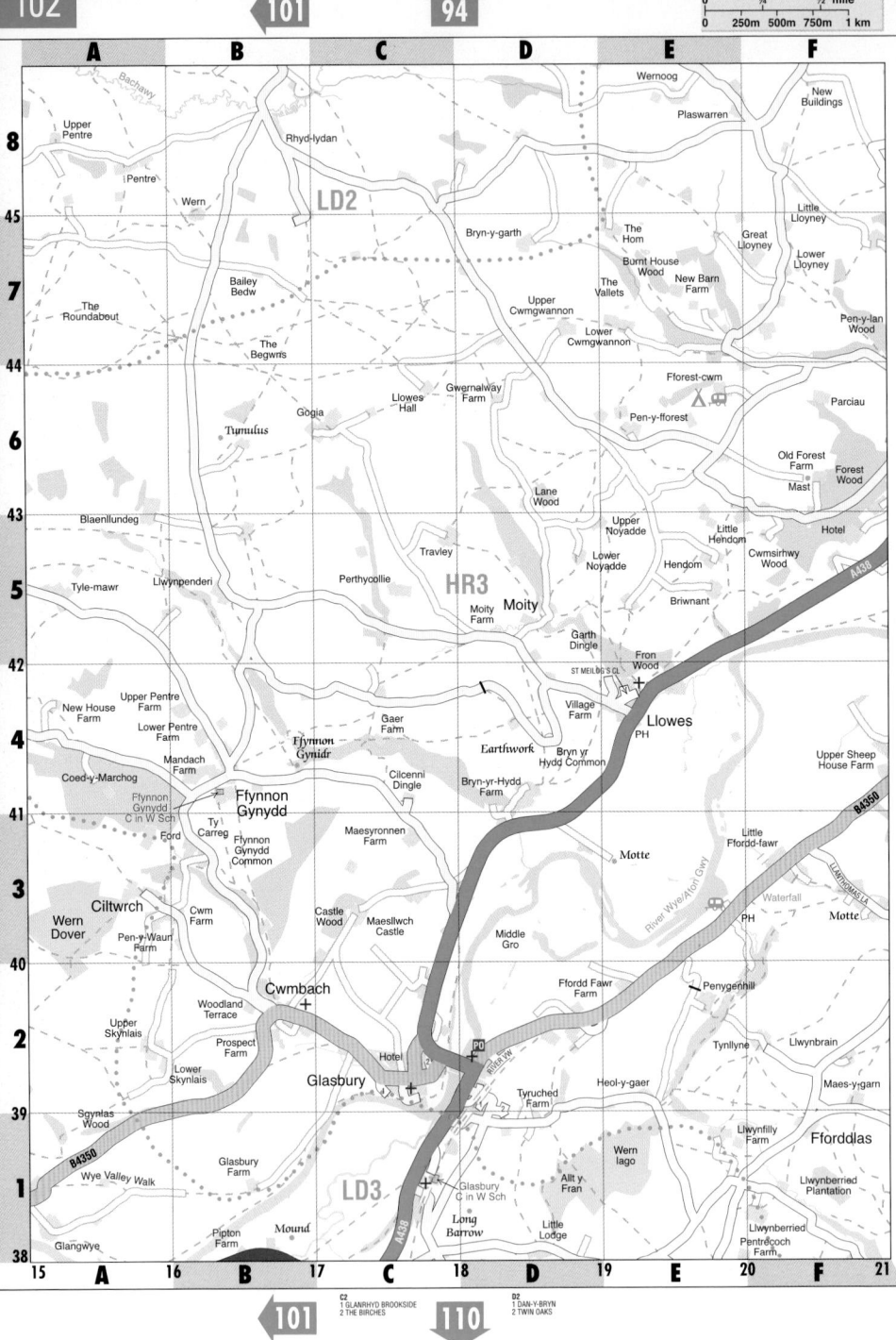

Scale: 1⅓ inches to 1 mile
0 ¼ ½ mile
0 250m 500m 750m 1 km

95

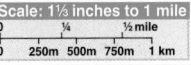

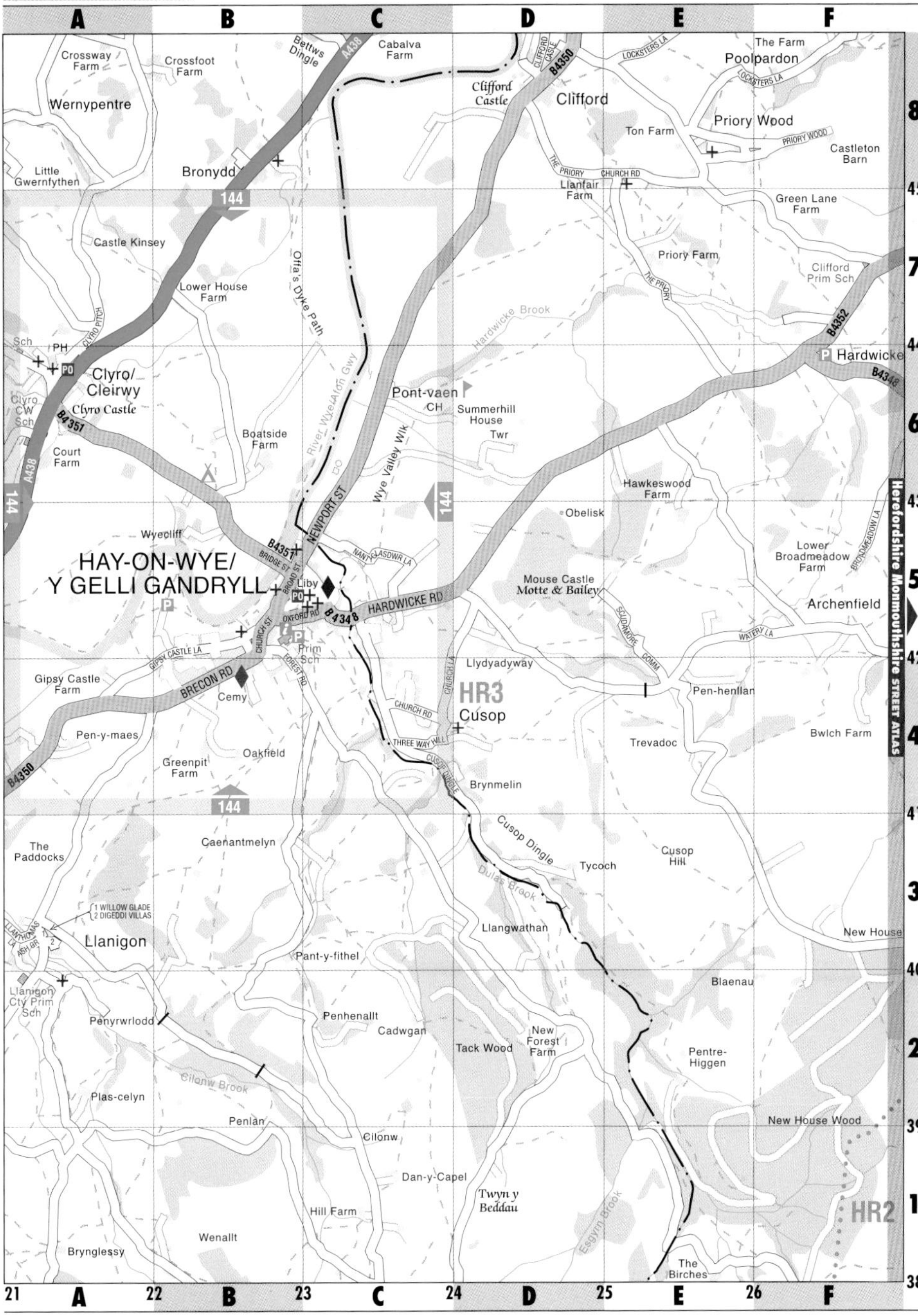

For full street detail of the highlighted area see page 144.

111

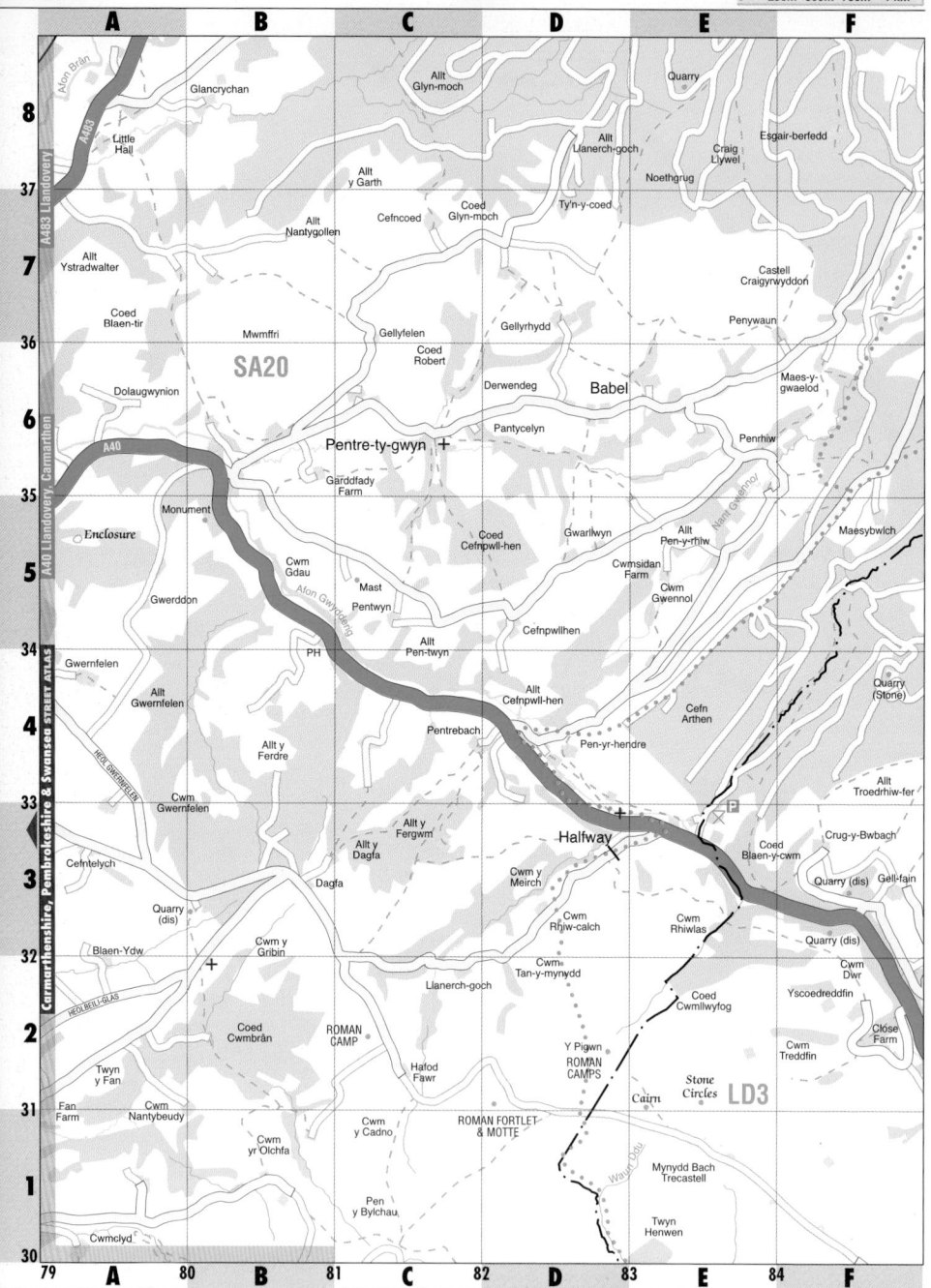

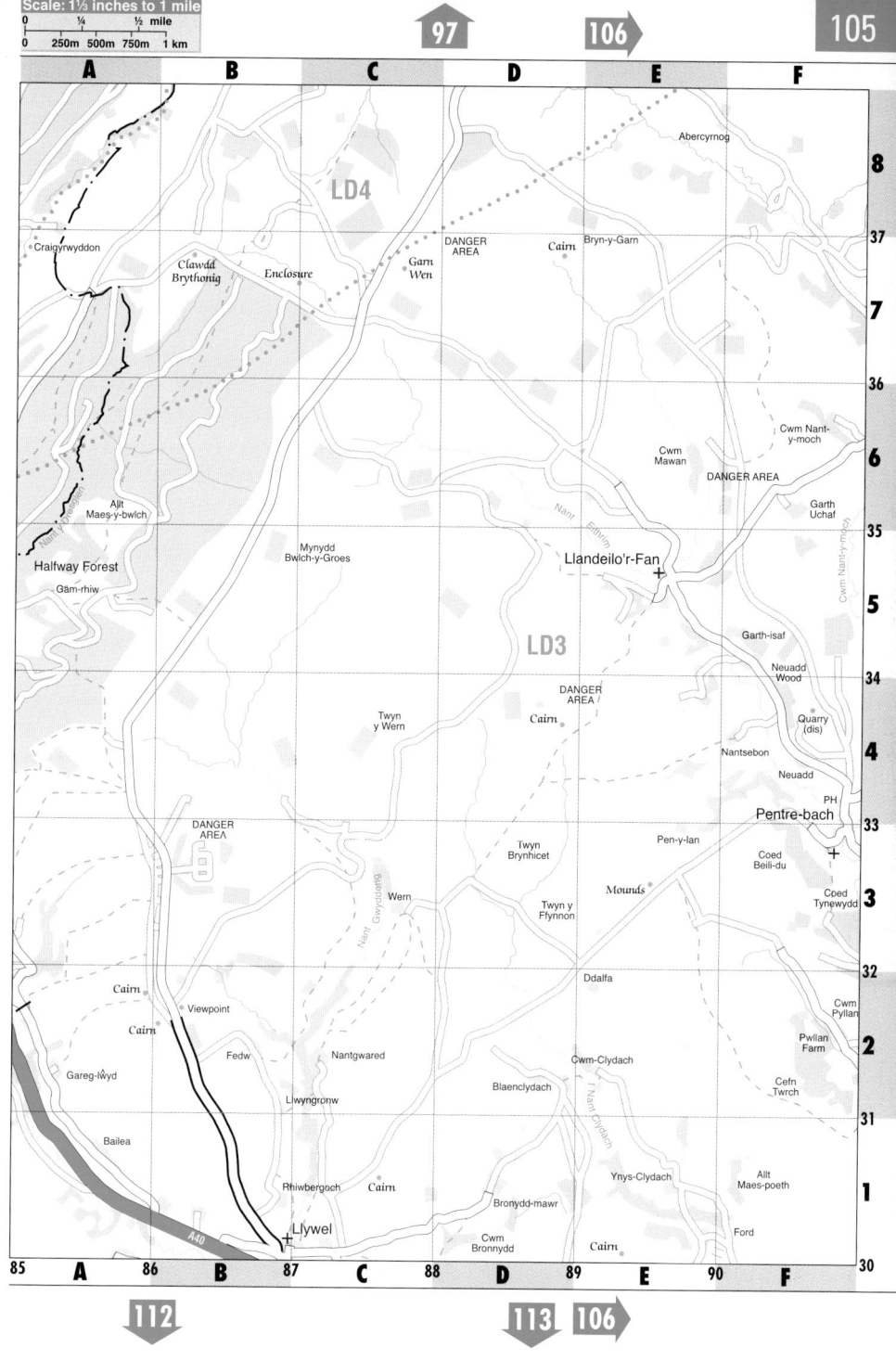

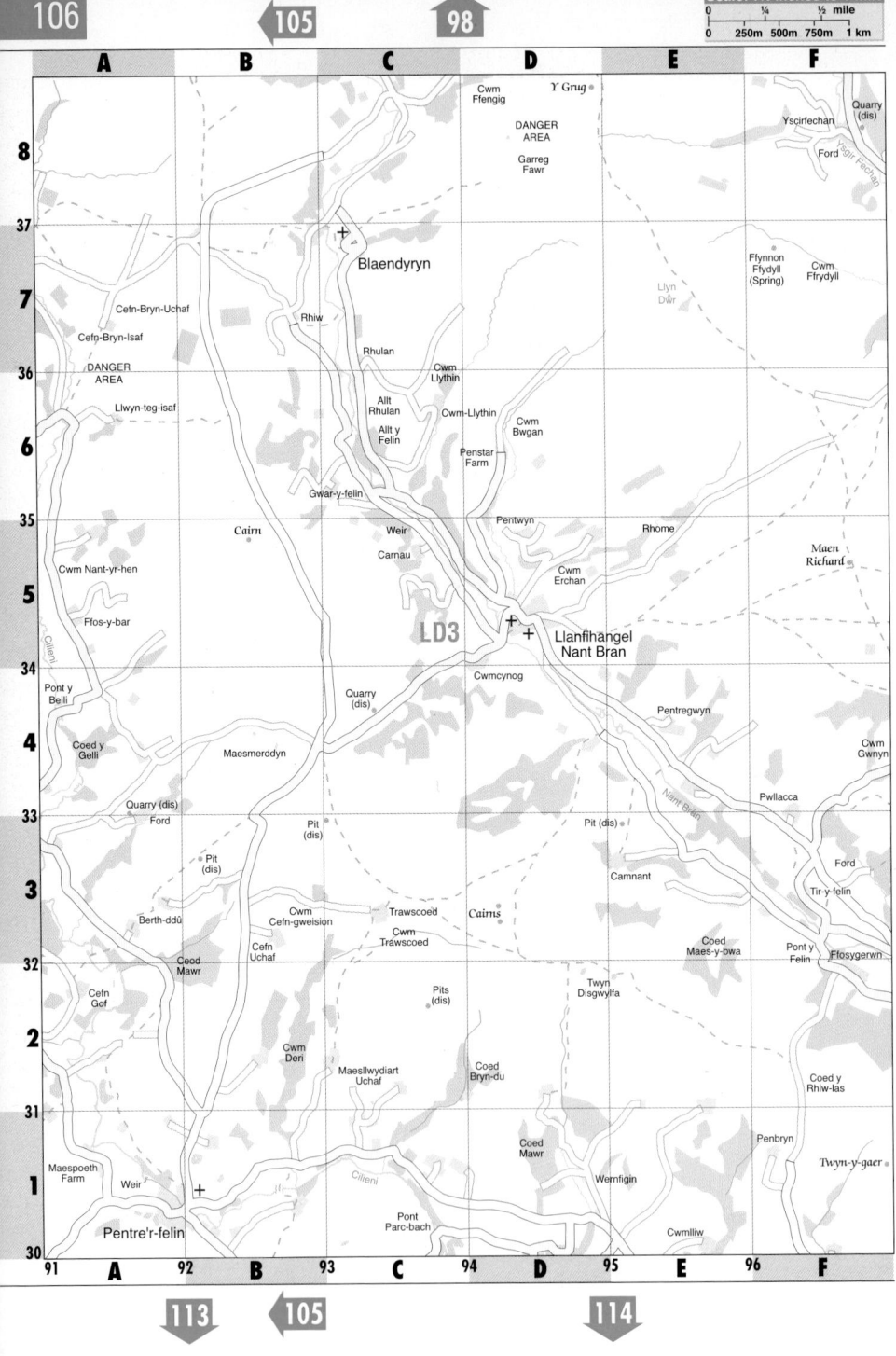

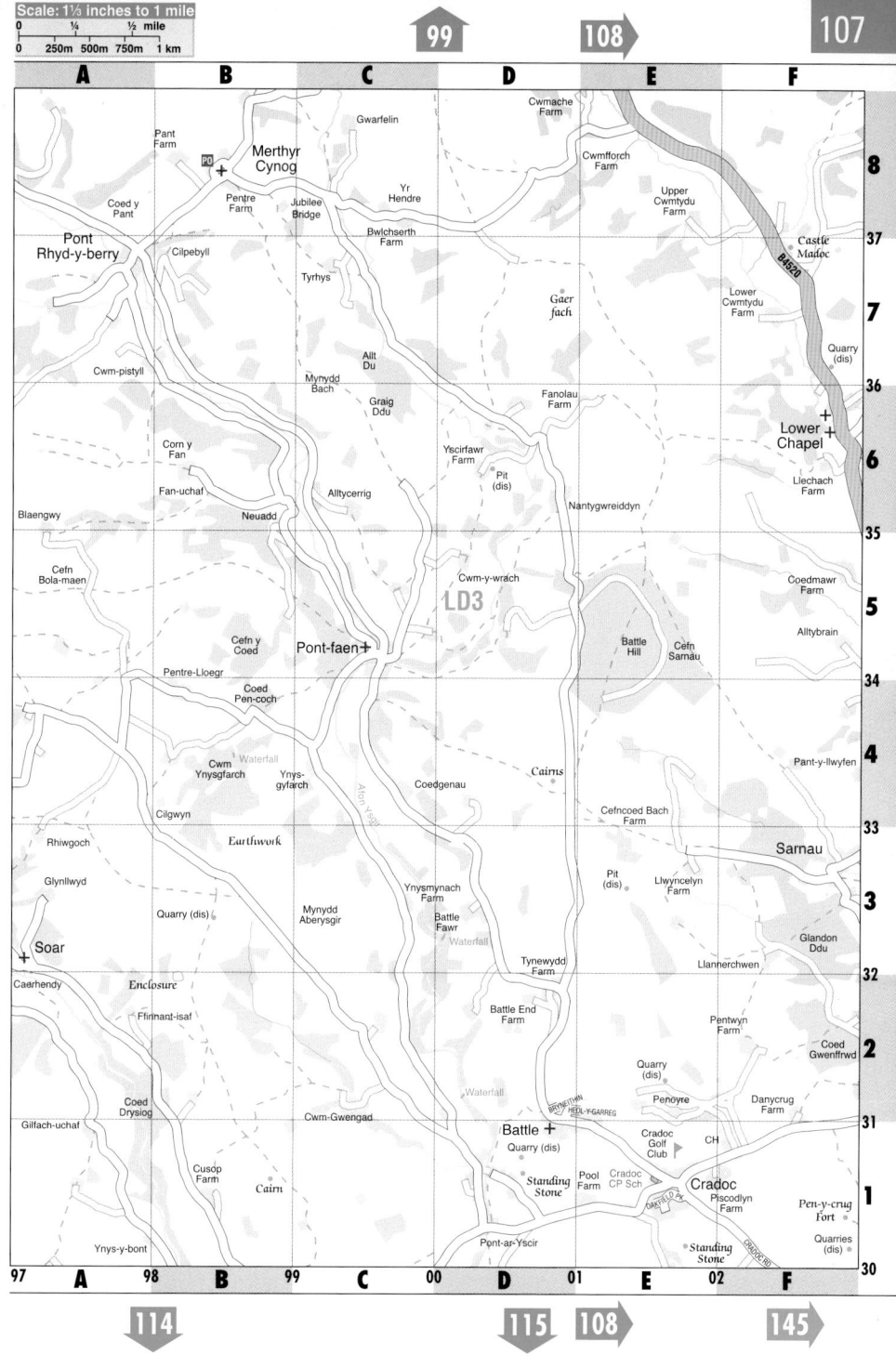

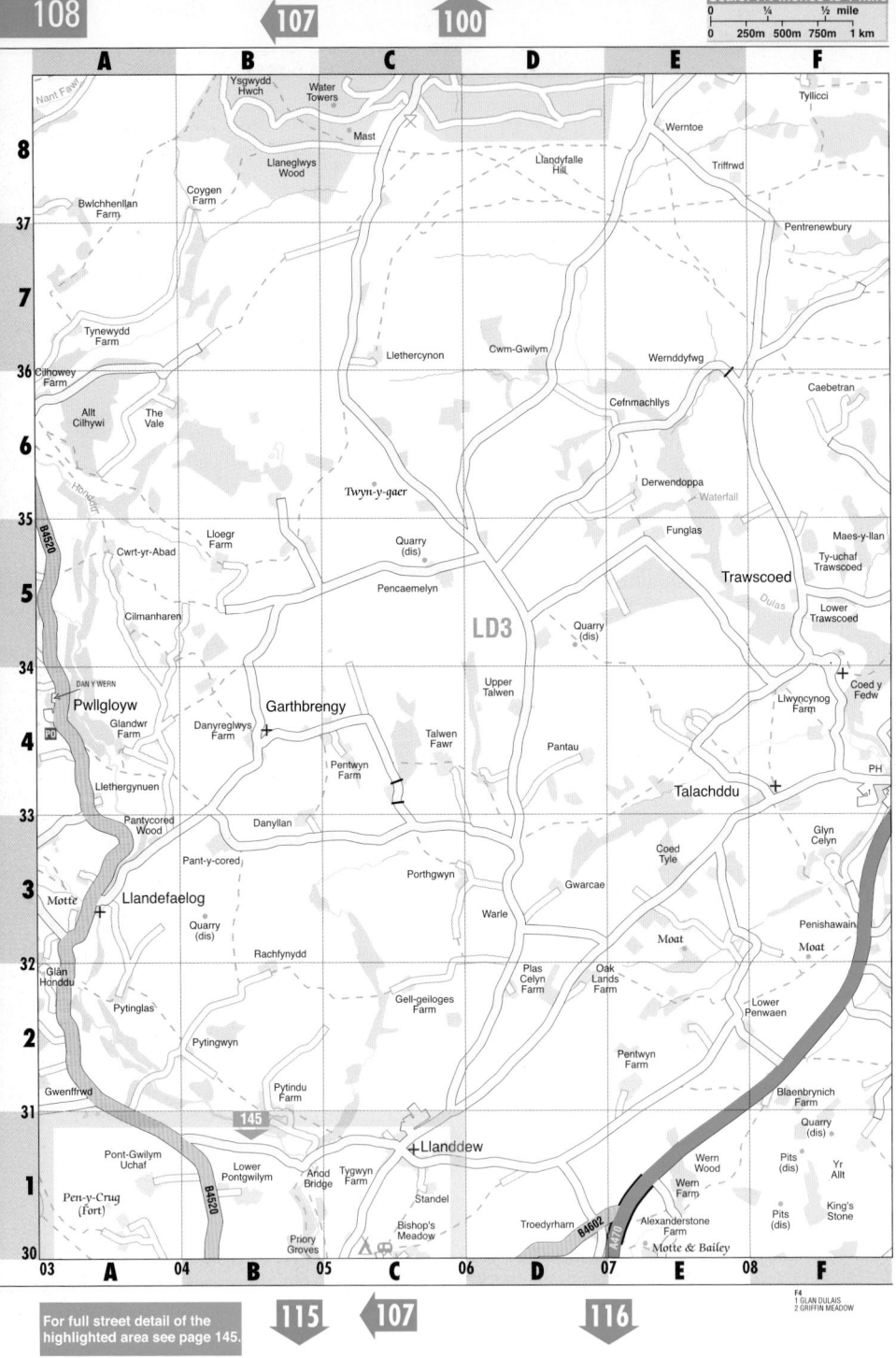

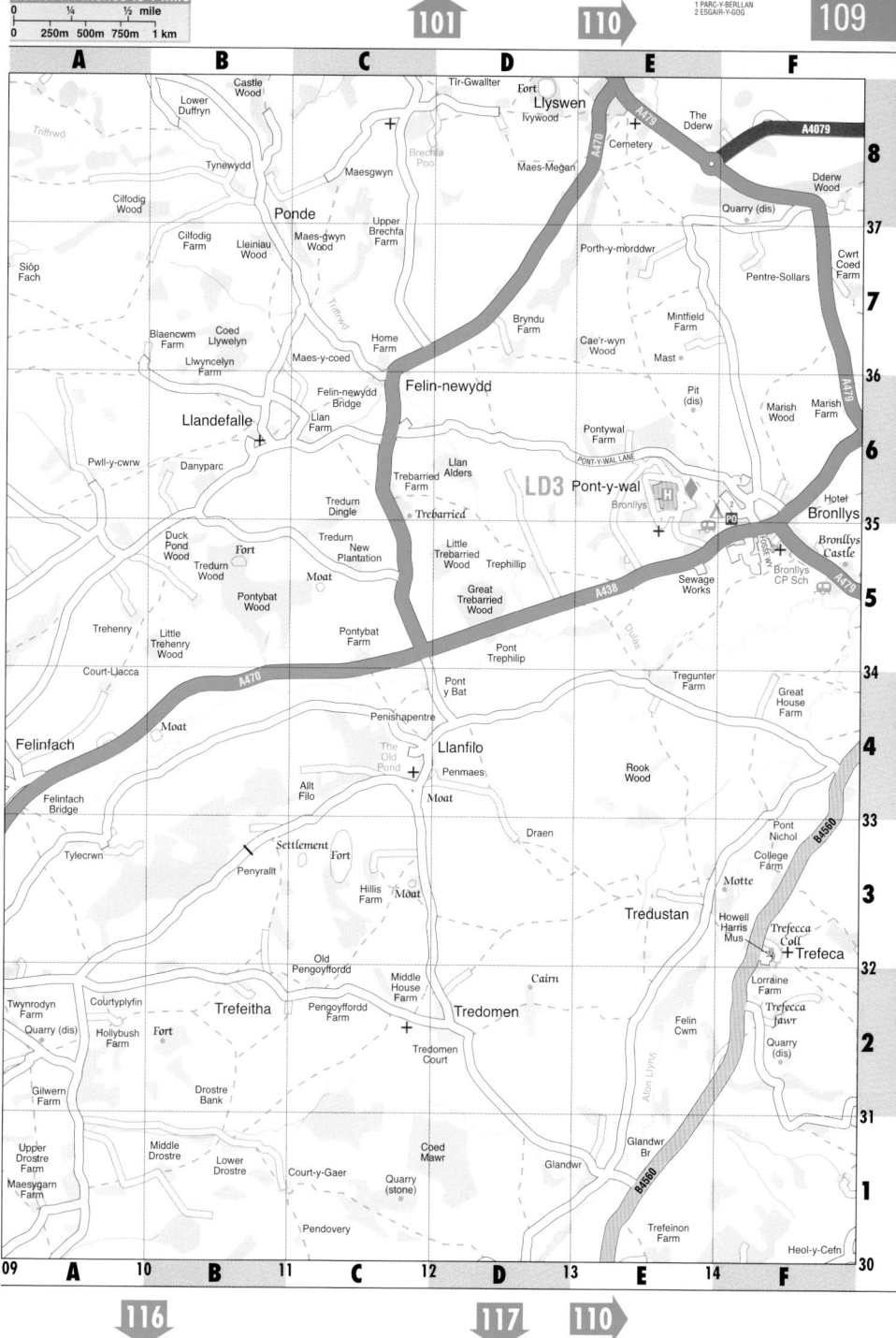

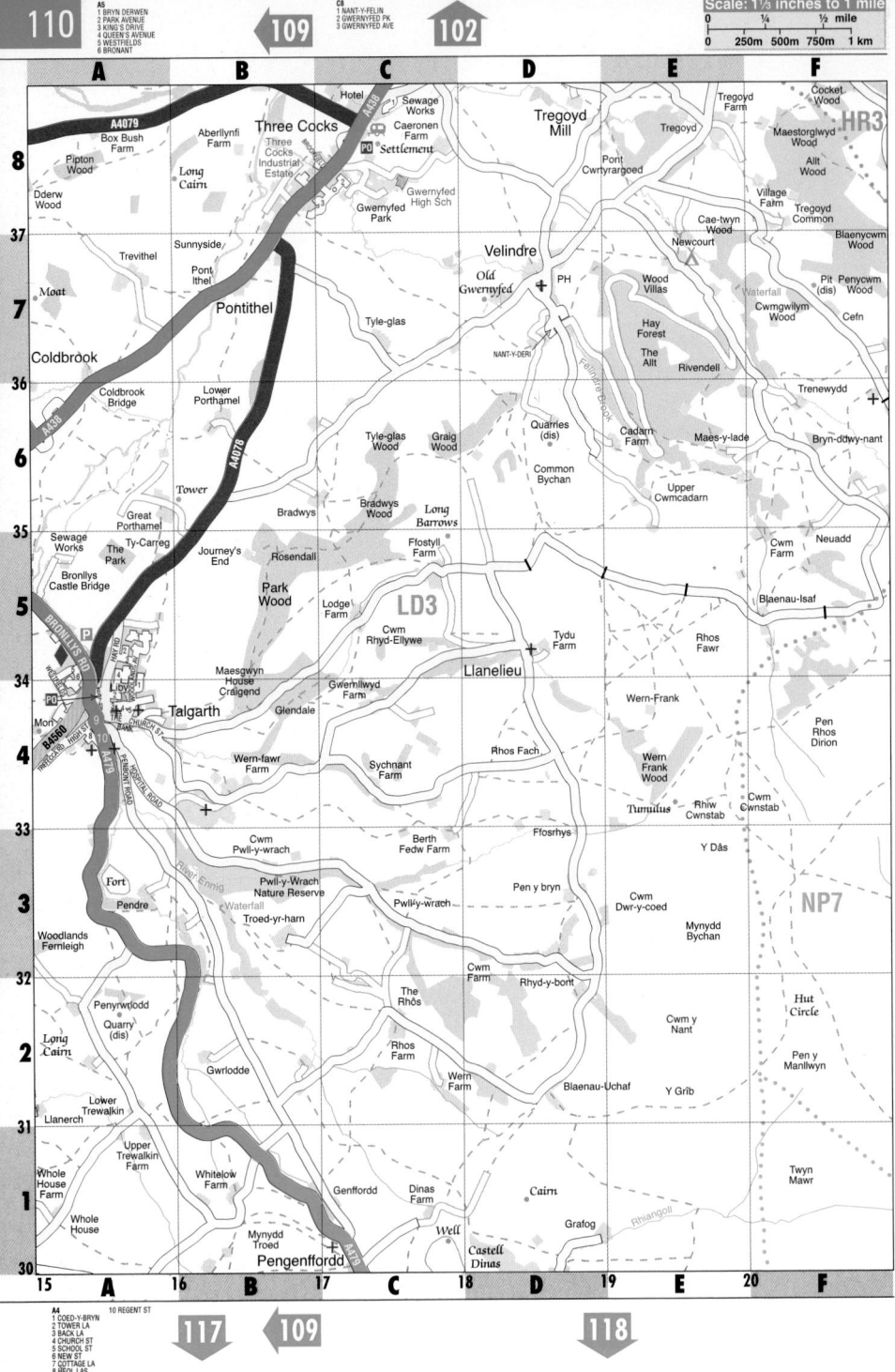

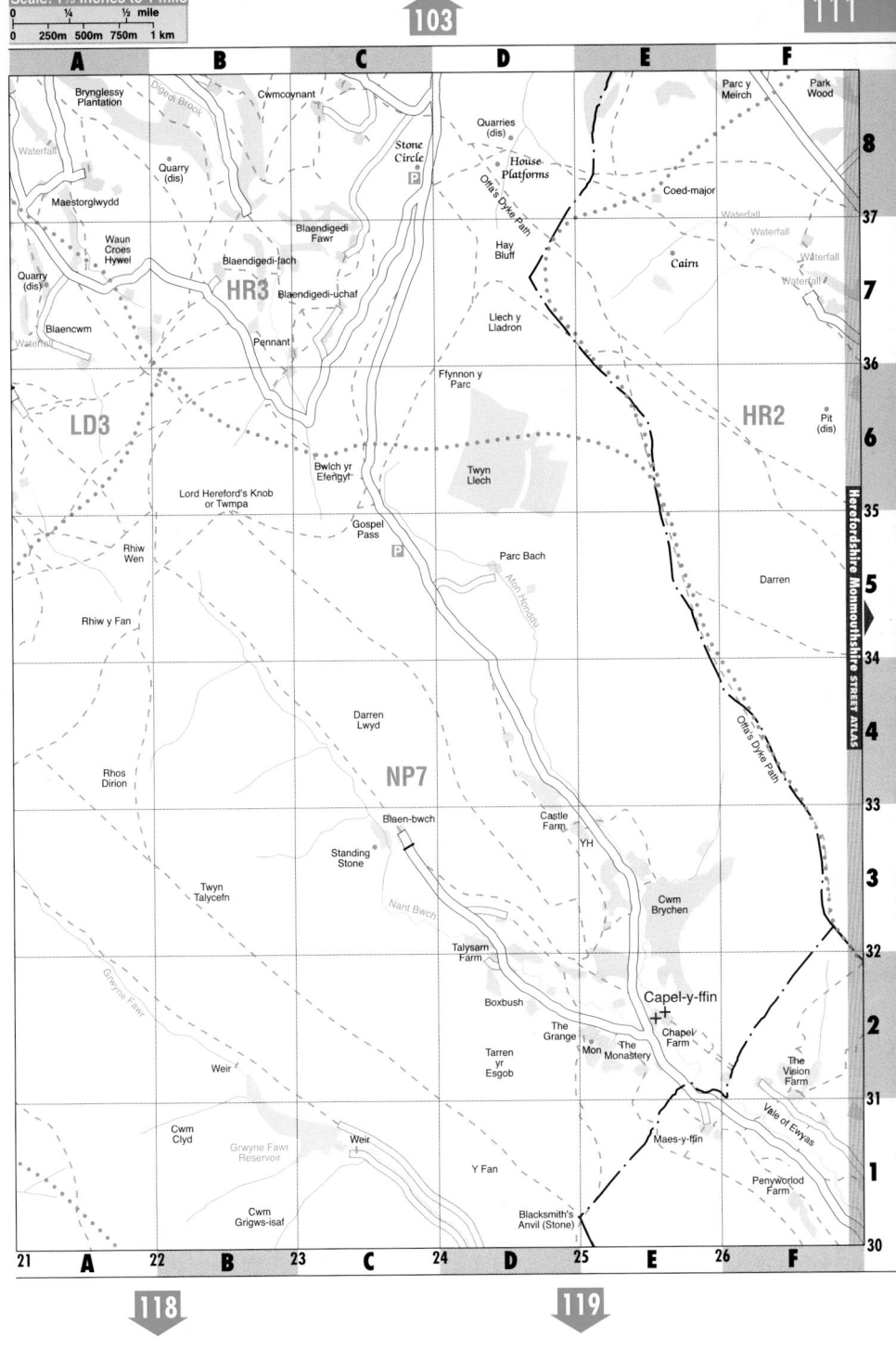

Scale: 1½ inches to 1 mile

0   ¼   ½ mile
0   250m 500m 750m 1 km

103

Herefordshire Monmouthshire STREET ATLAS

A B C D E F

8 37 7 36 6 35 5 34 4 33 3 32 2 31 1 30

Brynglessy Plantation
Digedi Brook
Cwmcoynant
Parc y Meirch
Park Wood

Waterfall
Quarries (dis)
Quarry (dis)
Stone Circle
P
House Platforms
Coed-major
Waterfall

Maestorglwydd
Blaendigedi Fawr
Hay Bluff
Waterfall
Waterfall

Waun Croes Hywel
Blaendigedi-fach
Offa's Dyke Path
Cairn
Waterfall

Quarry (dis)
HR3
Blaendigedi-uchaf
Llech y Lladron

Blaencwm
Pennant

Waterfall

Ffynnon y Parc

LD3
HR2
Pit (dis)

Bwlch yr Efengyl
Twyn Llech

Lord Hereford's Knob or Twmpa
Darren

Rhiw Wen
Gospel Pass
P
Parc Bach

Afon Honddu

Rhiw y Fan
Darren

Rhos Dirion
Darren Lwyd

NP7

Offa's Dyke Path

Twyn Talycefn
Blaen-bwch
Castle Farm
YH

Standing Stone

Nant Bwch
Cwm Brychen

Talysarn Farm

Boxbush
Capel-y-ffin

The Grange
Mon The Monastery
Chapel Farm

Weir
Tarren yr Esgob
The Vision Farm

Cwm Clyd
Grwyne Fawr Reservoir
Weir
Maes-y-ffin
Vale of Ewyas

Grwyne Fawr
Y Fan
Penyworld Farm

Cwm Grigws-isaf
Blacksmith's Anvil (Stone)

21 A 22 B 23 C 24 D 25 E 26 F

118

119

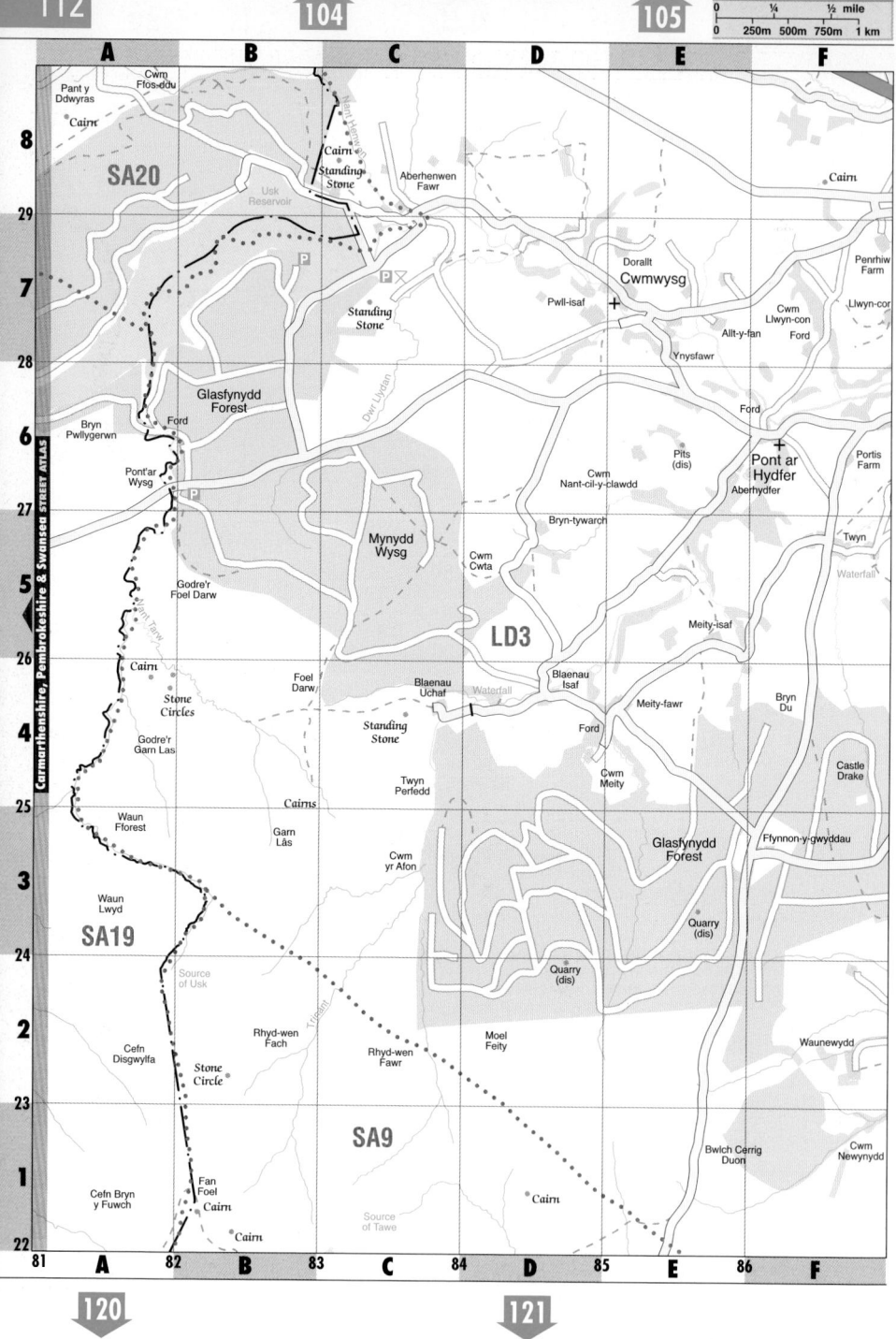

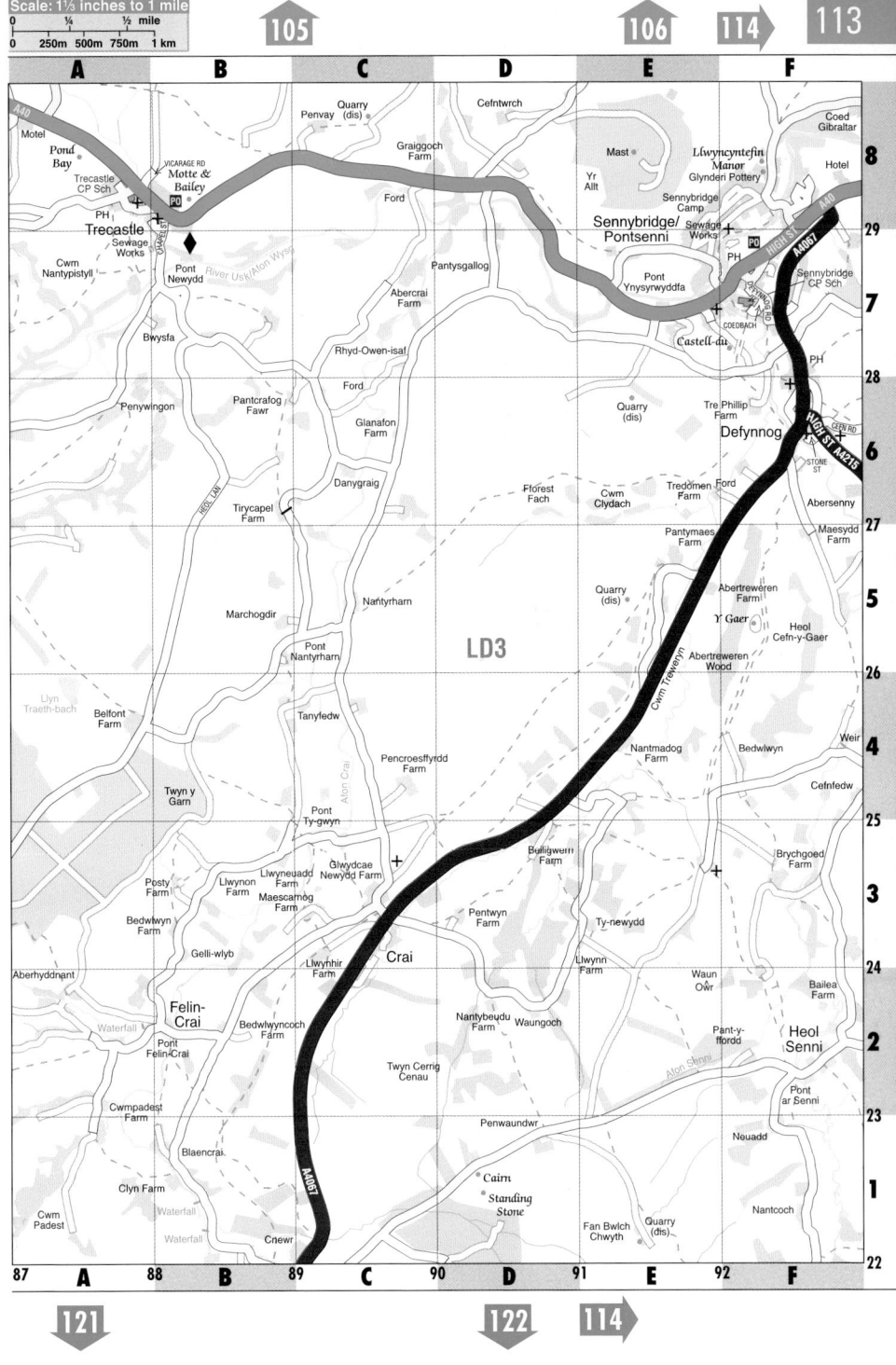

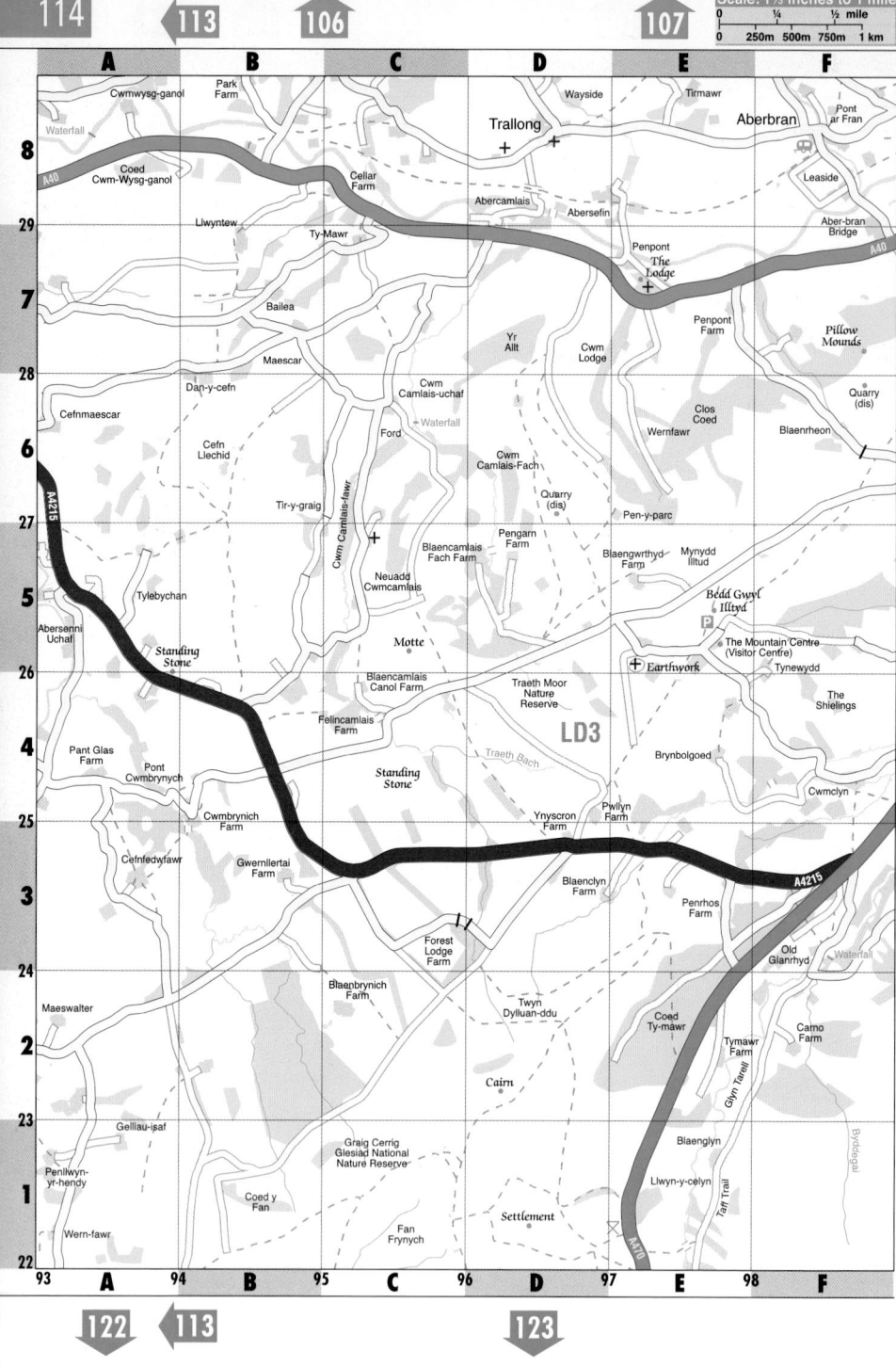

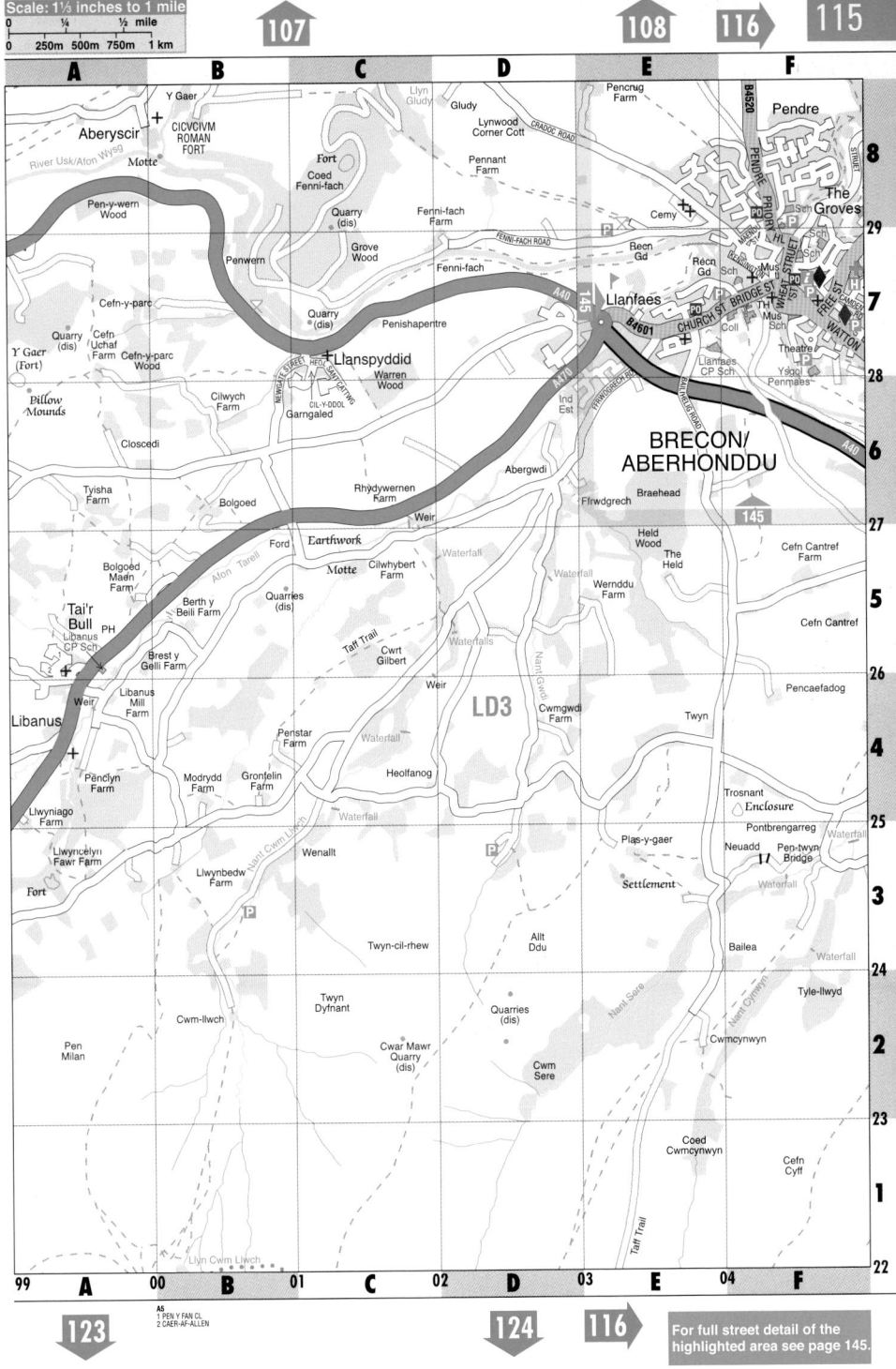

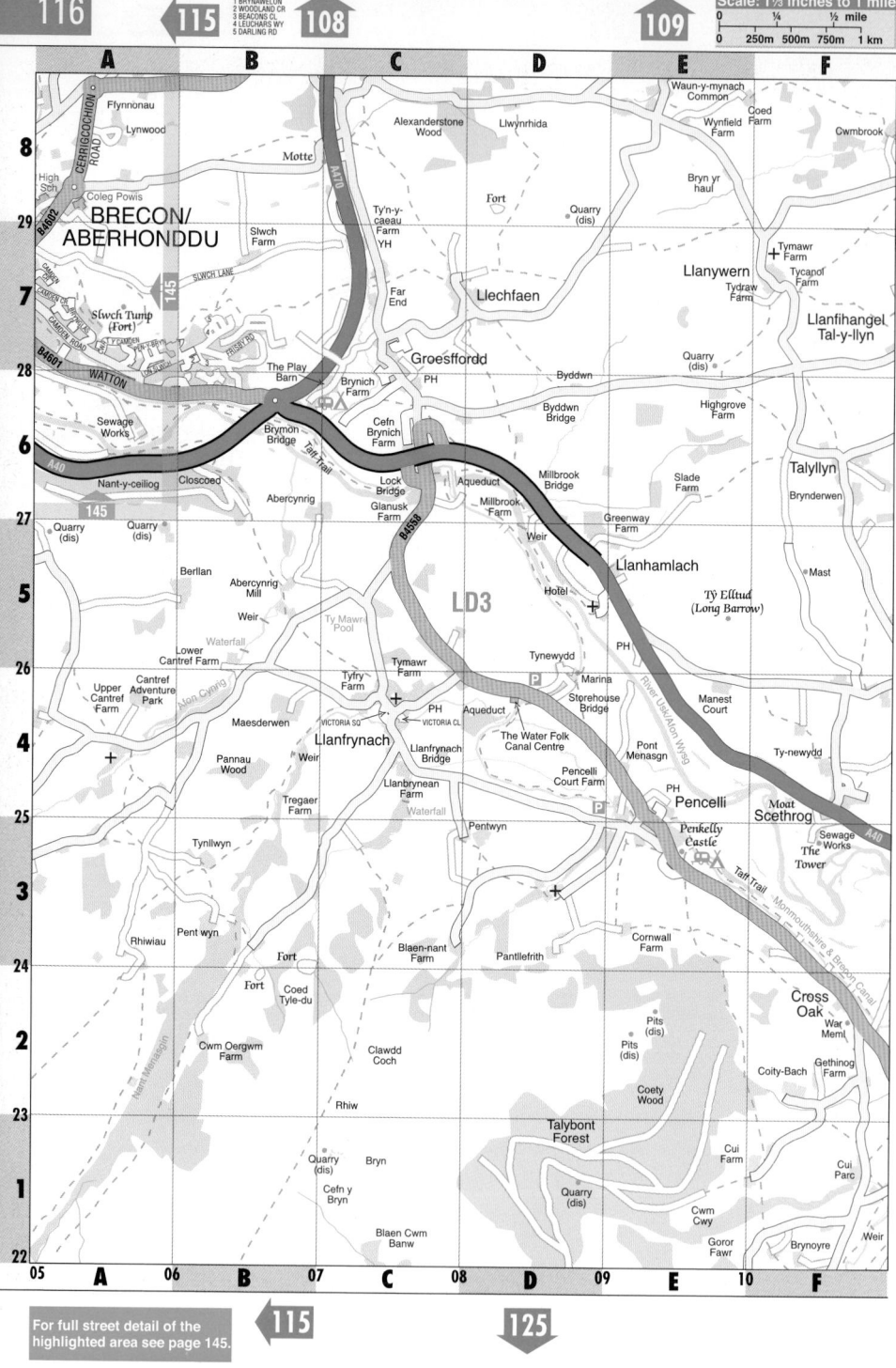

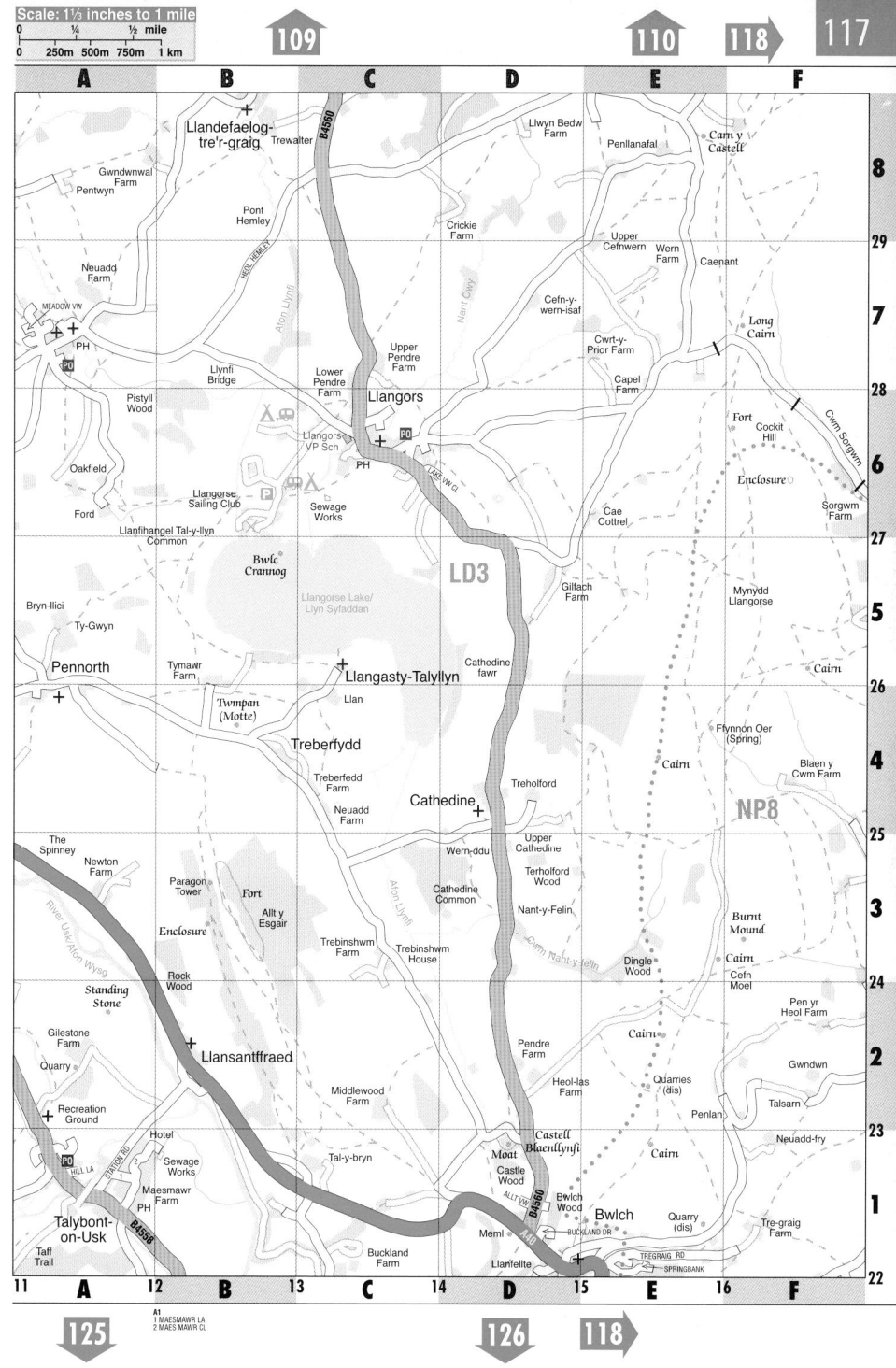

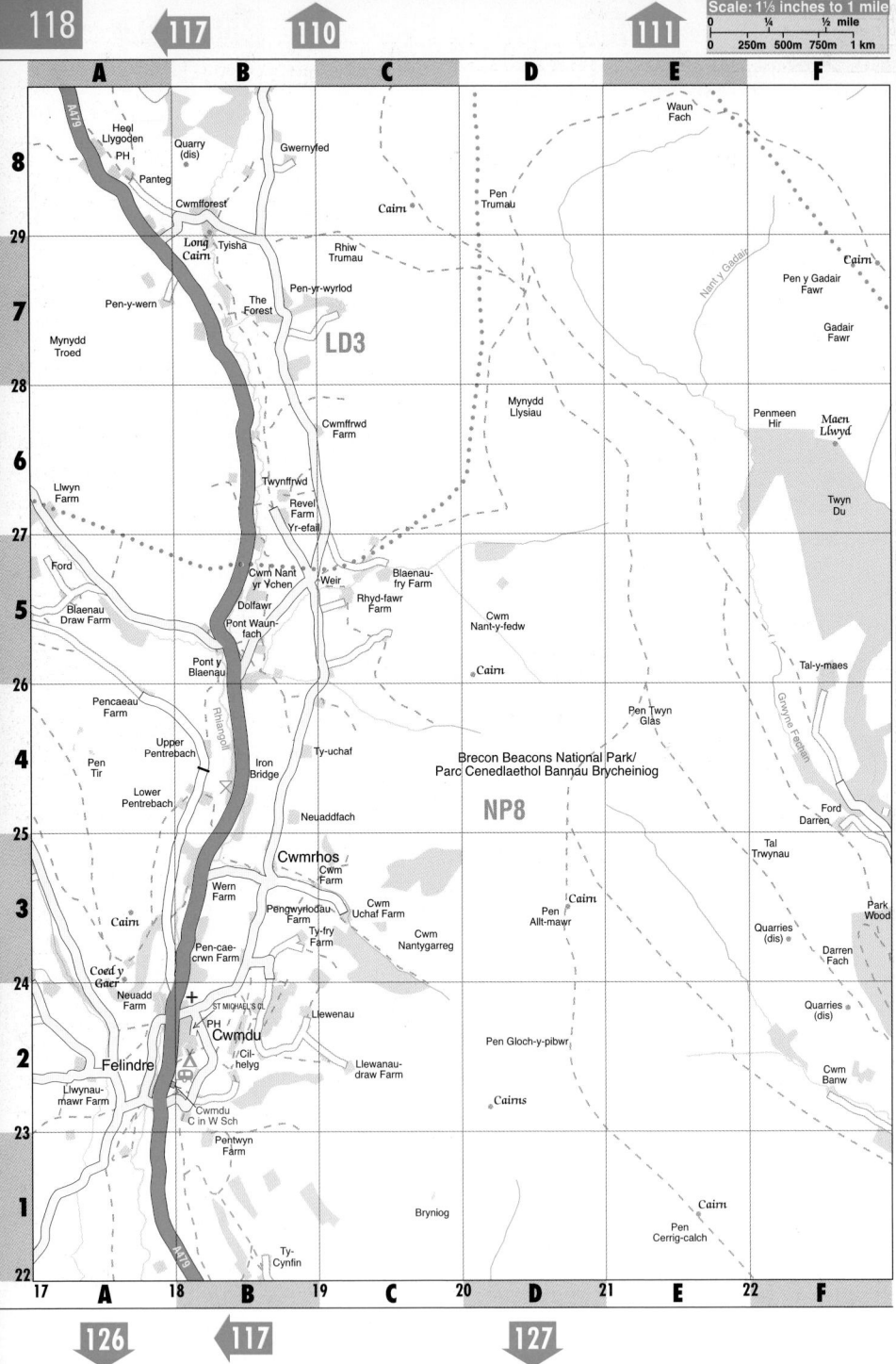

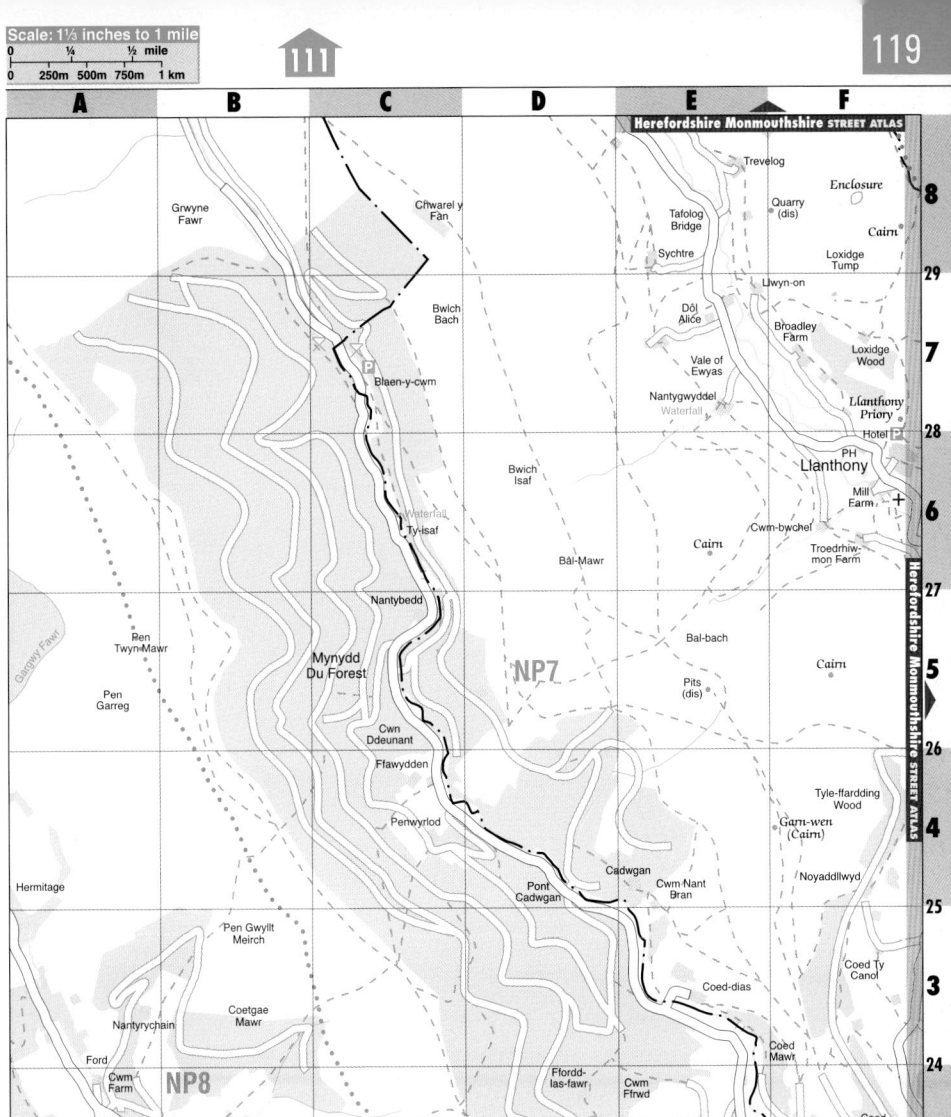

111

A   B   C   D   E   F

8   Grwyne
Fawr

Chwarel y
Fan

Trevelog

Enclosure

Quarry
(dis)

Cairn

Tafolog
Bridge

Sychtre

Loxidge
Tump

29   Bwlch
Bach

Llwyn-on

7   Blaen-y-cwm

Dôl
Alice

Vale of
Ewyas

Broadley
Farm

Loxidge
Wood

Nantygwyddel

Waterfall

Llanthony
Priory

Hotel

28   Bwlch
Isaf

PH

Llanthony

6   Waterfall

Ty-Isaf

Bàl-Mawr

Cairn

Cwm-bwchel

Mill
Farm

Troedrhiw-
mon Farm

27   Nantybedd

5   Pen
Twyn-Mawr

Mynydd
Du Forest

NP7

Bal-bach

Pits
(dis)

Cairn

Pen
Garreg

Cwn
Ddeunant

26   Ffawydden

Penwyrlod

Tyle-ffardding
Wood

4   Garn-wen
(Cairn)

Noyaddllwyd

Cadwgan

Cwm-Nant
Bran

25   Hermitage

Pont
Cadwgan

Coed Ty
Canol

3   Pen Gwyllt
Meirch

Coed-dias

Coetgae
Mawr

Coed
Mawr

24   Nantyrychain

Ford

Cwm
Farm

NP8

Fordd-
las-fawr

Cwm
Ffrwd

Upper
House

Coed
Robin

2   Blaenau

Llwyn-y-brain

Llanthony
Wood

Pentwyn

Gelli
Boeth

Cairn

Disgwylfa

Coed
Farm

23   Waterfall   Neuadd-
fawr

Bont

Partrishow

1   Penhoelmeirch   Milaid

Cwm Milaid

Crug
Mawr

Blaen-yr-
henbant

Ffynnon
Tshow

Ty'n-n-
llwyn

Ty-coch

22

23   A   24   B   25   C   26   D   27   E   28   F

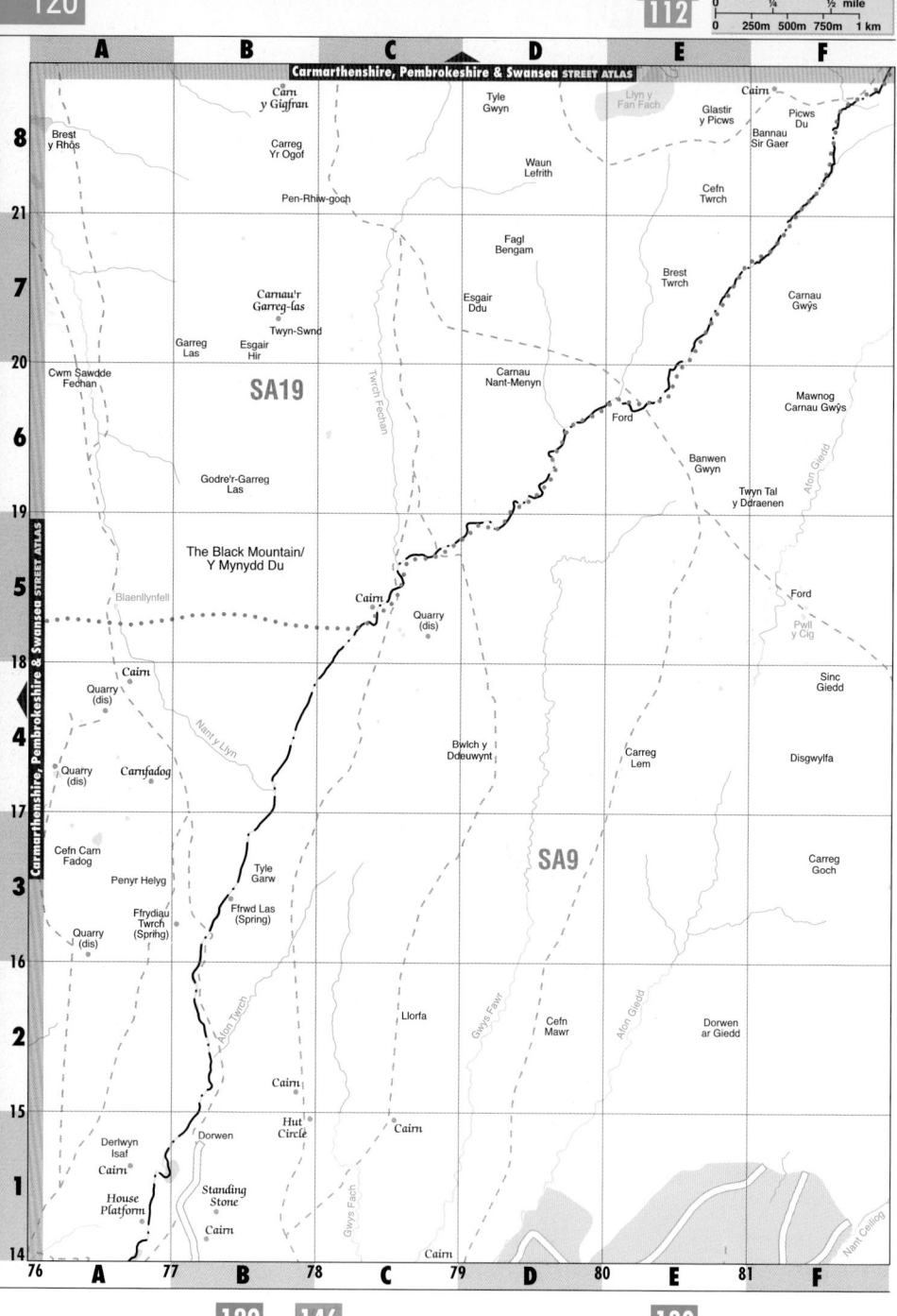

Carmarthenshire, Pembrokeshire & Swansea STREET ATLAS

Carmarthenshire, Pembrokeshire & Swansea STREET ATLAS

Brest
y Rhôs

Carn
y Gigfran

Tyle
Gwyn

Llyn y
Fan Fach

Glastir
y Picws

Cairn

Picws
Du

Carreg
Yr Ogof

Waun
Lefrith

Bannau
Sir Gaer

Pen-Rhiw-goch

Cefn
Twrch

Fagl
Bengam

Brest
Twrch

Carnau
Gwŷs

Carnau'r
Garreg-las

Esgair
Ddu

Garreg
Las

Esgair
Hir

Twyn-Swnd

SA19

Twrch Fechan

Carnau
Nant-Menyn

Mawnog
Carnau Gwŷs

Cwm Sawdde
Fechan

Ford

Godre'r-Garreg
Las

Banwen
Gwyn

Twyn Tal
y Ddraenen

Afon Giedd

The Black Mountain/
Y Mynydd Du

Cairn

Ford

Blaenllynfell

Cairn

Quarry
(dis)

Pwll
y Cig

Cairn

Nant y Llyn

Sinc
Giedd

Quarry
(dis)

Quarry
(dis)

Carnfadog

Bwlch y
Ddeuwynt

Carreg
Lem

Disgwylfa

Cefn Carn
Fadog

SA9

Penyr Helyg

Carreg
Goch

Tyle
Garw

Ffrydiau
Twrch
(Spring)

Ffrwd Las
(Spring)

Quarry
(dis)

Afon Twrch

Llorfa

Gwŷs Fawr

Cefn
Mawr

Afon Giedd

Dorwen
ar Giedd

Cairn

Derlwyn
Isaf

Dorwen

Hut
Circle

Cairn

Gwŷs Fach

Cairn

House
Platform

Standing
Stone

Nant Ceiliog

Cairn

Cairn

Cairn

129   146   130

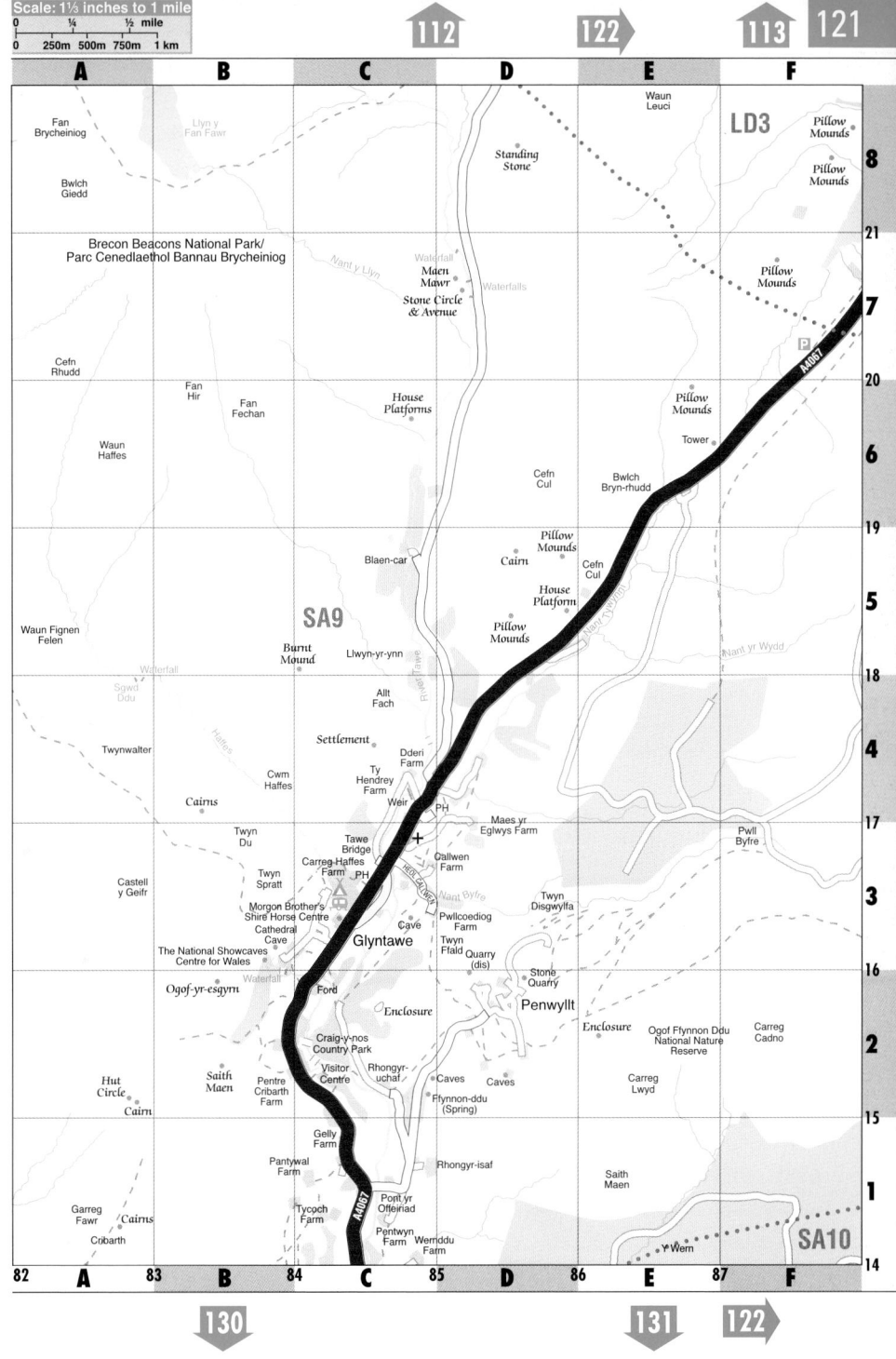

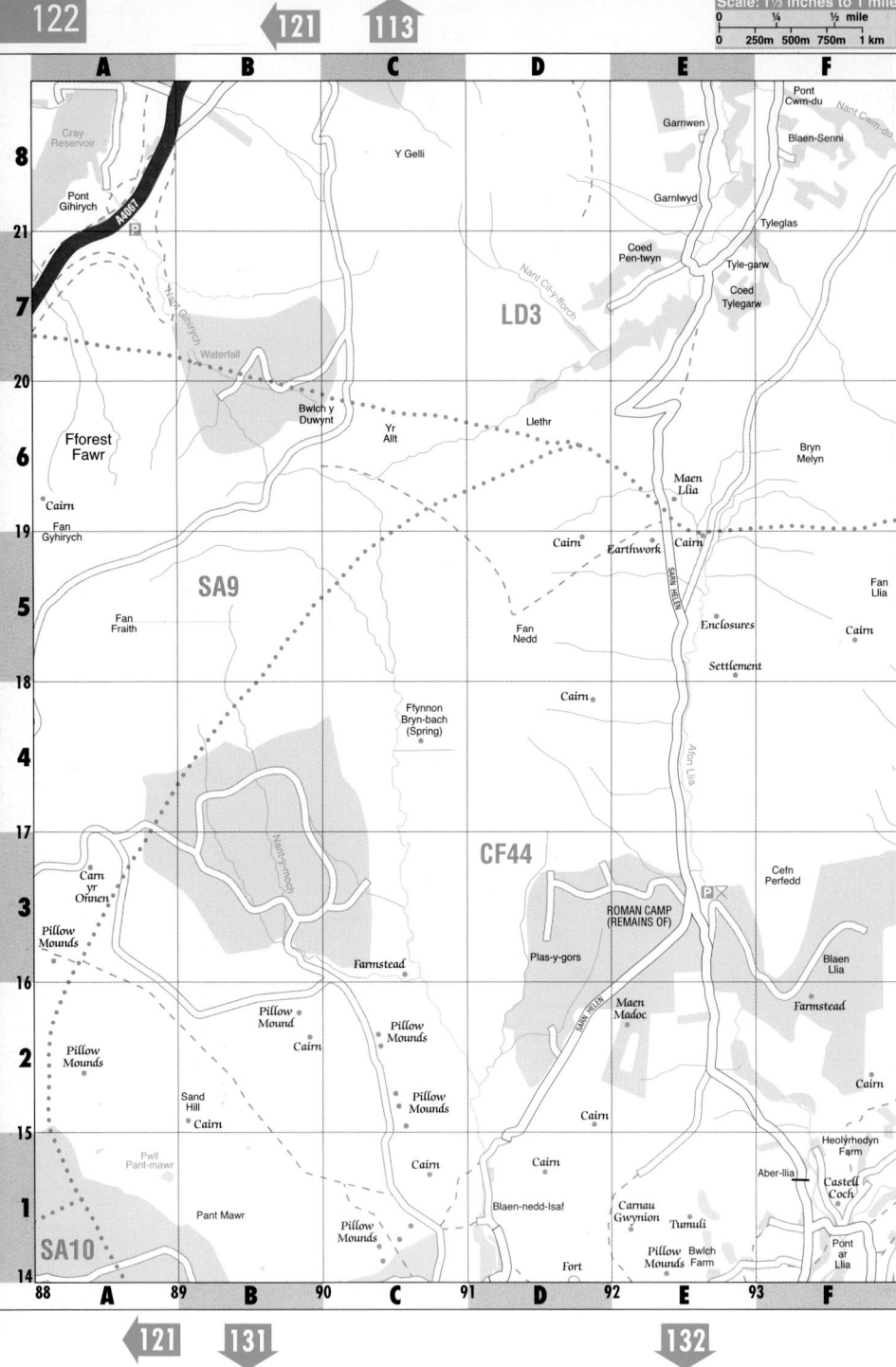

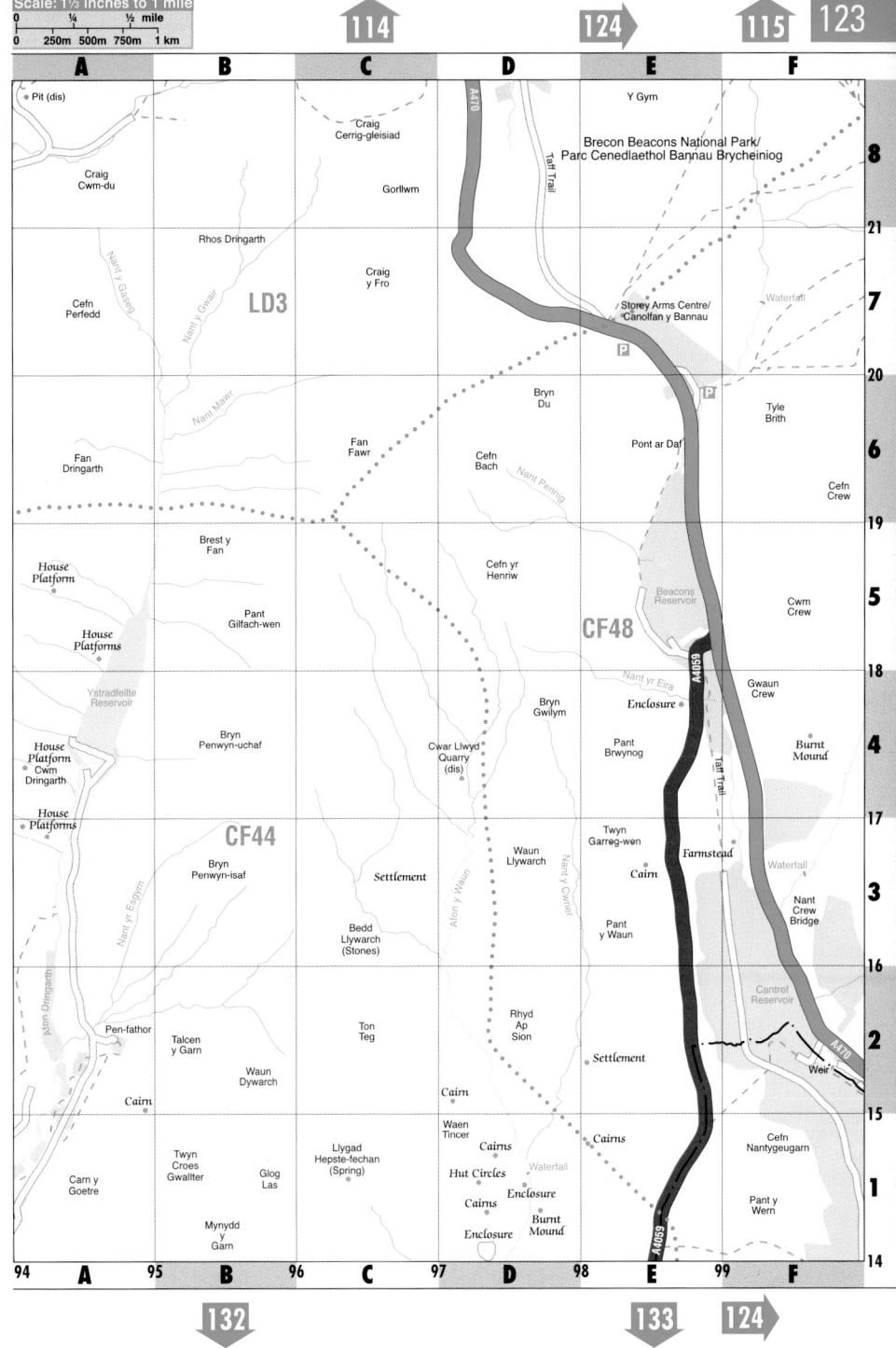

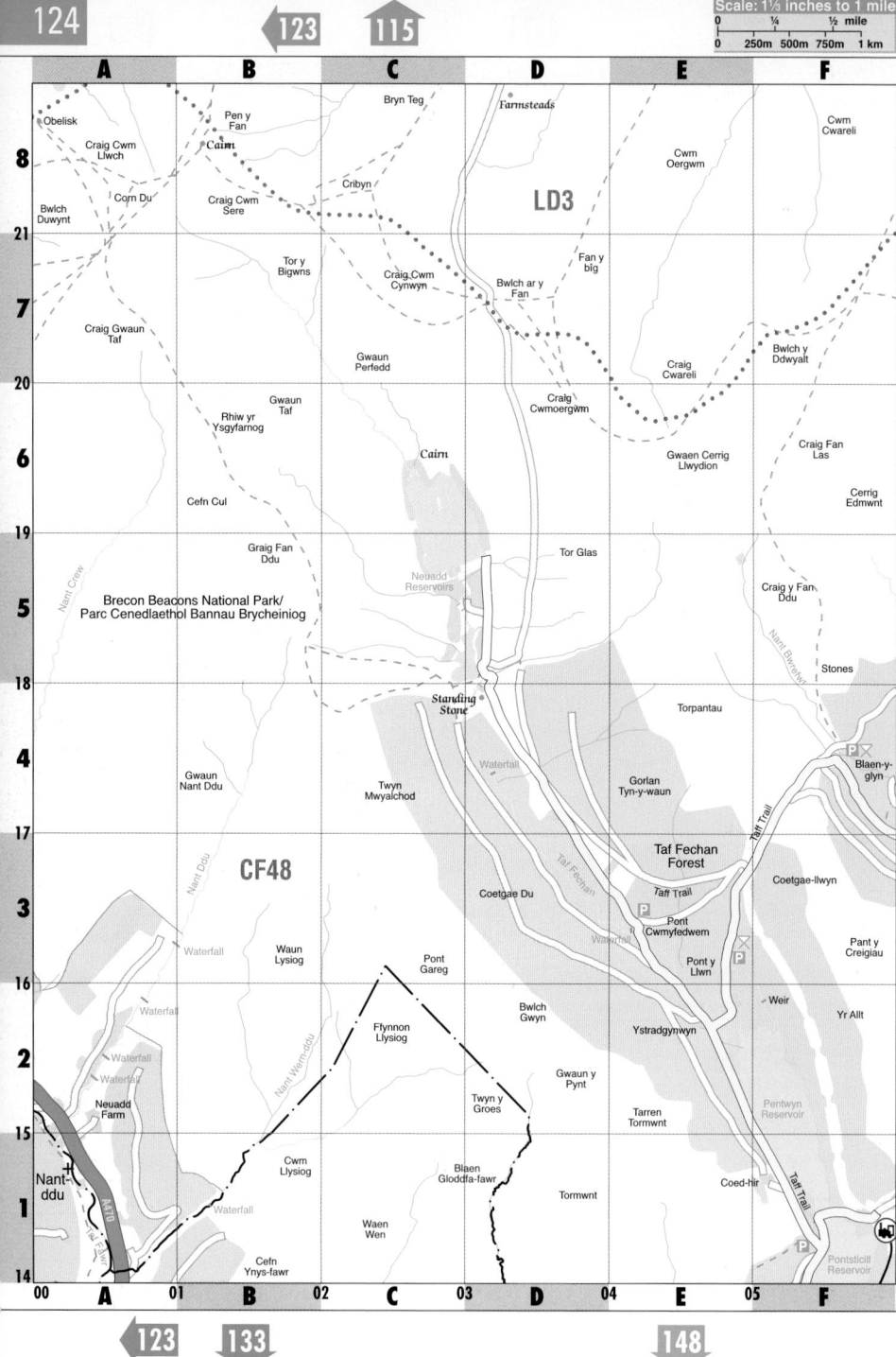

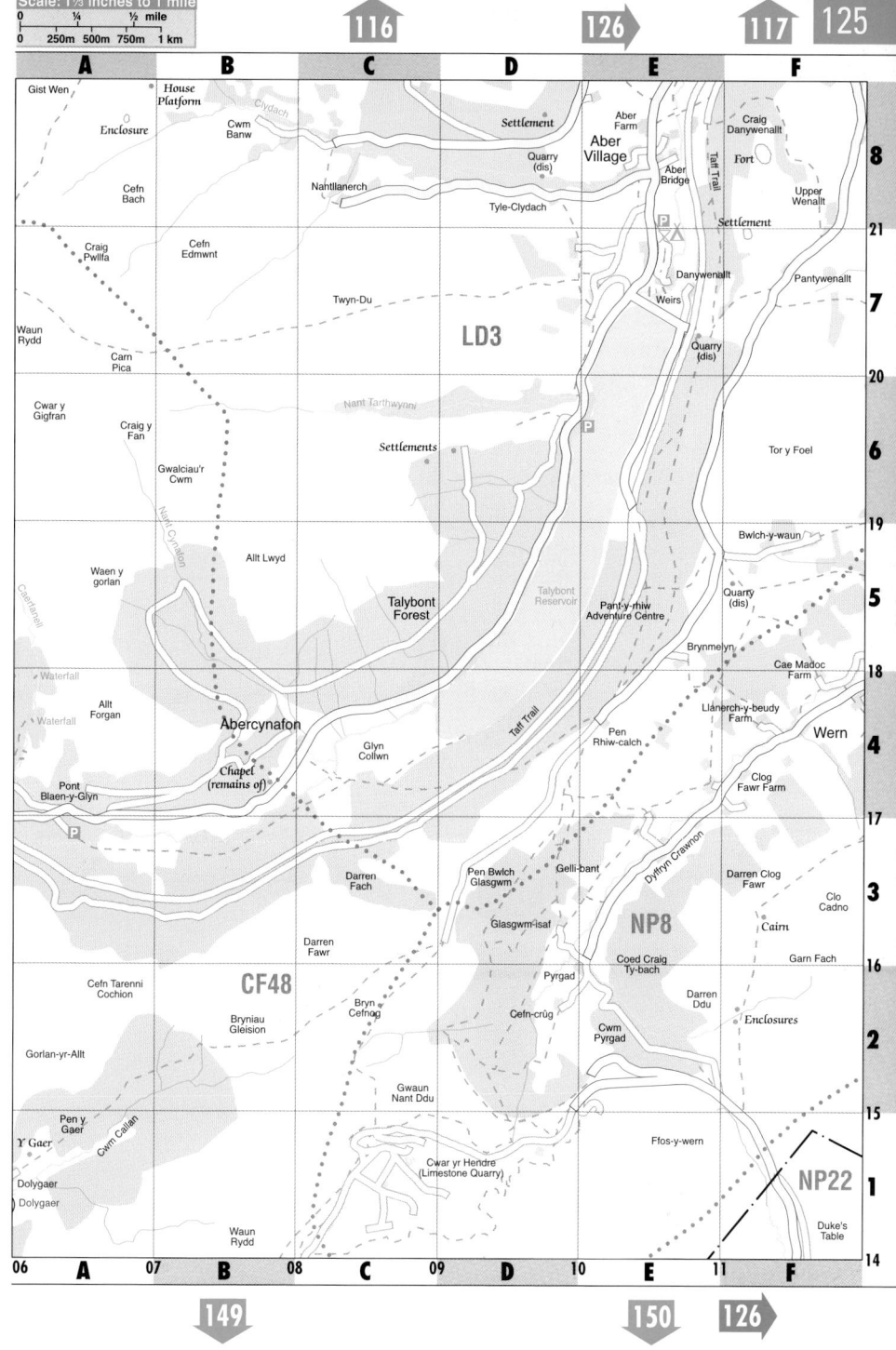

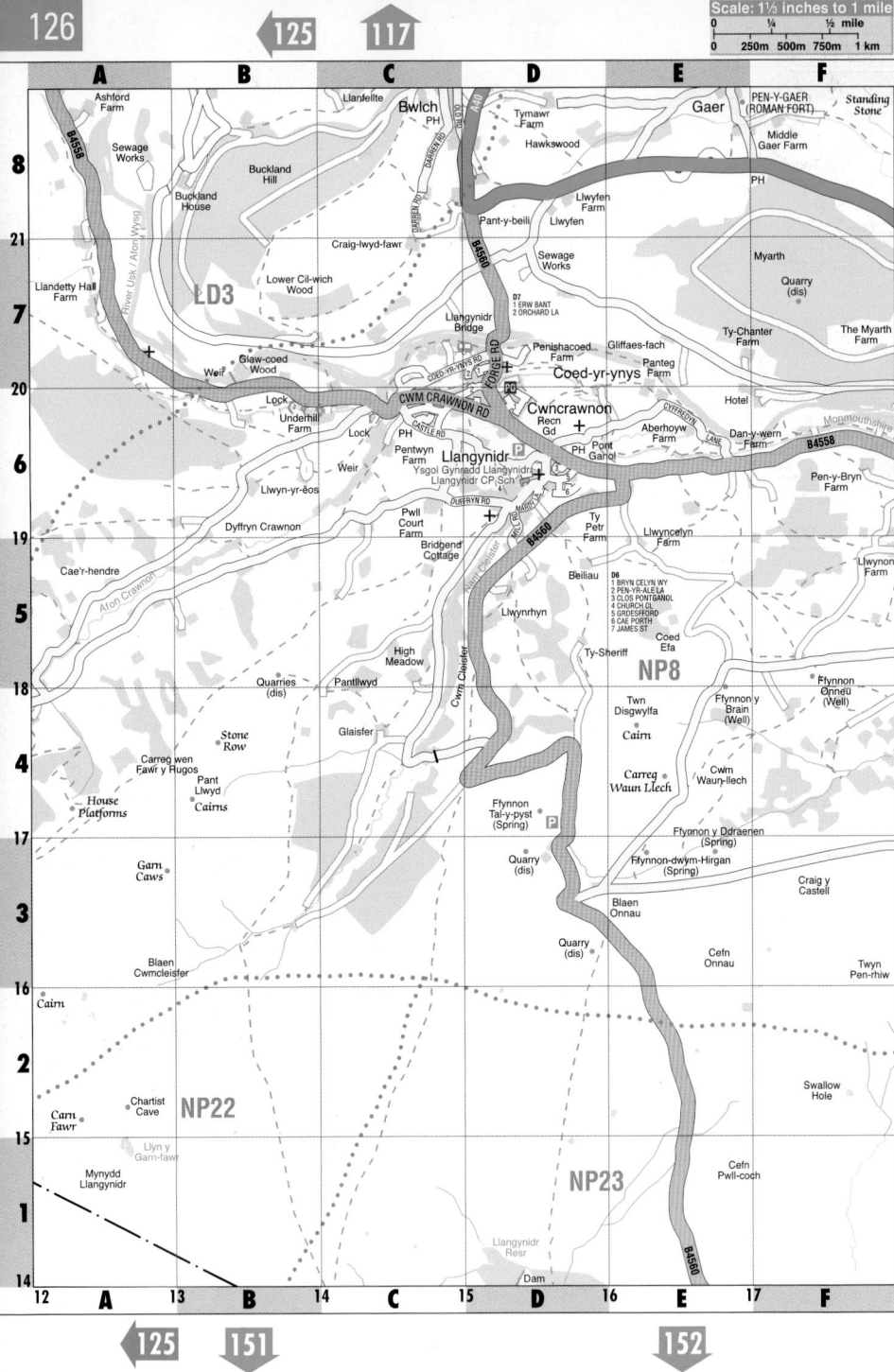

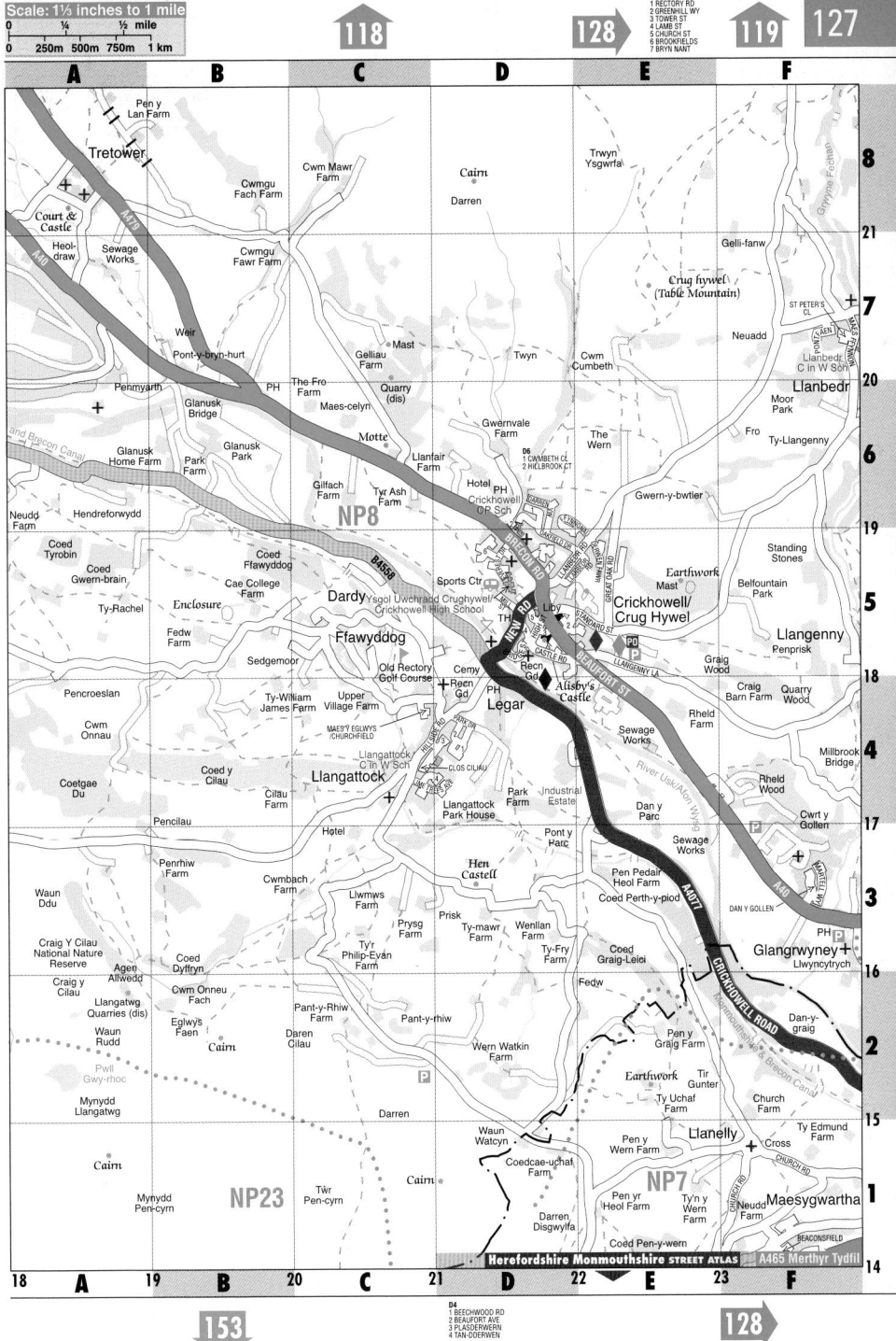

D5
1 RECTORY RD
2 GREENHILL WY
3 TOWER ST
4 LAMB ST
5 CHURCH ST
6 BROOKFIELDS
7 BRYN NANT

Pen y Lan Farm
Tretower
Court & Castle
Heol-draw
Sewage Works
Cwmgu Fach Farm
Cwm Mawr Farm
Cairn
Darren
Trwyn Ysgwrfai
Gelli-fanw
Crug hywel (Table Mountain)
ST PETER'S CL
Neuadd
Penmyarth
Weir
Pont-y-bryn-hurt
Cwmgu Fawr Farm
The Fro Farm
Gelliau Farm
Mast
Twyn
Cwm Cumbeth
Ty-Llangenny
Llanbedr C in W Sch
Llanbedr
Moor Park
Fro
PH
Maes-celyn
Quarry (dis)
Llanfair Farm
Gwernvale Farm

D6
1 CIMBETH CL
2 HILLBROOK CT

Glanusk Bridge
Glanusk Park
Motte
Hotel
Crickhowell CP Sch
PH
Gwernvale Farm
The Wern
Gwern-y-bwtler
Standing Stones
Neudd Farm
Glanusk Home Farm
Park Farm
Gilfach Farm
Tyr Ash Farm
NP8
Coed Tyrobin
Coed Gwern-brain
Cae College Farm
Coed Ffawyddog
Dardy
Ysgol Uwchradd Crughywel
Crickhowell High School
Sports Ctr
Libry
Crickhowell/Crug Hywel
Earthwork
Mast
Belfountain Park
Llangenny
Penprisk
Ty-Rachel
Fedw Farm
Enclosure
Ffawyddog
THI
Graig Wood
Hendreforwydd
Sedgemoor
Old Rectory Golf Course
Upper Village Farm
Cemy
Recn Gd
Legar
Alisby's Castle
Rheld Farm
Craig Barn Farm
Quarry Wood
Pencroeslan
Ty-William James Farm
PH
Recn Gd
Sewage Works
Cwm Onnau
MAES'Y EGLWYS /CHURCHFIELD
CLOS CILAU
Llangattock C in W Sch
River Usk/Afon Wysg
Rheld Wood
Millbrook Bridge
Coetgae Du
Coed y Cilau
Llangattock
Cilau Farm
Llangattock Park House
Park Farm
Industrial Estate
Dan y Parc
Cwrt y Gollen
Pencilau
Hotel
Hen Castell
Pont y Parc
Sewage Works
Waun Ddu
Penrhiw Farm
Cwmbach Farm
Llwmws Farm
Prisk
Pen Pedair Heol Farm
Coed Perth-y-piod
Dan y Gollen
PH
Craig Y Cilau National Nature Reserve
Tyr Philip-Evan Farm
Prysg Farm
Ty-mawr Farm
Wenllan Farm
Ty-Fry Farm
Coed Graig-Leici
Glangrwyney
Craig y Cilau Quarries (dis)
Agen Allwedd
Coed Dyffryn
Cwm Onneu Fach
Fedw
Dan-y-graig
Llwyncytrych
Waun Rudd
Llangattwg
Eglwys Faen
Cairn
Pant-y-Rhiw Farm
Daren Cilau
Pant-y-rhiw
Wern Watkin Farm
Pen y Graig Farm
CRICKHOWELL ROAD
Mynydd Llangattwg
Pwll Gwy-rhoc
Earthwork
Ty Gunter
Tir
Church Farm
Ty Edmund Farm
Cairn
Darren
P
Waun Watcyn
Pen y Wern Farm
Ty Uchaf Farm
Llanelly
Cross
CHURCH RD
Cairn
Mynydd Pen-cyrn
Twr Pen-cyrn
NP23
Coedcae-uchaf Farm
Pen yr Heol Farm
Darren Disgwylfa
Pen y Heol Farm
Coed Pen-y-wern
NP7
Ty'n y Wern Farm
Neudd Farm
Maesygwartha
BEACONSFIELD

D4
1 BEECHWOOD RD
2 BEAUFORT AVE
3 PLASDERWERN
4 TAN-DDERWEN

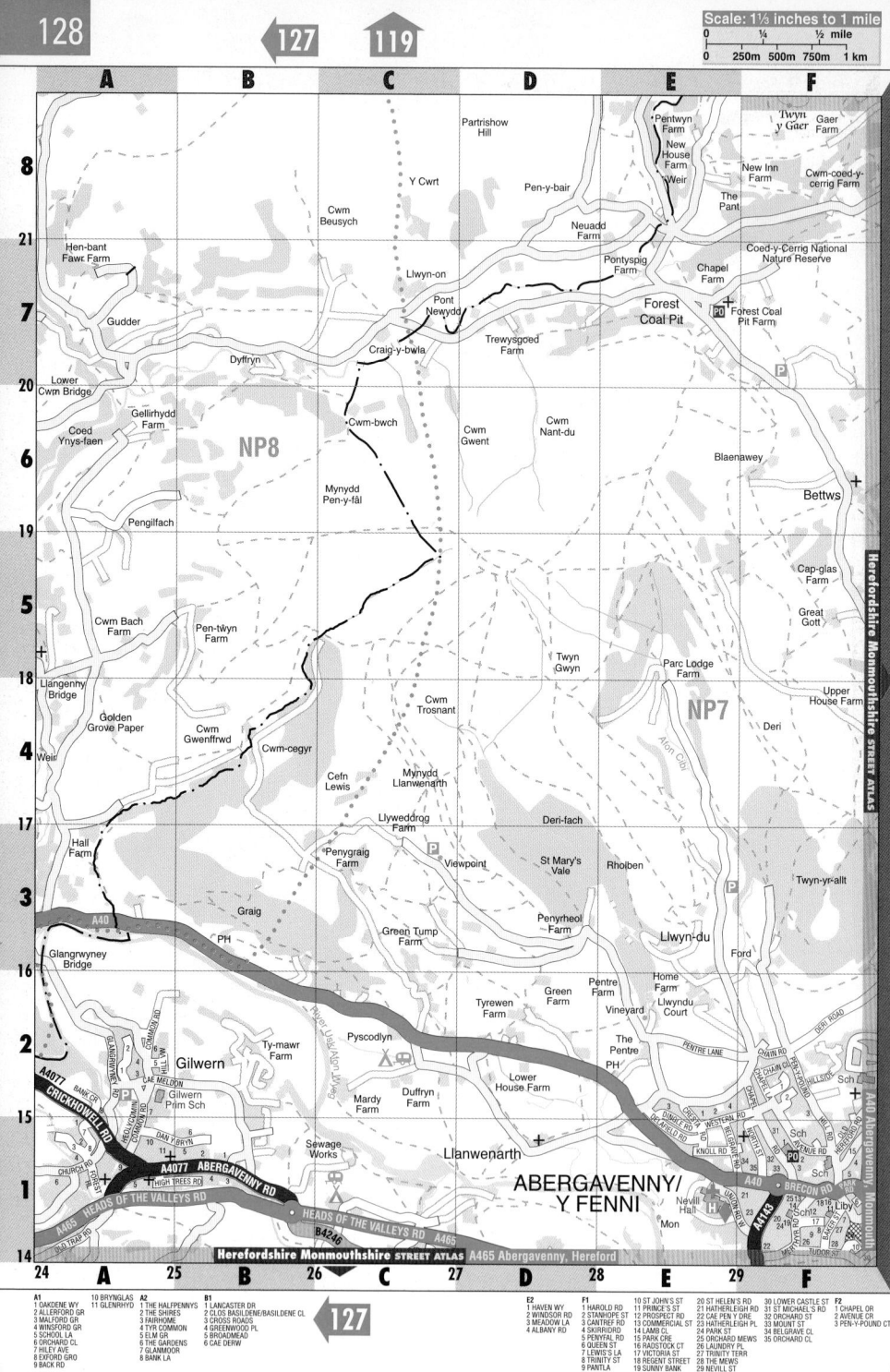

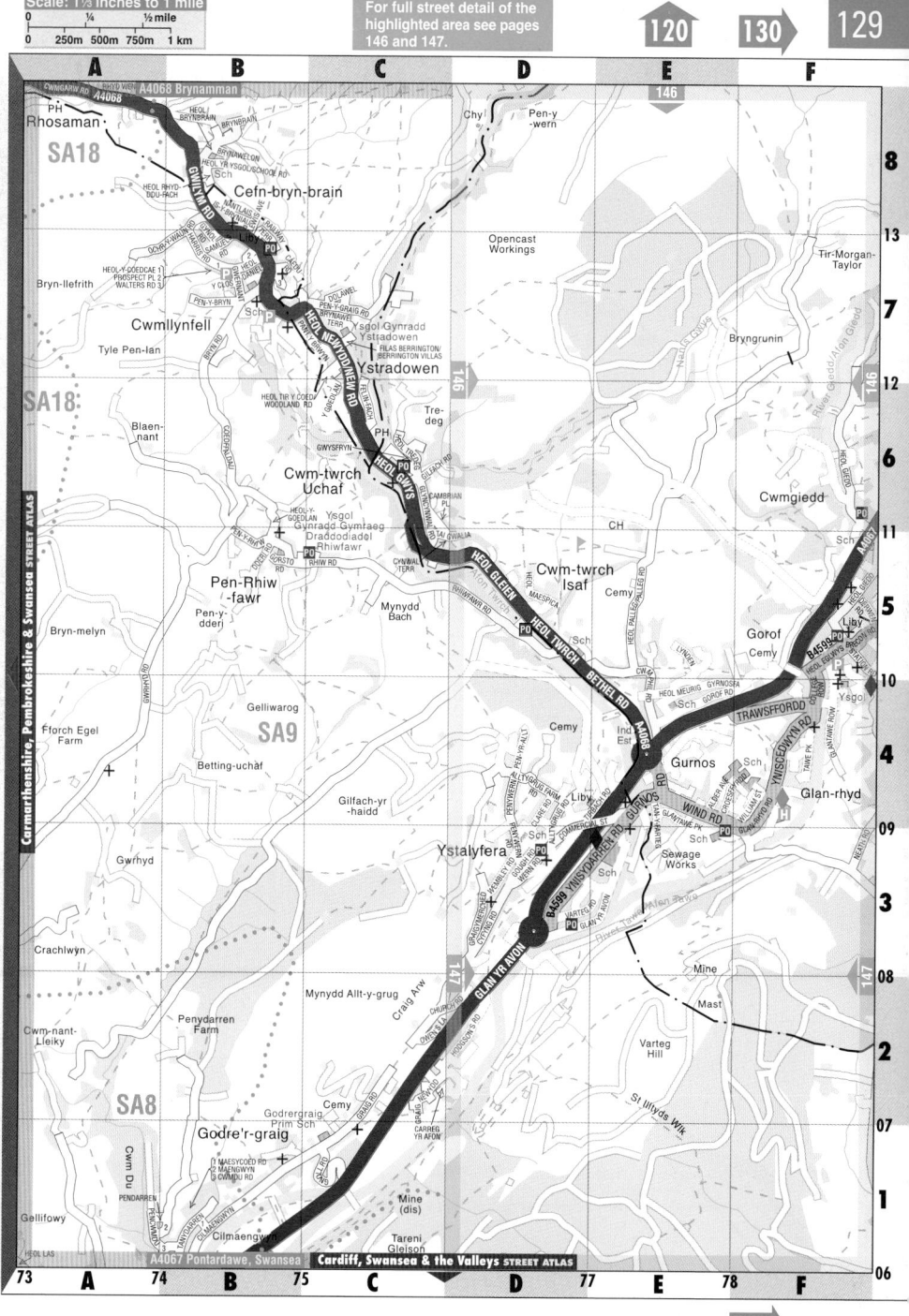

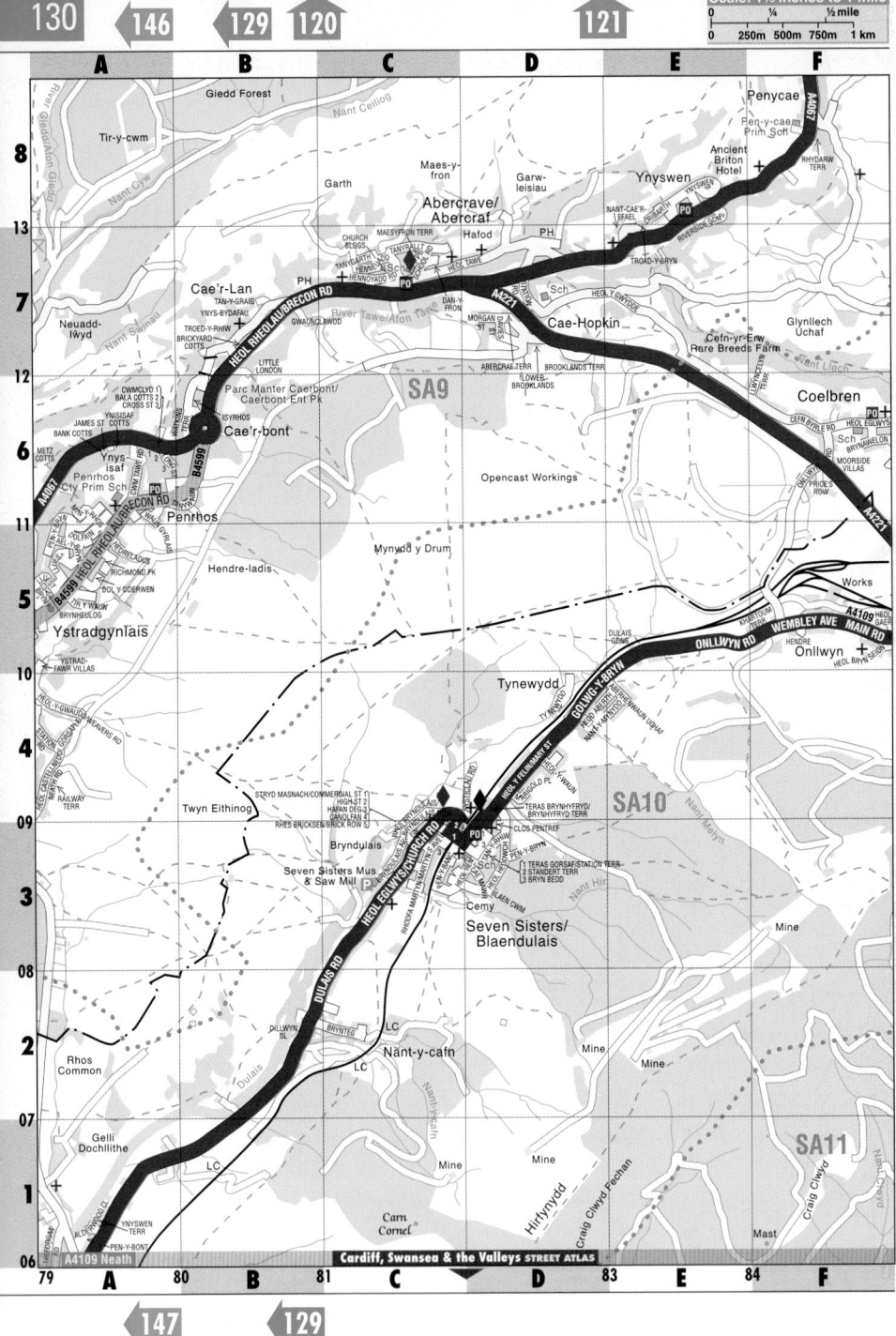

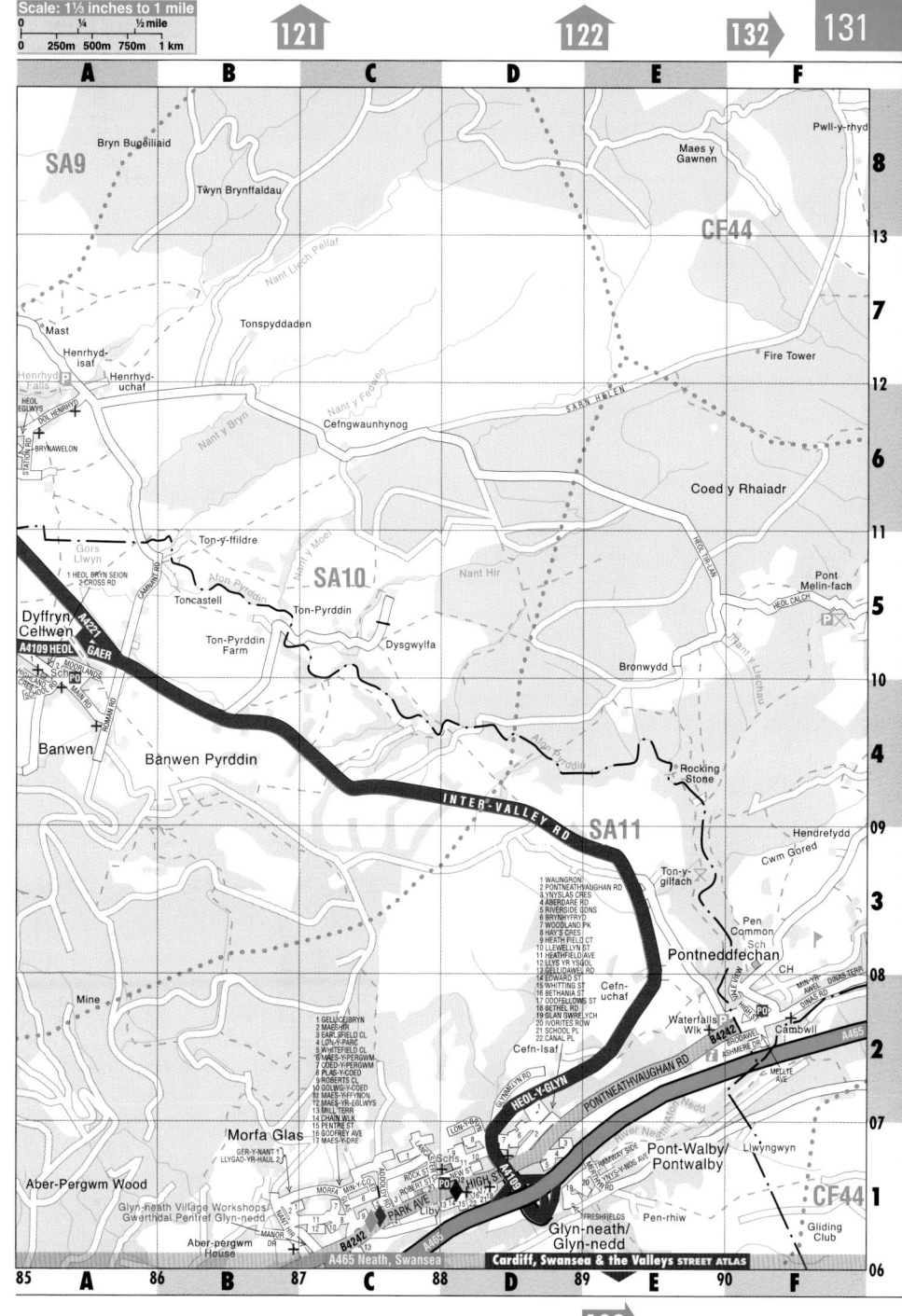

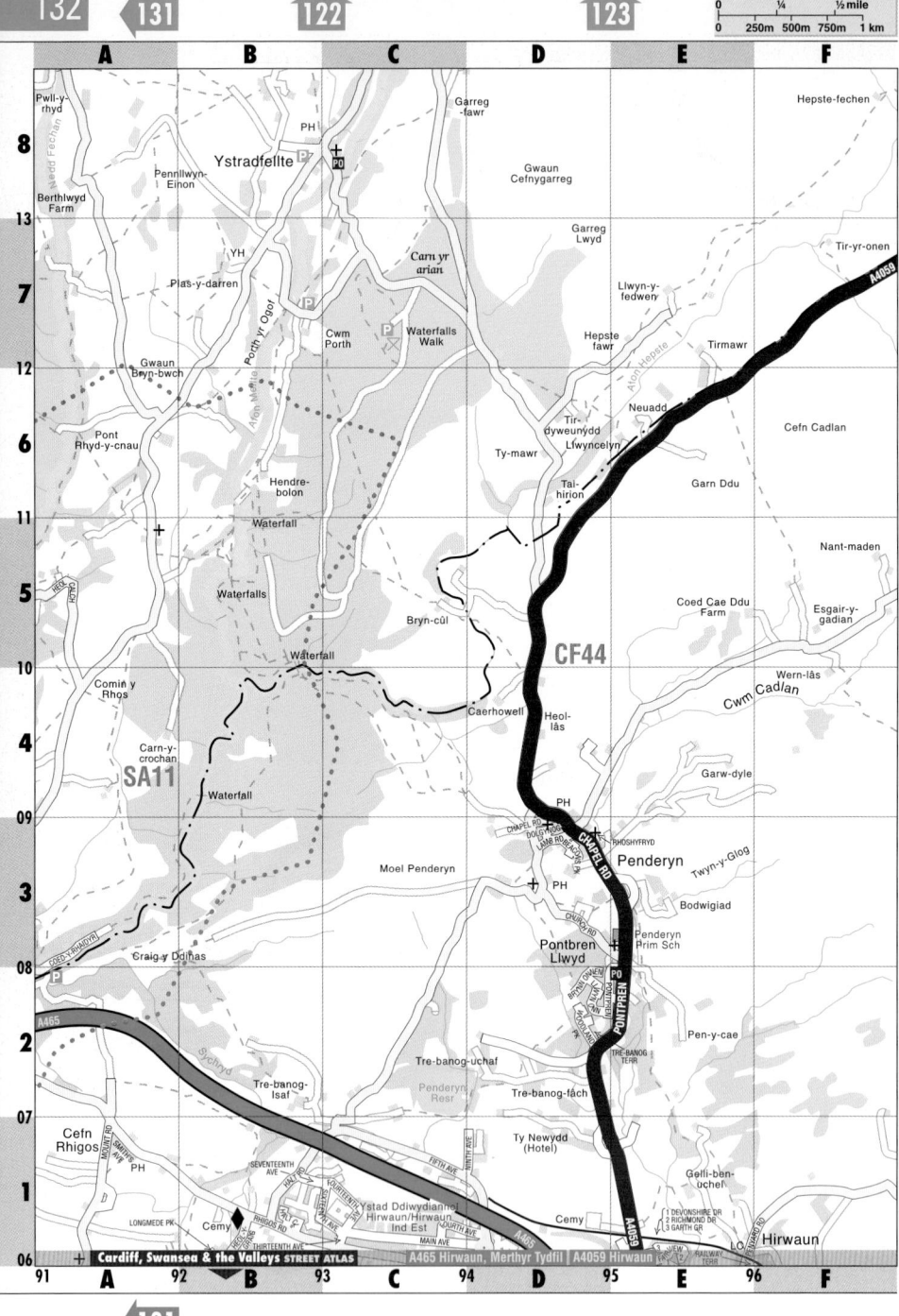

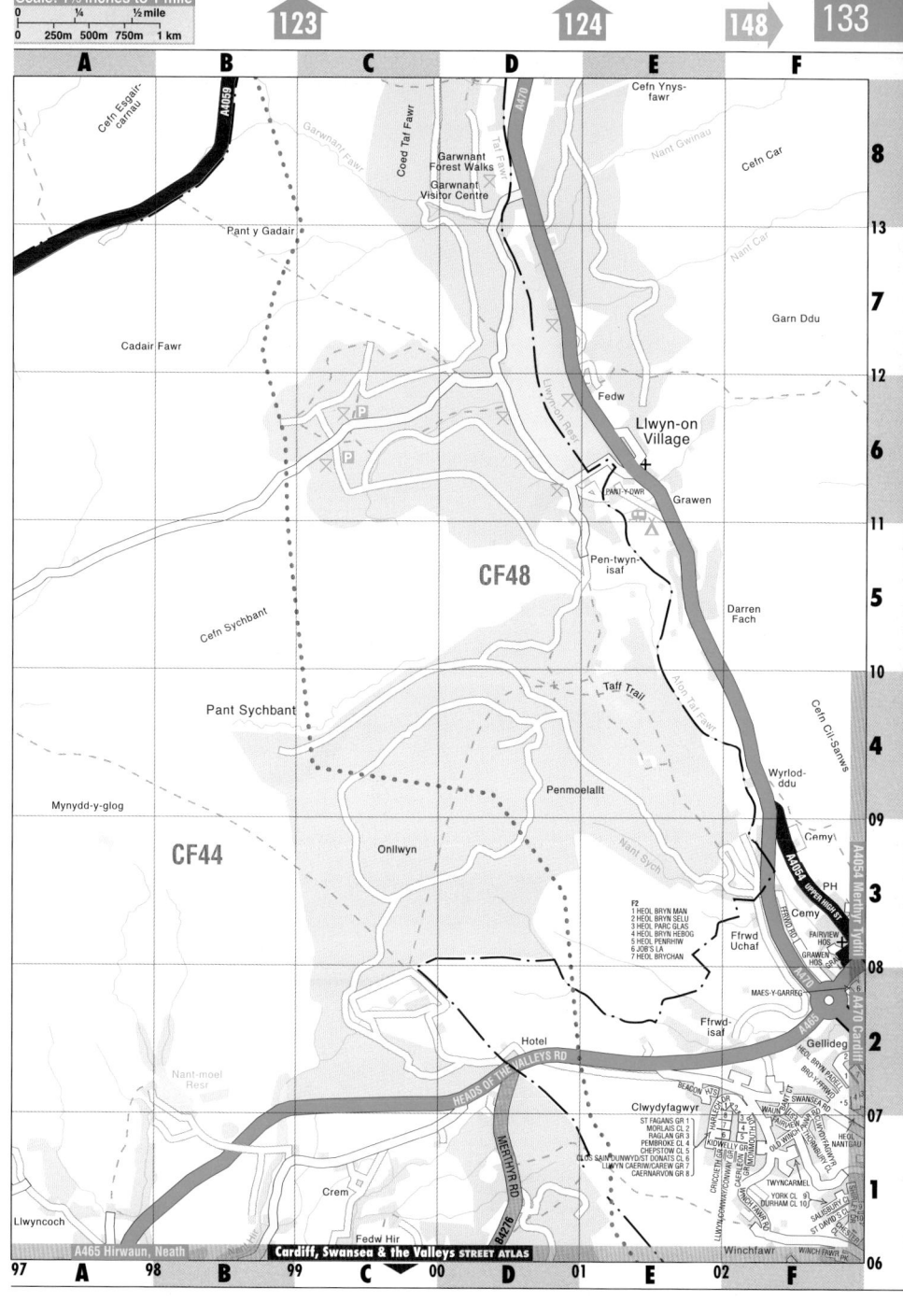

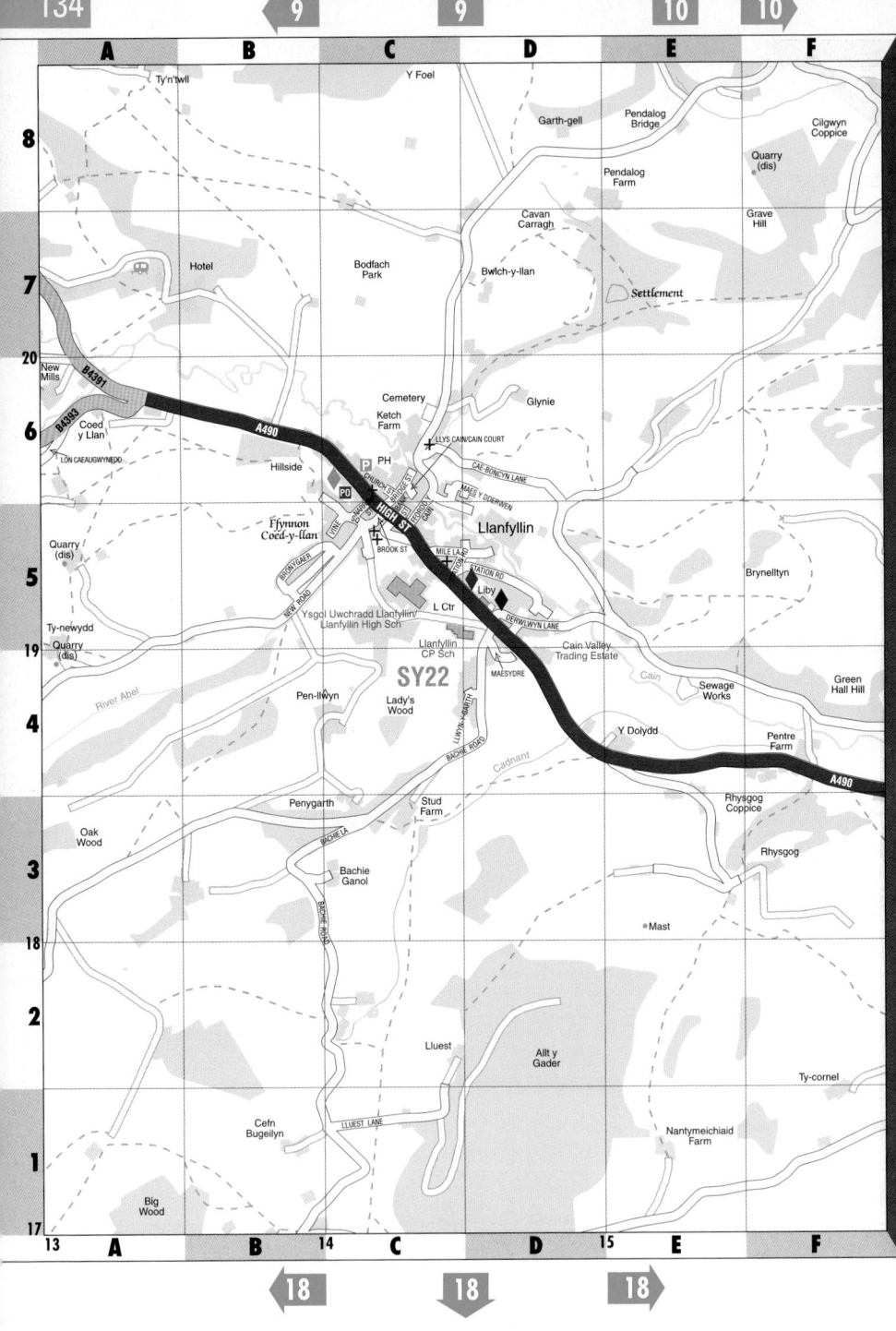

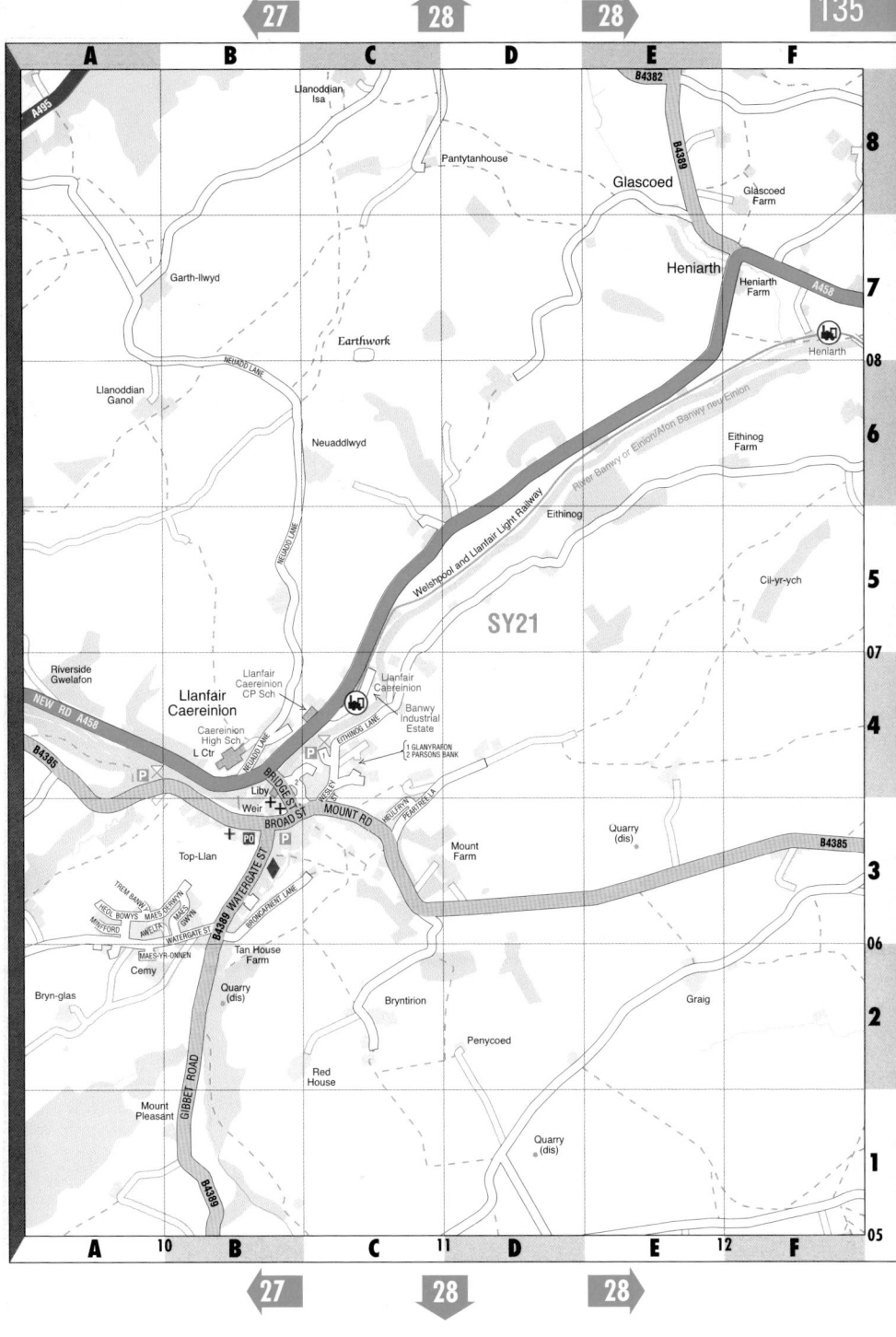

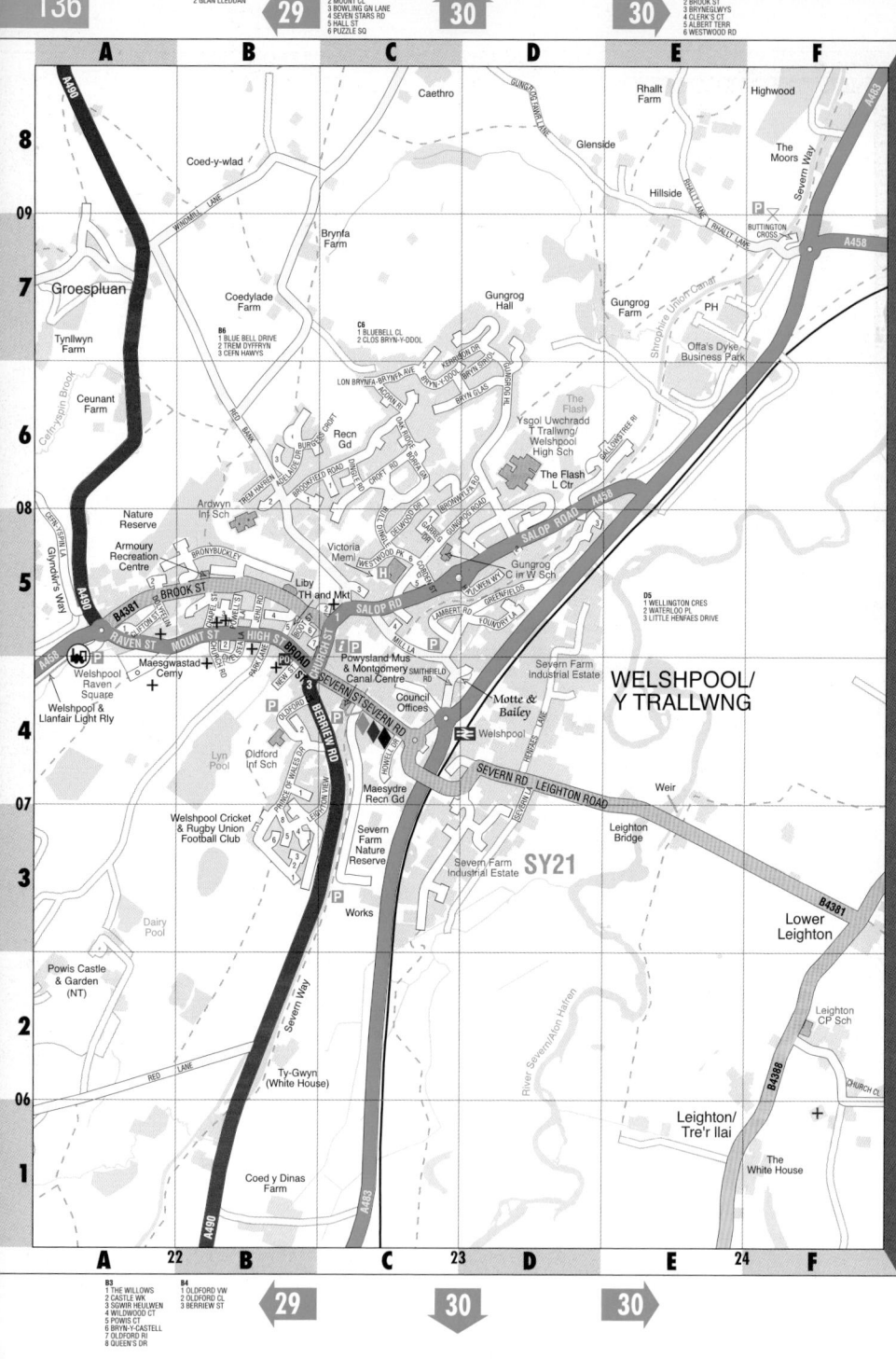

A5
1 RAVEN SQ
2 GLAN LLEDDAN

29

7 PARKER'S PL

B5
1 OLD TAVERN LA
2 MOUNT CL
3 BOWLING GN LANE
4 SEVEN STARS RD
5 HALL ST
6 PUZZLE SQ

30

30

C5
1 CHURCH BANK
2 BROOK ST
3 BRYNEGLWYS
4 CLERK'S CT
5 ALBERT TERR
6 WESTWOOD RD

7 MYRTLE DR

WELSHPOOL/
Y TRALLWNG

SY21

Lower
Leighton

Leighton/
Tre'r llai

B3
1 THE WILLOWS
2 CASTLE WK
3 SGWIR HEULWEN
4 WILDWOOD CT
5 POWIS CT
6 BRYN-Y-CASTELL
7 OLDFORD RI
8 QUEEN'S DR

B4
1 OLDFORD VW
2 OLDFORD CL
3 BERRIEW ST

29

30

30

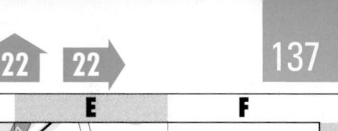

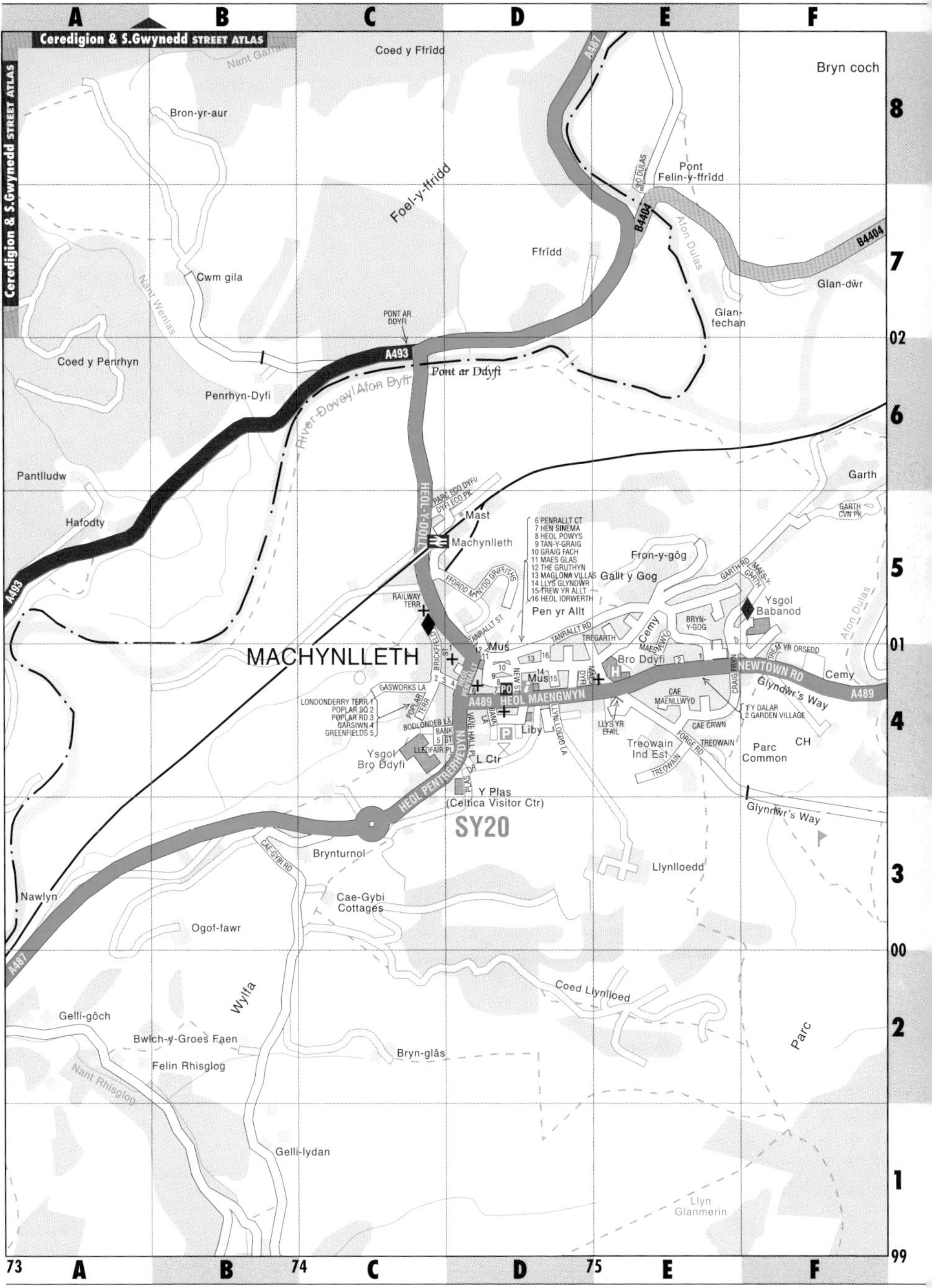

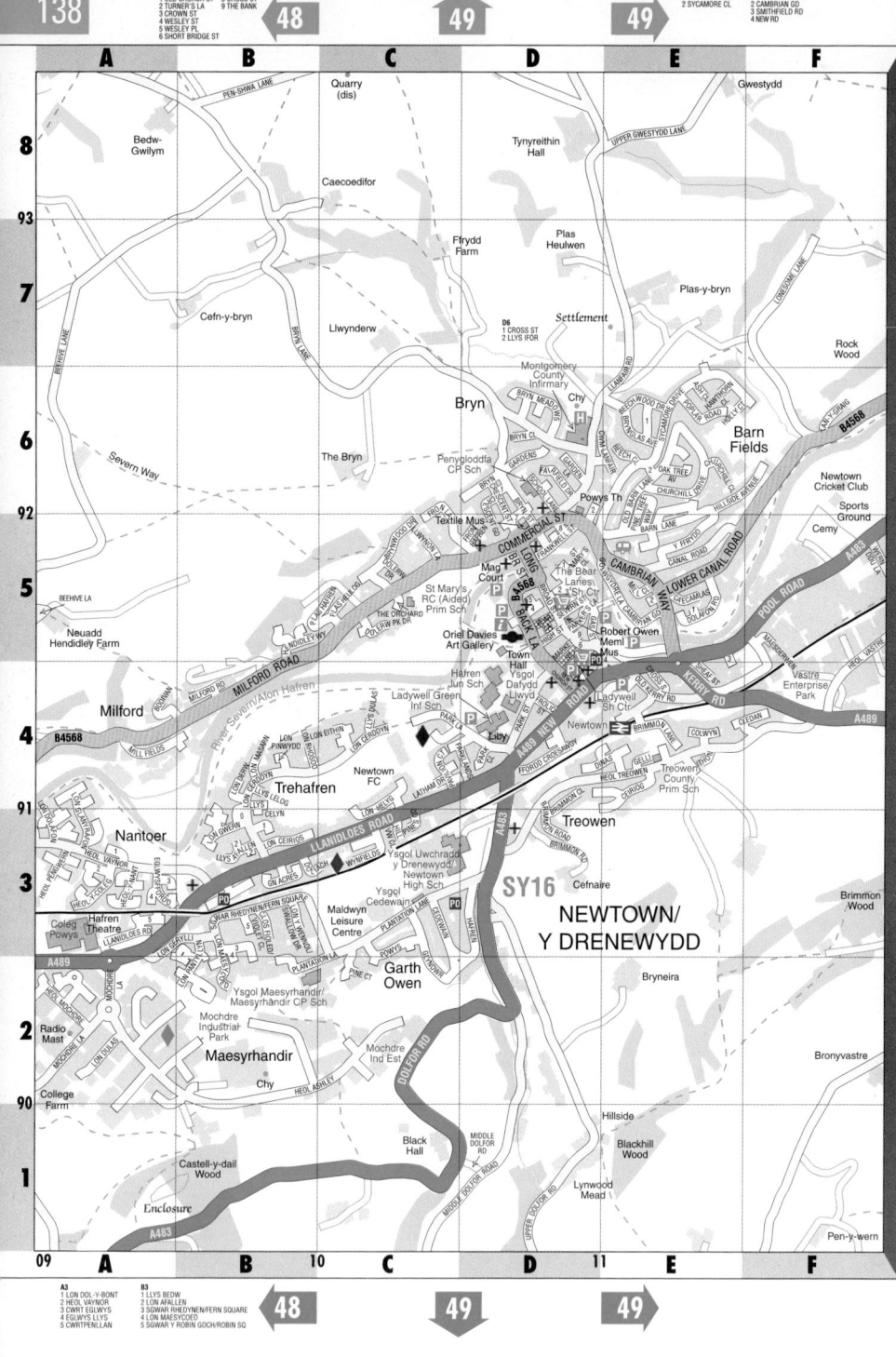

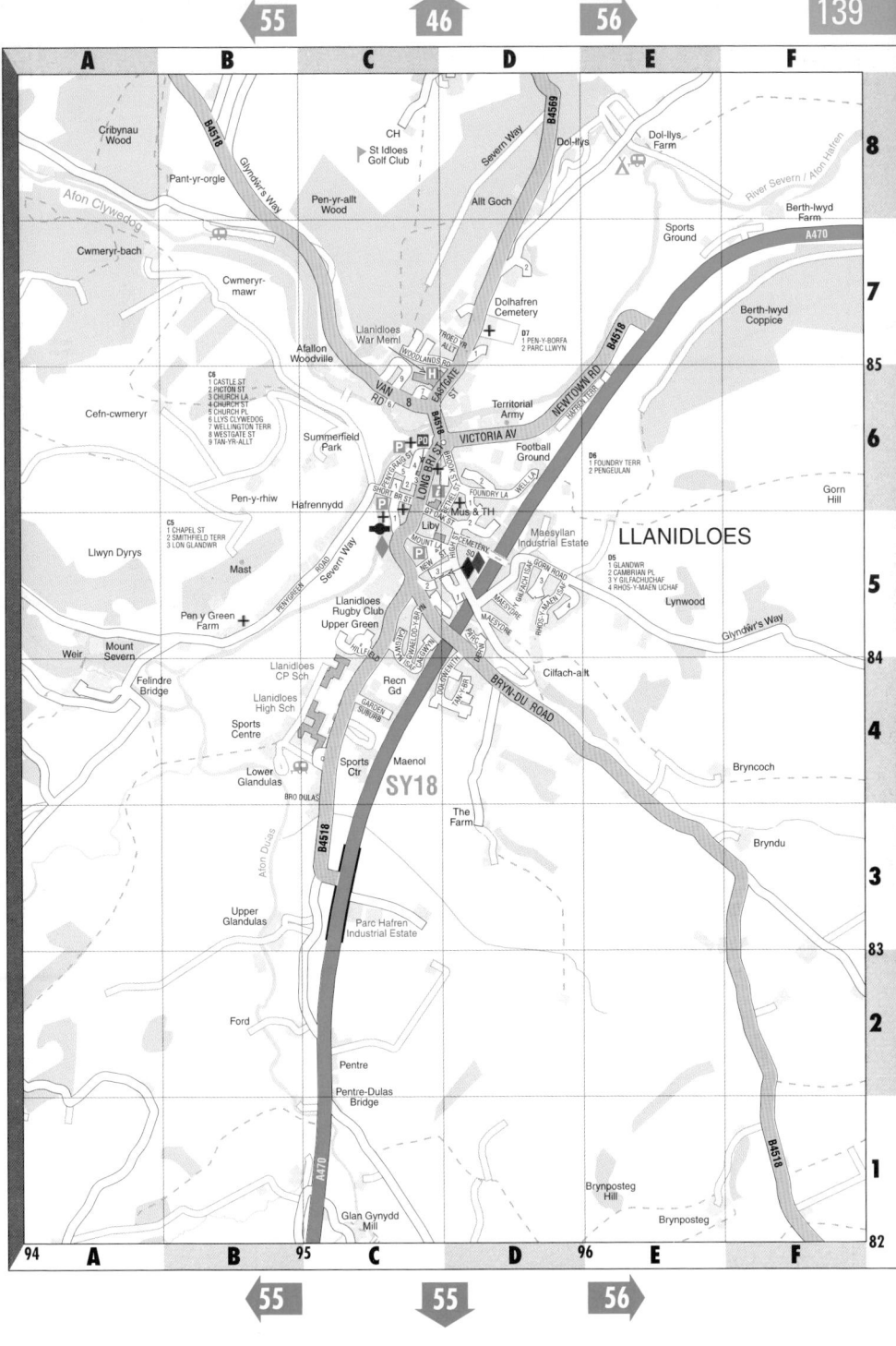

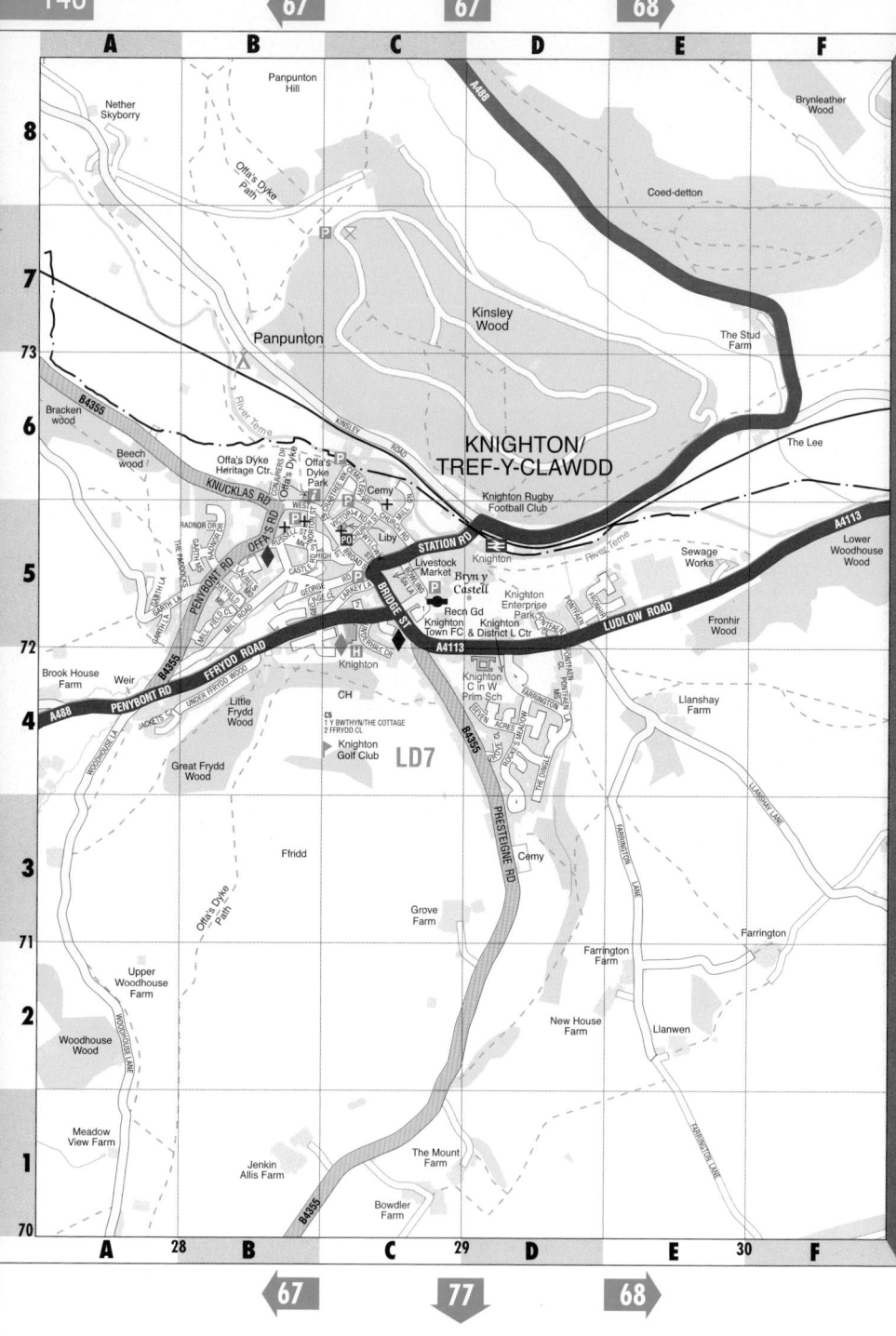

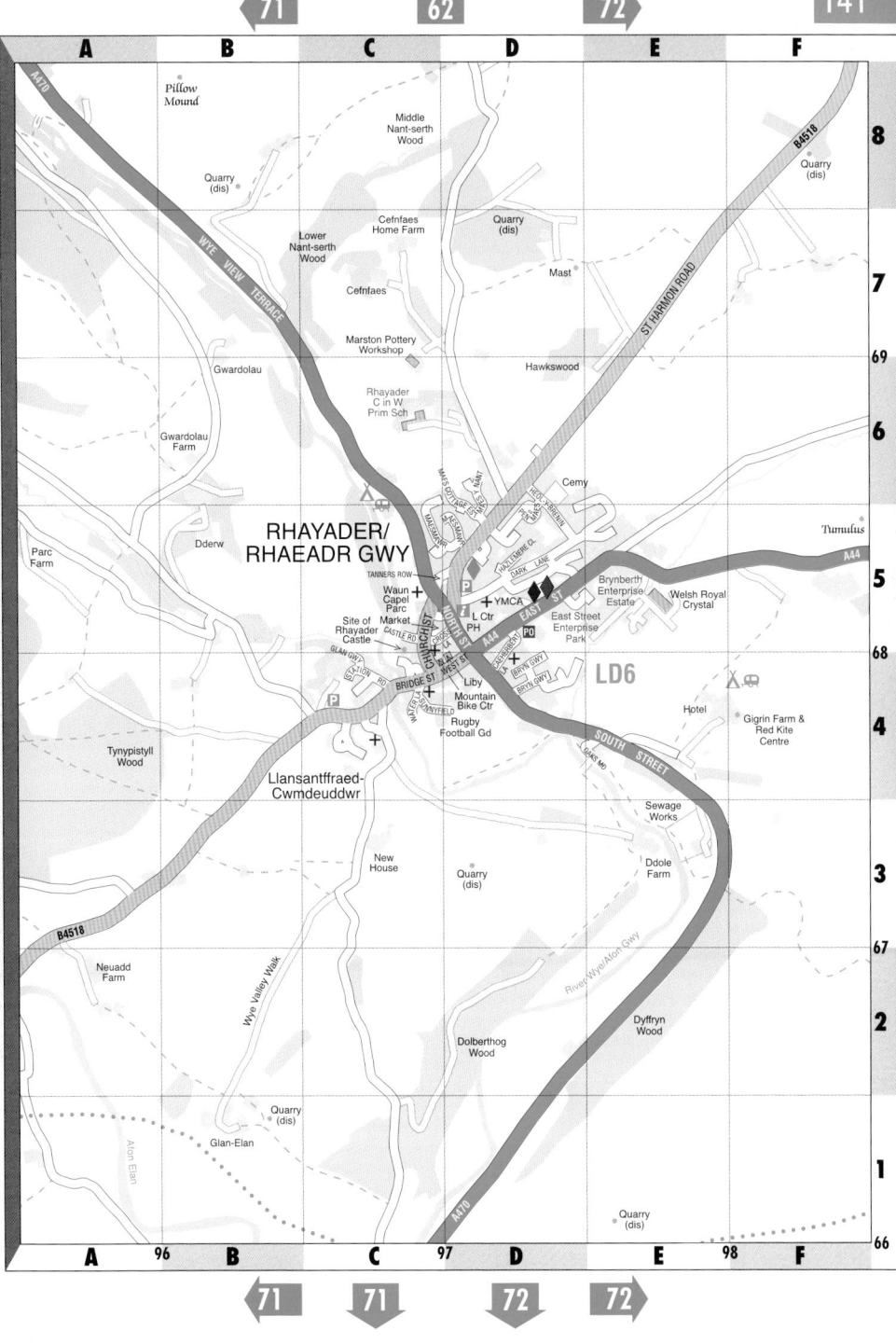

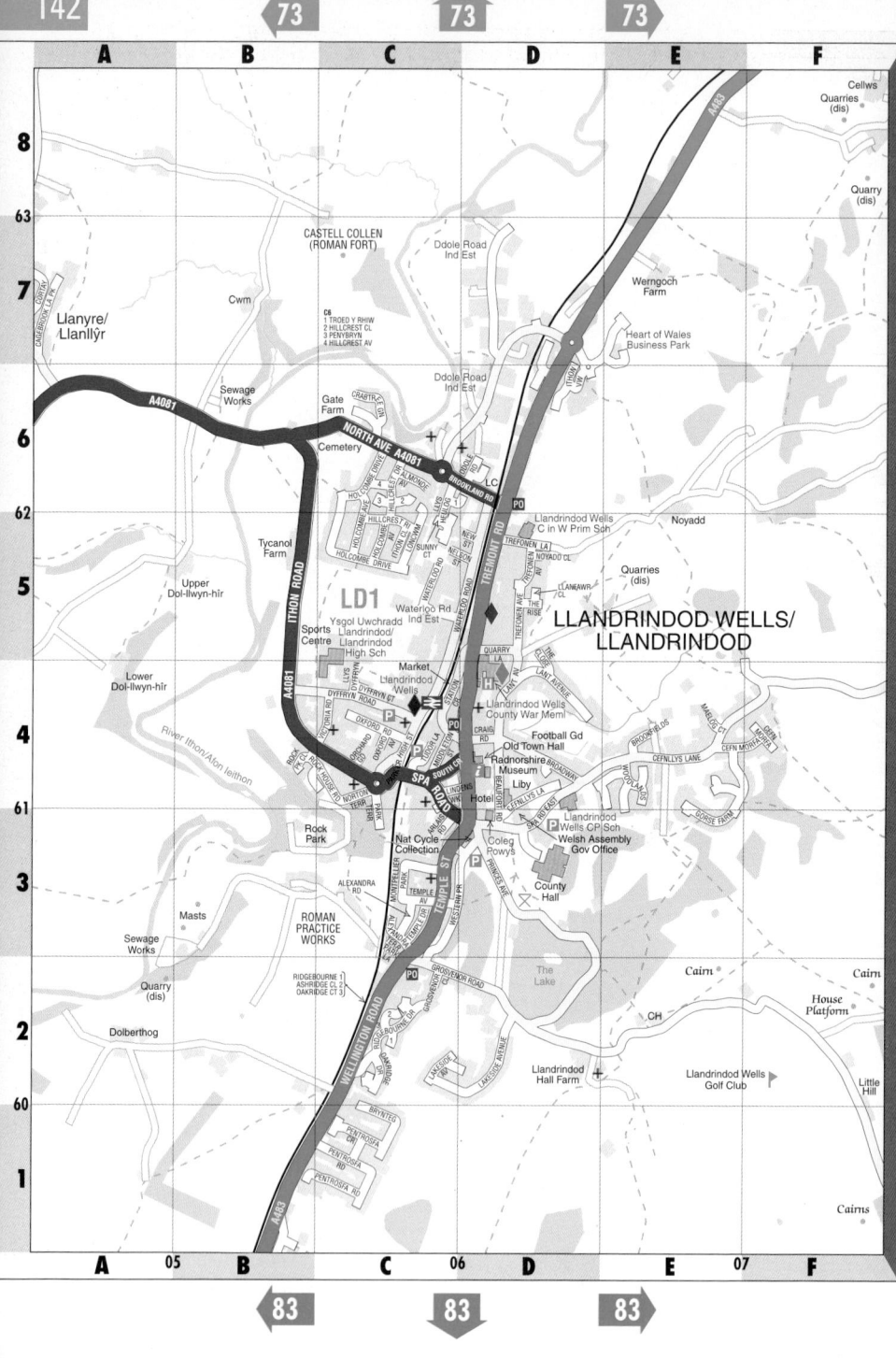

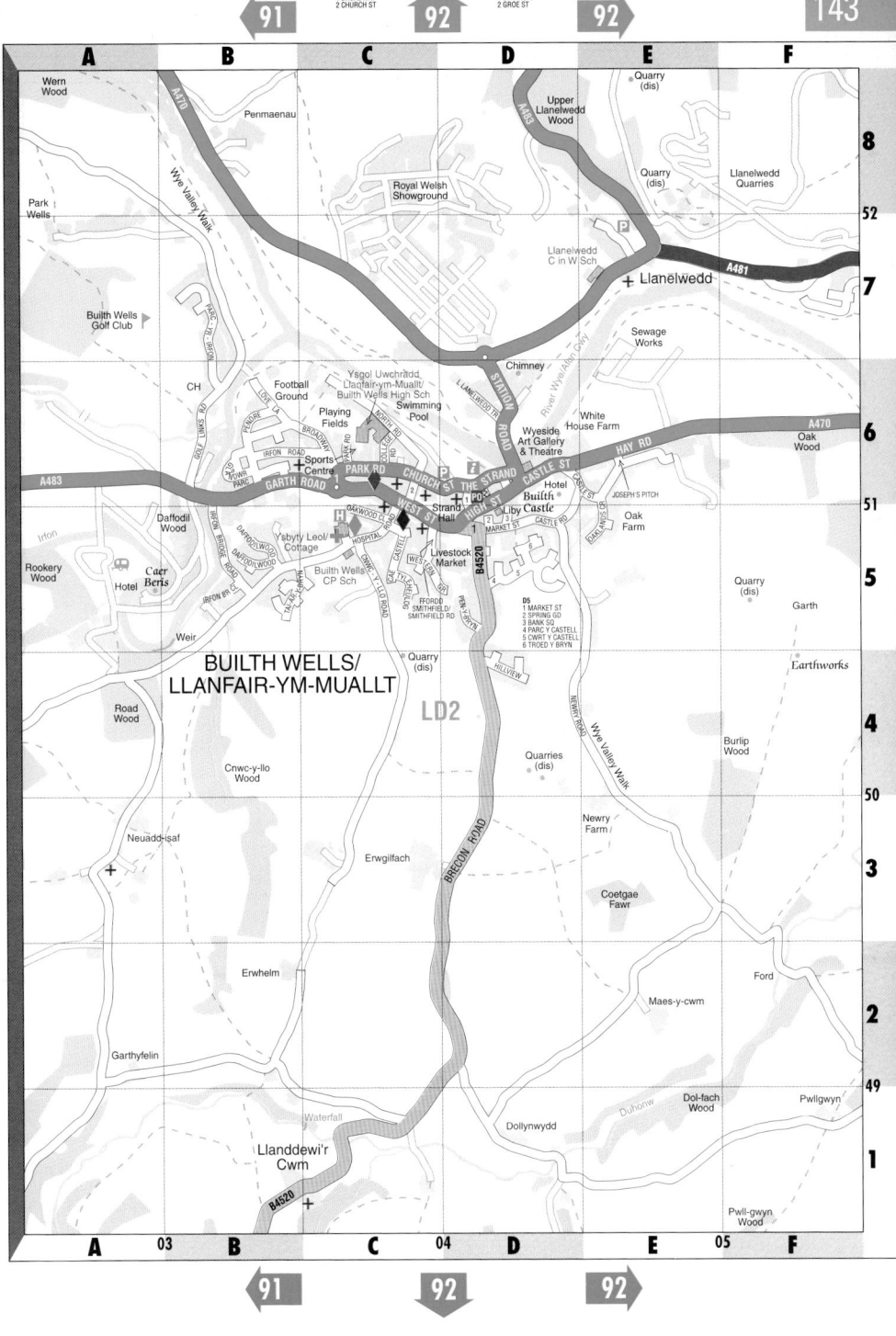

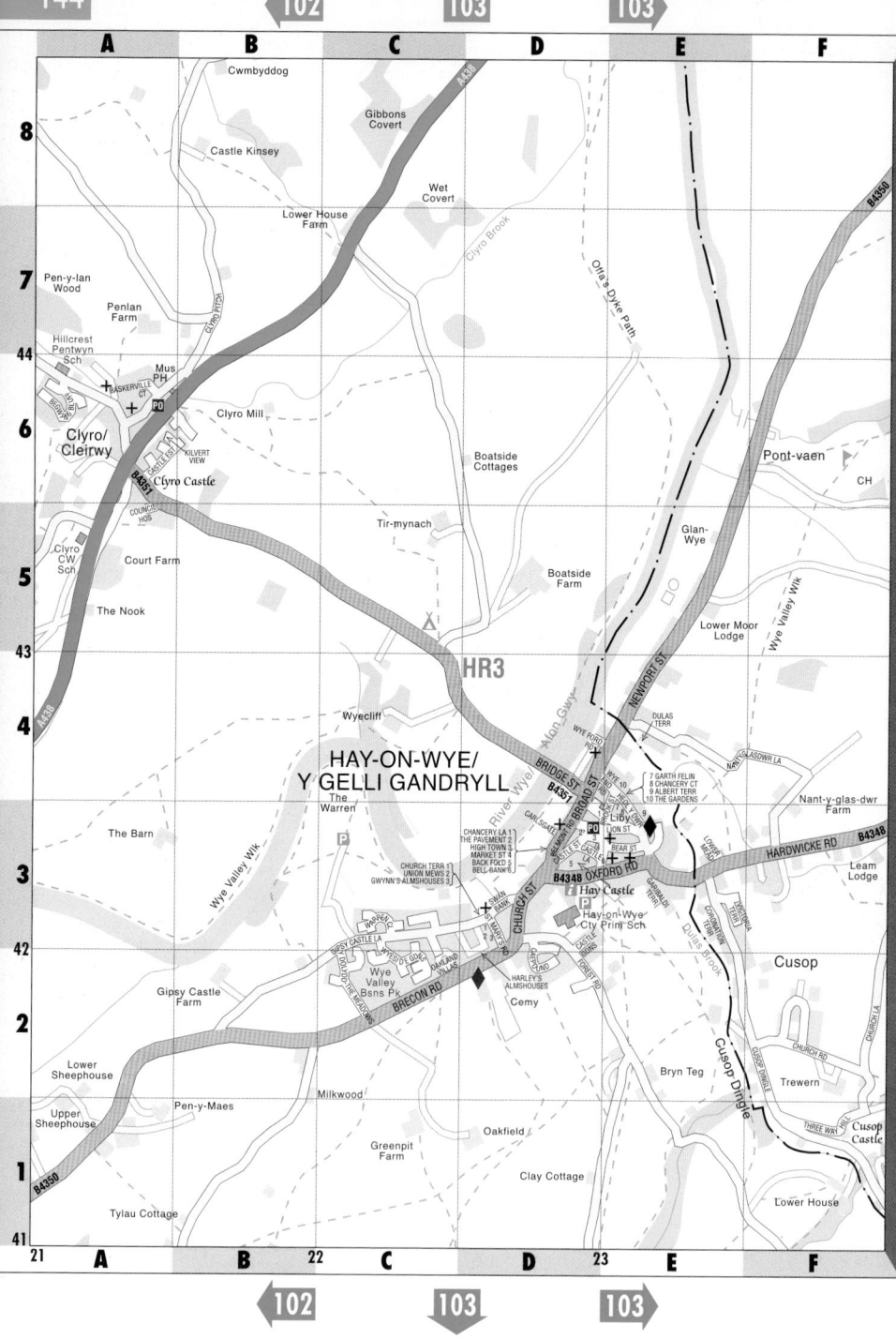

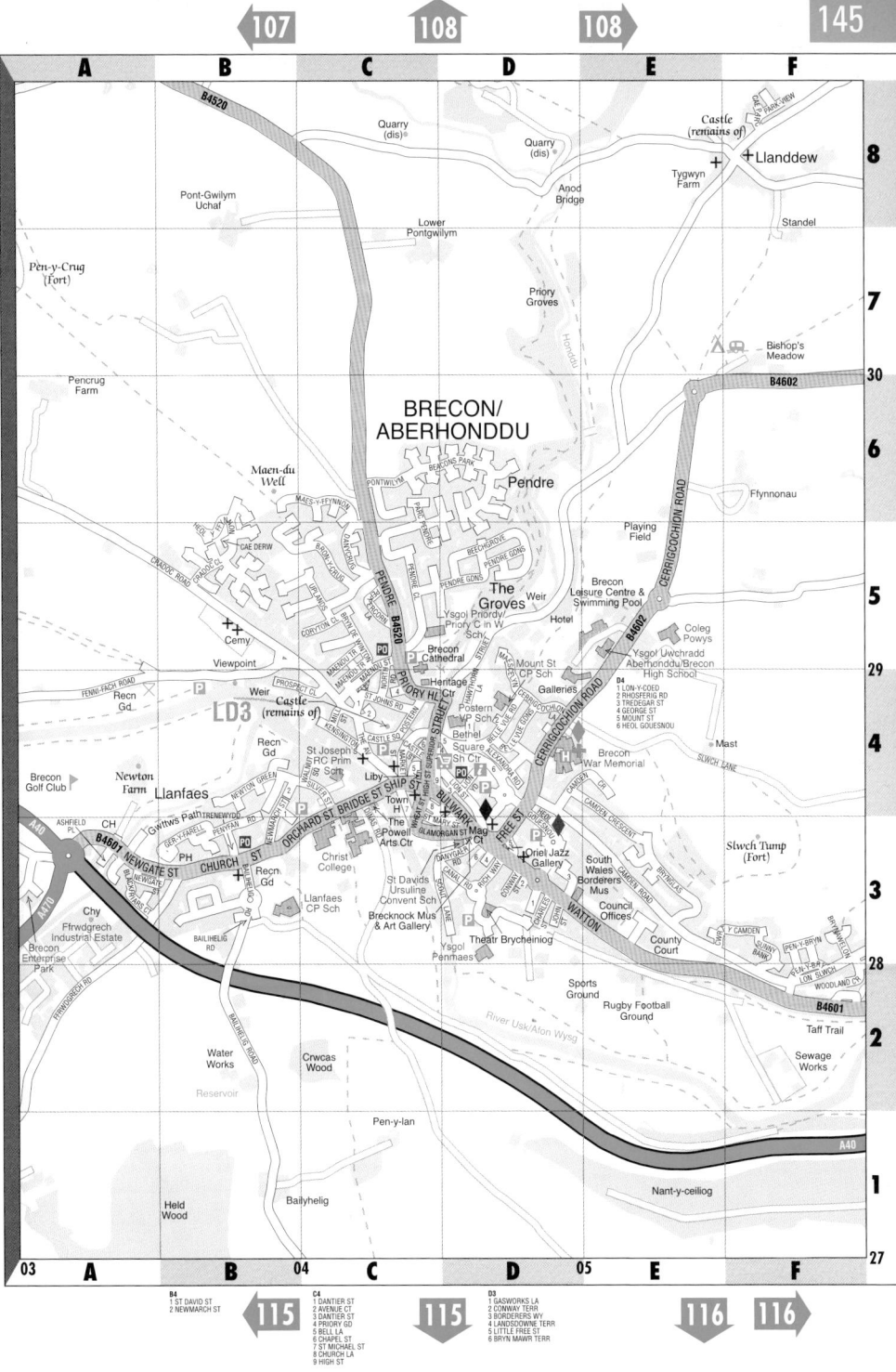

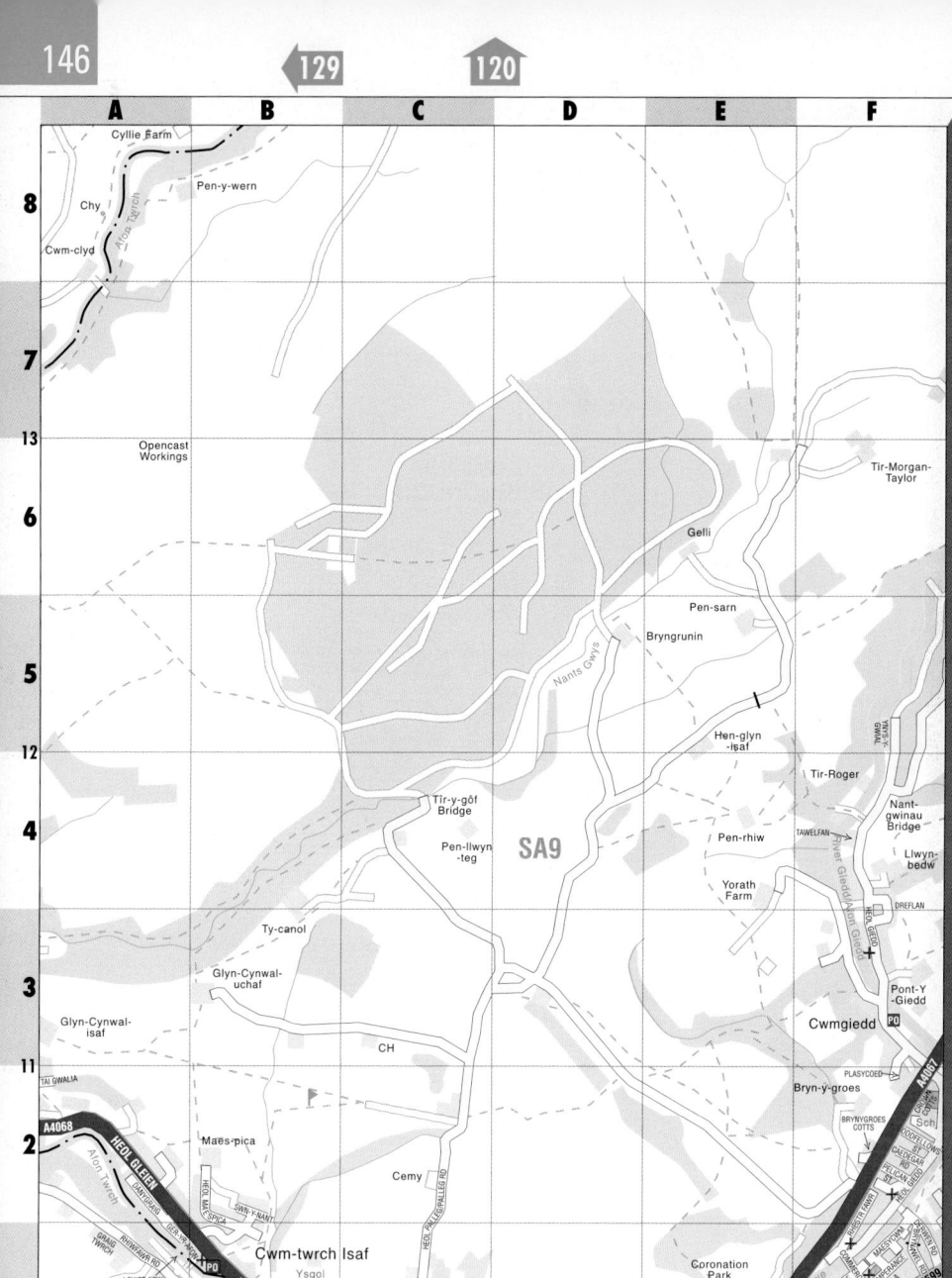

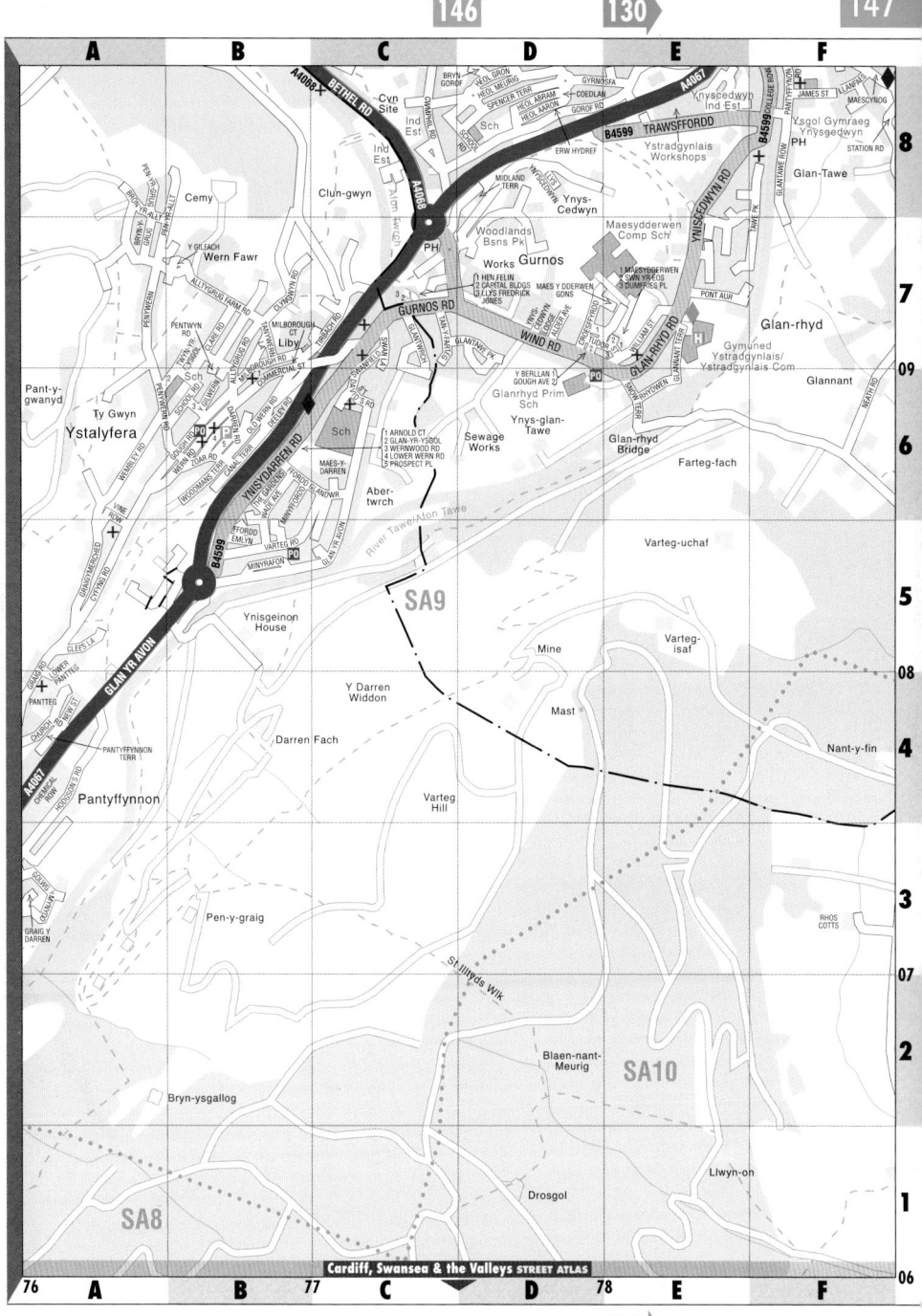

A B C D E F

8

Nant Rhyd-ddu

Boat House

Nant Car Fach

Cwm-Câr

Sailing Club

7

Twyn Croes

Pontsticill Resr

13

Llyngeren

Taff Trail

6

Carn-ddu

5

CF48

12

Bryn Glas

Nant y Firwrd

4

Nant Cwm-moel

TAF FACHAN HOS

Tredegar-fach
Pontsticill

Cwm Moel

Red Cow Hotel (PH)

Pont Sticill

BRYN TERR PH

CASTELL MORLAIS

3

Nant y Wern

Ty'n-y-fedw

Pengellifawr

MAC-CODU

EVANS HOS

PEN-Y-GARN

11

Blaenglais

Pencelly Fach

Penrhadw Farm

Nant y Glais

Maes-y-faenor

2

Berthlwyd

Rectory

Cwm

Llwyncilsanws

Blaen-y-dyffryn

Llwynybrain

Llwynrodin

Vaynor/ Faenor

Church Tavern (PH)

Taff Fachan

Cwm Taf Fechan

1

Ogof Rhyd-sych

Hy- Brasail

Cae Burtydd

Taff Trail

Pen-rhiw-gfais

10

03 A B 04 C D 05 E F

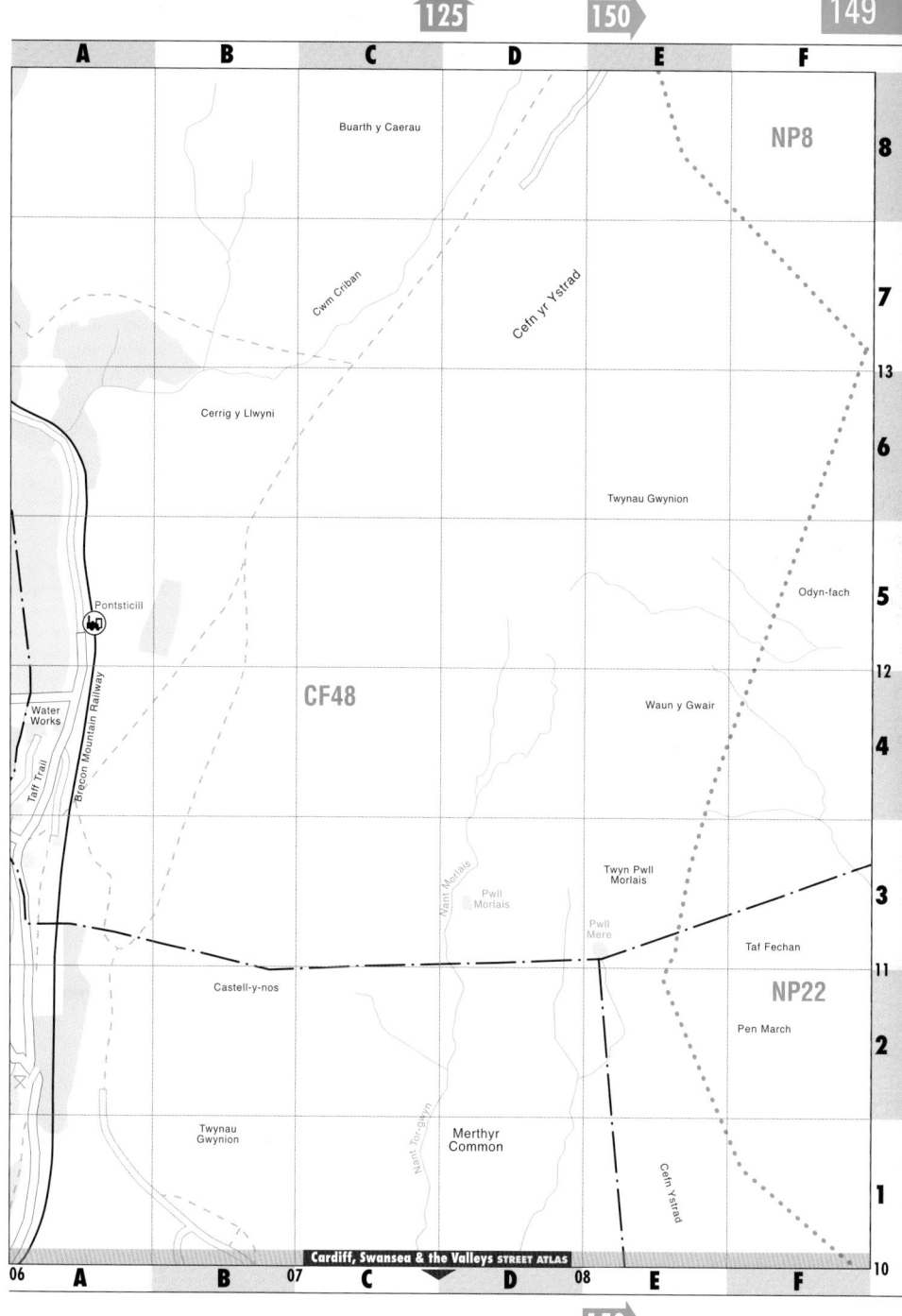

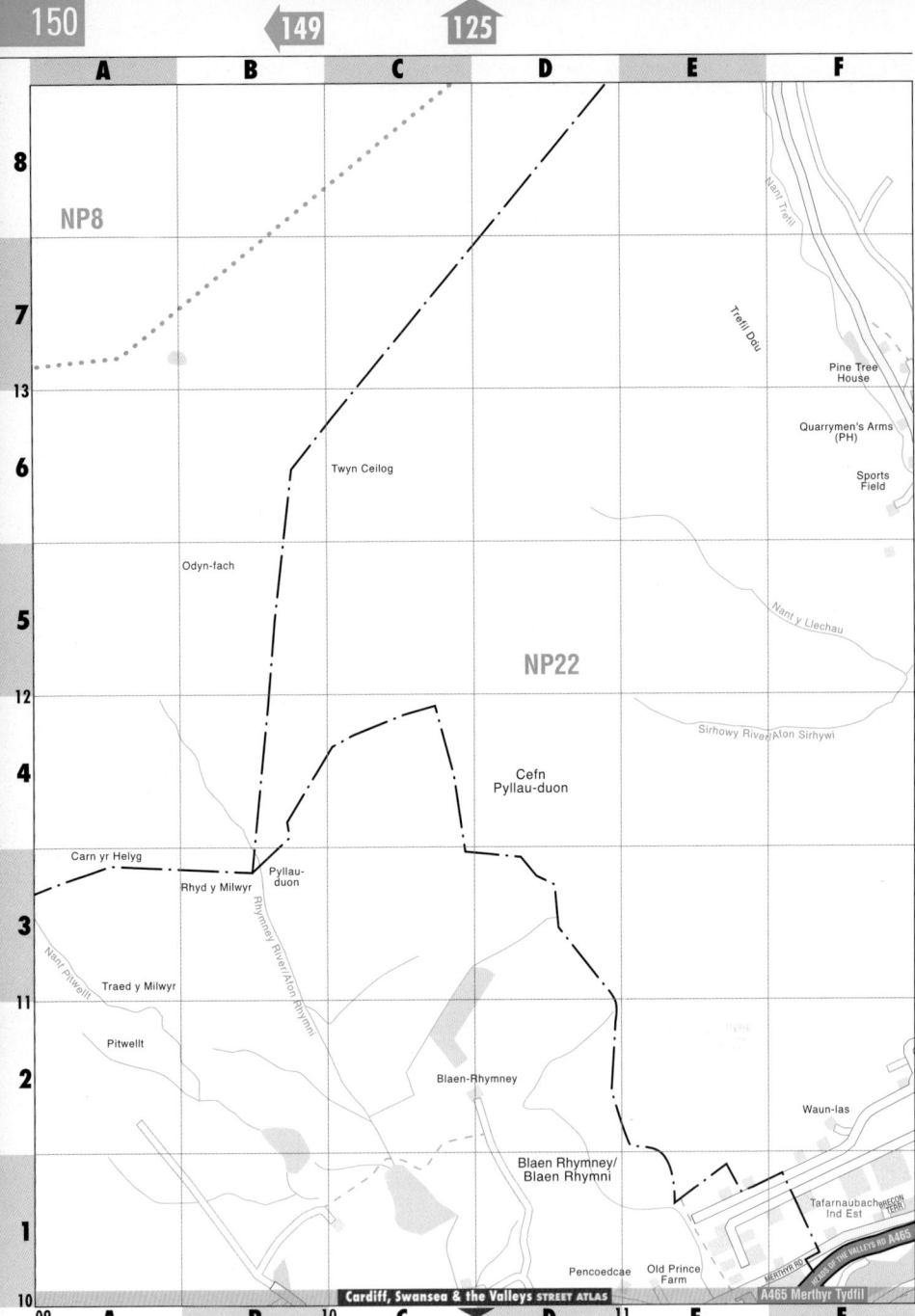

NP8

NP22

Trefil

Nant Trefil

Trefil Ddu

Pine Tree House

Quarrymen's Arms (PH)

Sports Field

Nant y Llechau

Twyn Ceilog

Odyn-fach

Cefn Pyllau-duon

Sirhowy River/Afon Sirhywi

Carn yr Helyg

Pyllau-duon

Rhyd y Milwyr

Rhymney River/Afon Rhymni

Traed y Milwyr

Nant Pitwellt

Pitwellt

Blaen-Rhymney

Waun-las

Blaen Rhymney/ Blaen Rhymni

Tafarnaubach Ind Est

BRECON TERR

Pencoedcae

Old Prince Farm

MERTHYR RD

HEADS OF THE VALLEYS RD A465

A465 Merthyr Tydfil

Cardiff, Swansea & the Valleys STREET ATLAS

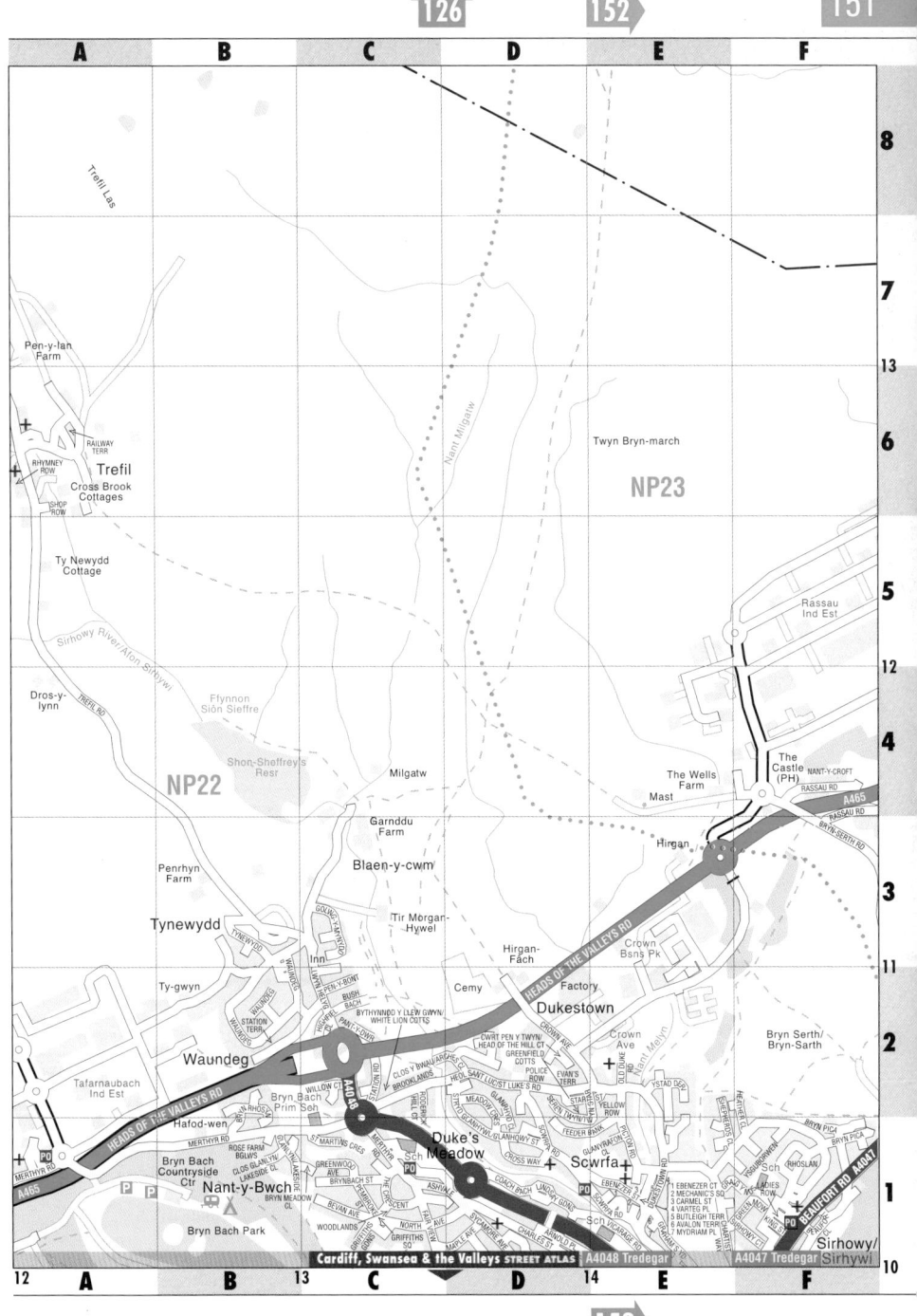

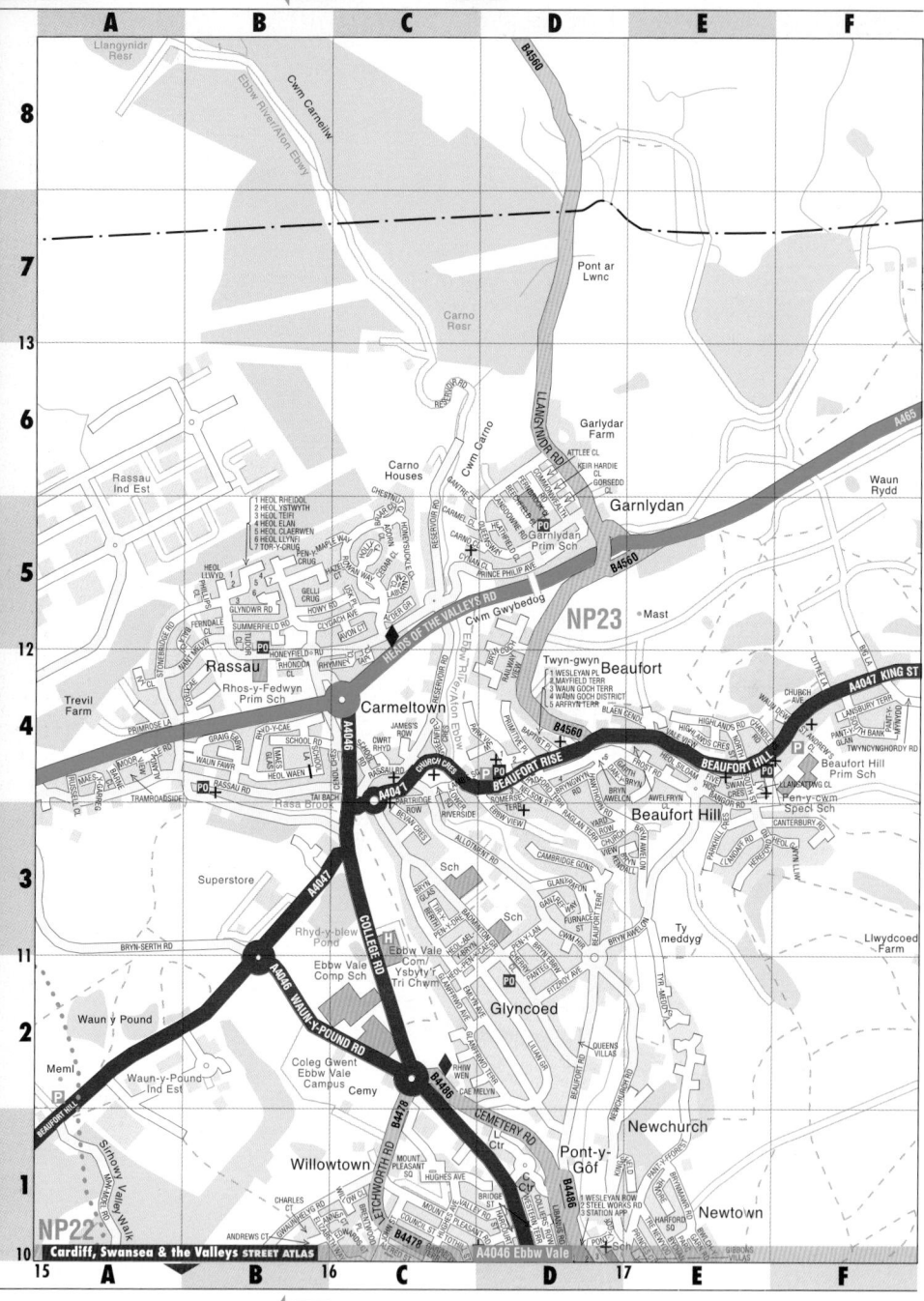

151 126 151

NP23

NP22

A4046 Ebbw Vale

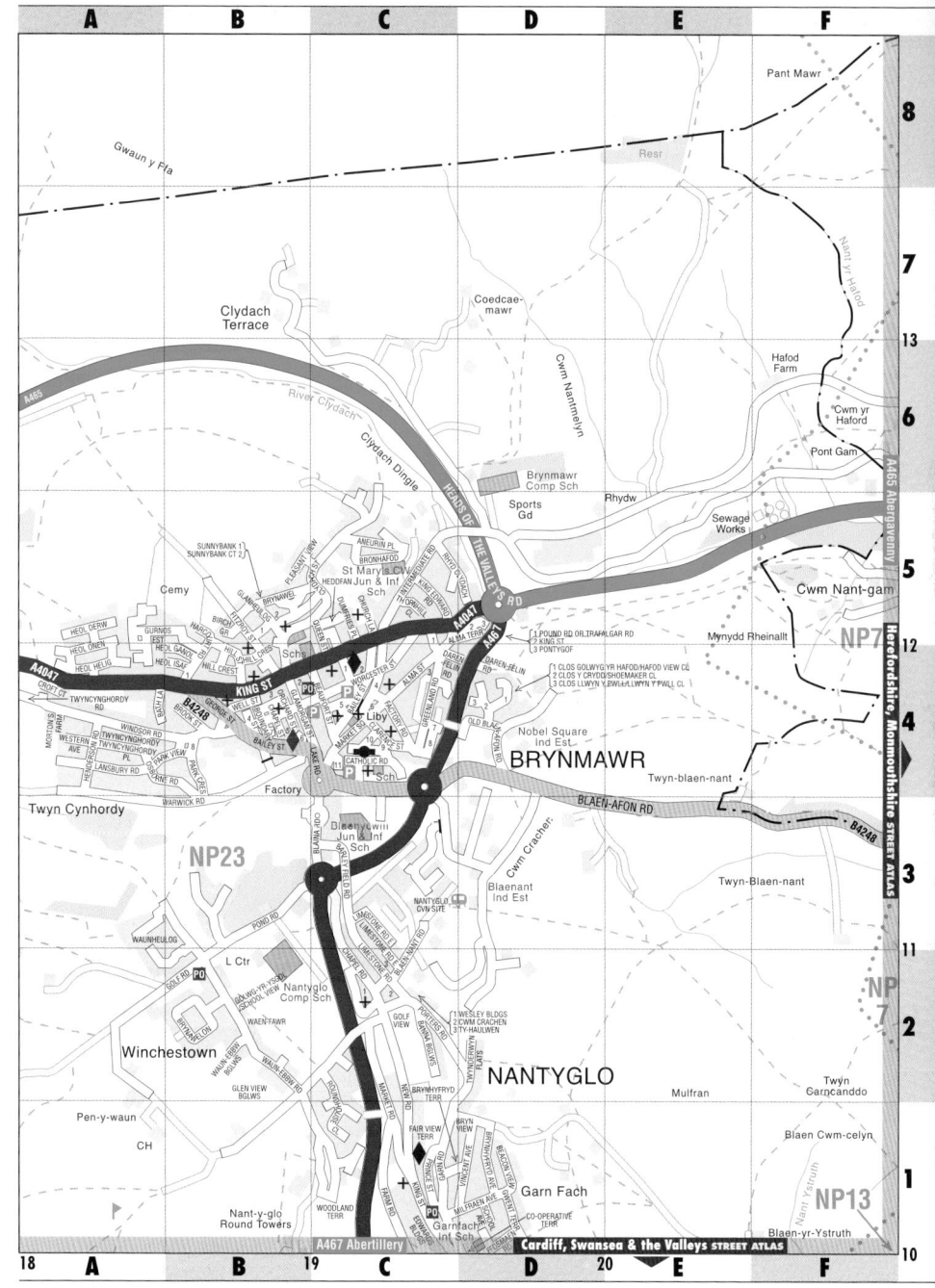

A B C D E F

8

7

13

6

Pant Mawr

Resr

Gwaun y Ffa

Clydach Terrace

Coedcae-mawr

Cwm Nantmelyn

Nant yr Hafod

Hafod Farm

Cwm yr Haford

A465

River Clydach

Clydach Dingle

Pont Gam

Brynmawr Comp Sch

Sports Gd

Rhydw

Sewage Works

A465 Abergavenny

Cwm Nant-gam

5

SUNNYBANK 1
SUNNYBANK CT 2

Cemy

St Mary's CW
HEDDFAN Jun & Inf Sch

ANEURIN PL
BRONHAFOD

Mynydd Rheinallt

NP7

12

HEOL DERW
HEOL ONEN
HEOL GANOL
HEOL HELIG
HEOL ISAF

GURNOS

NIEL CREST

A4047

TWYNCYNGHORDY RD
WINDSOR RD
TWYNCYNGHORDY PL
WESTERN AVE
LANSBURY RD

CROFT CT
MOUNT
DARK VIEW
LIME RD

KING ST

B4248

BAILEY ST

Factory

Twyn Cynhordy

1 POUND RD OR TRAFALGAR RD
2 KING ST
3 PONTYGOF

1 CLOS GOLWG YR HAFOD/HAFOD VIEW CL
2 CLOS Y CRYDD/SHOEMAKER CL
3 CLOS LLWYN Y PWLL/LLWYN Y PWLL CL

DAREN-FELIN

Nobel Square
Ind Est

CATHOLIC RD
Sch

OLD BLAE

Liby
P

BRYNMAWR

Twyn-blaen-nant

BLAEN-AFON RD

B4248

4

NP23

Blaenycwm
Jun & Inf Sch

Cwm Cracher

Blaenant Ind Est

Twyn-Blaen-nant

3

WAUNHEULOG

POND RD

NANTYGLO CVN SITE

GOLWG-YR-YSGOL
SCHOOL VIEW

Nantyglo
Comp Sch

LIMESTONE RD

11

L Ctr

GOLLOG PO

WAEN-FAWR

GOLF VIEW

1 WESLEY BLDGS
2 CWM CRACHEN
3 TY-HAULWEN

NP7

2

Winchestown

GLEN VIEW
BGLWS

WAUN EBBW
BGLWS

BRYNFYRYD TERR

BRYN VIEW

NANTYGLO

Mulfran

Twyn Garncanddo

Pen-y-waun

CH

FAIR VIEW TERR

MARKET RD

FARM RD

Garn Fach

Blaen Cwm-celyn

NP13

1

Nant-y-glo
Round Towers

WOODLAND TERR

MILFRAEN ROW

Garnfach
Inf Sch

CO-OPERATIVE TERR

Blaen-yr-Ystruth

A467 Abertillery

Index

Church Rd [6] Beckenham BR2......... **53** C6

Place name	Location number	Locality, town or village	Postcode district	Page and grid square
May be abbreviated on the map	Present when a number indicates the place's position in a crowded area of mapping	Shown when more than one place has the same name	District for the indexed place	Page number and grid reference for the standard mapping

Public and commercial buildings are highlighted in magenta. **Places of interest** are highlighted in blue with a star★

Abbreviations used in the index

Acad	**Academy**	Comm	**Common**	Gd	**Ground**	L	**Leisure**
App	**Approach**	Cott	**Cottage**	Gdn	**Garden**	La	**Lane**
Arc	**Arcade**	Cres	**Crescent**	Gn	**Green**	Liby	**Library**
Ave	**Avenue**	Cswy	**Causeway**	Gr	**Grove**	Mdw	**Meadow**
Bglw	**Bungalow**	Ct	**Court**	H	**Hall**	Meml	**Memorial**
Bldg	**Building**	Ctr	**Centre**	Ho	**House**	Mkt	**Market**
Bsns,Bus	**Business**	Ctry	**Country**	Hospl	**Hospital**	Mus	**Museum**
Bvd	**Boulevard**	Cty	**County**	HQ	**Headquarters**	Orch	**Orchard**
Cath	**Cathedral**	Dr	**Drive**	Hts	**Heights**	Pal	**Palace**
Cir	**Circus**	Dro	**Drove**	Ind	**Industrial**	Par	**Parade**
Cl	**Close**	Ed	**Education**	Inst	**Institute**	Pas	**Passage**
Cnr	**Corner**	Emb	**Embankment**	Int	**International**	Pk	**Park**
Coll	**College**	Est	**Estate**	Intc	**Interchange**	Pl	**Place**
Com	**Community**	Ex	**Exhibition**	Junc	**Junction**	Prec	**Precinct**

Prom	**Promenade**
Rd	**Road**
Recn	**Recreation**
Ret	**Retail**
Sh	**Shopping**
Sq	**Square**
St	**Street**
Sta	**Station**
Terr	**Terrace**
TH	**Town Hall**
Univ	**University**
Wk, Wlk	**Walk**
Wr	**Water**
Yd	**Yard**

Translations Welsh – English

Aber	**Estuary, confluence**	Cwm	**Valley**	Lôn	**Lane**	Rhiw	**Hill, incline**
Afon	**River**	Cwrt	**Court**	Maes	**Open area, field, square**	Rhodfa	**Avenue**
Amgueddfa	**Museum**	Dinas	**City**			Sgwâr	**Square**
Bro	**District, area**	Dôl	**Meadow**	Môr	**Sea**	Stryd	**Street**
Bryn	**Hill**	Eglwys	**Church**	Mynydd	**Mountain**	Swyddfa	**Post office**
Cae	**Field**	Felin	**Mill**	Oriel	**Gallery**		post
Caer	**Fort**	Fferm	**Farm**	Parc	**Park**	Tref, Tre	**Town**
Canolfan	**Centre**	Ffordd	**Road, way**	Parc busnes	**Business park**	Tŷ	**House**
Capel	**Chapel**	Gelli	**Grove**	Pen	**Top, end**	Uchaf	**Upper**
Castell	**Castle**	Gerddi	**Gardens**	Pentref	**Village**	Ysbyty	**Hospital**
Cilgant	**Crescent**	Gorsaf	**Station**	Plas	**Mansion, place**	Ysgol	**School**
Clôs	**Close**	Heol	**Road**	Pont	**Bridge**	Ystad, stad	**Estate**
Coed	**Wood**	Isaf	**Lower**	Prifysgol	**University**	Ystad ddiwydiannol	**Industrial estate**
Coleg	**College**	Llan	**Church, parish**	Rhaeadr	**Waterfall**		
		Llyn	**Lake**	Rhes	**Terrace, row**	Ystrad	**Vale**

Translations English – Welsh

Avenue	**Rhodfa**	Estuary	**Aber**	Mansion	**Plas**	Station	**Gorsaf**
Bridge	**Pont**	Farm	**Fferm**	Meadow	**Dôl**	Street	**Stryd**
Business Park	**Parc busnes**	Field	**Cae**	Mill	**Felin**	Terrace	**Rhes**
		Fort	**Caer**	Mountain	**Mynydd**	Top, end	**Pen**
Castle	**Castell**	Gallery	**Oriel**	Museum	**Amgueddfa**	Town	**Tref, tre**
Centre	**Canolfan**	Gardens	**Gerddi**	Parish	**Plwyf eglwys, llan,**	University	**Prifysgol**
Chapel	**Capel**	Grove	**Gelli**			Upper	**Uchaf**
Church	**Eglwys**	Hill	**Bryn, rhiw**	Park	**Parc**	Vale	**Ystrad, glyn, dyffryn**
City	**Dinas**	Hospital	**Ysbyty**	Place	**Plas, maes**		
Close	**Clôs**	House	**Tŷ**	Post office	**Swyddfa post**	Valley	**Cwm**
College	**Coleg**	Industrial estate	**Ystad ddiwydiannol**	River	**Afon**	Village	**Pentref**
Court	**Cwrt**			Road	**Heol, ffordd**	Waterfall	**Rhaeadr**
Crescent	**Cilgant**	Lake	**Llyn**	School	**Ysgol**	Way	**Ffordd**
District	**Bro**	Lane	**Lôn**	Sea	**Môr**	Wood	**Coed**
Estate	**Ystad, stad**	Lower	**Isaf**	Square	**Sgwâr, maes**		

Index of localities, towns and villages

A

Abbey-cwm-hir 63 E2
Aberangell 13 D1
Aberangell Glantwymyn ...23 E8
Aberbechan 49 E8
Aberbran 114 F8
Abercegir 34 A8
Abercraf / Abercrave ..130 C8
Abercrave / Abercraf ..130 C8
Abercynafon 125 B4
Aber-Cywarch 13 E6
Aberedw 92 F2
Abergavenny / Y Fenni .128 E1
Abergwesyn 89 A7
Aberhafesp 48 D7
Aberhonddu / Brecon ..145 D6
Aberhosan 34 B4
Aberllefenni 22 D8
Aber-miwl / Abermule .40 A1
Abermule / Aber-miwl .40 A1
Abernant 9 D4
Abernant 40 B4
Aberriw / Berriew 40 C7
Abertridwr 8 A2
Aber Village 125 E8
Aberyscir 115 A8
Adfa 38 B7
Alltforgan 6 F7
Alltmawr 92 E2
Alport 11 A1
Anchor 59 C8
Arddlîn / Arddleen ...20 C6
Arddleen / Arddlîn ...20 C6
Ashfield 12 E8
Ashvale 151 C1
Aston 52 C6

B

Babel 104 D6
Bacheldre 51 D7
Banwen 131 A4
Barland 77 B1
Barn Fields 138 F6
Battle 107 D1
Beaufort 152 D4
Beaufort Hill 152 E3
Beguildy 59 E2
Belan 29 F3
Bentlawnt 42 F8
Berriew / Aberriw ...40 C7
Berth-las 24 D1
Betton 31 D1
Bettws Cedewain 39 C4
Beulah 90 B6
Binweston 31 C3
Birtley 78 D8
Bishop's Castle 52 E3
Blaendulais /
   Seven Sisters 130 D3
Blaendyryn 106 C7
Blaen-y-cwm 151 C3
Bleddfa 75 F7
Bont Dolgadfan 35 C7
Boughrood 101 D2
Boughrood Brest 101 F1
Braichyfedw 45 E6
Brecon / Aberhonddu .145 D6
Bredward 87 B2
Brilley 95 F4
Brilley Mountain 95 F6
Broad Heath 78 A2
Brockton 31 D3
Bromlow 42 E8
Broneirion 47 E3
Bronllys 103 B8
Brooks 39 E6
Brunant 31 A8
Bryn 138 D6
Bryngwyn 94 D4
Brynmawr 153 D4
Bucknell 68 E4
Builth Road 91 F8
Builth Wells /
   Llanfair-Ym-Muallt .143 B4
Burgedin 20 A5
Burlingjobb 86 E5
Buttington 30 D7
Bwlch 117 E1
Bwlch-y-cibau 18 F8
Bwlchyddar 10 C4
Bwlch-y-ffridd 38 C2
Bwlch-y-Plain 67 A6
Bwlch-y-sarnau 63 C5
Byton 78 D2
Byton Hand 78 E2

C

Cabin 52 E4
Cae-Hopkin 130 D7
Cae'r-Lan 130 B7

Caersws
Caersws 47 F6
Camnant 84 A3
Capel-y-ffin 111 E2
Carmel 73 C5
Carmeltown 152 C4
Carno 36 D3
Cascob 76 C5
Castle Caereinion ...29 A4
Castlegreen 52 F4
Cathedine 117 D4
Cefn 20 D1
Cefn-bryn-brain 129 B8
Cefn-côch 3 E1
Cefn Canol 5 E6
Cefn Coch 27 B1
Cefn-gorwydd 97 F8
Cefn-llyfnog 19 B8
Cefn Rhigos 132 A1
Cegidfa / Guilsfield .19 E2
Cemmaes 23 D5
Cefn /
   Glantwymyn 23 C3
Ceri / Kerry 49 F4
Chapel Lawn 68 B7
Chirbury 41 E5
Church Stoke 41 E1
Churchtown 51 F2
Cilcewydd 30 B3
Cilmeri / Cilmery ...91 E6
Cilmery / Cilmeri ...91 E6
Ciltwrch 102 A3
City 51 A5
Clatter 37 B1
Clawdd-llesg 18 D2
Clifford 103 D8
Cloddiau 29 E8
Clwydyfagwyr 133 E2
Clydach Terrace 153 B7
Clyro 144 A6
Clyro /Cleirwy 144 A6
Cnwclas / Knucklas ..67 B5
Coedway 21 D5
Coed-yr-ynys 126 D7
Coelbren 130 F6
Coldbrook 110 A7
Colebatch 52 F2
Colva 94 F8
Combe 78 B2
Combe Moor 78 D2
Commins Coch 23 E2
Cornhill 101 E3
Corris 22 B6
Corris Uchaf 22 A7
Cradoc 107 E1
Crai 113 C3
Cregrina 93 D7
Crewgreen 21 C6
Crickheath 12 C5
Crickhowell /
   Crug Hywel 127 E5
Criggion 20 F6
Crossgates 73 F3
Cross Oaks 12 F2
Cross Oak 116 F2
Crossway 83 C4
Crossways 65 C5
Crowther's Pool 95 A3
Crug 66 B3
Crug Hywel /
   Crickhowell 127 E5
Cusop 144 F2
Cwm Aberhafesp 38 B2
Cwm Churchstoke 51 F5
Cwmbach 102 B2
Cwmbach Llechrhyd ..82 F1
Cwmbelan 55 D4
Cwm Cae 52 A6
Cwm Cewydd 13 C4
Cwmdu 118 B2
Cwmgiedd 146 F3
Cwm Irfon 89 A4
Cwmllynfell 129 B7
Cwm Nant-gam 153 F5
Cwmrhos 118 B3
Cwm-twrch Isaf 146 F1
Cwm-twrch Uchaf ...129 C6
Cwmwysg 112 E7
Cwncrawnon 126 D6
Cwrt 32 A7
Cyfronydd 28 E6
Cynghordy Hall 96 C2

D

Dardy 127 C5
Darowen 34 C8
David's Well 57 C1
Ddôl 58 D6
Ddôl Cownwy 16 B8
Deerfold 78 E6
Defynnog 113 F6
Derwenlas 32 E6
Deuddwr 20 A8
Dinas-Mawddwy 13 D5

Discoed
Discoed 77 A3
Disserth 83 A5
Dolanog 17 B4
Dolau 74 E6
Dol-fách 35 F8
Dol-fôr 23 B5
Dolfach 61 D8
Dolfor 49 B2
Dolley Green 77 B4
Dolwen 25 F6
Dol-y-cannau 94 F3
Dolyhir 86 D4
Dolymelinau 38 F6
Domgay 12 B2
Downton 86 C7
Duke's Meadow 151 C1
Dukestown 151 D2
Dutlas 66 C8
Dyffryn Cellwen 131 A5
Dylife 35 A1

E

Eglwys Fach 32 A2
Elan Village 71 C3
Erwood 101 B6
Esgairgeiliog Ceinws .22 C4
Evenjobb 76 E1

F

Faenor / Vaynor 148 D1
Felin-Crai 113 B2
Felindre Beguildy ...59 B4
Felindre Berriew 40 A8
Felindre Llanfihangel Cwmdu with
   Bwlch & Cathedine .118 A2
Felinfach 109 A4
Felin-newydd 109 D6
Felin Newydd / New Mills .39 A8
Ffawyddog 127 C5
Ffodun / Forden 41 A7
Fforddlas 102 F1
Ffridd 39 F2
Ffynnon Gynydd 102 B4
Fishpools 75 E7
Foel 15 F2
Forden / Ffodun 41 A7
Forge 33 C7
Four Crosses Llandysilio ..11 F1
Four Crosses
   Llanfair Caereinion ..27 B7
Frank's Bridge 84 C2
Frochas 20 F1
Fron Berriew 40 B4
Fron Forden with Leighton
   and Trelystan 30 D6
Fron Llanbadarn Fawr .74 A4
Furnace 32 A2

G

Gaer 126 E8
Garn 58 B4
Garn Fach 153 D1
Garnlydan 152 D5
Garth 90 E4
Garthbrengy 108 B4
Garthmyl 40 D6
Garth Owen 138 C2
Gaufron 72 D7
Geseilfa 46 F6
Geuffordd 19 D5
Gilwern 128 E2
Gladestry 86 C2
Glandyfi 32 B3
Glangrwyney 127 F3
Glanhanog 36 C6
Glanmule 50 B5
Glan-rhyd 147 F7
Glantwymyn /
   Cemmaes Road 23 C3
Glan-y-nant 55 C7
Glasbury 102 C2
Glascoed Kerry / Ceri ..48 F3
Glascoed Llangyniew .135 E8
Glascwm 94 A8
Glaspwll 32 F4
Gleiniant 47 A6
Glyn 46 B1
Glynbrochan 55 B6
Glyncoed 152 D2
Glynhafren 54 E7
Glyn-neath / Glyn-nedd .131 D1
Glyn-nedd / Glyn-neath .131 D1
Glyntawe 121 C3
Godre'r-graig 129 B1
Gorof 146 E1
Gravels 42 E7
Gravelsbank 42 E7
Great Cellws 73 E3
Green 41 F1
Gregynog 38 E4

Groesffordd
Groesffordd 116 C7
Groes-lwyd 19 C2
Groespluan 136 A7
Guilsfield / Cegidfa .19 E2
Gurnos 147 D7
Gwenddwr 100 D6
Gwernafon 46 B5
Gwerneirin 59 C3
Gwernydd 27 E1
Gwystre 73 D4

H

Haimwood 21 B7
Halfway 104 D3
Halfway House 21 E2
Hampton Beech 31 D4
Hardwicke 103 F6
Harpton 86 C6
Haughton 12 D1
Hay-on-Wye /
   Y Gelli Gandryll .144 C4
Hernford 42 E7
Hendomen 40 F4
Hengoed
   Michaelchurch-on-Arrow ..95 D6
Hengoed Newchurch ...95 B8
Heniarth 135 E7
Heol Senni 113 F2
Heyop 66 F5
Highgate 39 B2
Hirnant 8 B6
Hodley 50 B6
Hope 30 D6
Howey 83 C5
Hundred House 84 C1
Huntington 95 E8
Hurdley 42 B1
Hyssington 42 C1

K

Kerry / Ceri 49 F4
Kingswood 30 C1
Kington 87 D3
Kinnerton 76 D1
Knighton /
   Tref-y-Clawdd ...140 D6
Knill 87 C2
Knucklas / Cnwclas ..67 B5

L

Legar 127 D4
Leigh 31 F2
Leighton / Tre'r Ilai .30 E5
Libanus 115 A4
Limebrook 78 E5
Lingen 78 D6
Little London 48 B4
Little Worthen 31 F4
Llaithddu 57 E3
Llan 35 C7
Llanafan-fawr 81 F2
Llananno 64 D8
Llanarmon Dyffryn
   Ceiriog 4 D7
Llanbadarn Fynydd ...58 B1
Llanbadarn Fynydd ...64 D8
Llanbadarn-y-garreg ..93 C3
Llanbedr 127 F7
Llanbister 64 A6
Llanbrynmair 24 F1
Llancowrid 50 E6
Llanddew 145 F8
Llanddewi'r Cwm 143 B1
Llanddewi Ystradenni ..74 C7
Llandefaelog 108 A3
Llandefaelog-
   tre'r-graig 117 B8
Llandefalle 109 B6
Llandegley 74 F2
Llandeilo Graban ...101 A7
Llandeilo'r-Fan 105 E5
Llandinam 47 F3
Llandrindod /
   Llandrindod Wells .142 E5
Llandrindod Wells /
   Llandrindod 142 E5
Llandrinio 20 F7
Llandysilio 11 F2
Llandyssil 40 D2
Llangelwys 100 C1
Llanelieu 110 D5
Llanelly 127 E1
Llanelwedd 143 E7
Llanerch 52 B8
Llanerfyl 26 C6
Llanes 145 B4
Llanfair Caereinion .27 B6
Llanfair Waterdine ..67 A7
Llanfair-Ym-Muallt /
   Builth Wells 143 B4

Llanfaredd
Llanfaredd 92 E5
Llanfechain 10 D3
Llanfechan 91 A5
Llanfihangel-helygen ..73 B3
Llanfihangel Nant Bran .106 D5
Llanfihangel-
   nant-Melan 85 C5
Llanfihangel Rhydithon .75 A5
Llanfihangel Tal-y-llyn .116 F7
Llanfihangel-
   yng-Ngwynfa 17 C7
Llanfilo 109 D4
Llanfrynach 116 C4
Llanfyllin 134 D5
Llangadfan 16 B1
Llangammarch Wells ...90 D1
Llangasty-Talyllyn .117 C5
Llangedwyn 10 D7
Llangenny 127 F5
Llangors 117 C6
Llangunllo 66 D2
Llangurig 54 F2
Llangynidr 126 D6
Llangyniew 28 C8
Llanhamlach 116 E5
Llanidloes 139 E5
Llanifyny 54 B4
Llanigon 103 A3
Llanllugan 27 B1
Llanllwchaiarn 49 D7
Llanllwyd 59 D4
Llanllyr / Llanŷre .142 A7
Llanmerwig 50 A7
Llannerch-ym-
   Mochnant 4 A1
Llanrhaeadr-ym-
   Mochnant 9 D8
Llansantffraed 117 B2
Llansantffraed-
   Cwmdeuddwr 141 C4
Llansantffraed-in-Elwel .84 B1
Llansantffraid-ym-
   Mechain 11 B3
Llanslin 5 C3
Llanstephan 101 C7
Llanstephan 19 C5
Llanthony 119 F6
Llanwddyn 7 E1
Llanwenarth 128 D1
Llanwnog 47 F8
Llanwrin 22 E2
Llanwrthwl 72 A2
Llanwrtyd 89 B2
Llanwrtyd Wells 89 C2
Llanwyddelan 38 E8
Llanyblodwel 11 C6
Llanymynech 11 F4
Llany˜re / Llanllyr .142 A7
Llanywern 116 E7
Llawr-y-glyn 46 C6
Llechryd 152 D6
Llowes 102 E4
Lloyney 95 A6
Lloyney Beguildy 67 A6
Llwyndewi 29 E2
Llwyn-derw 55 A8
Llwyn-on-Village ...133 E6
Llwyn-y-go 12 E4
Llyswen Bronllys ...101 E1
Llyswen Bronllys ...109 D8
Llywel 105 C1
Lower Chapel 107 F6
Lower Hergest 87 A2
Lower Kinsham 78 C3
Lower Leighton 136 F3
Lyde 42 D8

M

Machynlleth 137 C4
Maesbrook 12 D4
Maesbury 10 B6
Maesbury Marsh 12 E8
Maesmynis 91 E2
Maesyfed / New Radnor .127 F1
Maesygwartha 127 F1
Maespandy 37 B2
Maesyrhandir 138 B2
Mainstone 52 A2
Mallwyd 13 E3
Manafon 28 B1
Marton 31 A1
Meadowtown 42 D8
Meifod 18 D4
Melinbyrhedyn 34 B6
Melin-y-ddôl 27 C6
Melverley 21 D7
Merthyr Cynog 107 B8
Michaelchurch-
   on-Arrow 95 D5
Middletown 21 A3
Milebrook 68 B3

Milford	138 A4
Milton	95 A5
Minllyn	13 D5
Mochdre	48 E3
Moity	102 D5
Monaughty	76 C7
Montgomery / Trefaldwyn	41 B4
Morfa Glas	131 B1
Morton	12 C7

N

Nant-ddu	124 A1
Nant-glas	72 D4
Nantgwyn	62 E7
Nantmawr	11 D7
Nantmel	72 F5
Nantoer	138 A3
Nant-y-Bwch	151 B1
Nant-y-cafn	130 C2
Nantyglo	153 D2
Nash	77 D1
Newbridge Llangyniew	18 B2
Newbridge Oswestry Rural	12 D8
Newbridge-on-Wye	82 F5
Newchapel	56 B6
Newchurch	152 E1
Newchurch	95 A5
New Invention	67 F8
New Mills / Felin Newydd	39 A8
New Radnor / Maesyfed	86 A8
Newton	78 E8
Newtown	152 E1
Newtown / Y Drenewydd	138 D3
New Wells	39 F3
Norton	77 D6

O

Oakley Park	47 B1
Obley	68 C8
Ochr Hen-fache	3 F2
Old Church Stoke	42 A1
Old Hall	54 F7
Old Neuadd	48 E1
Old Radnor	86 E6
Onllwyn	130 F5
Osbaston	12 E5

P

Pandy	24 E3
Panpunton	140 B7
Pant	12 A4
Pant-glâs	33 D4
Pant Mawr	53 F5

Pantperthog	22 A3
Pant-y-dwr	62 E5
Pant-y-ffridd	28 F1
Pantyffynnon	147 A4
Pedair-ffordd	9 C7
Penarron	49 E3
Pencelli	116 E4
Pencraig	2 E2
Penderyn	132 E3
Pendre	145 D6
Penffordd-Lâs / Staylittle	45 E7
Pengenffordd	110 B1
Pennal	32 C7
Pennant	35 B4
Pennant Melangell	2 C1
Pennorth	117 A5
Penrallt	46 E1
Pen-Rhiw-fawr	129 B5
Penrhos	130 B6
Pentre Forden with Leighton and Trelystan	30 C4
Pentre Llangynog	8 C8
Pentre Meifod	18 C4
Pentre Mochdre	48 D1
Pentre-bach	105 F4
Pentre Dolau Honddu	99 B6
Pentrefelin	10 B7
Pentreheyling	51 D8
Pentre Hodre	68 C7
Pentre Llifior	39 E5
Pentre-llwyn-llŵyd	81 E1
Pentre'r beirdd	19 B4
Pentre'r-felin	106 A1
Pentre-ty-gwyn	104 C6
Penwyllt	121 D2
Penybont	74 C3
Penybontfawr	9 A7
Pen-y-bont Llanerch Emrys	10 F6
Pen y Foel	11 F4
Penygarnedd	9 B6
Penygelli	49 E6
Pilleth	76 E7
Plas Llysyn	36 D4
Plas Meredydd	40 C4
Plasnewydd	36 F3
Plas-rhiw-Saeson	24 D4
Ponde	109 B8
Pont ar Hydfer	112 F6
Pontbren Llwyd	132 D3
Pont Crugnant	35 C2
Pontdolgoch	47 D8
Pont-faen	107 C5
Pontithel	110 B7
Pont Llogel	16 D6
Pontneddfechan	131 E3
Pont Rhydgaled	53 E5
Pont Rhyd-y-berry	107 A7
Pontrobert	17 F3
Pontsenni / Sennybridge	113 E8
Pontsticill	148 F4

Pont-Walby / Pontwalby	131 E1
Pont-y-Gôf	152 D1
Pont-y-wal	109 E6
Pool Quay	20 B2
Presteigne	77 E2
Presteigne / Llanandras	77 D2
Priest Weston	42 B4
Priory Wood	103 E8
Purlogue	67 E8
Pwll	29 D3
Pwllgloyw	108 A4

R

Rassau	152 B4
Refail	40 D7
Rhôs Common	12 B1
Rhaeadr Gwy / Rhayader	141 C5
Rhayader / Rhaeadr Gwy	141 C5
Rhiwargor	6 F7
Rhiwlas	5 B6
Rhos	20 D8
Rhos-goch	94 D2
Rhos-y-brithdir	9 E6
Rhos-y-meirch	77 A8
Rhulen	93 E4
Rhyd	36 F7
Rhydlydan	48 C8
Rhydspence	95 D2
Rhydspence	95 D5
Rhydyfelin	48 F7
Rodd	77 F1
Rodd Hurst	77 F1
Rorrington	42 B7
Rowley	31 C5

S

St Harmon	62 E3
Sarn	50 F5
Sarnau Honddu Isaf	107 F3
Sarnau Llandrinio	19 F6
Scethrog	116 F4
Scrwgan	10 D6
Scwrfa	151 D1
Sennybridge / Pontsenni	113 E8
Seven Sisters / Blaendulais	130 D3
Shelve	42 F6
Sirhowy / Sirhywi	151 F1
Sirhywi / Sirhowy	151 F1
Skyborry Green	67 C5
Slough	77 D2
Snead	52 E6
Soar	107 A3
Stanner	86 F5
Stapleton	77 F4

Staylittle / Penffordd-Lâs	45 E7
Stepaside	48 E4
Stockton	41 E8
Stowe	68 B4
Tafolwern	24 C1
Tai'r Bull	115 A5
Talachddu	108 E4
Talerddig	36 B7
Talgarth	110 B4
Talybont-on-Usk	117 A1
Talyllyn	116 F6
Tal-y-Wern	34 C7
Tan Hinon	54 E8
The Colony	77 E6
The Groves	145 D5
The Haim	21 C7
The Marsh	42 C4
Thorn	77 A2
Three Cocks	110 B8
Tirabad	97 C4
Trallong	114 D8
Trawscoed	108 F5
Treberfydd	117 C4
Trecastle	113 A7
Trederwen	20 D6
Tre-derwen	11 D2
Tredomen	109 D2
Tredustan	109 E3
Trefaldwyn / Montgomery	41 B4
Trefeca	109 F3
Trefeglwys	47 A5
Trefeitha	109 B2
Trefil	151 A6
Treflach	11 F8
Trefnanney	19 C6
Tref-y-Clawdd / Knighton	140 D6
Tregeiriog	4 F8
Tregoyd Mill	110 D8
Tregynon	38 F5
Trehafren	138 B4
Trelystan	30 D2
Treowen	138 D3
Tre'r llai / Leighton	136 E1
Tretower	127 A8
Trewern	20 E2
Trwstllewelyn	40 C5
Twyn Cynhordy	153 A3
Tycyrwyn	9 B1
Tyddyn	47 C2
Tylwch	56 A3
Tynewydd Seven Sisters / Blaendulais	130 D4
Tynewydd Tredegar	151 B3
Tyn-y-graig	91 E4
Tynyrwtra	54 D8

U

Upper Chapel	99 D3
Upper Hergest	86 E1
Upper Kinsham	78 D4

V

Van	46 D2
Varchoel	19 F3
Vaynor / Faenor	148 D1
Velindre	110 D7
Vennington	31 F8
Vron Gate	31 F8

W

Waen	11 C2
Waen-fâch	19 D8
Walton	86 E6
Warden	77 D3
Wattlesborough Heath	21 F2
Waundeg	151 B2
Welshpool / Y Trallwng	136 E4
Wern Carreghofa	11 E3
Wern Llandrinio	20 B4
Wern Llangynidr	125 F4
Wernlas	12 E3
Weston	68 C4
Weythel	86 C4
White Grit	42 D4
Whitney-on-Wye	95 F2
Whitton	77 A6
Wig	49 C2
Willowtown	152 B1
Winchestown	153 B2
Winchfawr	133 F1
Winllan	11 B4
Wollaston	21 D3
Womaston	86 F7
Worthen	31 F3
Wotherton	42 A7

Y

Yardro	86 B5
Y Drenewydd / Newtown	138 D3
Y Fenni / Abergavenny	128 E1
Ynyswen	130 E8
Ystalyfera	147 A6
Ystradfellte	132 B8
Ystradgynlais	130 A5
Ystradowen	129 C2
Ystrad Uchaf	27 D2
Y Trallwng / Welshpool	136 E4

A		
Abercrave Cty Prim Sch SA9	.130	C7
Abercrave Terr SA9	.130	D7
Aberdare Rd SA11	.131	D1
Aberedw Castle* LD2	.92	E2
Abergavenny Rd NP7	.128	B1
Aberhafesp CP Sch SY16	.48	C8
Aberhenwaun Uchaf SA10	.130	E4
Aberllefenni Forest Trail* SY20	.22	D8
Abermule Dolforwyn Prim Sch SY15	.40	A1
Abertridwr SY10	.8	A1
Acorn Cl NP23	.152	C5
Acorn Rise SY21	.136	C6
Acrefield Ave ❶ SA9	.19	E2
Addoldy Rd SA11	.131	C1
Adelaide Dr SY21	.136	B6
Aelybryn SY20	.22	C4
Ael-y-bryn Carno SY17	.36	D4
Ystradgynlais SA9	.130	A5
Agincourt Dr SY21	.19	E2
Alandale Rd NP23	.152	A4
Albany Rd ❹ NP7	.128	E2
Albert Terr Hay-on-Wye HR3	.144	E3
❺ Welshpool / Y Trallwng SY21	.136	C5
Albridge La SY10	.12	C8
Alder Ave SA9	.147	D7
Alder Gr NP23	.152	C5
Alder Way LD2	.82	E1
Alderwood Cl SA10	.130	A1
Alexander Cl LD8	.77	C5
Alexandra Rd Brecon / Aberhonddu LD3	.145	D4
Disserth & Trecoed LD2	.142	C3
Alexandra Terr LD2	.142	C3
Alexandra Terr ❽ NP23	.153	C4
Alfred St NP23	.152	C1
Allerford Gr ❷ NP7	.128	A1
Allotment Rd NP23	.152	C3
Allt View LD3	.117	D1
Allt-y-crug LD1	.72	A2
Alltygrug Farm Rd SA9	.147	B7
Alltygrug Rd SA9	.147	B7
Alma St SY21	.153	D5
Alma Terr NP23	.153	D5
Almonde Ave LD1	.142	C6
Andrews Ct NP23	.152	B1
Aneurin Pl NP23	.153	C5
Annes Ct NP23	.152	C1
Apostles La HR3	.95	F6
Appletree Mdw LD8	.77	F3
Archdeacon Griffiths C in W (A) Sch LD3	.101	D1
Arches Cl / Clos Y Bwau NP22	.151	D2
Arddleen Cty Prim Sch / Ysgol Gynradd Arddllin SY22	.20	B6
Arddlceen Rd SY21	.19	E2
Arddol Terr SY20	.22	B6
Ardwyn Infants Sch SY21	.136	B6
Arfryn Terr NP23	.152	D4
Arlais Rd LD1	.142	C3
Arnold Ct SA9	.147	B6
Arnold Pl NP22	.151	C6
Arrow Ct Ind Est HR5	.87	A1
Arrow View HR5	.87	A1
Arthurs Gate ❷ SY21	.41	A4
Arthur St SY15	.41	A3
Ash Cl SY16	.138	E6
Ashfield Dr ❷ SY22	.11	F3
Ashfield Pl LD3	.145	A3
Ash Gr HR3	.153	C4
Ashmere Dr SA11	.131	F2
Ashridge Cl LD2	.142	C2
Ashvale NP22	.151	C1
Attlee Cl NP23	.152	D6
Avalon Terr NP22	.151	E1
Avenue Cres ❷ NP7	.128	F2
Avenue Ct ❸ LD3	.145	C4
Avenue Rd NP7	.128	E1
Avenue The LD3	.145	C4
Avon Ct NP23	.152	C5
Avon St SA11	.131	C1
Awelfa SY21	.135	A3
Awelfryn Cl NP23	.152	E4

B		
Bachie La SY22	.134	B3
Bachie Rd SY22	.134	C4
Back Chapel St SY10	.4	A1
Back Fold HR3	.144	D3
Back La Bausley with Criggion SY5	.20	E6
❺ Montgomery / Trefaldwyn SY21	.41	A3
Newtown / Y Drenewydd SY16	.138	D5
Presteigne LD8	.77	E3
❸ Talgarth LD3	.110	A4
Back Rd ❾ NP7	.128	A1
Badminton Gr NP23	.152	D3
Bailey St Brynmawr NP23	.153	C4
Baillheilg Rd LD3	.145	B2
Baker St NP7	.128	F1
Bala Cl NP23	.152	A5

Bala Cotts SA9	.130	A6
Ball La SY10	.12	D8
Bangor Rd NP23	.152	E4
Bank Cotts SA9	.130	A6
Bank Cres NP7	.128	A2
Bank La ❽ Llanelly NP7	.128	A2
Machynlleth SY20	.137	D4
Bank Sq ❸ LD2	.143	D5
Bank St Llanfyllin SY22	.134	C5
Machynlleth SY20	.137	C4
Bank The Newtown / Y Drenewydd SY16	.138	D5
Talgarth LD3	.110	A4
Banley Dr ❽ HR5	.87	D3
Banna Bglws NP23	.153	C2
Banw CP Sch SY21	.16	A2
Banwy Ind Est SY21	.135	D4
Baptist Pl NP23	.152	D4
Barley Field Rd NP23	.153	C3
Barley Mdws SY22	.11	F3
Barnes Cl NP23	.152	A4
Barns La NP23	.138	E5
Barons Way LD8	.77	C5
Barton La HR5	.87	C3
Basildene Cl / Clos Basildene NP23	.128	B1
❶ Welshpool / Y Trallwng SY21	.136	C5
Baskerville Ct HR3	.144	A6
Bath La NP23	.153	A4
Beacon Hts CF48	.133	E2
Beacons Cl ❸ LD3	.116	B7
Beaconsfield NP7	.127	F1
Beacons Pk Brecon / Aberhonddu LD3	.145	C6
Penderyn CF44	.132	D3
Beacon View NP23	.153	D1
Bear Lanes SY16	.138	D5
Bear Lanes Sh Ctr The SY16	.138	D5
Bear St HR3	.144	E3
Beaufort Ave ❷ NP8	.127	D4
Beaufort Cl NP22	.151	F1
Beaufort Hill Ebbw Vale / Glyn Ebwy NP23	.152	E4
Tredegar NP22	.152	A1
Beaufort Hill Prim Sch NP23	.152	F4
Beaufort Rd Disserth & Trecoed LD1	.142	D4
Ebbw Vale / Glyn Ebwy NP23	.152	D2
Tredegar NP22	.151	F1
Beaufort Rise NP23	.153	C4
Beaufort St Brynmawr NP23	.153	C4
Crickhowell NP8	.127	D5
Beaufort Terr LD3	.110	A4
Beddoes View LD8	.77	E3
Bedw Hir Gdn* LD2	.100	C7
Beech Cl SY16	.138	E6
Beeches Pk LD3	.101	D1
Beechfield Cl NP23	.152	D6
Beech Gr SY16	.49	F5
Beechgrove LD3	.145	D5
Beechwood Dr SY16	.138	E6
Beechwood Rd ❶ NP8	.127	D4
Beehive La SY16	.138	A5
Beguildy C in W Sch LD7	.59	F7
Begwns Bluff HR3	.144	A6
Belan Fields SY21	.19	D2
Belan Sch La SY21	.29	E2
Belgrave Ct ❸ NP7	.128	F1
Belgrave Rd NP7	.128	E1
Bell Bank HR3	.144	D3
Belle Vue Gdns LD3	.145	D4
Belle Vue Rd LD3	.145	C4
Bell La ❾ LD3	.145	C4
Bell St ❸ LD3	.110	A4
Belmont Rd HR3	.144	D3
Berllan ❺ SY22	.11	F3
Berriew CP Sch SY21	.40	C8
Berriew Rd SY21	.136	B4
Berriew St ❸ SY21	.136	B4
Berrington Villas / Filas Berrington SY21	.129	C7
Berthllwyd ❸ LD5	.89	D1
Berwyn St SY10	.2	F1
Bethania St SA11	.131	D1
Bethania Terr SY20	.22	A7
Bethel Rd Glynneath SA11	.131	D1
Ystradgynlais SA9	.147	D8
Bethel Sq Sh Ctr LD3	.145	D4
Bethel St SY18	.139	D5
Betton Dingle Nature Reserve* SY5	.31	D1
Beulah Rd LD5	.89	C1
Bevan Ave NP22	.151	C1
Bevan Cres NP23	.152	F4
Big La NP23	.152	F4
Billingsley Cl ❷ SY9	.52	F3
Binweston La SY5	.31	B3
Birch Cl SY22	.12	A1
Birches The ❷ HR3	.102	C2
Birch Gr LD3	.153	B5
Birch Way LD2	.82	E1
Bishop's Castle Bsns Pk SY9	.52	F3
Bishop's Castle Prim Sch SY9	.52	F3
Bishops Castle Rly Mus* SY9	.52	F3
Bishops Castle St ❶ SY15	.41	A3
Black Barn ❼ HR5	.87	D3
Blackbridge La SY10	.12	A5
Black Bridge La SY17	.47	F4

Black Friars Ct LD3	.145	A3
Black La SY22	.19	F5
Blaen-Afon Rd NP7, NP23	.153	C3
Blaenant Ind Est NP23	.153	C3
Blaen Cendl NP23	.152	E4
Blaen Cwm SA10	.130	D3
Blaendulais Prim Sch SA10	.130	D3
Blaen-Nant Rd NP23	.153	C2
Blaenycwm Jun & Inf Sch NP23	.153	C3
Blaina Rd NP23	.153	C3
Blodwel Bank SY10	.11	E7
Bluebell Cl ❶ SY21	.136	D6
Blue Bell Dr ❶ SY21	.136	B6
Bodivan SY16	.138	A4
Bodlonden La SY20	.137	C4
Boot St SY21	.136	B5
Borderers Way ❸ LD3	.145	D3
Borfa Gn SY21	.136	B6
Boundary St NP23	.153	B4
Bowling Gn Cl ❹ SY9	.52	F3
Bowling Gn La Knighton / Tref-y-Clawdd LD7	.140	C5
❶ Welshpool / Y Trallwng SY21	.136	C6
Bradnor HR5	.87	C4
Bradnor Hill (NT)* HR5	.87	B5
Bradnor View Cl HR5	.87	C3
Braggington La SY21	.21	D5
Braich-Goch Terr SY20	.22	B6
Bramble Cl ❷ SY16	.138	E6
Brampton Rd ❾ SY9	.52	F2
Brecknock Mus & Art Gall* LD3	.145	C3
Brecon Cath* LD3	.145	D5
Brecon Ent Pk LD3	.145	A3
Brecon Her Ctr* LD3	.145	D4
Brecon High Sch / Ysgol Uwchradd Aberhonddu LD3	.145	D5
Brecon Leisure Ctr & Swimming Pool LD3	.145	E5
Brecon Mountain Railway* CF48	.149	A4
Brecon Rd Abergavenny / Y Fenni NP7	.128	F1
Builth LD2	.143	C6
Crickhowell NP8	.127	D6
Hay-on-Wye HR3	.144	C2
Ystradgynlais SA9	.146	F1
Brecon Rd / Heol Rheolau Abercrave / Aberhonddu LD3	.130	B7
Ystradgynlais SA9	.130	A5
Brecon Terr NP22	.150	F1
Brecon War Meml Hospl LD3	.145	E4
Breidden Ave LD3	.20	B6
Breidden Way SY21	.19	E2
Brentwood Pl NP23	.152	C1
Briar Cl NP23	.152	D5
Brickfield St SY20	.137	C4
Brick Row / Rhes Bricksen SA10	.130	D3
Brickyard Cotts LD3	.130	B7
Brickyard Rd HR5	.87	A2
Bridgeend La SY7	.68	E5
Bridge Sea Mdw SY7	.68	E5
Bridge St Brecon / Aberhonddu LD3	.145	C4
Caersws SY17	.48	A6
Corris SY20	.22	B6
Crickhowell NP8	.127	D5
Cwm-twrch Isaf SA9	.146	B1
Ebbw Vale / Glyn Ebwy NP23	.152	D1
Hay-on-Wye HR3	.144	D3
Kington HR5	.87	C3
Knighton / Tref-y-Clawdd LD7	.140	C5
Llanfair Caereinion SY21	.135	B3
Llanfyllin SY22	.134	C5
Rhayader / Rhaeadr Gwy LD6	.141	C4
Briggs La SY10	.12	A5
Brilley CE Prim Sch HR3	.95	F4
Brilley Prim Sch HR3	.95	F4
Brimmon Cl SY16	.138	D3
Brimmon La SY16	.138	D3
Brimmon Rd SY16	.138	D3
Brithdir La SY21	.29	C1
Broadaxe LD8	.77	E2
Broadaxe Bsns Pk LD8	.77	E2
Broadmead ❺ NP7	.128	B1
Broadmeadow LD3	.103	F5
Broad St Hay-on-Wye HR3	.144	D4
Knighton / Tref-y-Clawdd LD7	.140	C5
Llanfair Caereinion SY21	.135	B3
New Radnor / Maesyfed LD8	.86	A4
Newtown / Y Drenewydd SY16	.138	D5
Presteigne LD8	.77	E3
Welshpool / Y Trallwng SY21	.136	B5
Broadway ❶ Builth Wells LD2	.143	C6
Disserth & Trecoed LD2	.142	D4
Brockton Mdw SY5	.31	D3
Brodawel SA11	.131	F2

Bro Ddyfi Com Hospl / Ysbyty Gymuned Bro Ddyfi SY20	.137	E4
Bro Dulas Llangurig SY18	.139	B4
Machynlleth SY20	.137	E8
Bro Feiniog SY22	.17	E3
Bronant ❻ LD1	.143	C6
Broncaernant La SY21	.135	B3
Bronhafod NP23	.153	C5
Bronhaul SA20	.96	B2
Bronllys Castle* LD3	.109	F5
Bronllys CP Sch LD3	.109	F5
Bronllys Hospl LD3	.109	E6
Bronllys Rd LD3	.110	A5
Bronwylfa SY22	.11	F4
Bronwylfa Rd SY21	.136	B5
Bronybuckley SY21	.136	B5
Bron-y-crug LD2	.145	C5
Bronygaer SY22	.136	B5
Bron Yr Allt SA9	.147	A8
Brookfield LD3	.110	B8
Brookfield Rd NP23	.136	B6
Brookfields ❺ Crickhowell NP8	.127	C5
Disserth & Trecoed LD1	.142	C4
Llandrindod Wells / Llandrindod LD1	.83	D8
Brookland Rd LD1	.142	C6
Brooklands NP22	.151	C2
Brooklands Terr SA9	.130	C2
Brooklyn Rd SY10	.12	A5
Brookside ❺ SY5	.31	E3
Brook St Brynmawr NP23	.153	B4
Hay-on-Wye HR3	.144	E3
Llanfyllin SY22	.134	C5
Llandbees SY18	.139	C5
❷ Welshpool / Y Trallwng SY21	.136	C5
Brook Terr SY20	.13	D4
Bro-y-Ffrwd CF48	.133	F2
Brunley Cl HR3	.95	F4
Bryans Ground Gdns* LD8	.78	A3
Brydes Gate SY22	.20	E8
Brynafal Bridge Ct HR3	.95	D3
Brynawel NP23	.151	C2
Brynawelon Brecon / Aberhonddu LD3	.145	F3
Cefn-bryn-brain SA9	.129	B8
Coelbren SA10	.130	A5
❷ Llanwrtyd Wells LD5	.89	D1
Winchestown NP23	.153	B2
Bryn Awelon Beaufort Hill NP23	.152	E4
Ebbw Vale / Glyn Ebwy NP23	.152	E4
Brynawel Rd SA9	.146	F1
Brynawel Terr SA9	.129	C7
Bryn Bach Countryside Ctr* NP22	.151	B1
Bryn Bach Pk* NP23	.151	B1
Bryn Bach Prim Sch NP22	.151	C1
Brynbach St NP22	.151	C1
Brynbedd Enterprise Est LD3	.141	E5
Bryn Cain SY22	.11	A3
Bryn-Celyn SY10	.12	C6
Bryn Celyn Way ❶ NP8	.126	D6
Bryn Cl SY16	.138	D6
Bryn Coch NP23	.153	C5
Bryncoed SY5	.21	D5
Bryncriafol LD1	.74	C2
Bryn Derwen ❶ LD3	.110	A5
Bryn De Winton LD3	.145	D4
Bryndulais Ave SA10	.130	C3
Bryndulais Row / Rhes Bryndulais SA10	.130	C4
Bryn-du Rd SY18	.139	C5
Bryn Ebbw NP23	.152	C6
Brynegiwys ❸ SY22	.134	C5
Bryneithin LD3	.107	D2
Bryneithyn SA9	.146	C1
Brynfa Ave / Lon Brynfa SY21	.136	C6
Bryn Gdns SY16	.138	C6
Brynglas Brecon / Aberhonddu LD3	.145	B3
❶ Gwbert NP7	.128	A1
Bryn Glas Ebbw Vale / Glyn Ebwy NP23	.152	C2
Welshpool / Y Trallwng SY21	.136	C6
Bryn Gwyn LD6	.141	D4
Bryn Gwyn NP23	.152	D6
Brynhafren Cty Prim Sch SY5	.21	D5
Bryn Haul / Sun Hill LD6	.62	E4
Brynheulog SA10	.130	A3
Brynhyfryd Ave NP23	.131	D1
Brynhyfryd Rd NP23	.153	C1
Brynhyfryd Terr / Teras Brynhyfryd NP23	.130	D4
Bryn Kendall NP23	.152	C4
Bryn La Newtown & Llanllwchaiarn SY16	.138	B6
Trewern SY21	.30	D5
Bryn Llwyd SY19	.45	C7

Brynllywarch Hall Sch SY16	.50	A4
Brynmawr Comp Sch NP23	.153	D6
Brynmawr RC Jun & Inf Sch NP23	.153	C4
Brynmawr Rd ❻ LD3	.145	D3
Bryn Mdws SY16	.138	D6
Bryn Meadow Ct NP23	.151	C1
Bryn Nant ❼ NP23	.127	D5
Bryn Offa (Controlled) CE Prim Sch The SY10	.12	A4
Bryn Onnen CF44	.132	D2
Bryn Pica NP22	.151	F1
Bryn Rd Cwmllynfell SA9	.129	B7
Ystradgynlais SA9	.130	A5
Bryn Rhosys NP22	.151	B2
Bryn-Serth Rd NP23	.152	A3
Bryn Siriol ❶ Llansantffraid SY22	.11	A3
Welshpool / Y Trallwng SY21	.136	D6
Bryn St SY16	.138	D6
Brynteg Bettws SY16	.39	C3
Disserth & Trecoed LD2	.142	C1
Llandrindod Wells / Llandrindod LD1	.83	D6
Seven Sisters / Blaendulais SA10	.130	C2
Bryn Teg SY22	.20	B6
Bryn Terr CF48	.148	F3
Bryn View NP23	.153	D1
Brynwood Dr SY16	.138	C5
Bryn-y-castell ❻ SY21	.136	B3
Bryn-y-ddol SY21	.136	C6
Bryn-y-gog SY20	.137	D6
Brynygroes Cotts SA9	.146	F2
Bryn-y-Grug SY21	.147	A7
Buckland Dr LD3	.117	D1
Bucknell Sta SY7	.68	F4
Builth Castle* LD2	.143	D6
Builth Rd Sta LD2	.91	F8
Builth Wells CP Sch LD2	.143	C5
Builth Wells High Sch / Ysgol Uwchradd Llanfair-ym-muallt LD2	.143	C6
Builth Wells Sports Ctr LD2	.143	C6
Bull Dingle SY16	.136	C6
Bull La ❷ SY9	.52	F4
Bulwark LD3	.145	C4
Burgess Croft SY21	.136	B6
Burnt Hengoed HR3	.95	F6
Burnt La SY21	.20	C1
Bush Bach NP7	.151	C2
Butleigh Terr NP22	.151	C1
Buttington Cross SY21	.136	F7
Buttington Trewern CP Sch SY21	.20	D1
Bwlch-y-Garn Rd NP23	.152	A4
Bytheny SY5	.20	E4
Bythnnod Y Llew Gwyn / White Lion Cotts NP22	.151	C2

C		
Cae Bach / Paddocks The LD8	.77	E3
Cae-Boncyn La SY22	.134	D6
Cae Camlad ❸ SY15	.41	F1
Caecamlas SY16	.138	E5
Cae Capel / Chapel Field SY22	.20	B6
Cae Castell LD2	.143	C5
Cae Celyn SY21	.40	C7
Cae Coed SY15	.137	E4
Cae Crwn SY20	.137	E4
Cae Dafydd SY22	.18	D4
Caedogar Rd SA9	.146	F2
Cae Derw Brecon / Aberhonddu LD3	.145	B5
❻ Llanelly NP7	.128	B1
Caedu Rd SA9	.147	C8
Cae Elfan LD8	.77	D5
Caegwyn Cl LD3	.139	C4
Caegwyn Isaf SY18	.139	C5
Cae-Gybi Rd SY20	.137	B3
Cae Haidd SY21	.11	F3
Caeherbert La LD3	.141	D4
Caehopkin Cty Prim Sch SA9	.130	D7
Cae Llewellyn LD2	.91	D6
Cae Maenllwyd SY20	.137	E4
Cae Mawr SA10	.130	D3
Cae Meldon NP7	.128	A2
Cae Melyn Ebbw Vale / Glyn Ebwy NP23	.152	C2
❷ Tregynon SY16	.77	E3
Cae Parc LD3	.145	F8
Cae Pen Y Dre ❷ HR3	.144	D3
Cae Porth ❻ NP7	.128	A6
Caepound HR3	.144	D2
Caer-af-allen ❷ LD2	.115	A5
Caerbont Ent Pk / Parc Manter Caerbont SA9	.130	D6
Caereinion High Sch / Ysgol Uwchradd Caereinion SY21	.135	B4

Caereinion Leisure Center
SY21 ....135 B4
Caerhowel Mdws 3
SY15 ....40 E5
Caerleon Gr CF48 ....133 F1
Caernarvon Gr CF48 ....133 F1
Cae Robert SY22 ....18 D4
Caersws CP Sch SY17 ....48 A7
Caersws Sta SY17 ....47 F7
Cae-y-nant SY16 ....39 C3
Cagebrook La LD1 ....142 A7
Cain Ct / Llys Cain
SY22 ....134 C6
Cain Valley Trading Est
SY22 ....134 D4
Cambrian Gdns 2 SY16 ....138 E5
Cambrian Mill Heritage Ctr*
LD5 ....89 C2
Cambrian Pl
Cwm-twrch Uchaf SA9 ....129 C6
2 Llanidloes SY18 ....139 D5
Cambrian Way SY16 ....138 E5
Cambridge Gdns NP23 ....152 B3
Camden Cres LD3 ....145 D4
Camden Rd LD3 ....145 E3
Camlad Dr SY21 ....40 F6
Camlo Cl LD1 ....73 D4
Camnant Rd SA10 ....131 A5
Campion Cl 1 SY16 ....49 D7
Canal Pl SA11 ....131 D1
Canal Rd
Brecon / Aberhonddu LD3 ....145 D3
Llandysilio SY22 ....11 F1
SY16 ....138 E5
Canal Terr SA9 ....147 B6

Canolfan = centre

Canolfan SA10 ....130 C3
Canterbury Rd NP23 ....152 F3
Cantref Rd NP7 ....128 E2
Capital Bldgs SA9 ....147 C7
Carew Gr / Llwyn Caeriw
CF48 ....133 F1
Carlsgate HR3 ....144 D3
Carmel Cl NP22 ....152 C5
Carmel St NP22 ....151 E1
Carngafallt Nature Reserve*
LD1 ....71 D3
Carno Cl NP23 ....152 C5
Carno CP Sch SY17 ....36 D3
Carno Rd SY17 ....47 F6
Carreghofa La SY22 ....11 E3
Carregoffa CP Sch SY22 ....11 F3
Carreg Yr Afon SA9 ....129 C2
Castell Morlais CF48 ....148 F3
Castle Caereinion Sta
SY21 ....29 A4
Castle Est HR3 ....144 A6
Castle Gdns HR3 ....144 D3
Castle Gn 1 SY9 ....52 F4
Castle Hill 10 HR5 ....87 C3
Castlehill La SY21 ....11 F5
Castle La HR3 ....144 D3
Castle Mdw LD2 ....94 B1
Castle Rd
Builth Wells / Llanfair-Ym-Muallt
LD2 ....143 D5
Crickhowell NP8 ....127 D5
Knighton / Tref-y-Clawdd
LD7 ....140 B5
Llangynidr NP8 ....126 C6
Presteigne LD8 ....77 E3
Rhayader / Rhaeadr Gwy
LD6 ....141 C5
Castle Rd Bglws LD8 ....77 E3
Castle Sq LD3 ....145 C4
Castle St
Brecon / Aberhonddu LD3 ....145 C4
Builth Wells / Llanfair-Ym-Muallt
LD2 ....143 D6
Hay-on-W HR3 ....144 D3
1 Llanidloes SY18 ....139 C6
Castle Wlk 2 SY21 ....136 B3
Catholic Rd SY21 ....136 B3
Causemountain La SY5 ....31 E7
Cedar Cl
Ebbw Vale / Glyn Ebwy
NP23 ....152 C5
Presteigne LD8 ....77 E3
Cedewain SY16 ....138 C3
Cefn Byrle Rd SA10 ....130 A6
Cefn Crib Cvn Pk SY20 ....32 A6
Cefn Hawys 3 SY21 ....136 B6
Cefn La SY10 ....11 E7
Cefnllys La LD1 ....142 D3
Cefn Morfa LD1 ....142 E4
Cefn Rd Maescar LD3 ....113 F6
Michaelchurch-on-A HR3 ....95 D4
Cefn-yr-Erw Rare Breeds
farm* SA9 ....130 E7
Cefn-yspin La SY21 ....138 E4
Ceiriog SY16 ....138 E4
Celyn La SY21 ....19 E2
Cemetery La SY21 ....19 D2
Cemetery Rd
Ebbw Vale / Glyn Ebwy, Pont-y-Gof
NP23 ....152 A1
Knighton / Tref-y-Clawdd
LD7 ....140 C6
Cemetery Sq SY18 ....139 D5
Cemetrey Rd 1 NP23 ....153 B4

Cendl Cres NP23 ....152 C4
Centre for Alternative
Technology* SY20 ....22 B3
Cerrigcochan La LD3 ....145 D4
Cerrigcochan Rd LD3 ....145 C4
Chain Cl NP7 ....128 F2
Chain Rd NP7 ....128 F2
Chain Wlk SA11 ....131 C1
Chancery Ct HR3 ....144 E3
Chancery La HR3 ....144 D3
Chandlers Rd NP23 ....152 E4
Chapel Field / Cae Capel
SY22 ....20 B6
Chapel Fields SY21 ....40 D7
Chapel La
Abergavenny / Y Fenni
NP7 ....128 F2
Carreghofa SY22 ....11 F3
Chapel Orch 4 NP7 ....128 F2
Chapel Rd
Abergavenny / Y Fenni
NP7 ....128 F2
Nantyglo NP23 ....153 C2
Penderyn CF44 ....132 D3
Whitney-on-W HR3 ....95 F3
Chapel St
6 Brecon / Aberhonddu
LD3 ....145 C4
Brynmawr NP23 ....153 B4
Corris SY20 ....22 B6
1 Llanidloes SY18 ....139 C5
Llywel LD3 ....113 B7
Welshpool / Y Trallwng
SY21 ....136 B5
Charles Ct NP23 ....152 B1
Charles St
Brecon / Aberhonddu LD3 ....145 D3
Tredegar NP22 ....151 D1
Chartist Way NP22 ....151 E1
Chelsea La SY21 ....136 B4
Chemical Row SA9 ....147 A4
Chepstow Cl CF48 ....133 F1
Cherry Cl NP23 ....152 D2
Chester Cl CF48 ....133 F1
Chestnut Cl
Ebbw Vale / Glyn Ebwy
NP23 ....152 C5
9 Llandrinio SY22 ....12 A1
Chestnut Mdw SY7 ....68 F5
Chestnut View SY16 ....49 F4
Chirbury CE Prim Sch
SY15 ....41 E5
Chirbury Gate 1 SY15 ....41 A3
Chirbury Rd SY15 ....41 A3
Christ Coll LD3 ....145 C3
Church Ave NP23 ....152 F4
Church Bank
Bishop's Castle SY9 ....52 F3
8 Brecon / Aberhonddu
LD3 ....145 C4
Brynmawr NP23 ....153 C5
Cusop HR3 ....144 F2
2 Guilsfield SY21 ....19 D2
3 Llanidloes SY18 ....139 C6
Llansantffraid SY22 ....11 A3
Melverley SY22 ....21 D7
Whitney-on-W HR3 ....95 F2
Church Rd Bronllys LD3 ....101 E1
Clifford HR3 ....103 E8
Cusop HR3 ....144 F2
Gilwern NP7 ....128 A1
Kington HR5 ....87 C3
Knighton / Tref-y-Clawdd
LD7 ....140 C5
Llanelly NP7 ....127 F1
Penderyn CF44 ....132 D3
Welshpool / Y Trallwng
SY21 ....136 B5
Ystalyfera SA9 ....147 A4
Church St
7 Bishop's Castle SY9 ....52 F3
Brecon / Aberhonddu LD3 ....145 B3
8 Builth Wells /
Llanfair-Ym-Muallt LD2 ....143 C6
5 Crickhowell NP8 ....127 D5
Hay-on-W HR3 ....144 D3
12 Kington HR5 ....87 C3
Knighton / Tref-y-Clawdd
LD7 ....140 C5
Llanfyllin SY22 ....134 C6
Llangynog SY10 ....8 A1
4 Llanidloes SY18 ....139 C6
Llanrhaeadr-ym-Mochnant
SY10 ....4 A1
Presteigne LD8 ....77 E3
Rhayader / Rhaeadr Gwy
4 Talgarth LD3 ....110 A4

Church St continued
Welshpool / Y Trallwng
SY21 ....136 B4
Church Terr
1 Berriew SY21 ....40 C7
Hay-on-W HR3 ....144 D3
Church View
Ebbw Vale / Glyn Ebwy
NP23 ....152 D3
Llangynog SY10 ....2 F1
Presteigne LD8 ....77 E3
Cilmaengwyn SA8 ....129 B1
Cilmeri Sta LD2 ....93 F8
Cil-y-ddol LD3 ....115 C6
City La SY22 ....12 A1
Clarence St NP23 ....153 C4
Clare Rd SA9 ....147 B7
Clatterbrune LD8 ....77 F3
Clawdd La LD8 ....86 A7
Cledan SY16 ....138 E4
Clees La SA9 ....147 A5
Cleobury La LD7 ....66 F4
Clerk's Ct 4 SY21 ....136 C5
Clifford Casle HR3 ....95 D1
Clifford Castle HR3 ....103 D8
Clifford Prim Sch HR3 ....103 F7
Clifton St SY21 ....136 B6
Clos Basildene / Basildene Cl
2 NP7 ....128 B1
Clos Bryn-y-ddol 2
SY16 ....136 C6
Clos Ciliau NP8 ....127 D4
Close The LD1 ....142 D5
Clos Fioled / Violet Cl
SY16 ....138 B3
Clos Glandwr SY16 ....48 F5
Clos Glanllyn / Lakeside Cl
NP22 ....151 B1
Clos Golwyg Yr Hafod /
Hafod View Cl NP23 ....153 D4
Clos Llwyn Y Pwll / Llwyn Y
Pwll Cl NP23 ....153 D4
Clos Pentref SA10 ....130 E6
2 Pontganol 3 NP8 ....126 D6
Clos Sain Dunwyd / St
Donats Cl CF48 ....133 F1
Clos Y Berllan LD1 ....82 E5
Clos Y Bwau / Arches Cl
NP22 ....151 D2
Clos Y Crydd / Shoemaker Cl
NP23 ....153 D4
Club La Llanelwedd LD2 ....92 A8
Ystradgynlais SA9 ....146 F1
Clwydyfagwyr CF48 ....133 F1
Clydach Ave NP23 ....152 C5
Clydach St NP23 ....153 C5
Clyngwyn Rd SA9 ....147 B7
Clyro CW Sch HR3 ....144 A5
Clyro Pitch HR3 ....144 B7
Cnwc-y-llo Rd LD2 ....143 C5
Coach Bach NP7 ....151 D1
Cobden St SY21 ....136 C5
Coedbach LD3 ....113 F7
Coedcae NP23 ....152 B4
Coedffaldau SA9 ....129 B6
Coed La SY15 ....41 C1
Coedlan
Bausley with Criggion SY5 ....21 D5
Ystradgynlais SA9 ....147 D8
Coed-y-Bryn 1 LD3 ....110 A4
Coed-y-Cerrig National
Nature Reserve* NP7 128 F7
Coed-y-Glyn SY21 ....19 D2
Coed-y-Pergwm SA11 ....131 C1
Coed-y-Rhaidyr SA11 ....132 A3
Coed-yr-Ynys Rd NP7 ....126 C7
Coelbren Cty Prim Sch
SA10 ....130 F6

Coleg = college

Coleg Powys
Brecon / Aberhonddu LD3 ....145 C5
Newtown / Y Drenewydd
SY16 ....138 A3
College Rd
Builth Wells / Llanfair-Ym-Muallt
LD2 ....143 C6
Ebbw Vale / Glyn Ebwy
NP23 ....152 C3
College Row SY22 ....134 C6
Colltryn La SY22 ....19 C8
Colliers' Row NP23 ....152 D1
Colwyn SY16 ....138 D5
Colwyn Castle* LD1 ....93 C8
Commercial St
13 Abergavenny / Y Fenni
NP7 ....128 F1
Newtown / Y Drenewydd
SY16 ....138 D5
Ystalyfera SA9 ....147 B6
Ystradgynlais SA9 ....146 F1
Commercial St / Stryd
Masnach SA10 ....130 C3
Common Cl 3 HR5 ....87 C3
Common Rd
Kerry / Ceri SY16 ....49 F4
Common Rd / Heol Y Comin
NP7 ....128 A1
Commonwealth Rd
NP23 ....152 D6
Conjurers Dr LD7 ....140 B6
Conway Gr / Llwyn Conway
CF48 ....133 F1
Conway St LD3 ....145 D3
Conway Terr 2 LD3 ....145 D3

Co-operative Terr
NP23 ....153 D1
Copall Paddock 12 SY9 ....52 F3
Coppice La
2 Castle Caereinion SY21 ....29 A4
Welshpool / Y Trallwng
SY21 ....20 B3
Coricks Rise 1 SY9 ....52 F3
Corndon Dr / Rhodfa
Cornatyn 8 SY15 ....41 A3
Coronation Rd 3 HR5 ....87 D3
Coronation Terr HR3 ....144 E3
Corporation St 11 SY9 ....52 F3
Corris Craft Ctr* SY20 ....22 A6
Corris Cvn Pk SY20 ....22 B5
Corris Rly* SY20 ....22 B6
Corris Prim Sch / Ysgol
Gynradd Corris SY20 ....22 B6
Corris Rly* SY20 ....22 B6
Cortay Pk LD1 ....142 A7
Coryton Cl LD3 ....145 C5
Cosy Pl 2 NP23 ....153 B4
Cottage Hospl / Ysbyty Leol
LD2 ....143 C5
Cottage La 8 LD3 ....110 A4
Cottage The / Y Bwthyn 1
LD7 ....140 C5
Council Hos HR3 ....144 A5
Council St NP23 ....152 C1
Court Cl SY15 ....40 A1
Courthouse La SY22 ....11 E1
Crabtree Gn LD1 ....142 C6
Crabtree Rd 15 HR5 ....87 C3
Crabtree Wlk LD7 ....140 C5
Cradoc Cl LD3 ....145 B5
Cradoc Cty Prim Sch
LD3 ....107 E1
Cradoc Rd
Brecon / Aberhonddu LD3 ....145 A5
Yscir LD3 ....107 F1
Craig Fryn SY20 ....137 E4
Craignant LD1 ....72 E4
Craig Rd LD1 ....142 D4
Craig Y Ciliau National Nature
Reserve* NP8 ....127 A3
Crescent Gdns SY16 ....138 D6
Crescent St SY16 ....138 D6
Crescent The
11 Kington HR5 ....87 C3
Tredegar NP22 ....151 C1
Cresta Rd NP7 ....128 E2
Criban St LD3 ....130 E8
Criccieth Gr CF48 ....133 E1
Crickhowell CP Sch
NP8 ....127 D6
Crickhowell High Sch / Ysgol
Uwchradd Crughywel
NP8 ....127 D5
Crickhowell Rd
Llanelly NP7 ....128 A2
Llangattock NP8 ....127 E3
Crickhowell Sports Ctr
NP8 ....127 D5
Criggion Cl 1 SY22 ....12 A1
Criggion La
Bausley with Criggion SY5 ....20 F6
Trewern SY21 ....20 D2
Crossffrynd SA9 ....147 D7
Croes-Hir SY10 ....5 C2
Croes Stryt SY10 ....4 C1
Croft Cl SY21 ....153 A4
Croft Rd SY21 ....136 C6
Crossfield La LD8 ....76 C1
Crossgates Cty Prim Sch
LD1 ....73 F4
Cross La
Llansantffraid SY22 ....11 B2
Rhayader / Rhaeadr Gwy
LD6 ....141 D5
Cross of the Tree SY7 ....78 F6
Cross Oak SA10 ....131 A5
Cross Roads 3 NP7 ....128 B1
Cross St
1 Newtown / Y Drenewydd
SY16 ....138 D6
Ystradgynlais SA9 ....130 A6
Cross Way NP22 ....151 D1
Crown Ave
Tredegar, Dukestown
NP22 ....151 D2
Crown Bsns Pk NP22 ....151 E3
Crown Cotts SA9 ....146 F2
Crown St 3 SY16 ....138 D5
Crowthers Pool HR3 ....95 B3
Curzon St 9 NP23 ....153 C4
Cusop Dingle HR3 ....144 F2
Cutterbach La HR5 ....87 B3
Cwmbeth Cl 1 NP8 ....127 D6
Cwm Crachen NP23 ....153 C2
Cwm Crawnon Rd NP8 ....126 C7
Cwmdu C in W Sch NP8 ....118 B2
Cwmdu Rd SA8 ....129 B1
Cwmgarw Rd SA18 ....129 A8
Cwm Hir NP23 ....152 D3
Cwm La SY21 ....29 B4
Cwm Llanfair SY10 ....138 C6
Cwmmna Rd HR3 ....95 F6
Cwm Nedd Prim Sch
SA11 ....131 D1
Cwmphil Rd SA9 ....146 F1
Cwm Tawe Rd SA9 ....130 A6
Cwrt Dolafon 1 SY16 ....138 E5
Cwrt Eglwys 3 SY16 ....138 D5
Cwrt Penllan 2 SY16 ....138 A3
Cwrt Pen Y Twyn / Head of
the Hill Ct NP22 ....151 D2

Cwrt Rhyd NP23 ....152 C4
Cwrt Swswen SY17 ....48 A6
Cwrt Y Camden LD3 ....145 E3
Cwrt Y Castell 4 LD2 ....143 D5
Cyffredin La LD1 ....82 E5
Cyffredyn La NP8 ....126 E6
Cyfronydd Residential Sch
SY21 ....28 E7
Cyfronydd Sta SY21 ....28 E6
Cyfyng Rd SA9 ....147 A5
Cynan Cl NP23 ....153 C4
Cynghordy Sta SA20 ....96 B3
Cynwal Terr SA9 ....129 C5

D

Daffodil Wood LD2 ....143 B5
Dame Anna Child's Sch
LD3 ....77 A6
Dantier St 1 LD3 ....145 C4
Dan-y-Bryn 1 HR3 ....102 D2
Dan Y Bryn HR3 ....102 D2
Dan-y-coed CF48 ....148 F3
Danycrug LD3 ....145 C5
Dan-y-Fron SY24 ....130 C7
Danygaer Rd LD3 ....145 C4
Dan Y Gollen NP8 ....126 E2
Danygraig SA9 ....146 A2
Dan Y Wern LD3 ....148 A4
Daren-Felin Rd NP23 ....153 C4
Dark La LD3 ....141 D5
Darling Rd 5 LD3 ....116 B7
Darren Rd
Llanfihangel Cwmdu with
Bwlch & Catheoline LD3 ....126 C8
Ystalyfera SA9 ....147 B6
Darren View NP8 ....127 D6
Davies St
Abercrave / Abercrâf SA9 ....130 D7
8 Brynmawr NP23 ....153 C4
Dderi Rd SA9 ....129 B5
Ddole Rd LD1 ....142 D6
Ddole Rd Ind Est LD1 ....142 D6
Deeley Rd SA9 ....147 B6
Defynnog Rd LD3 ....113 F7
Delafield Rd NP7 ....128 E2
Dell The LD2 ....82 E1
Delwood Dr SY21 ....136 C5
Deri Rd NP7 ....128 E2
Derw SY18 ....139 D4
Derwen Fawr NP8 ....127 E6
Derwen Gn 10 SY22 ....12 A1
Derwen Rd SA9 ....146 F1
Derwlwyn La SY22 ....134 C6
Digeddi Villas HR3 ....103 A3
Dillwyn Cl SA10 ....130 B2
Dinas SY16 ....138 D4
Dinas Rd
Brecon / Aberhonddu LD3 ....145 C4
Pontnedddechan SA11 ....131 F1
Dinas Terr SA11 ....131 F2
Dingle Rd
Abergavenny / Y Fenni
NP7 ....128 E2
Welshpool / Y Trallwng
SY21 ....136 C6
Dingle The LD7 ....140 D4
Dog Kennel La SY7 ....68 F5
Dolafon Sta SY21 ....15 E2
Dolafon Rd SY16 ....138 E5
Dolau Sta LD1 ....74 E6
Dolawel SA9 ....129 C2
Dolecoed Rd LD5 ....89 C1
Dolerw Dr SY16 ....138 C5
Dolerw Pk Dr SY16 ....138 C5
Dolfach SY16 ....138 B3
Dolfain SA9 ....130 A5
Dolfor CP Sch / Ysgol
Gymunedol Gynradd Dolfor
SY16 ....49 B2
Dolforgan View SY16 ....49 F4
Dolfor Rd SY16 ....138 C4
Dolgoch SY10 ....12 A7
Dolgoch Quarry Nature
Reserve* SY10 ....12 A7
Dolgwenith SY18 ....139 D4
Dolgynog CF44 ....132 D3
Dolhendra SY10 ....2 F1
Dol Henhryd SA10 ....131 A6
Doli Villas SY15 ....40 A1
Dol-y-Bont SY10 ....4 A1
Dol Y Dderwen SA9 ....130 A5
Dolydd Hafren Nature
Reserve* SY21 ....40 E7
Dolyfelin SY21 ....136 A5
Dol Y Felin 2 SY15 ....40 A1
Dolygaer Sta CF48 ....125 A1
Dol-y-Wennol Mdw 4
SY21 ....29 A4
Domgay Pl 3 SY22 ....12 A1
Domgay Rd SY22 ....12 A1
Dovey Junction Sta SY20 ....32 B5
Dreflan SY9 ....52 F3
Drury La SY5 ....42 F8
Dyffryn Rd NP7 ....128 E2
Duke St HR5 ....87 C3
Dukestown Rd NP22 ....151 E1
Dulais Gdns SA10 ....130 C2
Dulais Rd SA10 ....130 C2
Dulas Terr HR3 ....144 E4
Dumfries Pl
Brynmawr NP23 ....153 C5
Ystradgynlais SA9 ....146 F1
Dunfield Cl LD3 ....87 A6
Dyffryn Cl LD3 ....145 B4
Dyffryn Foel SY22 ....11 A3

Dyffryn Ind Est SY16 49 D6
Dyffryn La SY21 40 D8
Dyffryn Rd LD1 142 C4
Dyfi Eco Pk / Parc Eco Dyfi SY20 137 C5
Dyfi Furnace (Mus)* SY20 32 A2
Dyfi Terr SY20 13 D5

E

Eardisley Rd HR5 87 D3
Earlsfield Cl SA11 131 C1
Eastgate St SY18 139 C6
East St LD6 141 D5
East St Enterprise Pk LD6 141 D5
Ebbw Vale Coll of F Ed NP23 152 C2
Ebbw Vale Com Hospl / Ysbyty'r Tri Chwm NP23 152 C3
Ebbw Vale Comp Sch NP23 152 C2
Ebbw View NP23 152 D3
Ebenezer Ct NP22 151 E1
Ebenezer St NP22 151 E1
Edwards Bldgs NP23 153 C1
Edwards Ct NP23 152 C1
Edward St SA11 131 D1
Edw Cres LD2 92 E2
Eglwys Ffordd SY16 138 A3
Eglwys Llys 4 SY16 138 A3
Eithinog La SY21 135 C4
Elan Valley Visitor Ctr* LD6 71 B3
Elizabeth Rd 5 HR5 87 D3
Elizabeth Way NP23 152 C1
Elm Gr 5 NP7 128 A2
Emlyn Ave NP23 152 C2
Erw Bant 1 NP8 126 D7
Erw Deg 1 SY21 26 F8
Erw Haf 1 LD5 89 D1
Erw Hydref SA9 147 D8
Erwood Sta Craft Ctr* LD2 101 A7
Esgair-y-Gog 2 LD3 109 F6
Estyn Pitch LD2 82 D4
Evans Hos CF48 148 F3
Evan's Terr NP22 151 D2
Everest Dr NP8 127 D5
Exford Gr 8 NP7 128 A1
Eywood La HR5 87 F6

F

Factory Rd NP23 153 C4
Fairfield SY16 49 F4
Fairfield Dr SY16 138 D6
Fairhome 3 NP7 128 A2
Fairview CF44 132 E1
Fair View NP22 151 C1
Fairview Ave SY21 19 D2
Fairview Est CF48 133 F1
Fairview Hos CF48 133 F3
Fair View Terr NP23 153 C1
Farrington La LD7 140 D4
Fawnog La SY22 19 D6
Feeder Bank NP22 151 D1
Felindre SY20 32 B7
Felin-fach SA9 129 C6
Fenni-fach Rd LD3 145 A4
Fernbrook Cl NP23 152 D6
Ferndale Cl
Ebbw Vale / Glyn Ebwy NP23 152 B5
7 Llandysilio SY22 12 A1
Fern Sq / Sgwar Rhedynen 3 SY16 138 B3
Ffinnant La SY22 10 E4

Ffordd = road, way

Ffordd Clawdd Offa / Offas Dyke Rd SY22 12 A1
Ffordd Croesawdy SY16 138 D4
Ffordd Emlyn SA9 147 B5
Ffordd Glandwr SA9 147 B6
Ffordd Glyndwr SY22 18 E3
Ffordd Goed SY10 8 F7
Ffordd Mynydd Griffiths SY20 137 D5
Ffordd Nant Goch SY21 16 A1
Ffordd Newydd SY16 39 B3
Ffordd Smithfield / Smithfield Rd LD2 143 C5
Ffordd Sugn SY10 5 A5
Ffordd Y Cain SY22 134 C5
Ffordd-y-Coedwyr SY19 45 C6
Ffosmaen Rd NP23 153 D1
Ffoss Rd 2 LD5 89 C1
Ffrwdgrech Ind Est LD3 145 A3
Ffrwdgrech Rd LD3 145 A2
Ffrwd Rd CF48 133 F3
Ffrydd Cl 2 LD7 140 C5
Ffrydd Rd LD7 140 B4
Ffynnonau NP8 127 D6
Ffynnon Ct 3 NP23 153 B4
Ffynnon Gynydd C in W Sch HR3 102 A4
Field La SY9 52 F3
Fifth Ave CF44 132 C1
Filas Berrington / Berrington Villas SA9 129 C7
Fir Ct Dr 2 SY15 41 F1
Firemans Ct 2 NP23 153 C4
Fisher Rd SY21 30 D7
Fitzroy Ave NP23 152 D2
Fitzroy St NP23 153 B5
Five Hos NP23 152 E4
Flash Leisure Ctr The SY21 136 D6
Folly La SY21 19 E2
Forden C in W Prim Sch SY21 41 A8
Forden Rd SY15 41 A4
Ford St LD8 77 E3
Forest Hill NP7 128 A1
Forest Rd HR3 144 D2
Forge Rd Llangynidr NP8 126 D7
Machynlleth SY20 137 E4
Fosse Way LD3 109 F5
Foul St SY22 9 A1
Foundry La
Llanidloes SY18 139 D6
Welshpool / Y Trallwng SY21 136 D5
Foundry Terr 1 SY18 139 D6
Four Crosses Bsns Pk SY22 12 B1
Fourteenth Ave CF44 132 C1
Fourth Ave CF44 132 C1
Foxen Manor Rd SY22 12 A1
Frank's Bridge Cty Prim Sch LD1 84 C3
Frankwell St SY16 138 D5
Free St LD3 145 D3
Freshfields SA11 131 D1
Frisby Rd LD3 116 B7
Frolic St SY16 138 D4
Fron Hafren SY16 138 D5
Fronhir LD7 140 D5
Fron La SY16 138 C5
Frost Rd NP23 152 E4
Furnace St NP23 152 D3

G

Gaer La SY22 19 C6
Galloping Dr The SY16 38 F4
Gallowstree Rise SY21 136 D6
Gantre Cl NP23 152 C5
Gantref Way NP23 152 D3
Gaol Rd 3 SY15 41 A3
Garden Cl SY16 49 F4
Garden La SY16 138 D6
Gardens The
6 Gilwern NP7 128 A2
Hay-on-W HR3 144 E4
Kerry / Ceri SY16 49 F4
Ystalyfera SA9 147 B6
Garden Suburb SY18 139 C4
Garden Village SY20 137 E4
Garfield Terr NP23 152 C1
Garibaldi Terr HR3 144 E3
Garneddwen SY20 22 C7
Garnfach Inf Sch NP23 153 D1
Garnlydan Prim Sch NP23 152 D5
Garn Rd NP23 153 C1
Garreg Bank SY21 20 E2
Garreg Dr SY21 136 C5
Garsiwn SY20 137 D4
Garth Cvn Pk SY20 137 F5
Garth Dan-y-Bryn NP23 152 D4
Garth Felin HR3 144 E3
Garth Gr CF44 132 E1
Garth La LD7 140 A5
Garth Mdws LD7 140 B5
Garth Rd
Builth Wells / Llanfair-Ym-Muallt LD2 143 B6
Machynlleth SY20 137 E5
Garth Sta LD4 90 E4
Garwnant Forest Walks* CF48 133 D8
Garwnant Visitor Ctr* CF48 133 D8
Gas St SY16 138 D5
Gasworks La
1 Brecon / Aberhonddu LD3 145 D3
Machynlleth SY20 137 C4
Gelli SY16 138 E4
Gelliceibryn SA11 131 C1
Gelli Crug NP23 152 B5
Gellidawel Rd SA11 131 D1
Gelli-lwyd La SY10 11 A6
George Cl LD7 140 B5
George Rd LD7 140 B5
George St
4 Brecon / Aberhonddu LD3 145 D4
Brynmawr NP23 153 B4
Gerddi Cledan SY17 36 D4
Ger-y-Farell LD3 145 B3
Ger-y-Nant SA11 131 B1
Ger-yr-Afon SA9 146 A1
Gibbet Rd SY21 135 B1
Gibbons Villas NP23 152 E1
Gibraltar La SY10 11 F8
Gilfach La SY16 49 E4
Gilfach Nature Reserve & Visitor Ctr* LD6 62 C2
Gilfach Rd SA9 129 C6
Gilwern Prim Sch NP7 128 B2
Gladestry C in W Sch HR5 86 C2
Glade The LD2 82 E1
Glade Willow HR3 103 A3
Gladstone St 10 NP23 153 C4
Glamorgan St
Brecon / Aberhonddu LD3 145 C3
Brynmawr NP23 153 B4
Glanaber Dr 2 SY21 19 E2
Glan Cerniog SY17 36 E3
Glanclegyr 1 SY19 24 D1
Glan Dorddu LD1 64 E4
Glan Dulais 1 LD3 108 F4
Glandulas Dr SY16 48 F5
Glandwr
1 Llanidloes SY18 139 D5
Newtown / Y Drenewydd SY16 48 F5
Glandwr Parc LD2 143 B6
Glanffrwd Ave NP23 152 C2
Glanffrwd Terr NP23 152 D2
Glangrwyney Rd NP7 128 A2
Glan Gwrelych SA11 131 D1
Glan Gwy LD6 141 C5
Glanheulog NP23 153 B5
Glanhowy Prim Sch NP22 151 E1
Glanhowy St / Stryd Glanhywl NP22 151 D1
Glan Lleddan 2 SY21 136 A5
Glanlyn / Lakeside NP22 151 B1
Glanmoor 7 NP7 128 A2
Glannant Terr SA9 147 E7
Glanrhyd Brookside 1 LD3 102 C2
Glanrhyd Cl NP22 151 D1
Glanrhyd Prim Sch SA9 147 D6
Glan-Rhyd Rd SA9 147 E7
Glansevern Hall Gdns* SY21 40 D7
Glantawe Pk SA9 147 D7
Glantawe Row SA9 147 F8
Glantwrch SA9 147 C7
Glan-y-Nant SY16 48 C8
Glanyrafon
Ebbw Vale / Glyn Ebwy NP23 152 D3
Llanfair Caereinion SY21 135 C4
Glanyrafon Cl NP22 151 E1
Glan Yr Avon
Pantyffynnon SA9 147 A5
Ystalyfera SA9 147 C5
Glan-yr-Ysgol SA9 147 B6
Glasbury C in W Sch LD3 102 D1
Glaslyn Nature Reserve* SY20 34 C1
Glebe The SY16 50 F6
Glendower Cvn Pk SY10 2 F1
Glenrhyd 11 NP7 128 A1
Glen View Bglws NP23 153 B2
Glyncoed Comp Sch / Ysgol Gyfun Glyncoed NP23 152 C3
Glyncoed Prim Sch / Ysgol Gynradd Glyncoed NP23 152 D3
Glyncynwal Rd SA9 129 C6
Glynderi Pottery* LD3 113 F8
Glynderwen SY20 32 E6
Glyndwr SY16 138 C3
Glyndwr Rd NP23 152 B5
Glynmelyn Rd SA11 131 D2
Glyn-neath Village Workshops / Gwerthdal Pentref Glyn-nedd SA11 131 C1
Gnoll Rd SA9 129 C1
Godrergraig Prim Sch SA9 129 C1
Golfa Cl SY21 21 A3
Golf Links Rd LD2 143 B6
Golf Rd NP23 153 B2
Golf View NP23 153 C2
Golwg-y-Bryn SA10 130 D4
Golwg-y-coed SA11 131 C1
Golwgydre La SY16 138 D5
Golwg Y Mynydd SA9 147 A3
Golwg-y-mynydd NP22 151 C3
Golwg-yr-Ysgol / School View NP23 153 B2
Golygfa Rodney / Rodney's View 3 SY22 12 A1
Gorn Rd SY18 139 D5
Gorof Rd SA9 147 D8
Gorsafle SA9 130 A4
Gorsedd Cl NP23 152 D5
Gorse Farm LD1 142 E3
Gorsto Rd SA9 129 B5
Gough Ave SA9 147 D7
Gough Rd SA9 147 B6
Graham's Yd NP22 151 E1
Graig Cerrig Glesiad National Nature Reserve* LD3 114 C1
Graig Ebbw NP23 152 B4
Graig Fach SY20 137 D4
Graig Newydd SA9 129 C2
Graig Rd SA9 129 C2
Graig Twrch SA9 146 A1
Graig Wood Nature Reserve* SY21 29 B7
Graig Y Darren SA9 147 A3
Graigymerched SA9 147 A5
Graig y Nos NP22 151 F1
Grange Gdns 15 SY9 52 F3
Grange Rd 3 SY9 52 E3
Gravel Hill 1 HR5 87 D3
Gravel Hill Dr 7 HR5 87 C3
Gravel Hill Rd HR5 87 C3
Gravel Rd LD1 73 D3
Grawen Hos CF48 133 F3
Grawen La CF48 133 F3
Grdesffordd 5 NP8 126 D6
Great Oak Rd NP8 127 E5
Great Oak St SY18 139 C5
Green Acres SY16 138 B3
Green End LD8 77 E3
Greenfield Cotts NP22 151 D2
Greenfield Cres NP23 152 C4
Greenfield Rd LD8 77 E3
Greenfields
Machynlleth SY20 137 C4
Welshpool / Y Trallwng SY21 136 D5
Greenfield Terr SY20 22 B6
Greenhill Way 2 NP8 127 D5
Green La Churchstoke SY15 41 F1
Titley LD8 87 E8
Greenland Rd NP23 153 C4
Green Mdw NP22 151 F1
Greenprice Cl LD8 77 C5
Green The LD2 82 E1
Greenwood Ave NP22 151 C1
Greenwood Pl 4 NP7 128 B1
Griffin Mdw 2 LD3 108 F4
Griffiths Gdns NP22 151 C1
Griffiths Sq NP22 151 C1
Groe St 2 LD2 143 D6
Grosvenor Cl LD2 142 C2
Grosvenor Rd
Disserth & Trecoed LD2 142 C2
Llandrindod Wells / Llandrindod LD1 83 C7
Grove Cl LD7 140 D4
Grove Farm Rd HR5 95 C7
Gruthyn The SY20 137 D4
Guidfa Mdws 2 LD1 73 F4
Guilsfield Cty Prim Sch SY21 19 D2
Gungrog C in W Sch SY21 136 D5
Gungrog Fawr La SY21 136 D8
Gungrog Hill SY21 136 D6
Gungrog Rd SY21 136 C5
Gurnos CP Jun Sch SA9 147 D8
Gurnos Est NP23 153 A5
Gurnos Rd SA9 147 C7
Gwaelod-y-Bryn SY18 139 C4
Gwaryffordd LD1 82 E5
Gwaunclawdd SA9 130 B7
Gwaun Helyg Rd NP23 152 B1
Gwelfryn SY22 11 E3
Gwent Terr NP23 153 D1
Gwernant SA9 129 B7
Gwernowddy La SY22 12 B1
Gwern-Y-Bwch HR5 95 D7
Gwernyfed Ave 3 LD3 110 C8
Gwernyfed High Sch LD3 110 C8
Gwernyfed Pk 2 LD3 110 C8
Gwern-y-Go La SY22 20 E8
Gwerthdal Pentref Glyn-nedd / Glyn-neath Village Workshops SA11 131 C1
Gwilym Rd SA9 129 B8
Gwreiddyn La SY21 19 D4
Gwrhyd Rd SA9 129 A4
Gwynn's Almshouses HR3 144 D3
Gwysfryn SA9 129 C6
Gynol Rd SA9 129 B7
Gypsy Castle La HR3 144 C3
Gyrnosfa SA9 147 D8

H

Hafan Deg SA10 130 C3
Hafan Y Dorlan 2 SY10 9 D8
Hafod Cl 3 SY22 11 F3
Hafod View Cl / Clos Golwyg Yr Hafod NP23 153 D4
Hafren SY16 138 D3
Hafren Jun Sch SY16 138 D4
Hafren Terr SY18 139 D6
Hafren Theatre* SY16 138 A3
Halfpennys The 1 NP7 128 A2
Hall Bank SY15 41 F1
Hall La 2 LD8 86 A7
Hall St 5 SY21 136 B5
Halmar Dr SY21 30 A2
Halt Cl CF44 132 B1
Halt Rd CF44 132 B1
Hanter La LD8 86 E5
Harcourt Rd NP23 153 B5
Harcourt St NP23 152 D1
Hardwicke Rd HR3 144 F3
Harford Sq NP23 152 E1
Harlech Dr CF48 133 E1
Harley Jenkins St 8 SY9 52 F3
Harley's Almshouses HR3 144 D2
Harold Rd 1 NP7 128 F1
Harold Rd Jun Sch NP7 128 F2
Harper's La LD8 77 E3
Harrison Dr 2 SY15 40 E5
Harris Rd SA9 129 B7
Hatfield Mdws LD7 140 B5
Hatherleigh Pl 23 NP7 128 F1
Hatherleigh Rd 21 NP7 128 F1
Hatter St 4 NP23 153 B4
Hatton Gdns HR5 87 D3
Hatton Gdns Ind Est HR5 87 D4
Haulwen Way SY21 136 D5
Haven Way 1 NP7 128 E2
Hawthorn Cl SY16 138 E6
Hawthorn Dr 1 SY15 40 D2
Hawthorn La LD3 145 D4
Hawthorn Rd NP23 152 D4
Hawthorns The SY5 31 D3
Hawthorn Villas SA9 146 F1
Hay-on-Wye Cty Prim Sch HR3 144 D3
Hay Rd
Builth Wells / Llanfair-Ym-Muallt LD2 143 E6
Talgarth LD3 110 A5
Hay's Cres SA11 131 D1
Hazel Cl SY21 20 D1
Hazel Ct NP23 152 C5
Hazlemere Cl LD6 141 D5
Headbrook HR5 87 D3
Head of the Hill Ct / Cwrt Pen Y Twyn NP22 151 D2
Heads Of The Valleys Rd
Brynmawr NP23 153 D5
Ebbw Vale / Glyn Ebwy NP23 152 C4
Llanelly NP7 128 A1
Tredegar NP22 151 D2
Heart of Wales Bsns Pk LD1 142 E7
Heathcote Cl 7 NP23 153 B4
Heath Dr SY5 21 E2
Heather Cl
Newtown & Llanllwchaiarn SY16 49 D7
Tredegar NP22 151 F1
Heatherwood 3 SY21 30 C1
Heathfield Ave SA11 131 D1
Heathfield Cl NP23 152 D5
Heath Field Ct SA11 131 D1
Heblands Bank SY9 52 F5
Hedd Aberth SA10 130 D4
Heddfan NP23 153 C5
Hedreladus SA9 130 A5
Heldre La SY21 20 D1
Henderson Rd NP23 153 A4
Hendidley Way SY16 138 B5
Hendre
Dyffryn Cellwen SA10 130 F5
Ebbw Vale / Glyn Ebwy NP23 152 E1
Hendre La SY22 12 A1
Henfaes La SY21 136 D4
Hen Felin SA9 147 C7
Heniarth Sta SY21 135 F7
Henneuadd SA9 130 C7
Hennoyadd Rd SA9 130 C7
Henrhyd Falls* SA10 131 A6
Henrhyd La SY21 28 F4
Hen Sinema SY20 137 D4
Heol Aaron SA9 147 D8
Heol Abram SA9 147 D8
Heol-Ael-y-Bryn NP23 152 C3
Heol Ashley SY16 138 B2
Heol Beili-glas SA20 104 A2
Heol Bowys SY21 135 A3
Heol Brychan CF48 133 F2
Heol Brynbrain SA9 129 B8
Heol Bryn Hebog 4 CF48 133 F2
Heol Bryn Man 1 CF48 133 F2
Heol Bryn Padell CF48 133 F2
Heol Bryn Seion SA10 130 F5
Heol Bryn Selu 2 CF48 133 F2
Heol Calch SA11 131 F5
Heol Callwen SA9 121 C3
Heol Castellnedd / Neath Rd SA9 130 A4
Heol Claerwen NP23 152 B5
Heol Daniel SA9 129 B7
Heol Derw NP23 153 A5
Heol Eglwys
Coelbren SA10 130 F6
Ystradgynlais SA9 146 F1
Heol Eglwys / Church Rd SA10 130 C3
Heol Elan NP23 152 B5
Heol Gaer SA10 131 A5
Heol Ganol NP23 153 B4
Heol Giedd
Cwmgiedd SA9 146 F3
Ystradgynlais SA9 146 F2
Heol Gleien SA9 146 A2
Heol Gouesnou 6 LD3 145 D4
Heol Gron SA9 147 D8
Heol Gwernfelen SA20 104 A4
Heol Gwyn Lliw NP23 152 F3
Heol Gwys SA9 129 C6
Heol Heddwch SA10 130 D3
Heol Helig NP23 153 A4
Heol Hemley LD3 117 B7
Heol Hen SA10 130 C3
Heol Iorwerth SY20 137 D4
Heol Isaf NP23 153 B4
Heol Joe Deakins / Joe Deakins Rd LD8 77 E2
Heol Lan LD3 113 B6
Heol Las 8 LD3 110 A4
Heol Llwyd NP23 152 B5
Heol Llynfi NP23 152 B5
Heol Maengwyn SY20 137 D4
Heol Maespica SA9 146 B2
Heol Maes-y-Dre SA9 146 F1
Heol Meurig SA9 147 D8
Heol Mochdre SY16 138 A2
Heol Newydd / New Rd SA9 129 C7
Heol Onen NP23 153 A4
Heol Palleg / Palleg Rd SA9 146 C2
Heol Parc Glas 3 CF48 133 F2
Heol Pengwern SY16 138 A3
Heol Pen'rallt SY20 137 D4

Heol Penrhiw 5 CF48 . . .**133** F2
Heol Pentrerhedyn
SY20 . . . .**137** C4
Heol-Pen-y-Cae NP23 . .**152** C2
Heol Philip SA9 . . . .**146** D1
Heol Powys NP23 . . . . . .**137** D4
Heol Rheidol NP23 . . . . .**152** B5
Heol Rheolau / Brecon Rd
Abercrave / Abercraf SA9 . .**130** B7
Ystradgynlais SA9 . . . .**130** A5
Heol Rhyd-Ddu-Fach
SA9 . . . .**129** B8
Heol Sant Cattwg LD3 . .**115** C2
Heol Sant Luc / St Luke's Rd
NP22 . . . .**151** D2
Heol Siloam NP23 . . . . .**152** B4
Heol Tair Y Beddau / Rd to
the Three Graves LD3 . .**99** E3
Heol Tawe SA9 . . . .**130** D7
Heol Teifi NP23 . . . .**152** B5
Heol Tir-Lan SA11 . . . . . .**131** E5
Heol Tir Y Coed / Woodland
Rd SA9 . . . .**129** C2
Heol Tredeg SA9 . . . .**129** C6
Heol Treowen SY16 . . . . .**138** D4
Heol Twrch SA9 . . . .**146** B1
Heol Vastre SY16 . . . .**138** F4
Heol Vaynor 2 SY16 . . . .**138** A3
Heol Waen NP23 . . . .**152** B4
Heol-y-Brenin LD6 . . . . .**141** D6
Heol-y-Coedcae SA9 . . . .**129** C2
Heol-y-Coleg SY16 . . . . .**138** A3
Heol Y Comin / Comm Rd
NP7 . . . .**128** A1
Heol-y-Doll SY20 . . . .**137** C5
Heol Y Felin / Mary St
SA10 . . . .**130** D4
Heol Y Ffynnon LD3 . . . . .**145** B5
Heol-y-Garreg LD3 . . . . .**107** D2
Heol-y-Glyn SA11 . . . . . .**131** D1
Heol-y-Goedlan SA9 . . . .**129** B6
Heol-y-Gwaudd / Weaver Rd
SA9 . . . .**130** D4
Heol Y Gwydde SA9 . . . . .**130** E7
Heol-y-Nant SY16 . . . . . .**138** A3
Heol Yr Ysgol / School Rd
SA9 . . . .**129** B8
Heol Ystwyth NP23 . . . . .**152** B5
Heol-y-Waun SA10 . . . . . .**130** D4
Hereford Rd NP23 . . . . . .**152** E3
Hereford St LD8 . . . .**77** E3
Hergest Ct HR5 . . . .**87** B2
Hergest Rd HR5 . . . .**87** B3
Heritage Gn 5 SY21 . . . .**30** C1
Heulfryn Aberangell SY20 . . .**13** C1
Esgairgeiliog Ceinws SY20 . .**28** B5
Llanfair Caereinion SY21 . . .**135** C3
Heyop Rd LD7 . . . .**67** A5
Highfield LD1 NP22 . . . . .**151** C2
Highland Cres NP23 . . . . .**131** A5
Highlands Cres NP23 . . . .**152** E4
Highlands Rd NP23 . . . . .**152** E4
High St
4 Bishop's Castle SY9 . . . .**52** F3
2 Brecon / Aberhonddu
LD3 . . . .**145** C4
Builth Wells / Llanfair-Ym-Muallt
LD2 . . . .**143** D5
Disserth & Trecoed LD1 . .**142** C4
Glynneath SA11 . . . .**131** D1
Kington HR5 . . . .**87** C3
Knighton / Tref-y-Clawdd
LD7 . . . .**140** B5
Llandrindod Wells / Llandrindod
LD1 . . . .**83** C8
Llanfyllin SY22 . . . .**134** C5
Llanidloes SY18 . . . .**139** D5
Maescar LD3 . . . .**113** F6
Meifod SY22 . . . .**21** C6
Newtown / Y Drenewydd
LD1 . . . .**83** C8
Pontmeddechan SA11 . . .**131** F2
Presteigne LD8 . . . .**77** E3
Sennybridge / Pontsenni
LD3 . . . .**113** F7
Seven Sisters / Blaendulais
SA10 . . . .**130** C3
Talgarth LD3 . . . .**110** A4
Welshpool / Y Trallwng
SY21 . . . .**136** B5
High Streetv NP8 . . . .**127** D5
High St Superior LD3 . . . .**145** C4
High Town HR3 . . . .**144** D3
High Trees Rd NP7 . . . . . .**128** A1
Hiley Ave NP7 . . . .**128** A1
Hillbrook Cl 2 NP8 . . . . . .**127** D6
Hill Cres NP23 . . . .**153** B4
Hillcrest SY16 . . . .**48** D7
Hill Crest NP23 . . . .**153** B4
Hillcrest Ave 4 LD1 . . . . .**142** C6
Hillcrest Cl 2 LD1 . . . . . .**142** C6
Hillcrest Dr LD1 . . . .**142** C6
Hillcrest Pentwyn Sch
HR3 . . . .**144** A6
Hillcrest Rise LD1 . . . . . .**142** C5
Hillfield SY18 . . . .**139** C5
Hill Gate LD8 . . . .**87** C5
Hill La LD3 . . . .**117** A1
Hill Rd NP7 . . . .**128** C2
Hillsborough Terr SY20 . .**22** A7
Hillside
Abergavenny / Y Fenni
NP7 . . . .**128** F2
Llanymynech & Pant SY10 . .**12** A5
Hillside Ave SY16 . . . .**138** E6
Hillside Dr LD8 . . . .**77** C5
Hillside Rd NP8 . . . .**127** C4
Hill St NP23 . . . .**153** B4
Hillview LD2 . . . .**143** D4
Hill View NP7 . . . .**128** A2
Hill View Cl SY16 . . . .**138** C3
Hirwaun Ind Est / Ystad
Ddiwydiannol Hirwaun
CF44 . . . .**132** C1
Hodgson's Rd SA9 . . . . . .**147** A4
Holborn La HR3 . . . .**95** F5
Holcombe Rd LD1 . . . . . .**142** C5
Holcombe Dr LD1 . . . . . .**142** B6
Holly Cl NP23 . . . .**152** C5
Holly Ct SY16 . . . .**138** E6
Holly View 4 SY21 . . . . . .**30** C1
Honeyfield Rd NP23 . . . . .**152** B4
Honeysuckle Cl NP23 . . .**152** C5
Hope Rd SY21 . . . .**30** C6
Horseshoe Rd SY16 . . . . .**138** E4
Hospital Rd
Builth Wells / Llanfair-Ym-Muallt
LD2 . . . .**143** C5
Talgarth LD3 . . . .**110** A4
House on Crutches Mus*
SY9 . . . .**52** E4
Howell Dr SY21 . . . .**136** C4
Howell Harris Mus*
HR3 . . . .**109** F3
Howy Rd NP23 . . . .**152** B5
Hughes Ave NP23 . . . . . .**152** C1

I
Idris St SY20 . . . .**22** B6
Idris Terr SY20 . . . .**22** A7
Intermediate Rd NP23 . . .**153** C5
Inter-Valley Rd SA10,
SA11 . . . .**131** D4
Irfon Bridge Cl LD2 . . . . .**143** B5
Irfon Bridge Rd LD2 . . . .**143** B5
Irfon Cres LD5 . . . .**89** C1
Irfon Rd LD2 . . . .**143** B6
Irfon Terr 4 LD5 . . . .**89** D1
Irfon Valley CP Sch LD4 . .**90** E4
Is-y-Bryniau SA7 . . . .**130** B6
Isyrhos SA9 . . . .**130** B6
Ithon SY16 . . . .**138** E4
Ithon Cl LD1 . . . .**142** C5
Ithon Rd LD1 . . . .**142** B5
Ithon View LD1 . . . .**142** D6
Ivorites Row SA11 . . . . . .**131** D1
Ivy Cl NP23 . . . .**152** A4

J
Jackets Cl LD7 . . . .**140** A4
Jack's Ditch La HR5 . . . . .**87** E1
James's Row NP23 . . . . . .**153** B4
James St Gorof SA9 . . . . . .**147** F8
7 Llangynidr NP8 . . . .**126** D6
Penrhos SA9 . . . .**130** A6
Jehu Rd SY21 . . . .**136** B5
Joe Deakins Rd (Heol Joe
Deakins) LD8 . . . .**77** E2
John Beddoes Sch LD8 . . .**77** E3
John St
Brecon / Aberhonddu LD3 .**145** D3
Ebbw Vale / Glyn Ebwy
NP23 . . . .**152** C1
Joseph's Pitch LD2 . . . . .**143** E6
Judge's Lodging Mus The*
LD8 . . . .**77** E3

K
Keir Hardie Cl NP23 . . . . .**152** D6
Kensington LD3 . . . .**145** C4
Kerrison Dr SY21 . . . .**136** C6
Kerry Gate 4 SY15 . . . . . .**41** A3
Kerry La 13 SY9 . . . .**52** F3
Kerry Rd SY15 . . . .**41** A3
Kerry Ridgeway SY9 . . . . .**52** A4
Khartoum Terr SA10 . . . .**130** F5
Kidwelly Gr CF48 . . . .**133** F1
Kilvert View HR3 . . . .**144** E3
King Arthur's Labyrinth*
SY20 . . . .**22** A6
King Edward Rd NP23 . . . .**153** C5
Kings Ct (Llys Y Brenin)
LD8 . . . .**77** E2
King's Dr 3 LD3 . . . .**110** A5
Kingsfield NP23 . . . .**152** E1
King St Brynmawr NP23 . . .**153** B4
Ebbw Vale / Glyn Ebwy
NP23 . . . .**152** F4
Nantyglo NP23 . . . .**153** C1
Tredegar NP22 . . . .**151** F1
Kingswood Rd HR5 . . . . . .**87** C2
Kington Cottage Hospl
HR5 . . . .**87** C4
Kington Cty Prim Sch
HR5 . . . .**87** B3
Kington Mus* HR5 . . . . . .**87** C3
Kinnerton Ct* LD8 . . . . . .**78** D1
Kinsley Rd LD7 . . . .**140** C6
Knaplands LD1 . . . .**82** E4
Knighton C in W Prim Sch
LD7 . . . .**140** D4
Knighton & District Leisure
Ctr LD7 . . . .**140** D5
Knighton Ent Pk LD7 . . . .**140** D5
Knighton Hospl LD7 . . . . .**140** C4
Knighton Rd LD8 . . . .**77** D3

Knighton Sta LD7 . . . .**140** D5
Knoll Rd NP7 . . . .**128** E1
Knucklas Rd LD7 . . . .**140** B6
Knucklas Sta LD7 . . . .**67** B4

L
Laburnam Ave NP22 . . . . .**151** D1
Laburnum Cl NP23 . . . . . .**152** C5
Laburnum Mdws SY22 . . . .**20** D8
Ladies Row NP22 . . . .**151** F1
Lady Hawkins' Sch HR5 . .**87** C3
Ladywell 1 SY7 . . . .**68** F4
Ladywell Gn Infants Sch
SY16 . . . .**138** C4
Ladywell Sh Ctr SY16 . . . .**138** C4
Lagden La SY9 . . . .**52** F1
Lake Rd NP23 . . . .**153** C4
Lakeside Ave
Disserth & Trecoed LD2 . . .**142** C2
Llandrindod Wells / Llandrindod
LD1 . . . .**83** C7
Lakeside Cl / Clos Glanllyn
NP22 . . . .**151** B1
Lakeside Dr LD8 . . . .**77** C5
Lakeside / Glanlyn
NP22 . . . .**151** B1
Lamb Cl LD3 . . . .**117** C6
Lamb La 14 HR3 . . . .**144** E3
Lambert Rd CF44 . . . .**132** D3
Lamb's Sq NP23 . . . .**152** C4
Lamb St 4 NP8 . . . .**127** D5
Lancaster Cl SA11 . . . . . .**131** C1
Lancaster Dr 1 NP7 . . . . .**128** B1
Landsdowne Terr 4
LD3 . . . .**145** D3
Lansbury Rd NP23 . . . . . .**153** A4
Lansbury Terr NP23 . . . . .**152** F4
Lansdowne Rd NP23 . . . .**152** D5
Lant Ave LD1 . . . .**142** D4
Larkey La LD7 . . . .**140** C5
Latham Dr SY16 . . . .**138** C4
Laundry La SY21 . . . .**19** B1
Laundry Pl 3 NP7 . . . . . .**128** B1
Laurels Mdw LD7 . . . .**140** B6
Lavender Bank 1 SY9 . . . .**52** E3
Lawnt Y Plas SY20 . . . . . .**13** D6
Layton Cl 1 LD5 . . . .**89** D1
Leigh Mdws 11 SY21 . . . . .**30** C1
Leighton CP Sch SY21 . . .**136** F2
Leighton Rd SY21 . . . .**136** D4
Leighton View SY21 . . . . .**136** B4
Letchworth Rd NP23 . . . .**152** C1
Leuchars Way 4 LD2 . . . .**116** B7
Lewis Ave SA9 . . . .**129** B8
Lewis Pl LD8 . . . .**86** A7
Lewis's La 7 NP7 . . . .**128** E1
Libanus Cty Prim Sch
LD3 . . . .**115** A5
Libanus Rd NP23 . . . .**152** D1
Lilian Gr NP23 . . . .**152** D2
Lime Kilns La SY21 . . . . . .**29** F4
Limestone Rd NP23 . . . . .**153** C2
Limestone Rd E NP23 . . .**153** C3
Lime Trees Ave NP8 . . . . .**127** C4
Lindens Wlk LD1 . . . .**142** C4
Lindsay Gdns NP22 . . . . .**151** E2
Lingen Gdns* SY7 . . . .**78** D5
Linley Dr SY5 . . . .**4** A4
Lion St
Brecon / Aberhonddu LD3 .**145** D4
Hay-on-W HR3 . . . .**144** E3
Lion Yd LD3 . . . .**145** D4
Little Free St 5 LD3 . . . . .**145** D3
Little Henfaes Dr 3
SY21 . . . .**136** D5
Little La NP23 . . . .**152** F4
Little London SA9 . . . .**130** B7
Llanafan Rd LD1 . . . .**82** E5
Llan Arrow HR5 . . . .**95** B4
Llanbedr C in W Sch
NP8 . . . .**127** F7
Llanbedr Rd NP8 . . . .**127** D5
Llanbister Cty Prim Sch
LD1 . . . .**64** A4
Llanbister Rd Sta LD1 . . . .**65** F2
Llandaff Rd SY21 . . . .**152** E3
Llandinam CP Sch SY17 . .**47** F3
Llandrindod High Sch /
Ysgol Uwchradd
Llandrindod LD1 . . . .**142** C5
Llandrindod Wells C in W
Prim Sch LD1 . . . .**142** D5
Llandrindod Wells CP Sch
LD1 . . . .**142** D4
Llandrindod Wells & Cty War
Meml Hospl LD1 . . . .**142** D4
Llandrindod Wells Sta
LD1 . . . .**142** C4
Llandysilio C in W Sch
SY22 . . . .**11** F1
Llanelwedd C in W Sch
LD2 . . . .**143** D7
Llanelwedd Terr LD2 . . . .**143** D6
Llanfaes LD3 . . . .**147** F8
Llanfaes CP Sch LD3 . . . .**145** C4
Llanfair Caereinion Prim Sch
SY21 . . . .**135** B4
Llanfair Rd SY16 . . . .**138** E1
Llanfair Cl LD1 . . . .**142** D5
Llanfechain C in W Sch /
Ysgol Gynradd Llanfechain
SY22 . . . .**10** D3
Llanfihangel C in W Sch
SY22 . . . .**17** C2

Llanfihangel Rhydithon Cty
Prim Sch LD1 . . . .**75** A6
Llanfyllin CP Sch SY22 . . .**134** C5
Llanfyllin High Sch / Ysgol
Uwchradd Llanfyllin
SY22 . . . .**134** C5
Llanfyllin Leisure Ctr
SY22 . . . .**134** C5
Llangammarch Sta LD4 . . .**90** C2
Llangattock C in W Sch
NP8 . . . .**127** C4
Llangattwg Cl NP23 . . . . .**152** E4
Llangedwyn Mill Craft Ctr*
SY10 . . . .**10** D6
Llangedwyn Prim Sch
SY10 . . . .**10** C7
Llangenny La NP8 . . . .**127** E5
Llangors VP Sch LD3 . . . .**117** C6
Llangurig Cty Prim Sch
SY18 . . . .**54** F3
Llangynidr CP Sch / Ysgol
Gynradd Llangynidr
NP8 . . . .**126** D6
Llangynllo Sta LD7 . . . . . .**66** D3
Llanidloes Cty Prim Sch
SY18 . . . .**139** A4
Llanidloes & District Sports
Ctr SY18 . . . .**139** B4
Llanidloes High Sch / Ysgol
Uwchradd Llanidloes
SY18 . . . .**139** B4
Llanidloes Mus* SY18 . . . .**139** D5
Llanidloes Rd SY16 . . . . .**138** A3
Llanidloes Sports Ctr
SY18 . . . .**139** C4
Llanidloes War Meml Hospl
SY18 . . . .**139** C7
Llanigon CP Sch HR3 . . . .**103** A2
Llanrhaeadr-ym-Mochnant
CP Sch SY10 . . . .**4** A1
Llanrwtyd Sta LD5 . . . . . .**89** D1
Llansantffraid C in W Sch
SY22 . . . .**11** B3
Llanshay La LD7 . . . .**140** F4
Llanthomas La
Llanigon HR3 . . . .**102** F3
Llanigon HR3 . . . .**103** A3
Lledfair Pl SY20 . . . .**137** D4
Lletty La SY22 . . . .**11** A2
Llewellyn St SA11 . . . .**131** D1
Llidiart-cae-hir LL20 . . . . .**4** C5
Lluest SA9 . . . .**130** A5
Lluest La SY22 . . . .**134** A6
Llugwy Estates SY20 . . . . .**32** D7
Llwybr Y Gath LD1 . . . . . .**63** E6
Llwyn Caeriw / Carew Gr
CF48 . . . .**133** F1
Llwyn Celyn LD1 . . . .**82** E5
Llwyncelyn Terr SA10 . . .**130** F6
Llwyn Conway / Conway Gr
CF48 . . . .**133** F1
Llwyn Helyg NP22 . . . . . .**151** C2
Llwynon La SY16 . . . .**138** C5
Llwyn Onn CF44 . . . .**132** D2
Llwyn Perthi SY22 . . . .**20** B6
Llwyn-y-garth SY22 . . . . .**134** C4
Llwyn Y Pwll Cl / Clos Llwyn
Y Pwll NP23 . . . .**153** D4
Llygad-yr-Haul SA11 . . . . .**131** B1
Llynclys Comm Nature
Reserve* SY10 . . . .**12** A6
Llynlloedd La SY20 . . . . . .**137** D4
Llys Afallen SY16 . . . .**138** B3
Llys Bedw 1 SY14 . . . . . .**138** B4
Llys Cain / Cain Ct
SY22 . . . .**134** C6
Llys Clywedog 6 SY18 . . .**139** C6
Llys Dulas SY16 . . . .**138** C4
Llys Dyffryn LD1 . . . .**142** C4
Llys Fredrick Jones
SA9 . . . .**147** C7
Llys Glyndwr SY20 . . . . . .**137** D4
Llys Heulog LD1 . . . .**142** C6
Llys Ifor 2 SY16 . . . .**138** B4
Llys Lelog SY16 . . . .**138** B4
Llys Rhufain SY17 . . . .**48** A7
Llys Tawel SY9 . . . .**146** F1
Llyswen La SY21 . . . .**19** D4
Llys Y Brenin / Kings Ct
LD8 . . . .**77** E2
Llys Ynyscedwyn SA9 . . .**147** D8
Llys yr Efail SY20 . . . .**137** D4
Llys Yr Ysgol SA11 . . . . . .**131** D1
Locksters La Clifford HR3 . .**95** F1
Whitney-on-W HR3 . . . . . .**95** F1
Logan Mus of Sculpture*
SY21 . . . .**30** C7
Lon Afallen 2 SY16 . . . . .**138** B3
Lon Brynfa / Brynfa Ave
SY21 . . . .**136** C6
Lon Caeaugwynedd
SY22 . . . .**134** A6
Lon Ceirios SY16 . . . .**138** B3
Lon Cerddyn SY16 . . . . . .**138** B4
Loncwm LD1 . . . .**142** C5
Lon Derw SY16 . . . .**138** B3
Lon Dol-y-bont 1
SY16 . . . .**138** A3
Londonderry Terr SY17 . . .**48** A7
Lon Dulas SY16 . . . .**138** C3
Lon Eithin SY16 . . . .**138** B3
Lonesome La SY16 . . . . . .**138** F7
Long Bridge St
Llanidloes SY18 . . . .**139** C6

Long Bridge St *continued*
Newtown & Llanllwchaiarn
SY16 . . . .**138** D5
Lon Gerylli SY16 . . . .**138** A2
Lon Glanyrafon 3 SY18 . .**139** C5
Lon Glanyrafon SY16 . . . .**138** A4
Long Length SY17 . . . .**48** B6
Longmede Pk CF44 . . . . . .**132** B1
Long St SA9 . . . .**130** A6
Lon Gwern SY16 . . . .**138** B3
Lon Helyg SY16 . . . .**138** C3
Lon Maesycoed 4 SY16 . .**138** B2
Lon Masarn SY16 . . . .**138** B3
Lon Pantyllyn SY16 . . . . .**138** B2
Lon Pinwydd SY16 . . . . . .**138** B4
Lon Rhosmari 1 SY16 . . .**138** F5
Lon Rhosod SY16 . . . .**138** B4
Lon Slwch LD3 . . . .**145** F2
Lon-y-Bryn SA11 . . . .**131** C1
Lon-y-coed 1 LD3 . . . . . .**145** D4
Lon-y-Nant SA11 . . . .**131** C1
Lon-y-Parc SA11 . . . .**131** C1
Lon Yr Ysgol / School La
LD8 . . . .**77** D6
Lon Y Wennol / Swallow Dr
SY16 . . . .**138** B3
Lordstone La SY5 . . . .**31** F1
Love La Bishop's Castle SY9 . .**52** F3
Builth Wells / Llanfair-Ym-Muallt
LD2 . . . .**143** B6
Kington HR5 . . . .**87** C3
Lower Bailey St 4
NP23 . . . .**153** C2
Lower Bridge St HR3 . . . . .**95** E3
Lower Brooklands SA9 . . .**130** D7
Lower Canal Rd SY16 . . . .**138** E5
Lower Castle St 10 NP7 . .**128** F1
Lower Cwrt SY20 . . . .**32** A7
Lower Gwestydd La SY16 . .**49** D8
Lower Mead HR3 . . . .**144** E3
Lower New Hos SA9 . . . . .**146** C1
Lower Pantteg SA9 . . . . . .**147** A4
Lower Sq NP23 . . . .**152** C4
Lower Wern Rd SA9 . . . . .**147** B6
Ludlow Rd LD7 . . . .**140** B5
Lugg View LD8 . . . .**77** E3
Lymore View SY15 . . . .**41** A3
Lynden SA9 . . . .**146** D1

M
Machynlleth Music Festival
(Mus)* SY20 . . . .**137** D4
Machynlleth Sta SY20 . . . .**137** C5
Maelog Ct
Disserth & Trecoed LD1 . . .**142** E4
Llandrindod Wells / Llandrindod
LD1 . . . .**83** D8
Maendu St LD3 . . . .**145** C4
Maendu Terr LD3 . . . .**145** C4
Maenygwyn SA8 . . . .**129** B3
Maerdy La SY22 . . . .**20** B7
Maesanwion SY17 . . . .**48** A7
Maes Awyr Canolbarth Cymru
Maldwyn / Mid Wales
Airport SY21 . . . .**30** A3
Maesbury Prim Sch SY10 . .**12** D8
Maesbury Rd SY10 . . . . . .**12** D8
Maes Castell SY21 . . . .**30** A1
Maescelyn LD3 . . . .**145** D5
Maes Chwarae 1 SY15 . . .**41** F1
Maes Cottage Est LD6 . . .**141** C6
Maescynog SA9 . . . .**146** F1
Maes Derw SY22 . . . .**20** C1
Maesderwen SY16 . . . . . .**138** F5
Maes Derwyn SY21 . . . . .**135** A3
Maes Dinas SY22 . . . .**10** E3
Maes Dyfi SY20 . . . .**137** D4
Maes Ffynnon NP8 . . . . . .**127** F7
Maesgarmon Cl 3 SY21 . .**29** A4
Maes Glas Clawddnewydd SY11 . .**48** A7
Ebbw Vale / Glyn Ebwy
NP23 . . . .**152** B4
Machynlleth SY20 . . . .**135** B3
Maes Gwyn SY15 . . . .**21** C6
Maes Hafren SY5 . . . .**21** C6
Maeshir SA11 . . . .**131** C1
Maesmarchog Prim Sch
SA10 . . . .**131** A5
Maesmawr LD6 . . . .**141** C5
Maes Mawr Cl 2 LD3 . . . .**117** A1
Maes Mawr La 1 LD3 . . . .**117** A1
Maesnewydd SY20 . . . . . .**137** E5
Maes Offa / Offas Gn
LD8 . . . .**77** D6
Maes Teg SY20 . . . .**32** C2
Maes Uchaf 3 SY22 . . . . .**11** A3
Maes Watkin SY16 . . . . . .**10** D7
Maes-y-Celyn SY21 . . . . . .**19** E2
Maesycoed Rd SA8 . . . . . .**129** B1
Maes Y Darren SY22 . . . . .**17** A6
Maes-y-darren SA9 . . . . .**147** C6
Maesydderwen SA7 . . . . .**130** A5
Maes-y-Dderwen 2
SY19 . . . .**24** D1
Maes Y Dderwen
Llanfyllin SY22 . . . .**134** D6
Llanrhaeadr-ym-Mochnant
SY10 . . . .**4** A1
Maes Y Dderwen Gdns
SA9 . . . .**147** E7
Maesyddinas SY17 . . . . . .**48** A7
Maesydre Caersws SY17 . . .**48** A7
Llanfyllin SY22 . . . .**134** D4

Maesydre continued
Llanidloes SY18 ....**139** D5
Maesydre Ind Est LD5 ....**89** D1
Maes Y Eglwys / Churchfield
NP8 ....**127** C4
Maes-y-Felin SY21 ....**40** F6
Maes-y-Ffynnon LD3 ......**145** B6
Maes-y-Ffynon SA11 ......**131** C1
Maes Y Foel SY22 ....**11** A3
Maesyfron Terr SA9 ....**130** C7
Maes-y-Garreg
Ebbw Vale / Glyn Ebwy
NP23 ....**152** A4
2 Llansantffraid SY22 ....**11** A3
Merthyr Tydfil / Merthyr Tudful
CF48 ....**133** F2
Maes-y-Garth SY20 ....**137** F5
Maes-y-Gof SY21 ....**15** F2
Maes-y-Granllyn SY21 ....**19** E2
Maesyllan SY21 ....**26** F8
Maes-y-Llan Corris SY20 ...**22** B6
Llansantffraid SY22 ....**11** A3
Maes y Llan SY10 ....**5** D2
Maes-y-Llan SY21 ....**18** D4
Maes-Y-llan SY17 ....**36** E3
Maesyllan Ind Est SY18 ...**139** D5
Maes Y Nant LD6 ....**141** D5
Maes-y-Neuadd SY17 .....**48** A6
Maes-Yr-Afon LD7,LD8 ....**7** A6
Maes-yr-Efail SY19 ....**24** D1
Maes-yr-Eglwys
Glynneath SA11 ....**131** C1
4 Llansantffraid SY22 ....**11** A3
Maes Yr Esgob **1** SY19 ....**9** D8
Maesyrhandir Cty Prim Sch /
Ysgol Maesyrhandir
SY16 ....**138** B2
Maes- Y-Rhiw **2** SY21 .....**40** C7
Maes-yr-Onnen SY21 ......**135** A2
Maes Yr Orsaf SY20 ....**22** C8
Maes-yr-Ysgol **1** SY22 ...**10** E3
Maglona Villas SY20 ....**137** D4
Mahollan Rd
Huntington SY8 ....**86** F1
Huntington HR5 ....**95** E8
Main Ave CF44 ....**132** C1
Main Rd SA10 ....**131** A4
Main St SY17 ....**48** A6
Mais-Einion LL20 ....**4** F8
Maldwyn Leisure Ctr
SY16 ....**138** C3
Maldwyn Way **7** SY21 ....**41** A3
Malford Gr **3** NP7 ....**128** A1
Malt Rise SY21 ....**21** C6
Manor Cl LD8 ....**77** C5
Manor Dr SA11 ....**131** B1
Manthrig La SY17 ....**48** A6
Maple Ave NP22 ....**151** D1
Maple Way NP23 ....**152** C5
Marcella Cl **3** SY21 ....**19** E2
Marche La SY5 ....**21** D1
Mardy La NP8 ....**126** D6
Marian Terr SY20 ....**32** B7
Marigold Pl SA10 ....**130** D4
Market Hall St **8** HR5 .....**87** C3
Market Rd NP23 ....**153** C2
Market Sq
3 Bishop's Castle SY9 ...**52** F3
Brynmawr NP23 ....**153** C4
Market St
Brecon / Aberhonddu LD3 ..**145** C4
1 Builth Wells /
Llanfair-Ym-Muallt LD2 ...**143** D5
Hay-on-W HR3 ....**144** D3
Knighton / Tref-y-Clawdd
LD7 ....**140** B5
Llanrhaeadr-ym-Mochnant
SY16 ....**138** D5
Markwick Cl **9** HR5 ....**87** C3
Marston Pottery Workshop*
LD6 ....**141** C7
Martell War Mus **4** NP22 ...**127** F3
Martindale Cl **7** NP22 .....**151** D1
Martyn's Ave / Rhodfa
Martyn SA10 ....**130** C3
Mary St / Heol Y Felin
SA10 ....**130** D4
Mawddwy Cotts SY20 ......**13** D5
MawddwyTerr SY20 ....**13** D5
Mayfield Terr NP23 ....**152** D4
Meadow Cl LD8 ....**77** C5
Meadow Cres NP22 ....**151** D2
Meadow La **3** NP7 ....**128** E2
Meadow The **1** SY10 ....**8** F7
Meadow Vale HR5 ....**86** C1
Meadow View
SY22 ....**20** E8
Llangors LD3 ....**117** A7
Meads Cl **3** HR5 ....**87** D3
Meads The HR5 ....**87** D3
Mechanic's Sq NP22 ......**151** E1
Meeting House La LD8 ....**77** D7
Meifod Cty Prim Sch
SY22 ....**18** D4
Meirion Woollen Mill*
SY20 ....**13** D4
Melite Ave SA11 ....**131** F2
Melverley Craft Ctr*
SY22 ....**21** D7
Melverley View SY5 ....**21** D6
Merthyr Rd
Abergavenny / Y Fenni
NP7 ....**128** F1
Pontwalby SA11 ....**131** E1

Merthyr Rd continued
Tredegar, Llechryd NP22 ...**150** F1
Metz Cotts SA9 ....**130** A6
Mews The **26** NP7 ....**128** F1
Middle Dolfor Rd
Kerry / Ceri SY16 ....**49** B3
Newtown & Llanllwchaiarn
SY16 ....**138** C1
Middleton St LD1 ....**142** C4
Midland Terr SA9 ....**147** D8
Mid Wales Airport / Maes
Awyr Canolbarth Cymru
Maldwyn SY21 ....**30** A2
Milbank Est LD8 ....**77** D5
Milborough Cl SA9 ....**147** B7
Milborough Rd SA9 ....**147** B7
Mile La SY22 ....**134** C5
Milford Rd SY16 ....**138** B4
Milfraen Ave NP23 ....**153** D1
Mill Cl SY16 ....**138** E5
Mill Field Cl LD7 ....**140** B5
Mill Fields SY16 ....**138** A4
Mill Gn LD7 ....**140** C5
Mill La Guilsfield SY21 .....**19** D2
Presteigne LD8 ....**77** D3
Welshpool / Y Trallwng
SY21 ....**136** C5
Mill Rd
Knighton / Tref-y-Clawdd
LD7 ....**140** B5
Llangynidr NP8 ....**126** D6
Mill St Bettws SY16 ....**20** C3
Brecon / Aberhonddu LD3 ..**145** C4
Crickhowell NP8 ....**127** D5
Kington HR5 ....**87** C3
Millstream SY5 ....**31** E3
Millwalls SY21 ....**40** C8
Minafon Rd SY22 ....**40** C8
Mineah Dr SY21 ....**19** D2
Minffordd SY15 ....**135** A3
Minffordd St SY20 ....**22** B6
Min-y-Coed SA11 ....**131** C1
Min-y-Ddol SY20 ....**22** C2
Minyffordd SY9 ....**147** B6
Minyrafon SA9 ....**147** B8
Min-yr-awel SA11 ....**131** F2
Min-y-Rhos SA9 ....**130** A6
Moat Hill SY9 ....**52** C4
Moat La SY17 ....**48** A5
Mochdre Ind Est SY16 ....**138** C2
Mochdre Ind Pk SY16 .....**138** B2
Mochdre La
Newtown & Llanllwchaiarn
SY16 ....**48** F4
Newtown / Y Drenewydd
SY16 ....**138** A2
Monmouth Dr CF48 ....**133** F1
Montfort Rd HR5 ....**87** B3
Montgomery Castle*
SY15 ....**40** F3
Montgomery C in W Sch
SY15 ....**41** A3
Montgomery Coll of Further
Ed SY16 ....**48** F5
Montgomery Cty Infmy
SY16 ....**138** D6
Montpellier Pk LD1 ....**142** C3
Moorlands SA10 ....**130** D4
Moorside Villas SA10 .....**130** F6
Moor View SY22 ....**20** E8
Morben-isaf Cvn Pk
SY20 ....**32** C5
Morfa Glas SA11 ....**131** C1
Morgans Orch **14** HR5 ...**87** C3
Morgan St SA9 ....**130** D7
Morgan Brother's Shire
Horse Ctr* SA9 ....**121** B3
Morlais Cl CF48 ....**133** F2
Morton's Farm NP23 .....**153** A4
Mountain Ctr (Visitor Centre)
The* LD3 ....**114** E5
Mountain View
5 Brynmawr NP23 ....**153** B4
Llandrinio SY22 ....**20** B6
Mount Cl **2** SY21 ....**136** B5
Mount La SY18 ....**139** C5
Mount Pleasant Rd
NP23 ....**152** C1
Mount Pleasant Sq
NP23 ....**152** C1
Mount Rd
Llanfair Caereinion SY21 ...**135** C3
Rhigos CF44 ....**132** A1
Mount St
32 Abergavenny / Y Fenni
NP7 ....**128** F1
5 Brecon / Aberhonddu
LD3 ....**145** D4
Welshpool / Y Trallwng
SY21 ....**136** A5
Mount St CP Sch LD3 .....**145** D5
Mount View LD2 ....**110** D3
Museum of Mechanical
Magic* SY19 ....**24** D2
Mutton Dingle LD8 ....**85** F8
Mydriam NP22 ....**151** E1
Mynd Rd LD8 ....**77** D6
Myrtle Dr **7** SY21 ....**136** C5

N

Nant-cae'r-efael SA9 ...**130** E8
Nant Hir SA11 ....**131** B1
Nant Irfon National Nature
Reserve* LD5 ....**79** F1
Nantlais SA9 ....**129** B8
Nantmawr Bank SY10 ...**11** E7

Nantmawr Quarry (Outdoor
Activity Centre)* SY10 **11** D7
Nantmel C in W Sch LD1 ..**73** A5
Nant Melyn NP23 ....**152** B4
Nant-y-croft NP23 ....**151** F4
Nant-y-Deri LD3 ....**110** D7
Nant-y-Felin **8** LD3 ....**110** C8
Nantyglasdwr La HR3 .....**144** F4
Nantyglo Comp Sch
NP23 ....**153** B2
Nantyglo Cvn Site NP23 .**153** C3
Nant-y-glo Round Towers*
NP23 ....**153** B1
Nant-y-Mynydd SA10 .....**130** E4
Narrow St SY22 ....**136** C5
National Cycle Collection*
LD1 ....**142** C3
National Showcaves Ctr for
Wales The* SA9 ....**121** B3
Neath Rd SA9 ....**147** F6
Neath Rd / Heol Castellnedd
SA9 ....**147** F6
Nelson St
Disserth & Trecoed LD1 ...**142** C5
Ebbw Vale / Glyn Ebwy
NP23 ....**152** D4
Neuadd La SY21 ....**153** B1
Nevill Hall Hospl NP7 .....**128** E1
Nevill St **25** NP7 ....**128** F1
Newbridge-on-Wye CP Sch
LD1 ....**82** F4
Newchurch Rd NP23 .....**153** D2
New Church St SY16 ......**138** D4
Newgate La LD8 ....**85** F7
Newgate St
Brecon / Aberhonddu LD3 ..**145** A3
Glyn Tarell LD3 ....**115** B6
Newmarch St **2** LD3 .....**145** A4
Newport St HR3 ....**144** E4
New Rd Crickhowell NP8 ...**127** D5
Llanfair Caereinion SY21 ...**135** C3
Llanfyllin SY22 ....**134** B5
Montgomery / Trefaldwyn
SY15 ....**41** A4
Nantyglo NP23 ....**153** C2
4 Newtown / Y Drenewydd
SY16 ....**138** D4
New Rd / Heol Newydd
SA9 ....**129** C2
Newry Rd LD2 ....**143** C6
New St
6 Bishop's Castle SY9 ...**52** F3
Disserth & Trecoed LD1 ...**142** C5
Llanidloes SY18 ....**139** C5
Machynlleth SY20 ....**137** D4
6 Talgarth LD3 ....**110** A4
Welshpool / Y Trallwng
SY21 ....**136** C5
Ystalyfera SA9 ....**147** A4
Newton Gn LD3 ....**145** B4
Newton Rd
Kington Rural HR5 ....**87** B4
Norton LD8 ....**77** D5
Newtown High Sch / Ysgol
Uwchradd y Drenewydd
SY16 ....**138** C3
Newtown Rd
Llanidloes SY18 ....**139** D6
Machynlleth SY20 ....**137** F4
Newtown Sta SY16 ....**138** C4
Nicholas Way LD2 ....**82** E1
Ninth Ave CF44 ....**132** D1
Nobel Square Ind Est
NP23 ....**153** D4
North Ave
Disserth & Trecoed LD1 ...**142** C6
Llandrindod Wells / Llandrindod
LD1 ....**73** C1
Tredegar NP22 ....**151** C1
North Rd
Brecon / Aberhonddu LD3 ..**145** C4
Builth Wells / Llanfair-Ym-Muallt
LD2 ....**143** D6
Pant SY22 ....**11** F4
North St
Abergavenny / Y Fenni
NP7 ....**128** F1
Ebbw Vale / Glyn Ebwy
NP23 ....**152** E4
Rhayader / Rhaeadr Gwy
LD6 ....**141** C5
Norton Rd SA10 ....**130** C3
Norton Terr LD1 ....**142** C4
Novers The **5** SY9 ....**52** E3
Noyadd Cl LD1 ....**142** D5

O

Oak Cl SY22 ....**12** A1
Oakdene Way **1** NP7 ....**128** A1
Oak Dr SY16 ....**49** F5
Oakfield Dr
Crickhowell NP8 ....**127** D5
Guilsfield SY21 ....**19** D2
Oakfield Pk LD3 ....**145** D4
Oakfields SY22 ....**11** B3
Oak La **1** Guilsfield SY21 .**19** D2
Oswestry Rural SY10 ....**11** D3
Oaklands Cres LD2 ....**143** E5
Oakland Villas HR3 ....**144** C2
Oak Mdw **2** SA9 ....**52** F4
Oak Rise SY22 ....**136** C6
Oakridge Ct LD2 ....**142** C2
Oakridge Dr
Disserth & Trecoed LD2 ...**142** C2

Oakridge Dr continued
Llandrindod Wells / Llandrindod
LD1 ....**83** C6
Oaks Mdw LD6 ....**141** D4
Oak Tree Ave SY16 ....**138** E6
Oaktree View LD1 ....**74** A3
Oak Way LD2 ....**82** E1
Oakwood Cl LD2 ....**143** C5
Ochr-y-Waun Rd SA9 .....**129** B7
Oddfellows St SA11 ....**131** D1
Oddfellows' St SA9 ....**146** F2
Offas Cl SY10 ....**11** E8
Offa's Dyke Bsns Pk
SY21 ....**136** E7
Offas Dyke Rd / Ffordd
Clawdd Offa SY22 ....**12** A1
Offas Gn (Maes Offa)
LD8 ....**77** D6
Old Barn La SY16 ....**138** E5
Old Bedstone Rd **8** SY7 ...**68** F4
Old Bell Mus* SY15 ....**41** A3
Old Blaen-Afon Rd
Brynmawr NP23 ....**153** C4
Old Church St 1 SY16 ....**138** D5
Old Duke Rd SY20 ....**151** E2
Oldford Cl **2** SY21 ....**136** B4
Oldford View **7** SY21 ....**136** B4
Old Hereford Rd NP7 .....**128** F1
Old Kerry Rd SY16 ....**138** E4
Old Mill Cl **8** SY5 ....**31** E3
Old Moat La SY17 ....**48** B5
Old Oak La SY5 ....**21** F7
Old Tavern La **1** SY21 ...**136** B5
Old Trap Rd NP7 ....**128** A1
Old Wern Rd SA9 ....**147** B6
Old Winch Fawr Rd
CF48 ....**133** F1
Ongar St SY7 ....**78** F6
Onllwyn Rd
Coelbren SA10 ....**130** F6
Dyffryn Cellwen SA10 .....**130** C5
Orchard Cl
38 Abergavenny / Y Fenni
NP7 ....**128** F1
6 Gilwern NP7 ....**128** A1
Presteigne LD8 ....**77** E3
Orchard Croft SY22 ....**20** D8
Orchard Gdns LD1 ....**142** C4
Orchard Gn **1** SY22 ......**11** B3
Orchard La **2** NP8 ....**126** C7
Orchard Mews NP7 ....**128** F1
Orchard St SY21 ....**21** B3
Orchard St
32 Abergavenny / Y Fenni
NP7 ....**128** F1
Brecon / Aberhonddu LD3 ..**145** B3
Brynmawr NP23 ....**153** B4
Orchard The SY16 ....**138** C5
Orchard View SY18 ....**76** F1
Oriel Davies Art Gall*
SY16 ....**138** C4
Oriel Jazz Gall* LD3 .....**145** D3
Osborne Rd NP23 ....**153** A4
Our Lady & St Michael's Prim
Sch NP7 ....**128** F1
Owen's La SA9 ....**129** C2
Owl's La SY15 ....**52** F6
Oxford Ave LD1 ....**142** C4
Oxford La **5** HR5 ....**87** C3
Oxford Rd
Disserth & Trecoed LD1 ...**142** C4
Hay-on-W HR3 ....**144** D3

P

Paddocks The
Knighton / Tref-y-Clawdd
LD7 ....**140** A5
Presteigne LD8 ....**77** E3
Paddocks The / Cae Bach
LD8 ....**77** E3
Palleg Rd / Heol Palleg
SA9 ....**147** C6
Pandy Rd SY19 ....**24** C2
Panteg NP23 ....**152** D2
Pant La **9** NP7 ....**128** F1
Pantteg SA9 ....**147** A4
Pant Y Brwyn SA9 ....**129** C7
Pant-y-Dwr
Merthyr Tydfil / Merthyr Tudful
CF48 ....**133** E6
Tredegar NP22 ....**151** C2
Pant-y-Fforest NP23 ......**152** E1
Pantyffynnon Terr SA9 ...**147** A4
Pant-y-Glan NP23 ....**147** F8
Pant-y-Mynydd SY21 .....**135** C3
Pant-y-Rhiw Adventure Ctr
LD3 ....**139** D5
Panthyriwen La LD1 ....**73** A1
Pant SY22 ....**11** F4
Parc Bychan NP23 ....**152** E1
Parc Caradog SY21 ....**20** D7
Parc Eco Dyfi / Dyfi Eco Pk
SY20 ....**137** C5
Parc Hafod **3** SY16 ....**38** F5

Parc Hafren Ind Est
SY18 ....**139** C3
Parc Llwyn **2** SY18 ....**139** D7
Parc Manter Caerbont /
Caerbont Ent Pk SA9 ......**130** B6
Parc Offa **12** SY22 ....**12** A1
Parc Pendre LD8 ....**145** C6
Parc-y-Berllan **1** LD3 ....**109** F6
Parc Y Castell **4** LD2 ....**143** D5
Parc-yr-Irfon LD2 ....**143** B7
Park Ave Glynneath SA11 .**131** C1
Kerry / Ceri SY16 ....**49** F5
Kington HR5 ....**87** C3
2 Talgarth LD3 ....**110** A5
Park Cl SY16 ....**138** D4
Park Cres
18 Abergavenny / Y Fenni
NP7 ....**128** F1
Brynmawr NP23 ....**153** B4
Disserth & Trecoed LD1 ...**142** C4
Park Dr NP8 ....**127** D4
Park Dulas SY20 ....**22** B5
Parker's La SY16 ....**138** D5
Parker's Pl **7** SY21 ....**136** B5
Parkhill Cres NP23 ....**152** E3
Park La
Disserth & Trecoed LD2 ...**142** C3
Newtown / Y Drenewydd
SY16 ....**138** C4
Welshpool / Y Trallwng
SY21 ....**136** B4
Parklands SY16 ....**138** C4
Park Rd
Abergavenny / Y Fenni
NP7 ....**128** F1
Builth Wells / Llanfair-Ym-Muallt
LD2 ....**143** C6
Guilsfield SY21 ....**19** D2
Kington HR5 ....**87** C3
Park St
Abergavenny / Y Fenni
NP7 ....**128** F1
Llanrhaeadr-ym-Mochnant
SY10 ....**4** A1
Newtown / Y Drenewydd
SY16 ....**138** D4
Park Stile Mill
Huntington HR5 ....**86** F1
Huntington HR5 ....**95** F8
Park St Infants Sch NP7 ...**128** F1
Park Terr
Disserth & Trecoed LD1 ...**142** C3
Llandrindod Wells / Llandrindod
LD1 ....**83** C7
Park View
Brynmawr NP23 ....**153** B4
Ebbw Vale / Glyn Ebwy
NP23 ....**152** D4
Park-View LD3 ....**145** F8
Parsons Bank SY21 ....**135** B4
Parson's La SY22 ....**11** F2
Partridge Row NP23 ......**152** C4
Pavement The HR3 ....**144** D3
Pavilion Ct SY16 ....**138** C4
Peartree La SY21 ....**135** C3
Pecknall La SY16 ....**21** E4
Pelican St SA9 ....**146** F2
Pembroke Cl CF48 ....**133** F1
Pembroke St NP22 ....**151** C1
Penarron Dr SY16 ....**49** F4
Penarth Dr LD1 ....**74** A4
Penbont Rd LD3 ....**110** A4
Penbrey SY21 ....**27** F3
Pencwmdu SA8 ....**129** A1
Pendarren SA8 ....**129** B1
Penderyn Prim Sch
CF44 ....**132** C3
Pendre
Brecon / Aberhonddu LD3 ..**145** C4
Builth Wells / Llanfair-Ym-Muallt
LD2 ....**143** B6
Pendre Cl LD3 ....**145** D5
Pendre Gdns LD3 ....**145** D5
Pengeulan **8** SY18 ....**139** D6
Pengorof Ct SA9 ....**146** E1
Penmaen Cvn Pk SY20 ...**32** A5
Penmaendovey Cctry Club
SY20 ....**32** A6
Penmaes LD6 ....**141** D5
Penrallt Ct SY20 ....**137** D4
Pen-Rhos SY20 ....**22** B7
Penrhos Cty Prim Sch
SA9 ....**130** A6
Pensarn SY20 ....**22** D8
Pen-Shwa La SY16 ....**138** B8
Penthryn La SY22 ....**20** B7
Pentre Barog SY22 ....**18** D4
Pentre Clawdd SY22 .....**18** D4
Pentre Farm La HR3 ......**95** C3
Pentre Gr HR3 ....**95** C3
Pentre La NP7 ....**128** E2
Pentrosfa Cres LD2 ....**142** C1
Pentrosfa Rd LD2 ....**142** B1
Pen-Twyn HR3 ....**95** B3
Pentwyn Rd SA9 ....**147** B7
Penyard Rd CF44 ....**132** E1
Pen-y-Banc SA10 ....**130** C3
Pen-y-Bont
Crynant SA10 ....**130** A1
Tredegar NP22 ....**151** C2
Penybont Rd
Knighton / Tref-y-Clawdd
LD7 ....**140** A4
Whitton LD7 ....**77** A6

Pen-y-Bont Sta LD1 ......74 B3
Pen-y-Borfa **1** SY18 ...139 D7
Penybryn **8** LD1 ......142 C6
Pen-y-Bryn
  Brecon / Aberhonddu LD3 .145 F3
  Builth LD2 ......143 D5
  Cwmllynfell SA9 ......129 B7
Pen Y Bryn LD4 ......90 C2
Pen-y-Bryn
  Seven Sisters / Blaendulais
  SA10 ......130 A5
  Ystradgynlais SA9 ......130 A5
Penycae Prim Sch SA9 ...130 F8
Pen-y-Crug NP23 ......152 B5
Pen-y-cwm Specl Sch
  NP23 ......152 F4
Pen-y-Ddol SY21 ......15 F2
Pen-y-Dre NP23 ......152 C3
Penyfal Rd **5** NP7 ...128 F1
Pen Y Fan Cl **1** LD3 ...115 A5
Penyfan Rd LD3 ......145 B3
Pen-y-garn CF44 ......148 F2
Penygarreg Cl **1** SY10 ...12 A5
Penygarreg La SY10 ......12 B5
Penygarreg Rise SY10 ...12 A5
Penygloddfa Cty Prim Sch
  SY13 ......138 D6
Pen-y-Graig Rd SA9 ...129 C7
Penygraig St SY18 ......139 C6
Penygreen Rd SY18 ...139 B5
Pen-y-lan NP23 ......152 D3
Pen-y-Maes **2** SY22 ...10 E3
Pen-y-Maes La SY22 ...11 C4
Pen-y-Pound NP7 ......128 F2
Pen-y-Pound Ct **3** NP7 .128 F2
Pen-yr-Ale La **2** NP8 ...126 C7
Pen-yr-Allt SA9 ......147 B8
Pen-yr-Grug SA9 ......147 A8
Pen-y-Rhiw SA9 ......129 B5
Penywern SA9 ......147 A7
Penywern Rd SA9 ......147 A6
Peppercorn La LD3 ...145 C5
Perseverence CF HR5 ...87 C3
Phillips Cl NP23 ......152 B5
Piccadilly HR5 ......87 B2
Picton Rd NP22 ......151 E1
Picton St **2** SY18 ......139 C6
Pine Ct SY16 ......138 C2
Pines Gdns SY16 ......138 C3
Pine Tree Way SY16 ...138 E6
Pistyll Rhaeadr* SY10 ...3 B4
Pitts La LD7 ......68 B2
Plantation La LD8 ......138 B2
Plantation The LD8 ...77 F3
Plasderwern **3** NP8 ...127 C4
Plas Dr SY20 ......137 D4
Plas Hafren SY16 ......138 B5
Plas Heulog SY16 ......138 C4
Plas Talgarth SY20 ......32 B6
Plasycoed SA9 ......146 F2
Plas-y-Coed SA11 ......131 C1
Play Barn The* LD3 ...116 B7
Pleasant View NP23 ...153 B5
Police Row NP22 ......151 D2
Pond Rd NP23 ......153 B3
Pont ar Ddyfi SY20 ...137 C6
Pont Aur SA9 ......147 E7
Pontfaen
  Knighton / Tref-y-Clawdd
  LD7 ......140 D5
  The Vale of Grwyney NP8 .127 F7
Pontfaen Cl LD7 ......140 D4
Pontfaen Mdws LD7 ...140 D4
Pont Minllyn* SY20 ...13 E4
Pontneathvaughan Rd
  SA11 ......131 E2
Pontpren CF44 ......132 E2
Pontrobert CP Sch SY22 .17 E3
Pontsticill Sta* CF48 ...149 A4
Pontwilym LD3 ......145 C6
Pontygof NP23 ......153 D5
Pont-y-Gof NP23 ......152 D1
Pontygof Prim Sch
  NP23 ......152 D1
Pont-y-Wal La LD3 ...109 E6
Pool Rd
  3 Montgomery / Trefaldwyn
  SY15 ......41 A3
  Newtown / Y Drenewydd
  SY16 ......138 F5
Poplar Rd
  Machynlleth SY20 ......137 D4
  Newtown / Y Drenewydd
  SY16 ......138 E6
Poplar Sq SY20 ......137 C4
Poplar Terr SY20 ......137 C4
Porters Rd NP23 ......153 C2
Porth-y-cwm LL20 ......4 D7
Postern LD3 ......145 C5
Postern VP Sch LD3 ...145 D4
Post Office La SY17 ......36 E3
Pound Cl **1** SY9 ......52 F3
Pound Cvn Pk The HR3 ...95 F2
Pound La Presteigne LD8 .77 E3
  Welshpool / Y Trallwng
  SY21 ......29 D2
Pound Rd or Trafalgar Rd
  NP23 ......153 C5
Powell Arts Ctr The*
  LD3 ......145 C3
Powell's La SY21 ...136 B5
Powis Castle & Gdn (NT)*
  SY21 ......136 A2
Powis Ct **5** SY21 ......41 A3
Powys SY16 ......138 C2

Powysland Mus &
  Montgomery Canal Ctr*
  SY21 ......136 C4
Powys Theatre* SY16 ...138 D6
Presteigne Ind Est LD8 ...77 E3
Presteigne Prim Sch LD8 .77 E3
Presteigne Rd LD7 ...140 D3
Price's Row SA10 ......130 F6
Primitive NP23 ......152 D4
Primrose Dr SY16 ......49 D7
Primrose La LD3 ......143 D5
Prince of Wales Dr
  SY21 ......136 B3
Prince Philip Ave NP23 .152 D5
Princes Ave LD1 ......142 D3
Princes Ct NP23 ......152 E1
Princes's Ct SY5 ......21 D5
Princes St SY5 ......41 A3
Prince's St **11** NP7 ...128 F1
Prince St NP23 ......153 C1
Priory C in W Sch / Ysgol
  Priordy LD3 ......145 C5
Priory Gdns LD1 ......145 C4
Priory Hill LD3 ......145 C4
Priory The HR3 ......103 E7
Priory Wood HR3 ......103 F8
Prospect Cl LD3 ......145 B4
Prospect Pl
  Cwmllynfell SA9 ......129 B7
  4 Kington HR5 ......87 C3
Prospect Rd
  12 Abergavenny / Y Fenni
  NP7 ......128 F1
  1 Kington HR5 ......87 C3
Puzzle Sq **6** SY21 ...136 B5
Pwll Penarth Nature
  Reserve* SY16 ......49 E7
Pwll-y-Wrach Nature
  Reserve* LD3 ......110 B3

Q

Quarry La LD1 ......142 D5
Queen's Ave **4** LD3 ...110 A5
Queen's Dr **8** SY21 ...110 A5
Queen Sq **6** NP23 ...153 B4
Queen St
  6 Abergavenny / Y Fenni
  NP7 ......128 F1
  Brynmawr NP23 ......153 C5
Queens Villas NP23 ...152 D2
Queensway NP23 ......152 D5

R

Radford Terr NP23 ...152 D4
Radnor CP Sch LD8 ......86 A7
Radnor Dr LD7 ......140 E5
Radnorshire Mus* LD1 .142 D4
Radstock Cl **18** NP7 ...128 F1
Raglan Gr CF48 ......133 F1
Raglan Terr NP23 ......152 D3
Railway Terr
  Cwmllynfell SA9 ......129 B7
  Hirwaun CF44 ......132 E1
  Machynlleth SY20 ......137 C5
  Tredegar NP22 ......151 A6
  Ystradgynlais SA9 ......130 A4
Railway View NP23 ...152 D4
Rassau Ind Est NP23 ...152 A6
Rassau Rd NP23 ......152 B4
Raven Sq **1** SY21 ...136 A5
Raven St SY21 ......136 A5
Raylaw Ave SY21 ......136 A4
Rdgross SY5 ......20 E6
Rectory Gdns **4** SY5 ...31 E3
Rectory La
  1 New Radnor / Maesyfed
  LD8 ......86 A7
  4 Pant SY22 ......11 F3
Rectory Rd **1** NP8 ...127 D5
Red Bank SY21 ......136 B6
Red La Rhydspence HR3 ...95 B4
  Welshpool / Y Trallwng
  SY21 ......136 A2
Redlake Mdw **2** SY7 ...68 B7
Reeves La LD7 ......68 D2
Regent St
  Abergavenny / Y Fenni
  NP7 ......128 F1
  10 Talgarth LD3 ......110 A4
Reservoir Rd NP23 ...152 C5
Rest Rd The HR3 ......95 F4
Rhallt Dr **4** SY21 ......19 F4
Rhallt La SY21 ......136 F7
Rhayader C in W Prim Sch
  LD6 ......141 D5
Rhayader Leisure Ctr
  LD6 ......141 D5
Rhes Bricksen / Brick Row
  SA10 ......130 C3
Rhes Bryndulais / Bryndulais
  Row SA10 ......130 C4
Rhestr Fawr SA9 ......146 F2
Rhiwfawr Rd SA9 ......146 A1
Rhiw Rd SA9 ......129 C5
Rhiw Refail SY22 ......12 A4
Rhiw Wen SY21 ......152 C2
Rhodfa Cornatyn / Corndon
  Dr **8** SY15 ......41 A3
Rhodfa Martyn / Martyn's
  Ave SA10 ......130 C4
Rhondda Cl LD7 ......140 C4
Rhos Cotts SA10 ......147 F3
Rhosferig Rd **2** LD3 ...145 D4

Rhosgoch Cty Prim Sch
  LD2 ......94 D2
Rhos Goch National Nature
  Reserve* LD2 ......94 E3
Rhoshyfryd CF44 ......132 D3
Rhos La LD8 ......76 F2
Rhoslan Guilsfield SY21 ...19 D2
  Tredegar NP22 ......151 F1
Rhos-y-Fedwyn Prim Sch
  NP23 ......152 B4
Rhos-y-Maen Isaf SY18 .139 D5
Rhos-y-Maen Uchaf **4**
  SY18 ......139 D5
Rhydarw Terr SA9 ......130 F8
Rhyd Clydach NP23 ...153 D5
Rhyd-Esgyn La SY21 ...20 C5
Rhydwen SY9 ......147 E6
Rhyd Wen SA18 ......129 A8
Rhyd-y-Cae NP23 ......152 B4
Rhymney Cl NP23 ......152 C4
Rhymney Row NP22 ...152 C5
Richmond Dr CF44 ...132 E1
Richmond Pk SA9 ......130 A5
Rich Way LD3 ......145 D3
Ridgebourne LD1 ......142 C2
Ridgebourne Dr LD2 ...142 C2
Ridgebourne Rd HR5 ...87 B3
Ridge The **4** SY9 ......147 E6
Ripley Ct LD3 ......145 D5
Riverside NP23 ......152 C4
Riverside Gdns
  Abercrave / Abercraf SA9 .130 F8
  Glynneath SA11 ......131 D1
River View HR3 ......95 F2
Road to the Three Graves /
  Heol Tair Y Beddau LD3 .99 E3
Robert Owen Meml Mus*
  SY16 ......138 D5
Roberts Cl SA11 ......131 C1
Robert St SA11 ......131 C1
Robin Sq / Sgwar Y Robin
  Goch **5** SY16 ......138 B3
Rockbridge Pk LD8 ......77 C4
Rocke's Mdw LD7 ......140 D4
Rock House Rd LD7 ...140 D4
Rock Pk Cl LD1 ......142 B4
Rock St LD1 ......74 A4
Rock St SA11 ......131 C1
Rockwell La **5** SY10 ...12 A5
Roderick Hill Ct SY21 ...12 A5
Rodney's View / Golygfa
  Rodney **3** SY22 ......12 A1
Roman Rd SA10 ......131 A4
Rose Farm Bglws NP22 .151 B1
Rose Mount Dr **4** SY10 .12 A5
Rose Way **2** SY5 ......31 E3
Roundhouse Cl LD7 ......3 B4
Roundton Hill National
  Nature Reserve* SY15 ...42 B1
Rowan Cl **4** SY22 ......12 A1
Rowan Ct SY16 ......49 F5
Rowan Way NP23 ...152 C5
Rusbock LD8 ......87 C5
Russell Cl NP23 ......152 A4
Russell St LD7 ......140 B5

S

St Andrew's Cl NP23 ...152 F4
St Bride's Way SY21 ...11 B3
St David's Cl CF48 ...133 F1
St David's Rd SA9 ...147 C6
St David's St LD8 ......77 E3
St David St **1** SY21 ...136 A4
St Davids Ursuline Convent
  Sch LD3 ......145 C3
St Donats Cl / Clos Sain
  Dunwyd CF44 ......133 F1
St Fagans Gr CF48 ...133 F1
St Harmon Rd LD6 ...141 E7
St Helen's Rd NP7 ...128 F1
St Johns Rd LD3 ......145 C4
St John's St **11** NP7 ...128 F1
St Joseph's RC Prim Sch
  LD3 ......145 C4
St Joseph's RC Sch
  NP22 ......151 C1
St Luke's Rd / Heol Sant Luc
  NP22 ......151 D2
St Martins Cres NP22 ...151 C1
St Mary's Cl SY16 ...138 D5
St Mary's C in E Prim Sch
  SY7 ......68 F4
St Mary's CW Jun & Inf Sch
  NP23 ......153 C4
St Mary's RC (Aided) Prim
  Sch SY16 ......138 C3
St Mary's Rd HR3 ...144 D3
St Mary St LD3 ......145 C4
St Meilog's Cl HR3 ...102 D4
St Michael's Cl NP8 ...118 B2
St Michael's Rd **1** NP7 .128 F1
St Michael St **7** LD3 ...145 C4
St Peter's Cl NP8 ......127 F7
Sale La SY21 ......20 D1
Salisbury Cl CF48 ...133 F1
Salop Rd SY21 ......136 C5
Salop St **3** SY9 ......52 F4
Samuels Rd SA9 ......129 B7
Sarn CE Sch SY16 ......30 C1
Sarn Helen
  Pontneddfechan SA10,
  CF44 ......131 F4
  Ystradfellte CF44 ......122 D2
School Ave NP23 ......153 C4
School Bank **11** SY15 ...41 A3
Schoolhouse La SY9 ...52 F4

School La
  5 Bishop's Castle SY9 ...52 F3
  Ebbw Vale / Glyn Ebwy
  NP23 ......152 B4
  8 Gilwern NP7 ......128 A1
  Llanymynech & Pant SY10 ..12 A6
  New Radnor / Maesyfed
  LD8 ......86 A7
  Newtown / Y Drenewydd
  SY16 ......138 D6
  Norton LD8 ......77 D6
School Lane (Lon Yr Ysgol)
  LD8 ......77 D6
School Pl SA11 ......131 D1
School Rd
  Abercrave / Abercraf SA9 .130 C7
  Dyffryn Cellwen SA10 ...131 A4
  Ebbw Vale / Glyn Ebwy
  SY16 ......152 B4
  Ystalyfera SA9 ......147 B8
  Ystradgynlais SA9 ......147 D8
School Rd / Heol Yr Ysgol
  SA9 ......129 B8
School Rd The HR3 ...95 D7
School St SD8 ......110 A4
School View /
  Golwg-yr-Ysgol NP23 .153 B2
Scottleton St LD8 ......77 E3
Scout La LD3 ......145 C4
Scudamore Comm HR3 .103 E5
Scwrfa Rd NP22 ......151 E1
Sennybridge Camp LD3 .113 E8
Sennybridge CP Sch
  LD3 ......113 E8
Seren Twyn / Twyn Star
  NP22 ......151 D1
Seven Acres LD7 ......140 D4
Seven Sisters Mus & Saw
  Mill* SA10 ......130 C3
Seven Stars Rd **4** SY21 .136 B5
Seventeenth Ave CF44 .132 E1
Severn Cl **1** SY15 ......40 E5
Severn Farm Ind Est
  SY21 ......136 D3
Severn Farm Nature
  Reserve* SY21 ......136 C3
Severn La SY21 ......136 D4
Severn St Caersws SY17 ..48 A6
  Newtown / Y Drenewydd
  SY16 ......138 D5
  Welshpool / Y Trallwng
  SY21 ......136 B4
Severn Way **4** SY22 ...12 A1
Sgwar Rhedynen / Fern Sq
  3 SY16 ......138 B3
Sgwar Y Robin Goch / Robin
  Sq **5** SY16 ......138 B3
Sgwd Gwladus Waterfalls
  Wlk* SA11 ......131 E2
Sgwyr Heulwen **3** SY21 .136 A5
Sheaf St SY16 ......138 E4
Shepherds Cl NP22 ...151 E1
Ship St LD3 ......145 C4
Shires The **2** NP7 ...128 A2
Shoemaker Cl / Clos Y Crydd
  NP23 ......153 D4
Shop Row NP22 ......151 A6
Short Bridge St
  Llanidloes SY18 ......139 C6
  6 Newtown / Y Drenewydd
  SY16 ......138 D5
Silla Mdw LD8 ......77 E3
Silver St LD3 ......145 C4
Sirhowy Ct NP22 ......151 F1
Sirhowy Inf Sch NP22 ...151 F1
Sixteenth Ave CF44 ...132 E1
Skirrid Rd **4** NP7 ...128 F1
Slough Rd LD8 ......77 D3
Slwch La LD3 ......145 E4
Small Breeds Farm Pk &
  Animal Ctr* HR5 ......87 C1
Smelt House La **3** SY10 ..12 A5
Smithfield
  8 Newtown / Y Drenewydd
  SY16 ......138 E5
Smithfield Rd / Ffordd
  Smithfield LD3 ......143 C5
Smithfield Terr **3** LD8 ...138 C5
Smith's Ave CF44 ......132 A1
Snow Terr SA9 ......147 B8
Somerset St LD7 ......153 C4
Somerset Terr NP23 ...152 F4
South Bank HR3 ......95 F4
South Cres LD1 ......142 C4
South St
  Ebbw Vale / Glyn Ebwy
  NP23 ......152 B4
  Rhayader / Rhaeadr Gwy
  LD6 ......141 C4
South Wales Borderers
  Mus* LD3 ......145 E3
Spaceguard Ctr The*
  LD7 ......68 A1
Spa Rd LD1 ......142 C4
Spa Rd E LD1 ......142 D3
Spencer Terr SA9 ......147 D8
Springbank NP8 ......127 F8
Spring Bank SY16 ......50 F5
Spring Fields SY16 ...50 F5
Spring Gdns **2** LD2 ...143 D5
Spruce Way LD2 ......82 E1
Square The HR5 ......87 C3
Squirrels Way LD2 ......82 E1
Standard St NP8 ......127 D5

Standert Terr SA10 ...130 D3
Stanhope St **2** NP7 ...128 F1
Stargarreg La SY10 ...12 A5
Star St NP22 ......151 D2
Station App NP23 ......152 D1
Station Cres
  Disserth & Trecoed LD1 ...142 C4
  Llandrindod Wells / Llandrindod
  LD1 ......83 D8
Station Rd
  Abercrave / Abercraf SA9 .130 D7
  11 Brynmawr NP23 ...153 C4
  Builth Wells / Llanfair-Ym-Muallt
  LD2 ......143 D6
  Caersws SY17 ......48 A6
  Coelbren SA10 ......131 A6
  Glan-rhyd SA9 ......147 F8
  Glasbury LD3 ......101 D1
  Knighton / Tref-y-Clawdd
  LD7 ......140 C5
  Llanfyllin SY22 ......134 C5
  Llanwrtyd Wells LD5 ...89 D1
  3 Montgomery / Trefaldwyn
  SY15 ......41 A3
  Pant SY22 ......11 F3
  3 Pen-y-bont-Fawr SY10 ...8 F7
  Presteigne LD8 ......77 E3
  Rhayader / Rhaeadr Gwy
  LD6 ......141 C4
  Talybont-on-Usk LD3 ...117 A1
  Tredegar NP22 ......151 C2
  Ystradgynlais SA9 ......146 F1
Station Sq SY9 ......52 F3
Station Terr NP22 ......151 A6
Station Terr / Teras Gorsaf
  SA10 ......130 D3
Stokes Lonp SY17 ......47 A4
Stonebridge Rd NP23 ...152 A4
Stone House Ct **2** SY21 ...30 C1
Stone House Hospl SY9 ...52 F3
Stone St LD3 ......113 F6
Stoney Rd SY10 ......11 E8
Strand St **1** LD2 ......143 D6
Strand The LD2 ......143 D6
Street The SY22 ......11 F2
Struet LD3 ......145 C4
Stryd Glanhywl / Glanhowy
  St NP22 ......151 D1
Stryd Masnach / Commercial
  St SA10 ......130 C3
Sugar Loaf Sta LD5 ......96 F6
Summerfield Rd NP23 ...152 B5
Sun Hill / Bryn Haul LD6 .62 E4
Sun La **8** HR5 ......87 C3
Sunnybank NP23 ......153 B5
Sunny Bank
  Abergavenny / Y Fenni
  NP7 ......128 F1
  Brecon / Aberhonddu LD3 .145 F3
Sunnybank Rd NP23 ...153 B5
Sunnyfield Ct LD1 ......141 C4
Swallow Dr / Lon Y Wennol
  SY16 ......138 B3
Swallows **6** 29 A4
Swan Bank HR3 ......144 D3
Swan Cres NP23 ......152 E4
Swanfield SA9 ......147 B8
Swan La SA9 ......147 C7
Sweep's La SY21 ......29 F3
Swn-y-Nant SA9 ......146 B2
Swn yr Eos SA9 ......147 E7
Sycamore Ave NP22 ...151 D1
Sycamore Cl
  8 Llandysilio SY22 ......12 A1
  2 Newtown / Y Drenewydd
  SY16 ......138 E6
Sycamore Dr SY16 ...138 E6
Sycamore Fields SY10 ...12 D8
Sycamores The LD1 ......74 F5
Sychpant LD1 ......82 E5

T

Tafarnaubach Ind Est
  NP22 ......151 A2
Taf Fachan Hos CF48 ...148 F4
Taff Cl NP23 ......152 C4
Tai-ar-y-Bryn LD2 ......143 B5
Tai Bach NP23 ......152 B4
Tai Gwalia SA9 ......129 C5
Tan-dderwen **4** NP8 ...127 F7
Tan House Mdws **6** HR5 .87 D3
Tanners Row LD6 ......141 C5
Tanrallt St SY20 ......137 D5
Tanrallt St SY20 ......137 D5
Tan-y-Bryn SY18 ......139 D4
Tandarren SA8 ......129 B1
Tan-y-Farteg SA9 ......147 C7
Tanrallt SY20 ......32 A2
Tan-y-Foel Dr SY22 ...11 F3
Tanygarth SA9 ......130 C7
Tan-y-Graig
  Abercrave / Abercraf SA9 .130 B7
  Machynlleth SY20 ......137 D4
  Newtown / Y Drenewydd
  SY16 ......138 F6
Tan-y-Groes SY18 ......54 F3
Tan-y-Llan **4** SY16 ......38 F5
Tan Y Mur SY15 ......41 A3
Tanyrallt SA9 ......130 C7
Tan-yr-Allt Corris SY20 ...22 B7
  8 Llanidloes SY18 ......139 C6
Tan-yr-Eglwys **6** SY16 ...38 F5
Tan-y-Rhiw SA9 ......130 C8
Tanywaun SA9 ......130 B6
Tanywern La SA9 ......147 B7

Tawelfan SA9 ....146 F4
Tawe Pk SA9 ....147 F7
Temperance La SA9 ....146 F1
Temple Ave LD2 ....142 C3
Temple Dr LD2 ....142 C3
Temple St LD2 ....142 C3
Teras Brynhyfryd /
  Brynhyfryd Terr SA10 .130 D4
Teras Gorsaf / Station Terr
  SA10 ....130 D3
Terrace The LD8 ....77 D5
Textile Mus* SY16 ......138 D5
Theatr Brycheiniog*
  LD3 ....145 D3
Thirteenth Ave CF44 ...132 C1
Thornbury Cl CF48 .....133 F1
Thornhill Cl NP23 ......153 C5
Three Cocks Ind Est
  LD3 ....110 B8
Three Tuns Brewing Mus*
  SY9 ....52 F4
Three Way Hill HR3 ....144 F1
Tirbach Rd SA9 ....147 C7
Tir-y-Berth NP23 ......152 C3
Tir Y Waun SA9 ....130 A5
Top of Belan SY21 ......29 D2
Tor-y-Crug NP23 ......152 B5
Tothill St NP23 ....152 C1
Tower La LD3 ....110 A4
Tower Rd SY20 ....32 B7
Tower St NP8 ....127 D5
Townend LD3 ....77 E3
Traeth Moor Nature
  Reserve* NP23 ......114 D4
Trafalgar Cl NP23 .....153 C4
Tramroadside NP23 ....152 A4
Tramway Side SA11 ....131 E1
Trawsffordd SA9 ......147 E8
Tre-banog Terr CF44 ...132 D2
Trecastle CP Sch LD3 ..113 A8
Tredegar St LD3 ....145 D4
Trederwen La SY22 ......20 C6
Trefecca Rd LD3 ....144 C4
Trefeglwys Rd SY17 .....47 F6
Trefil Rd NP22 ....151 A4
Trefnanney CP Sch SY22 .19 C6
Trefonen Ave LD1 ......142 D5
Trefonen La LD1 ....142 D5
Treforgan Rd SA10 ....130 A1
Treganol SY16 ....38 C8
Tregarth SY20 ....137 E5
Tregarthen La SY10 ....12 A5
Tregraig Rd NP8 ....117 E1
Tregynon Hall Sch SY16 .38 E4
Trelydan La SY21 ....19 E2
Trem Banwy SY21 .....135 A3
Trem Dyffryn NP21 ....136 B6
Trem Hafren SY21 .....136 B6
Tremont Rd LD1 ....142 D5
Trem Y Coed LD3 ......137 E4
Trenynoddfa SY17 .....36 D3
Trem yr Allt SY20 .....137 D4
Trem yr Orsedd SY20 ..137 F4
Trenewydd LD3 ....145 B3
Tre Newydd NP23 .....152 E1
Treowain SY20 ....137 E4
Treowain Ind Est SY20 .137 E4
Treowen Cty Prim Sch
  SY16 ....138 E4
Trewylan La SY21 ......19 E8
Trinity St NP7 ....128 F1
Trinity Terr NP7 ....128 F1
Troad-y-Bryn SA9 .....130 E7
Troed Y Bryn LD2 .....143 D5
Troed Yr Allt SY18 ....139 D7
Troed-y-Rhiw SA9 ....130 A1
Troed Y Rhiw LD1 .....142 C6
Tudor Cl NP23 ....152 B5
Tudor Cres SA9 ....153 B4
Tudor La LD1 ....142 C4
Tudor St
  Abergavenny / Y Fenni
  NP7 ....128 F1
  Ystradgynlais SA9 ...147 E7
Turners La SY10 ....142 A6
Turner's La SY16 ......138 D5
Twin Oaks HR3 ....102 D1
Twyncarmel CF48 ......133 F1
Twyncynghordy NP23 ..153 A4
Twyncynghordy Pl
  NP23 ....153 A4
Twyncynghordy Rd
  Brynmawr NP23 .....153 A4
  Ebbw Vale / Glyn Ebwy
  NP23 ....152 F4
Twynderwen Flats
  NP23 ....153 D2
Twyn Star / Seren Twyn
  NP22 ....151 D1
Twyn-yr-Ysgol SA9 ....147 B7

Ty = house

Ty Brith Mdws Nature
  Reserve* SY22 ....20 A8
Ty Gwyn Rd SY17 ......48 A7
Ty-Haulwen NP23 .....153 C2
Tyleheulog LD2 ....143 C5
Ty-mawr La SY22 ......10 F1
Tynewydd NP22 ....151 B3
Ty Newydd SA10 ......130 D4
Tynllan Ct SY21 ....29 A4

Tyr Comm 4 NP7 ....128 A2
Tyr-Meddyg NP23 .....152 E2
Tywyn Uchel 2 LD1 ....73 B1

U

Uchel Dr SY16 ....49 F4
Under Ffrydd Wood
  LD7 ....140 B4
Underhill Cres LD07 ...140 C5
Union Mews HR3 ......144 D3
Union Rd W NP7 ......128 E1
Union St
  7 Bishop's Castle SY9 .52 F3
  7 Newtown / Y Drenewydd
  SY16 ....138 D5
Uplands LD3 ....138 D1
Upper Dolfor Rd SY16 .138 D1
Upper Gn SY18 ....139 C5
Upper Gwestydd La
  SY16 ....138 A8
Upper Hengoed HR5 ...95 D7
Upper Hergest HR5 .....87 A2
Upper High St CF48 ...133 F3
Usk Pl NP23 ....152 C5

V

Vale View
  Ebbw Vale / Glyn Ebwy
  NP23 ....152 E4
  Pontneddfechan SA11 .131 F2
Valley Rd NP23 ....152 D1
Vane Hall Pl SY20 .....137 D4
Van Rd SY18 ....139 C6
Varchoel La SY21 ......19 F3
Varteg Pl NP22 ....151 E1
Varteg Rd SA9 ....147 B5
Vaste Ind Est SY16 .....49 D6
Vastre Ent Pk SY16 ...158 F1
Verlon Cl SY15 ....41 A4
Vicarage Rd Llywel LD3 .113 B8
  Tredegar NP22 ......151 E1
Victoria Ave SY18 ....139 D6
Victoria Cl LD3 ....116 C4
Victoria Ct 2 HR5 ......87 D3
Victoria Meml Hospl
  SY21 ....136 C5
Victoria Rd
  Disserth & Trecoed LD1 .142 C4
  Kington HR5 ....87 C3
  Knighton / Tref-y-Clawdd
  LD7 ....140 C5
  Llanwrtyd Wells LD05 ..89 C1
Victoria Sq LD3 ....116 C4
Victoria St 17 NP7 ....128 F1
Victoria Terr HR3 .....144 E3
Village Cl 1 LD1 ....73 F3
Village Gn 2 SY15 .....40 D2
Vincent Ave NP23 ....153 D1
Vine Row SA9 ....147 A6
Vine Sq SY22 ....134 C5
Violet Cl / Clos Fioled
  SY16 ....138 B3
Vyrnwy Cres SY22 .....12 A1

W

Wade Ave SA9 ....147 B6
Waen-Fawr NP23 .....153 B2
Waen La SY17 ....47 E3
Walnut Gdns 2 HR5 ...87 C2
Walnut Sq LD3 ....145 C4
Walters Rd SA9 ....129 B7
Wapley Hill Forest Walks*
  HR6 ....78 D1
Warden Cl LD8 ....77 D3
Warden Rd LD8 ....77 C3
Warren Cl HR3 ....144 C3
Warwick Rd NP23 .....153 B2
Waterfall St SY17 ....4 A1
Water Folk Canal Ctr The*
  LD3 ....116 D4
Watergate St SY21 ....135 B3
Water La LD6 ....141 C4
Watery La Cusop HR5 ..87 B6
  Old Radnor LD8 ......86 F7
  Trewern SY21 ....20 C2
Watkins Terr SA9 .....130 D4
Watton LD3 ....145 D3
Waunbant Ct CF48 ....133 F2
Waundeg NP22 ....151 B2
Waun Dew NP23 ......152 F4
Waun-Ebbw Bglws
  NP23 ....153 B2
Waun-Ebbw Rd NP23 .153 B2
Waun Fawr NP23 .....152 B4

Waun Goch District
NP23 ....152 D4
Waun Goch Terr NP23 .152 D4
Waungron SA11 ....131 D1
Waun Gyrlais SA9 ....130 A6
Waunheulog NP23 ....153 A3
Waun-y-Pound Ind Est
  NP23 ....152 A2
Waun-y-Pound Rd
  NP23 ....152 B2
Weaver Rd / Heol-y-Gwaudd
  SA9 ....130 A4
Wellington Cres 1
  SY21 ....136 D5
Wellington Rd LD2 ....142 C2
Wellington Terr 7
  SY18 ....139 C6
Well La SY18 ....139 D6
Well St Brynmawr NP23 .153 B4
  8 Montgomery / Trefaldwyn
  SY15 ....41 A3
Welsh Harp Hollow SY17 .30 E6
Welshpool High Sch / Ysgol
  Uwchradd T Trallwng
  SY21 ....136 D6
Welshpool & Llanfair Light
  Rly* SY21 ....136 A3
Welshpool Raven Sq Sta
  SY21 ....136 A4
Welshpool Sta SY21 ...136 C5
Welsh Royal Crystal*
  SY21 ....141 E5
Welsh St SY9 ....52 E4
Wembley Ave SA10 ...130 F5
Wern Ave SA9 ....147 A6
Wern Ddu La
  Newtown & Llanllwchaiarn
  SY16 ....49 D6
  Newtown / Y Drenewydd
  SY16 ....138 F5
Wern Rd SA9 ....147 B6
Wernwood Rd SA9 ...147 B6
Wern Y Wennol Mdw 6
  SY21 ....136 A4
Wern Y Wiel SY21 .....11 F7
Wesleyan Pl NP23 ....152 D4
Wesleyan Row NP23 ..152 D1
Wesley Bldgs NP23 ...153 C2
Wesley Ho 6 NP23 ....153 C4
Wesley St
  Llanfair Caereinion SY21 .135 C3
  4 Newtown / Y Drenewydd
  SY16 ....138 D5
Western Ave NP23 ....153 A4
Western Gr LD2 ....143 C5
Western Prom
  Disserth & Trecoed LD2 .142 C3
  Llandrindod Wells / Llandrindod
  LD1 ....128 E1
Western Rd NP7 ......128 E1
Western Terr NP23 ....152 D1
Westfields 5 LD3 ......110 A5
Westgate St 8 SY15 ...19 A5
Weston Rd SY7 ....68 F4
West St
  Builth Wells / Llanfair-Ym-Muallt
  LD2 ....143 C6
  Knighton / Tref-y-Clawdd
  LD7 ....140 B5
  Rhayader / Rhaeadr Gwy
  LD6 ....141 D4
West Wall LD8 ....77 E3
Westwood Pk SY21 ...136 C5
Westwood Rd 6 SY21 .136 C5
Wheat St LD3 ....145 C3
Whip La SY10 ....12 E6
Whitefield Cl SA11 ....131 C1
White Lion Cotts / Bythynnod
  Y Llew Gwyn SY22 ....152 C1
Whitney Court Rd HR3 ..95 F3
Whitney Village Rd HR3 .95 F2
Whitting St SA11 ......131 D1
Whitton Sch LD7 ......77 A6
Wig La SY17 ....47 E7
Wigmore La SY5 ....21 F2
Wildwood Ct 4 SY21 ..136 B3
Willans Ct SY16 ....49 F5
Willans Dr SY16 ....49 F5
William St SA9 ....147 E7
Willow Cl
  Ebbw Vale / Glyn Ebwy
  NP23 ....152 D3
  Llandrinio SY22 ......12 A1
Willow Ct NP22 ......151 C2
Willows The 1 SY16 ...49 F5
Will's View LD8 ....77 D5
Wilson Terr LD3 ......145 A4
Winch Fawr Pk CF48 ..133 F1
Winch Fawr Rd CF48 ..133 F1
Windmill La SY7 ......68 C2
Wind Rd SA9 ....147 D7
Windsor Rd
  2 Abergavenny / Y Fenni
  NP7 ....128 E2
  Brynmawr NP23 .....153 A4
Winllan La SY22 ....11 A5
Winllan Rd SY22 ......11 A5
Winsford Gr 4 NP21 ..128 A1
Withy Ave 3 SY21 .....30 B1
Withy Cl 2 SY21 ....30 B1
Withy Ct 1 SY21 ......30 C1

Womaston Sch LD8 ....86 F7
Woodbatch Rd 2 SY9 ..52 E3
Woodbine Cl 1 SY5 ....31 E3
Woodhouse La
  Knighton / Tref-y-Clawdd
  LD7 ....140 A4
  Whitton LD7 ....77 A8
Woodland Cres LD3 ..145 F2
Woodland Dr
  Glynneath SA11 .....131 D1
  Penderyn CF44 ......132 D2
Woodland Rd / Heol Tir Y
  Coed SA9 ....129 C7
Woodlands
  Disserth & Trecoed LD1 .142 E4
  Tredegar NP22 ......151 C1
Woodlands Ave LD3 ..110 A4
Woodlands Bsns Pk
  SA9 ....147 D7
Woodland Terr LD3 ..139 C7
Woodland Terr NP23 ..153 C1
Woodland Way LD8 ....77 C5
Woodland Way / Y Lon Goed
  3 SY16 ....49 D7
Woodmans Terr SA9 ..147 B6
Wood Road The HR3 ...95 F3
Woodside HR3 ....95 E2
Woolston Rd LD3 ......12 F7
Worcester St NP23 ...153 C4
Worthen CE Prim Sch
  SY5 ....31 E3
Wye End Rd HR3 .....144 E4
Wye Ford Rd HR3 ....144 D4
Wyeside Art Gall & Theatre*
  LD3 ....143 D6
Wyeside Gdns HR3 ...144 C2
Wye Valley Bsns Pk
  HR3 ....144 C2
Wylcwm St LD7 ......140 C5
Wylecop St SY20 ....13 D5
Wynfields SY16 ....138 C3

Y

Yard Row NP23 ....152 D3
Y Berllan Llangedwyn SY10 .10 D7
  Ystradgynlais SA9 ...147 D7
Y Bwthyn / The Cottage 6
  SA9 ....147 E7
Y Clos SA9 ....129 B7
Y Dalar SY20 ....137 E4
Y Ddol 2 SY10 ....0 F7
Y Dolydd-The Meadows
  HR3 ....144 C2
Yeld La HR5 ....87 A4
Yellow Row NP22 .....151 C2
Y Fryd SY16 ....138 E5
Y Gilfach SA9 ....147 B7
Y Gilfach Isaf SY13 ...139 D5
Y Gilfach Uchaf 3
  SY18 ....139 D5
Y Gilwern SA9 ....147 B6
Y Goedlan SA9 ....129 C6
Y Lon Goed / Woodland Way
  3 SY16 ....49 D7
Ynyscedwyn Rd SA9 ..147 E8
Ynisisaf Cotts SA9 ...130 A6
Ynisydarren Rd SA9 ..147 B6
Ynys-bydafau SA9 ....130 B7
Ynyscedwyn Ind Est
  SA9 ....147 E8
Ynys-Cedwyn Lodge
  SA9 ....147 D7
Ynys-fr Nature Reserve*
  SY20 ....32 A3
Ynyslas Cres SA11 ....131 D1
Ynyswen SA9 ....130 E8
Ynyswen Terr SA10 ...130 A1
Ynys-y-gwial SA9 ....146 F5
Ynys-y-Nos Ave SA11 ..131 E1
Y Plas (Celtica Visitor Ctr)*
  SY20 ....137 D4

Ysbyty = hospital

Ysbyty Gymuned Bro Ddyfi /
  Bro Ddyfi Com Hospl
  SY20 ....137 E4
Ysbyty Gymuned
  Ystradgynlais SA9 ...147 E7
Ysbyty Leol / Cottage Hospl
  SY21 ....143 C5
Ysbyty'r Tri Chwm / Ebbw
  Vale Com Hospl NP23 .152 C3

Ysgol = school

Ysgol Babanod SY20 ..137 F5
Ysgol Bro Cynllaith SY10 .5 D3
Ysgol Bro Ddyfi SY20 ..137 E4
Ysgol Cedewain SY16 .138 C3
Ysgol Cefnbrynbrain
  SA9 ....129 B8
Ysgol Cynlais Prim Sch
  SA9 ....146 F2
Ysgol Dafydd Llwyd
  SY16 ....138 D4
Ysgol Dinas Mawddwy
  SY20 ....13 D5
Ysgol Dolafon LD5 .....89 C1

Taw – Zoa 163

Ysgol Dyffryn Trannon
  SY17 ....47 A5
Ysgoldy'r Cwm (Outdoor
  Pursuits Centre) SY19 .25 A5
Ysgol Efyrnwy Llanwddyn
  ....8 A2
Ysgol Gyfun Glyncoed /
  Glyncoed Comp Sch
  NP23 ....152 C3
Ysgol Gyfun Ystalyfera
  SA9 ....147 C6
Ysgol Gymraeg Brynmawr
  Jun & Inf Schs NP23 ..153 B4
Ysgol Gymraeg Cwmtwrch
  SA9 ....146 B1
Ysgol Gymraeg Ynysgedwyn
  SA9 ....147 F8
Ysgol Gymraeg Y Wern
  SA9 ....147 B6
Ysgol Gymunedol Gynradd
  Dolfor / Dolfor CP Sch
  SY16 ....49 B2
Ysgol Gynradd Ardd-lin /
  Arddleen Cty Prim Sch
  SY20 ....20 B6
Ysgol Gynradd Corris /
  Corris Prim Sch SY20 ..22 B6
Ysgol Gynradd Glyncoed /
  Glyncoed Prim Sch
  NP23 ....152 D3
Ysgol Gynradd Gymraeg
  Cwmnedd SA11 ......131 D1
Ysgol Gynradd Gymraeg
  Draddodiadol Rhiwfawr
  SA9 ....129 B5
Ysgol Gynradd Gymraeg
  Draddodiadol Cwmllynfell
  SA9 ....129 B7
Ysgol Gynradd Llanfechain /
  Llanfechain C in W Sch
  SY22 ....19 C4
Ysgol Gynradd Llangynidr /
  Llangynidr CP Sch
  NP8 ....126 D6
Ysgol Gynradd Pennal
  SY20 ....32 B7
Ysgol Gynradd Ystradowen
  SA9 ....129 C7
Ysgol Llanarmon Dyffryn
  Ceiriog LL20 ....4 D7
Ysgol Llanerfyl SY21 ...26 H1
Ysgol Maesyrhandir /
  Maesyrhandir Cty Prim Sch
  SY16 ....138 B2
Ysgol Pennaes LD5 ....145 D3
Ysgol Pennant SY10 ....8 F7
Ysgol Priordy / Priory C in W
  Sch LD3 ....145 D5
Ysgol Rhiw Bechan SY16 .38 F5
Ysgol Thomas Stephens
  SA11 ....131 F3
Ysgol Uwchradd Aberhonddu
  / Brecon High Sch
  LD3 ....145 D5
Ysgol Uwchradd Caereinion /
  Caereinion High Sch
  SY21 ....135 B4
Ysgol Uwchradd Crughywel /
  Crickhowell High Sch
  NP8 ....127 D5
Ysgol Uwchradd Llandrindod
  / Llandrindod High Sch
  LD1 ....142 C5
Ysgol Uwchradd
  Llanfair-ym-Muallt / Builth
  Wells High Sch LD2 ...143 C6
Ysgol Uwchradd Llanfyllin /
  Llanfyllin High Sch
  SY22 ....134 C5
Ysgol Uwchradd Llanidloes /
  Llanidloes High Sch
  SY18 ....138 A5
Ysgol Uwchradd T Trallwng /
  Welshpool High Sch
  SY21 ....136 D6
Ysgol Uwchradd y
  Drenewydd / Newtown High
  Sch SY16 ....138 C3
Ysguborwen NP22 ....151 F1

Ystrad = estate

Ystrad Ddwydiannol Hirwaun
  / Hirwaun Ind Est
  CF44 ....132 C2
Ystrad Deri NP22 .....151 E2
Ystrad-Fawr Villas SA9 .130 A5
Ystradgynlais Workshops
  SA9 ....147 E8
Ystrad Hir SY19 ....45 C6
Ystryd Ddu SY10 ....8 F7
Ystryd Y Ceunant SY21 .10 E4

Z

Zion St 1 LD5 ....89 C1
Zoar Rd SA9 ....147 B6

Addresses

Name and Address	Telephone	Page	Grid reference

Any feature in this atlas can be given a unique reference to help you find the same feature on other Ordnance Survey maps of the area, or to help someone else locate you if they do not have a Street Atlas.

The grid squares in this atlas match the Ordnance Survey National Grid and are at 500 metre intervals. The small figures at the bottom and sides of every other grid line are the National Grid kilometre values (**00** to **99** km) and are repeated across the country every 100 km (see left).

To give a unique National Grid reference you need to locate where in the country you are. The country is divided into 100 km squares with each square given a unique two-letter reference. Use the administrative map to determine in which 100 km square a particular page of this atlas falls.

The bold letters and numbers between each grid line (**A** to **F**, **1** to **8**) are for use within a specific Street Atlas only, and when used with the page number, are a convenient way of referencing these grid squares.

Example   The railway bridge over DARLEY GREEN RD in grid square B1

Step 1: Identify the two-letter reference, in this example the page is in **SP**

Step 2: Identify the 1 km square in which the railway bridge falls. Use the figures in the southwest corner of this square: Eastings **17**, Northings **74**. This gives a unique reference: **SP 17 74**, accurate to 1 km.

Step 3: To give a more precise reference accurate to 100 m you need to estimate how many tenths along and how many tenths up this 1 km square the feature is (to help with this the 1 km square is divided into four 500 m squares). This makes the bridge about **8** tenths along and about **1** tenth up from the southwest corner.

This gives a unique reference: **SP 178 741**, accurate to 100 m.

Eastings (read from left to right along the bottom) come before Northings (read from bottom to top). If you have trouble remembering say to yourself "Along the hall, THEN up the stairs"!

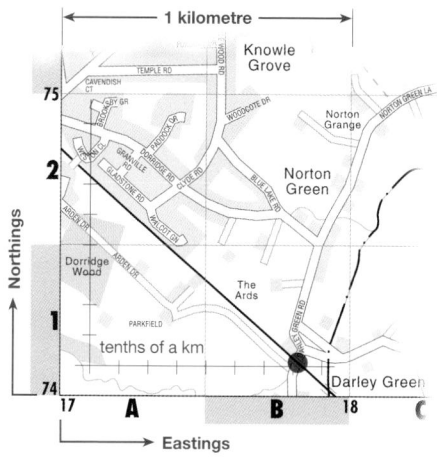

PHILIP'S MAPS

the Gold Standard for serious driving

- ◆ Philip's street atlases cover every county in England and Wales, plus much of Scotland.
- ◆ All our atlases use the same style of mapping, with the same colours and symbols, so you can move with confidence from one atlas to the next
- ◆ Widely used by the emergency services, transport companies and local authorities.
- ◆ Created from the most up-to-date and detailed information available from Ordnance Survey
- ◆ Based on the National Grid

For national mapping, choose **Philip's Navigator Britain** – the most detailed road atlas available of England, Wales and Scotland. Hailed by Auto Express as 'the ultimate road atlas', this is the only one-volume atlas to show every road and lane in Britain.

Currently available street atlases

England

Bedfordshire
Berkshire
Birmingham and West Midlands
Bristol and Bath
Buckinghamshire
Cambridgeshire
Cheshire
Cornwall
Cumbria
Derbyshire
Devon
Dorset
County Durham and Teesside
Essex
North Essex
South Essex
Gloucestershire
North Hampshire
South Hampshire
Herefordshire Monmouthshire
Hertfordshire
Isle of Wight
East Kent
West Kent
Lancashire
Leicestershire and Rutland
Lincolnshire
London
Greater Manchester
Merseyside
Norfolk
Northamptonshire
Nottinghamshire
Oxfordshire
Shropshire
Somerset
Staffordshire
Suffolk
Surrey
East Sussex
West Sussex
Tyne and Wear Northumberland
Warwickshire
Birmingham and West Midlands
Wiltshire and Swindon
Worcestershire
East Yorkshire Northern Lincolnshire
North Yorkshire
South Yorkshire
West Yorkshire

Wales

Anglesey, Conwy and Gwynedd
Cardiff, Swansea and The Valleys
Carmarthenshire, Pembrokeshire and Swansea
Ceredigion and South Gwynedd
Denbighshire, Flintshire, Wrexham
Herefordshire Monmouthshire
Powys

Scotland

Aberdeenshire
Ayrshire
Edinburgh and East Central Scotland
Fife and Tayside
Glasgow and West Central Scotland
Inverness and Moray

All England and Wales coverage

How to order

Philip's maps and atlases are available from bookshops, motorway services and petrol stations. You can order direct from the publisher by phoning **01903 828503** or online at **www.philips-maps.co.uk** For bulk orders only, phone 020 7644 6940